Cooperation for
International Development

Cooperation for International Development

The United States and the Third World in the 1990s

edited by
Robert J. Berg
David F. Gordon

Lynne Rienner Publishers ⸏ Boulder & London

Published in the United States of America in 1989 by
Lynne Rienner Publishers, Inc.
1800 30th Street, Boulder, Colorado 80301

and in the United Kingdom by
Lynne Rienner Publishers, Inc.
3 Henrietta Street, Covent Garden, London WC2E 8LU

Library of Congress Cataloging-in-Publication Data
Cooperation for international development.
    Includes bibliographical references.
    1. Economic assistance, American—Developing
countries. 2. Developing countries—Economic conditions.
3. United States—Foreign economic relations—Developing
countries. 4. Developing countries—foreign economic
relations—United States. I. Berg, Robert J.
II. Gordon, David F.
HC60.C65725   1989   338.9'17301724   89-10808
ISBN 1-55587-166-6   (alk. paper)
ISBN 1-55587-167-4   (pbk.:alk. paper)

British Cataloguing in Publication Data
A Cataloguing in Publication record for this book
is available from the British Library.

Printed and bound in the United States of America

The paper used in this publication meets the requirements
of the American National Standard for Permanence of
Paper for Printed Library Materials Z39.48-1984.

Contents

PART FOUR
Appendixes

Tables and Figures

Preface

This book grows out of a national project organized by Michigan State University to study and advise on U.S. policies of economic cooperation with the Third World. The project was the most extensive of its kind ever undertaken; it involved 11 cooperating institutions, more than 100 papers, and more than 800 individuals from around the world. Fifteen symposia were held, leading to a national conference at MSU in May 1988 at which a summary of recommendations reflecting the project work was extensively reviewed. The report of that review, prepared by Ralph Smuckler and Robert Berg with David Gordon, was later published under the title "New Challenges, New Opportunities: U.S. Cooperation for International Growth and Development in the 1990s" and has become a key document in ongoing discussions—official as well as private—on future policies. Highlights of this report appear as Appendix One in this book.

The project involved experts across the fields of international development. Among the active participants were present and former leading officials in the U.S. Agency for International Development, senior policymakers from a range of other U.S. government agencies, leaders from international organizations, key figures from the profit and nonprofit private sectors, and numerous senior development experts from the Third World. We thank them all for sharing their professional knowledge so candidly and generously.

Each chapter in this book was especially commissioned as part of the project. Drafts were first presented at a series of meetings in East Lansing and Washington, D.C., between May 1986 and May 1988. At these meetings each paper was thoroughly discussed, and has been revised and updated for this book. We thank each author for excellent thinking, willingness to consider suggestions, and continuing goodwill.

A distinctive feature of the project was the active participation of the following U.S. institutions, which sponsored symposia and colloquia on specific sectors and problems as part of the broader study: the Association for Women in Development, the Board on Science and Technology for International Development of the National Research Council, The Futures Group, the Institute of International Education, The Johns Hopkins University School of Hygiene and Public Health, the Midwest Universities Consortium for International Activities, the Overseas Development Council, the U.S. Council for International Business, the Virginia Tech College of Architecture and Urban Studies in cooperation with the Washington Chapter of the Society for International Development, the Winrock International Institute for Agricultural Development, the World Resources Institute, and MSU's Center for Advanced Study of International Development. Appendix Two contains a full list of the papers presented at these meetings; the papers, or summaries of them, are available from the institutions that hosted their original presentation.

We appreciate the cooperation of all these institutions in contributing to the analyses presented here, and to the overall project. In each case, the leaders of these institutions played an active role both in their specific colloquium and in the activities of the larger project. The financial contributions of several foundations facilitated the organization of the various colloquia.

The editors owe special gratitude to our late friend, Paxton Dunn, who until his untimely death was vice-president of the U.S. Council for International Business. Paxton showed continuous enthusiasm and commitment to the project and, despite his illness, actively participated in numerous meetings all around the United States. He brought to the project both the perspective of the U.S. private sector and his own wealth of experience and wisdom drawn from a long career in business and in diplomacy.

The editors gratefully acknowledge the continuing support of Michigan State University in bringing this volume to fruition. Ralph H. Smuckler, dean and assistant to the president for international studies and programs, has been the leading force behind the entire project; it is no exaggeration to say that the enterprise would not exist without him. Ralph has been a trusted colleague and a good friend to both of us. Tom Carroll, director of the Center for Advanced Study of International Development (CASID), worked closely with us through the entire process of editing this book, as did Doris Scarlett, CASID's able program coordinator. We thank both of them for their help and their friendship. Katherine McCracken, our editorial assistant at CASID, had the unenviable task of reconciling the styles and terminology of our contributors and made an excellent contribution to the final product. Ruth Marlatt did yeomanly work entering and transferring the various word-processing disks; she worked with competence and grace under considerable pressure from editors and publisher.

We thank Lynne Rienner for her enthusiasm about our work, and also Martha Peacock and Gia Hamilton at Lynne Rienner Publishers for their outstanding help in bringing the manuscript to publication.

Generous support for the core costs of the project was provided by the MSU Foundation, the John D. and Catherine T. MacArthur Foundation, the Carnegie Corporation of New York, and The Pew Charitable Trusts. We thank each institution for faith in us.

We take full responsibility, with our distinguished group of contributors, for the analyses presented and any errors that might be contained within.

We urge reflection on the subjects in this book and on the public policy implications that flow from these presentations.

Robert J. Berg
David F. Gordon

ONE

Introduction and Overview

ROBERT J. BERG
DAVID F. GORDON

Forty years after President Harry S Truman first articulated the United States' commitment to promoting economic development in the Third World, the nation stands at a crossroads in its relations with the developing countries of Africa, Asia, Latin America, and the Middle East. U.S. policies toward the developing world fall short of meeting U.S. economic, environmental, and humanitarian interests and, unless fundamentally changed, will be unable to respond to the disparate challenges of the 1990s that demand cooperation between the United States and the Third World.

In 1949, Point Four of President Truman's historic inaugural address extended the concept of Marshall Plan support to key countries in the Third World, particularly those surrounding the Soviet bloc. The Point Four program recognized the important link between U.S. economic growth and security and the need to generate economic development in the Third World. It brought together the United States' humanitarian concerns and its national security interests as the richest and most powerful nation in the world. While the world has changed dramatically in the 40 years since Point Four, and our contemporary concept of national security needs to be broadened to include economic and environmental themes, the basic rationale for Truman's policy remains unchanged.

John F. Kennedy began a new era of U.S.–Third World cooperation with a series of initiatives: establishment of the U.S. Agency for International Development (USAID), the Peace Corps, and the Alliance for Progress. President Kennedy's bold moves brought an official U.S. presence on development issues to virtually all parts of the Third World. The first half of the 1960s was an era of optimism and high expectations for international development, both in the United States and in the Third World. This was the only time when a true national consensus in favor of active development cooperation with the Third World prevailed in the Congress. This consensus brought together those motivated by security concerns and the threat of Soviet communism with those motivated by humanitarianism and a belief in

1

the United States' interest in a rapidly expanding and more equal world economy.

The domestic consensus favoring development cooperation was broken in the late 1960s by the deepening commitment of the United States to the war in Vietnam. Vietnam shattered the postwar bipartisan consensus on foreign policy and ended the period of congressional acquiescence to executive branch initiatives in foreign affairs. In the area of international development, congressional distrust arose against both President Johnson and President Nixon because of the way their administrations distorted the U.S. aid program in making it part of the war effort. In the early 1970s, Congress repudiated the official foreign assistance program, delivering the final blow to the coalition based on linking U.S. security interests and humanitarian concerns.

The early 1970s were a period of sober reassessment of international development and the role of the United States. In the Third World, voices were raised against the use of foreign aid as an instrument of power. In the United States, there was concern about whether the benefits of development in the Third World were reaching the poor. There was a strong feeling in Congress that stricter guidelines on the use of foreign assistance were needed to guard against a repeat of executive branch misuse of the program. Out of this crisis emerged a new legislative coalition that set U.S. policy in "new directions" toward a people-oriented philosophy aimed at meeting "basic human needs." This approach focused on specific poverty problems: food production, population growth, health, and education.

The basic human needs coalition succeeded in establishing legislative guidelines for their approach in 1973 but was unable to provide durable support and direction for U.S. policies of economic cooperation in the Third World. The practical life of the basic human needs approach was less than a decade. While the legislation generated by the coalition still provides the official basis for U.S. policy, the actual program has become a victim of dramatically changed circumstances in the Third World and diminished congressional interest in, and support for, development cooperation. In addition, the guidelines adopted in the legislation have been virtually ignored by the executive branch.

Expansion of basic human needs programs seemed reasonable in the context of sustained rapid economic growth that marked the Third World at the time of the New Directions legislation. While the goals of improving conditions for the poor in the Third World proved hard to achieve in the short run, real progress was made in the first phases of implementation. But in the late 1970s and 1980s, economic expansion gave way to the debt crisis and economic recession in much of the Third World. As economies shrank, meeting basic human needs became far more problematical.

At the same time, under President Ronald Reagan, the uses of U.S. foreign assistance became much more strategic and ideological. There was an increasing disjuncture between the original legislative guidelines and the actual content of the program. The Foreign Assistance Act became a jumble of conflicting goals and guidelines, lending no real direction to the executive branch. The Reagan administration's almost cavalier change of directions in its economic policies with the Third World met initially with remarkable passivity in Congress and major constituent groups. But by the mid-1980s, Democrats in Congress and the constituent groups that have traditionally supported foreign assistance were increasingly critical of the Reagan administration's overall approach to international development. In this context, the current crisis of foreign assistance and U.S. policies toward the Third World ensued.

The past few years have seen a remarkable rebirth of serious thought and debate about international development cooperation. Policy leaders here and abroad have come to realize that new challenges and new opportunities abound for which policy responses are needed. The geopolitical foundations of U.S. foreign policy—the East-West conflict—seem to be shifting beneath our feet, forcing new perspectives on a range of international issues. The "short-term" debt crisis of the early 1980s has turned into a seemingly permanent condition for much of Africa and Latin America. The varied dimensions of the population and environment crises are increasingly taking center stage. The impetus to popular participation in the political and economic life of nations challenges the usual ways in which economic and social business has been conducted. And perhaps most fundamental is the subtle, pervasive psychological climate of a far more interdependent world heading, in less than a decade, into a new millennium.

These factors all lead U.S. programs of international development cooperation into a new conjuncture where fundamental policies are again under discussion and new courses are being proposed. Indeed, in the 1988–1989 transition year of a new administration in Washington, a real cottage industry of analysts proposing new policies for the new government arose. Leaders in Congress, the main environmental groups, academic centers, think tanks of various political plumage, and officials of the outgoing Reagan and incoming Bush administrations were all at work producing their own "definitive" analyses of where the United States is and where it should be going vis-à-vis the Third World.

Is it audacious to offer yet another analysis? Perhaps so, but the effort that forms the basis for this book was the first major study of the topic aimed at the new administration; it was the broadest study of U.S.-Third World economic cooperation ever conducted, involving the largest number of analyses and analysts ever gathered on the topic; and it has been a base point for a large number of follow-up studies undertaken from disparate viewpoints. We are pleased that our initiative has generated such wide interest and response. Indeed, we believe that a lot of rethinking by leaders in the public and private sectors is needed: fundamental issues need to be reconsidered; major challenges are being taken too lightly, and major opportunities are being missed. And we are concerned that, unless the issues raised in this book are faced more directly than at present, there is a real danger that the United States will be less relevant to the rest of the world in the 1990s, to the detriment of all concerned.

The analyses offered in this book delineate a "centrist perspective" on U.S. international development cooperation. The centrist perspective incorporates a wide range of viewpoints, but excludes thinking from the radical right and the radical left. The latter viewpoints are interesting and at times illuminating, but the U.S. public has accepted neither perspective and neither, we believe, offers the basis for effective and sustainable policies and programs. Both the hard left and hard right essentially believe that it is wrong for the U.S. government to have active policies of economic cooperation with the Third World.

The right holds that the private sector is the appropriate locus for most development initiatives, that the U.S. government lacks competence in these matters, and that few Third World countries merit cooperation because of distortions in their policies that favor statist solutions to problems in their economy and society. The left is equally critical, holding that the U.S. government is all too effective a force in the Third World, backing governments that are far too conservative, backing programs that are effective in denying political, social, and economic rights to the poor, and reinforcing the worst tendencies in U.S. life: amorality, greed, and exploitation.

The extremes of both the right and the left believe the United States, led by its government, has unique power to misshape the Third World, particularly through its aid programs. One could call this "negative power," as both the left and the right see U.S. power largely in its ability to do harm. They see a continuation of officially backed economic cooperation as a sure way to immiserate the Third World and tend to see in the cessation of such cooperation the way to a more flourishing Third World.

The authors in this volume do not share these fringe perspectives. Having observed the United States in a wide variety of Third World relationships, in closer detail than most of the critics, we do not see evidence that the U.S. government is an inherently evil force. Development cooperation efforts, both officially sponsored and privately supported, have surely made their share of mistakes. But there is simply no credible evidence that U.S. programs of economic cooperation with the Third World consistently fail, as the right argues, or that they constitute the "evil empire" of the West, as the left believes.

Prior to a dozen years ago, sweeping condemnations of U.S.–Third World programs of economic cooperation might have had some standing because careful evidence of their effectiveness and efficiency had not been collected. But today, there are evaluation systems in place in our official programs, in the programs of many other international and bilateral donor agencies, in most of the important private programs of development cooperation, and within some Third World governments. Together, there is a very impressive body of evidence that gives confidence that success generally outweighs failure, and that fine-tuning of strategies and programs can be elevated beyond mere statements of philosophy.

The record of past cooperation is not nearly so bad as to argue against future cooperation. Neither is it so good as to make for complacency. Tomorrow's programs cannot be designed to respond to yesterday's conditions and problems. The development enterprise of the last 40 years can claim some real success, but for all too many people in the Third World, basic conditions of life have not improved. In the course of a wide set of activities much has been learned. We know that donors, partners, and investors from the United States do better in some fields than in others. As the authors in this book suggest, some strategies and some institutions succeed better than do others. And there is strong evidence that the United States has learned, improving its performance, just as the learning curves in most Third World nations have been positive.

Indeed, one reason to strive to improve U.S. policies further in these areas is that U.S. cooperation for development is needed and desired by the Third World. The centrist perspective articulated here intersects substantially with the domestic policy environments in most developing countries, where radical themes and anti-Westernism have substantially moderated in recent years. Development cooperation is not something that the United States is imposing on the Third World; rather, virtually all developing countries seek to expand their development linkages with the United States. Thus, we believe it timely and appropriate to explore in depth centrist policies that are supportable in the United States and that will find a receptive audience abroad.

As we discuss below, there have been major changes in both the United States and the Third World that impel both sides to cooperate more closely with each other in facing mutual problems of significance to all societies. In confronting these problems, the United States will need to exercise its unique public-private partnerships in its cooperation with the Third World. But given current circumstances, it is unrealistic to expect the U.S. private commercial sector to expand its role in most of the Third World. Investments here at home, in a uniting Europe, and in the advanced Third World nations are too attractive, and the risks in the rest of the Third World are too great to make these areas a likely target for substantially increased foreign direct investment (though India might be an exception). Programs to engage the pluralistic strengths of the United States to help Third World peoples have been remarkably successful and ought to continue. In particular, the energies of the noncommercial private sector—private voluntary organizations—must be stimulated. Over the longer run, as more Third World nations progress into industrial and information-based economies, it will be both possible and desirable to shift much of the burden of U.S. economic cooperation to the private commercial sector.

Thus, in the immediate future, leadership in development cooperation will have to come from official programs. Indeed, the nature of many of the problems being faced in the Third World (many of which have an impact upon U.S. society as well) generally require public sector leadership. For example, nowhere in the world has the private sector led the cleanup of the environment. No country has a primary education system in private hands. And no country has left basic policies regarding forests, infrastructure, and public health entirely in private hands. If the United States is to continue to be relevant to the central issues facing the developing countries, it will take an active U.S. government mobilizing public resources and private initiatives.

It is timely and important that U.S. policies of economic cooperation with the Third World be crafted for the 1990s and beyond. This book brings together the papers commissioned for the national project led by Michigan State University on the future of U.S. economic cooperation with the Third World and addresses three broad themes: (1) the international context in which development activities will occur in the 1990s; (2) U.S. interests in the Third World and the capacities of U.S. institutions, public and private, for involvement in international development; and (3) issues involved in the organization and implementation of U.S. policies and programs for international development cooperation.

Cooperation for International Development explores the changed international context for development cooperation. In the 1970s and 1980s, profound transformations in the world economy ended U.S. economic supremacy. This was generally a result of the success of the international economic order that was created, under U.S. leadership, in the aftermath of World War II. The revolution in communications and organization has created private economic entities (multinational corporations and international banks) whose interests transcend national borders. The world economy now includes a number of regional centers (North America, Europe, eastern Asia) and is marked by the unprecedented linking of trade, private investment, and global financial transfers.

Evolving patterns of global politics match the changes in the international economy. A multipolar world is rapidly replacing the U.S.-Soviet rivalry; the ideological conflicts of global liberalism versus global socialism are increasingly passé; and the leadership of Mikhail Gorbachev in the Soviet Union may well open up possibilities for more pragmatic treatment of world issues and a wider agenda between the superpowers. The Third World, chastened by its failure to generate a new international economic order, is seeking a redefinition of its own political role.

Linda Y. C. Lim, professor of business and East Asian Studies at the University of Michigan, addresses the issue of the opportunities and constraints that developing countries face in the contemporary world economy. Lim argues that a wide range of policies and economic outcomes in the industrialized countries (in particular the United States) influence prospects for the developing countries. She suggests that lowering the U.S. budget deficit and increasing consumer demand in Germany and Japan could substantially stimulate Third World growth in the coming decade.

Lim examines in detail the opportunities for export-led growth in developing countries. She foresees a continuing trend away from raw materials to trade in manufactures and services. The prospects for both agricultural commodities and metals are poor, because of both protectionism and overproduction. But Lim is far more optimistic about the prospects for Third World countries to expand their trade in manufactured goods and even in services. She notes that while protection for manufactures may help new entrants (mostly poorer developing countries) since it is usually directed against specific countries who have already achieved a strong market share, the Third World has an interest in free trade, since managed trade is more likely to be controlled by those countries with the most political clout.

Percy Mistry of Oxford University (formerly a senior official in the World Bank) explores the issues involved in financing international development in the 1990s. Mistry suggests that the international public finance system created after World War II worked remarkably well in promoting Third World development until the financial and communications revolutions of the 1970s and the rise of OPEC led to a burst of private lending by commercial banks. Mistry believes that these institutions became involved in a context that they knew very little about. The result of the incursion of commercial banks was the very rapid build-up of debt by Third World countries and the swamping of the carefully constructed system of sustainable international financing of Third World development.

The most pressing task facing international development is to solve the debt crises in Latin America and Africa. The international response to the debt crises of the 1980s has been programs of economic stabilization and adjustment supported both by the multilateral financial institutions and the bilateral donors. Both have tried to help developing countries reorient their policies to face the constraints of debt and an increasingly volatile international economy. While Mistry acknowledges the role of the international financial institutions in keeping the debt crises from hobbling the entire global financial system, he is critical of the strategy of muddling through by means of ad hoc rescheduling and austerity programs. In the 1990s, for a substantial number of Latin American and African countries, real development progress will depend upon reducing the burden of debt service. Mistry suggests the creation of a debt-restructuring facility, publicly funded, that would facilitate the further expansion of the secondary market for Third World debt.

Mistry also suggests that only through expanding and streamlining the public international financial system will adequate funding be forthcoming to finance development in the 1990s. In this process, he sees a key role for the regional development banks, which he proposes should double their share of total multilateral lending. Mistry also suggests that regionalization of bilateral aid portfolios might better utilize the limited volume of this form of financial transfer.

Finally, Mistry argues that, in general, the outlook for external financing of Third World development is poor. The implication is that developing countries must find ways to generate substantially higher levels of domestic savings and investment. One of the tasks of development cooperation in the 1990s is assisting in this, both through technical assistance to the public sector and in supporting developing countries' efforts to promote private investment within their own borders through instruments such as stock exchanges, capital markets, and other similar mechanisms.

Among the most important changes in the global context of development is the increasing diversity of the Third World and the new issues that are coming to the fore in different regions of the developing world. A striking change in the Third World has been the rapid growth of the newly industrialized countries—South Korea, Taiwan, Brazil, and others. Colin I. Bradford of Yale University argues that the United States has interpreted the rise of the newly industrialized countries in ideological terms, as a vindication of free market philosophy, rather than in realistic terms that assess the potential for cooperation or conflict between the United States and such countries. Bradford argues that not only is the ideological interpretation at odds with reality, but that it is itself an obstacle to real understanding between the United States and the newly industrialized countries and to the likelihood of good relations of mutual benefit. Several other authors also argue for a more active U.S. approach to such countries and to the other advanced developing countries.

But change in the Third World has not been confined to the newly industrialized countries. John Stover, of the Futures Group, provides an overview of crosscutting changes occurring in the developing countries. Stover focuses on demographic changes, quality-of-life issues, and political trends. He notes that population trends are sharply differentiated by region, with the demographic transition in full swing in Latin America and much of Asia, while in Africa high rates of population growth remain the norm. Rates of urbanization remain high all over the Third World, and the 1990s will see the Third World become the site of the largest urban agglomerations on the face of the earth. Stover poses the question whether these megacities will serve as breeding grounds for political turmoil or offer new opportunities for increasing the pace of growth and development. Urbanization will no doubt pose a challenge to the United States, whose development cooperation programs have become less urban-oriented in recent years.

In health and education, dramatic improvements occurred from the 1950s through the 1970s but slowed dramatically in the 1980s. Stover fears that AIDS, already recognized as a severe threat in Africa, may become the development issue of the 1990s. In education, the problem in many countries is the need to balance the aspirations of parents for their children with the requirements of the national economy, both in numbers of graduates and the specialties they pursue.

Stover sees political life in the developing countries becoming increasingly diverse in the 1990s. Islamic fundamentalism will provide a continuing challenge in countries with substantial Muslim populations. Many countries that have been under stable political leadership will face transitions as the old generation of leaders passes on. Finally, the sustained economic recession that many nations have faced in the 1980s has weakened their political and institutional environments and may lead to instability and rapid shifts in policy.

One of the most significant changes in the Third World in recent years is the emergence of environmental concerns and the linking of the issues of economic growth with those of protection of the global commons. Within the Third World, environmental problems were formerly seen as something that could be addressed only in the aftermath of successful economic development. There is now more and more realization that successful development will be achieved only by protecting the global environment and by balancing population and resources. William U. Chandler, of the Batelle Institute, addresses the issues of environment and development, focusing his attention on energy issues, tropical deforestation, and population growth. Linking development with the imperative for conservation will require pricing natural resources to reflect their replacement cost and environmental impact, as well as setting limits on consumption that do not exceed sustainable yields or destroy the natural resource base of the global economy.

Threats to the global environment give the United States a stake in promoting sustainable development in the Third World. Chandler argues that the United States will have to pay more sustained attention to the environmental impacts of its development projects and should assist developing countries in undertaking structural reforms designed to reduce economic and resource waste at the same time.

One of the most troubling changes in the Third World in recent years is the emergence of a set of countries that appear to be falling further and further behind in the quest for development. In an increasingly competitive international economy, there is a real danger that these "Fourth World" countries will become more and more marginalized unless their special problems are recognized and more effectively addressed, both by their own governments and by the international community.

Paul Streeten of Boston University addresses the issues of promoting growth in the poorest nations. Streeten questions the conventional wisdom that outward-oriented trade policies are the key to success for the poorest developing countries. He focuses instead on the supply-side constraints to growth—lack of skills and capital, poor motivation, the strength of traditional attitudes. While the problems of poverty remain in all of the developing countries, they are most formidable in the least developed. There, Streeten maintains, poverty itself continues to be a major brake on basic economic growth. Foreign assistance must focus on alleviating poverty, for both humanitarian and developmental reasons.

Streeten argues that expanding foreign aid and investment will be important if these countries are to escape the vicious circles in which they find themselves, but he warns that history suggests that financial support, while necessary, will not work unless it is more effectively supervised. Streeten proposes that in these countries traditional foreign assistance can play a key role as a transitional support for rigid and inflexible economies that face imperatives for adjustment. He argues that in the provision of aid to these countries, aid organizations must become more rather than less directly involved, because of the lack of technical and managerial expertise. To enhance the attractiveness of foreign investment, he proposes joint ventures that give increasing ownership to the country through a process of gradual buy-out of the foreign-owned interest.

During the past 40 years, one of the most radical transformations in history has gathered momentum: the transformation of women's roles and opportunities in society. The special role of women in meeting the development challenges of the Third World has been increasingly recognized, particularly in the fields of agricultural production. But greater progress toward the empowerment of women will be needed if they are to reach their development potential.

Another significant change in the developing countries is that larger numbers of nongovernmental organizations are emerging with capacity to plan and carry out programs in low-cost and participatory ways that conventional development projects have sometimes had difficulty attaining. In many of the developing countries, there is a parallel increase in managerial, technical, and scientific capacity. The existence of indigenous organizations and this core of trained and skilled personnel necessitates new norms of equality in programs of cooperation for international development and opens up a range of potential relationships based upon more direct mutual benefit and lying beyond the framework of foreign assistance as it has hitherto been practiced.

Changes in the international environment and in the developing countries are matched by changes in the global position of the United States and evolving patterns of U.S.—Third World relations. If power is defined in a purely relative manner, then one nation's success diminishes that of any other. But the entire postwar experience challenges so narrow a concept of power. U.S. success contributed to the success of other nations and then drew strength from their advances. The result of these successes is that the world is a much more competitive place, and the dominance of a single country—the United States—has ended. But is the implication of this that the world should be seen as dangerous, a place to be avoided? We think not. The challenge of statesmanship in the 1990s will be to blend the competitive elements of international relations with the cooperative ones. This will be as true in relations with the Third World as it is in other areas.

The U.S. budget, trade, and financial imbalances threaten its long-term future and, as Lim points out, have an important impact on the developing world. Conversely, the long-term prospects for the U.S. economy are bound up in the global economy of which the Third World is a significant part. The United States' capacity to participate effectively in development cooperation activities with the Third World has grown. Particularly in areas of applied science and technology, U.S. universities, research institutes, and corporations are at the forefront of expanding scientific knowledge of direct concern to a wide range of developing countries. But the ability of the United States to harness this capacity has been constrained by the budget deficit, waning domestic support for foreign assistance, and official attitudes toward the Third World.

Charles William Maynes, editor of *Foreign Policy,* explores the roots of the U.S. public's ambivalent attitudes toward the Third World and addresses the evolving nature of U.S. interests. Maynes points out a basic paradox in the role of the Third World in U.S. foreign policy and politics: Since World War II, the bulk of U.S. interest and concern has focused on Europe and on the West's conflict with the USSR, yet the greatest challenges facing the United States have come in the Third World. Presidential candidates risk their popularity if they appear too sensitive to the Third World, yet political survival in office may depend on the success or failure of executive Third World policies.

Maynes argues that growing international economic competitiveness, hostile rhetoric in the United Nations, and mounting cost—in blood, money, and pride—have undermined traditional U.S. humanitarian concern for developing countries. But Maynes believes that more accepting racial attitudes at home, the emergence of Third World leaders who appeal to the average U.S. citizen, the growing presence of Third Worlders here in the United States, and the increasing experience U.S. citizens have acquired in developing countries are forces that can, and should, balance the hostility toward the Third World.

Both Maynes and Princeton N. Lyman, a high-level State Department official, stress the broadening nature of U.S. interests in the Third World and in international development. At one time, U.S. interests might have centered around strategic and humanitarian concerns, but a variety of other economic, political, security, and shared social considerations have come to supplant the old rationales. The United States has both an economic and a humanitarian interest in seeing that the world grows economically with a minimum of damage to the natural environment. It shares an interest with the developing countries in maintaining an open international trading system and effective international economic and financial institutions. It has political interests in helping to resolve regional conflicts that endanger lives and threaten escalation and international involvement. It also has an interest in furthering the exciting trends toward pluralism and democratization in the Third World. Finally, Lyman identifies a U.S. interest in resolving a series of pressing contemporary problems that also involve developing countries: drugs, international crime, infectious diseases, and the challenge of international terrorism, among others.

But, unlike our relations with the Soviet Union, there is on the horizon no sign of dramatic improvement in U.S. relations with the Third World. Issues such as debt, the drug trade, migration, and environmental degradation provide a shared set of concerns but not necessarily a shared set of interests. Maynes, in fact, believes that U.S. relations with the developing world are going to become more difficult and complicated, which is why realistic attitudes and a serious interest commensurate with the scale of the issues are so important. If the United States is to maintain constructive relations with the Third World that will serve both its interests and meet those of the developing countries, it must forge a new national consensus on the importance of Third World issues and international development goals. Further, the United States must chart its course sensitively, marshaling its capabilities in the face of resource and budget constraints.

These changes in the international context of development, in the Third World itself, and in U.S. interests and capacities provide the backdrop for assessing appropriate policies and strategies for the United States in international development cooperation in the 1990s. The authors in this book address a number of issues fundamental to crafting improved policies. They do not, however, prescribe specific sectoral emphases and strategies. The Project on Cooperation for International Development included a series of meetings, undertaken by Michigan State's partner institutions in the project, that focused on sectoral issues and strategies and policies to address them. A summary of the sectoral and other recommendations from this exercise is found in Appendix One. In Appendix Two, we list information about the specific sectoral and other analyses generated in this comprehensive study of future U.S. economic cooperation with the Third World.

The consensus that emerged from the project was that special attention needed to be given to three urgent problems that go beyond the traditional boundaries of development cooperation: Third World debt, which endangers the basic growth potential of much of Africa and Latin America and threatens the basic credibility of the international financial system; Africa, where the degradation of the environment, poverty, and institutional deterioration imperil human life itself; and global deterioration of the environment, which requires unprecedented levels of international cooperation.

The project also generated a broad consensus that future U.S. programs should focus on four substantive areas in which needs in the Third World and U.S. experience and skills are particularly well matched: (1) enhancing physical well-being through improved health systems and population planning; (2) working for sustainable agricultural systems, particularly emphasizing food supplies and forestry; (3) developing environmental programs and policies that will protect natural resources and, through emphasizing renewable supplies and conservation, assure better energy security; and (4) fostering sound urban development policies.

In each of these four areas there are compelling reasons for serious U.S. interest in cooperation with the Third World, and in each of these areas we believe that there are significant U.S. capabilities to help Third World nations address their challenges and opportunities. The four themes reflect both continuity with long-standing U.S. priorities in international development and important changes. The first two have been continuing emphases of U.S. programs, while the latter two are new emphases and reflect the changing needs of the present and future. U.S. capabilities to address these four substantive areas are particularly strong in the crosscutting approaches of human resource development, science and technology, and policy and institutional development. In addition, the United States is particularly capable of fostering pluralism to mobilize diverse capabilities for addressing the substantive problems. These diverse energies include the private commercial sector, nongovernmental organizations, and the special role of women in development.

In a sense, the content of U.S. foreign aid programs has been less contentious than have the mechanisms and modalities chosen to implement them. In this book, several authors examine the range of issues involved in how the United States should actually carry out its aid programs. In examining future programs for U.S. economic cooperation with the Third World, it is important to consider how this cooperation will take place, what will be the basic policies guiding this cooperation, and what institutional and partnership modalities will be supported to foster this cooperation.

Much as the "development community" would wish otherwise, the realistic starting point for such policy considerations must be U.S. interests in the Third World. As discussed earlier, these interests have been expanding greatly in recent years. Further complicating the picture is the fact that the traditional preoccupations of U.S. foreign policy—East-West relations and relations with our European allies—are taking new directions whose shape is not yet very clear. In the past, the focus of the United States on the Soviet Union, Japan, and its European allies has tended to obscure the importance of the Third World. This should be corrected, as Lyman suggests, through a fundamental reassessment, led by the White House, of U.S. interests in the Third World. This kind of study would be particularly timely for the early 1990s, coming at a time of new regimes in the Third World and sharply deescalating East-West tensions. For the first time in decades, the United States is at a point in its national history where it faces considerable choice in the basic direction in which it is headed.

The wide range of interests we have identified call for a pluralistic response from the United States. Lyman, a former high U.S. aid official, points out that these relationships go well beyond what can reasonably be lodged in a foreign assistance agency. Indeed, they go well beyond what is possible and reasonable for the government to undertake and will depend upon the nurturing of a wide range of relationships by the private commercial sector, nongovernmental organizations, universities, and research institutions.

One key choice facing the United States in its development cooperation with the Third World is whether caution or boldness is required. It would be possible to review the opportunities for U.S.–Third World cooperation and choose a cautious course for the future, reflecting preoccupations with domestic and traditional foreign policy concerns. We do not need to imagine this option since it largely fits the current pattern of U.S. policy: being near the bottom of OECD economic cooperation programs in percentage of GNP devoted to aiding the Third World; having existing programs heavily skewed to just a few countries (e.g., Israel and Egypt) and to a few issues (e.g., security and drugs); and having a focus that is both overly narrow and mismatched with U.S. strengths (e.g., a fixation on structural adjustment). Some would say that this is a recipe for relationships by a second power.

Joseph C. Wheeler, chairman of the OECD Development Assistance Committee, presents a more ambitious agenda for the United States. Basing his recommendations both on the need for the United States to pull its own weight in the world and on a long view of U.S. interests in the Third World, he recommends a series of actions by which the United States "can make a real difference" and where its leadership is wanted and needed. In financial terms, this would mean an added expenditure of 1 percent of the federal budget to bring the United States to the average level of aid given by major OECD donors (again, in percentages of GNP given for official development assistance). Wheeler argues that the significance in political terms would more than match the cost, putting the United States in leading positions on such issues as agriculture in Africa and poverty in India.

The world is not sitting idly by while the United States decides whether to be cautious or bold. Indeed, Japan is already moving aggressively in its aid programs in countries such as India, where its levels of gross aid disbursements are six times those of the United States, and on a net basis (i.e., after accounting for India's paybacks of past U.S. aid loans) 35 times as great. Cautious U.S. responses at this time will send the wrong signals about the United States' role in the world. Thus, the question is not what "go it alone" policies the United States should pursue, but what policies in concert with other donors and the Third World the United States can pursue that have real worth both to it and to the Third World.

Whether or not the U.S. government continues a cautious international development program or embarks on more ambitious courses, there is common agreement that intragovernmental coordination of U.S. programs must be improved. For this Maurice J. Williams of the Overseas Development Council develops a strategy that is both an informed primer on how coordination now takes place and a set of recommendations for improvements. Among the issues that Williams explores is the balance between military and security assistance, on the one hand, and development assistance, on the other. Given the huge swing toward military/security assistance in the 1980s, this may be the most important coordination issue that needs to be addressed. The thrust of Williams' argument, implicitly backed by Maynes and Lyman as well, is that security interests need to be redefined to take into account economic and environmental themes and that the benefits of traditional "security" assistance need to be more carefully ascertained than at present.

The proliferation of U.S. interests in the Third World has brought numerous federal government departments and agencies into various programs and policies in the Third World. Many more have articulated interests in policies, even when not directly involved. There is wide agreement that, for efficiency's sake alone, better coordination is needed. Lyman points to the State Department to take a far more prominent role in this; Williams points to the White House. We believe that the scope of the interests involved demand active involvement from the very top of our political system, and we therefore endorse a strong White House role. In a sense, the options need not be mutually exclusive. One could easily envision stronger roles both for the State Department and for the White House.

Another key policy issue is the allocation of U.S. resources between its bilateral programs and the multilateral system. There has been an almost 180 degree shift in official U.S. attitudes toward the multilateral system during the 1980s. The Reagan administration came into office with great hostility to the multilateral banks and to the UN system. But, with the onset of the debt crisis in 1982, the administration began to realize the value of the multilateral financial system. By the latter years of the decade, antagonism to the UN system institutions also began to wane. At the end of the Reagan years there was something of a reapproachment: Some arrears to the United Nations had been paid, a large increase in the World Bank's authorized capital was approved, and the United States supported the efforts of the UN secretary-general in regional conflict resolution in several Third World hot spots.

The growing concern with global environmental issues may lead the Bush administration to invest more authority and resources in the multilateral system. That is a bridge yet to be crossed. Certainly it will be impossible for the United States simultaneously to follow Gramm-Rudman budget guidelines, maintain huge military/security aid commitments, maintain a bilateral development program, *and* maintain, let alone increase, commitments to the multilateral system. While none of our authors provides an escape from this dilemma, both Williams and David Shear suggest ways in which a far more productive collaboration can be achieved between the bilateral U.S. program and the multilateral system.

None of the authors in this book dispute the need for the United States to have a bilateral aid program. But they offer a range of competing ideas about what a U.S. development agency should do and how it should be organized. For Wheeler, the aid agency would be even yeastier than it was in the heyday of foreign aid in the 1960s and 1970s—a virtual organ board of programs with full stops out. Williams proposes retaining a traditional agency for the poorest and nearest countries (in Africa, the Caribbean, and Central America), while cutting back on foreign missions and expanding a more broad-based policy role for the agency in relation to the better-off parts of the developing world.

The most detailed vision of a future development agency is spelled out by Shear, a former senior aid official now with a private consulting firm. Like other contributors, Shear sees the need for a wide-ranging program. He goes on to suggest that pluralistic mechanisms are necessary to deliver pluralistic programs. He believes that vibrant programs should involve not only technical and capital assistance, but food aid and support for policy reform. Given the fact that these programs need to be crafted for a wide variety of circumstances in the Third World, the content and implementing dynamics of specific programs will vary widely. Alas, there is no magic development button or any magic development program.

Reform of the U.S. development program must go further than updating organizational functions and the division of labor between the development agency and different delivery agents. Reform of the incentive structure, the bureaucratic roles, and the program cycles must also be undertaken, according to Allan Hoben, a Boston University anthropologist who has been a participant observer within USAID. Hoben argues that there is excessive compartmentalization in USAID, that the program cycle is overly complicated, and that the on-the-ground operating procedures are inefficient and, in some cases, self-defeating. Hoben suggests how these factors can be reworked so that a more professionally motivated staff is better focused on more effectively helping Third World development. It will not be an easy task.

After 40 years of active U.S. participation in international development cooperation, during which time much progress has been made and a great deal has been learned about development and foreign assistance, the political support for, and popular belief in, these activities remains fragile at best. Part of the reason for this is that the link between the public and the government has been broken and that there is a debilitating climate of distrust between Congress and the executive branch. Journalist, historian, and aid executive John Maxwell Hamilton, currently with the World Bank, addresses the issue of creating a public commitment for international development cooperation. Tracing historical motivations going back to the early years of the nation and moving up through recent polling information, Hamilton finds that U.S. citizens have not ranked foreign aid high on their list of priorities and tend to perceive it as counter to U.S. interests. Hamilton fears that there is a real danger that just as the "national interest" rationale for development cooperation becomes stronger, popular support will continue to weaken. Hamilton suggests ways to counter this possibility, including a clearer articulation of goals and strong leadership from the highest political level.

Hamilton highlights the special relevance of changes in U.S. society that provide a basis for building constituencies. He argues for a self-interest that is not selfish: effective but modest approaches and programs that can be seen as part of a coherent approach to the rest of the world. Even so, there will still be a need for more education of the U.S. public on why such programs are necessary. Hamilton forces us to recognize the weak links between the international affairs constituency and the domestic education and media communities. Linkages between these two communities may well need to be greatly strengthened before the basic nature of many U.S. development cooperation endeavors are recast and strengthened.

Several of the contributors to this book emphasize the need for far greater cooperation between the executive branch and the Congress. The consensus that there was in the early days of U.S. foreign aid is no longer there. Partisanship, conflict between the branches, and intercommittee bickering has increased. Under these circumstances, major legislative reform may be less feasible than is pursuing reforms through administrative actions. But that can be only a short-term approach. In the long run, the interests of the United States demand that decisive steps be taken to coordinate more effectively the range of congressional committees involved in international development issues and, more important, to reestablish an enduring relationship between Congress and the administration on crucial issues of international economic cooperation. This necessitates a fundamental revision of the legislation that governs U.S. development cooperation activities.

What is at stake is not a series of small actions that,—if gulped down hard, can be swallowed. At stake is the character of U.S. relations with most of the peoples and countries of the world. Also at stake, whether the U.S. people and government recognize it or not, is the possibility, if the United States acts well, of improving the condition of much of humanity as we enter the twenty-first century. This is a time for the best possible mixture of global concern and national patriotism. In the end, thankfully, we do not have to choose between doing well and doing good.

PART ONE

The Global Context

TWO

The Impact of Changes in the World Economy on Developing Countries

_____ LINDA Y. C. LIM

Developing countries are deeply affected by changes in the international economic environment, but this does not mean that events in these countries depend only or even mainly on what happens in the world economy. Internal changes are also important, and they both influence and are affected by global economic change. My task in this chapter, however, is one-sided: to consider only how changes in the world economy might affect developing countries in the 1990s. I will discuss not what will happen, but rather what events will affect what will happen in these countries in the next decade.

The developing countries are a heterogeneous group, including—at the extremes—poor, stagnant, agrarian nations in Africa and relatively high-income, high-growth, newly industrializing countries (NICs) in Asia. Different types of countries will be differently affected by the various changes in the world economy and will have a different capacity to deal with these changes. At the same time, the developed countries that dominate the world economy are themselves diverse: within the First World, Western European nations, the United States, and Japan face somewhat different economic problems and prospects and will exert varying influences on the world economy and on developing countries. Changes in the world economy involve both market forces and government policies, in both the developed and developing countries, that are ever-changing and difficult to predict even over the short run. This complex matrix—not to mention internal changes in individual developing countries—must be borne in mind.

MACROECONOMIC DEVELOPMENTS

The Industrial Economies

Because of their generally heavy dependence on external trade, developing countries' growth is directly related to the growth of world output and trade. This in turn depends on what happens in the industrial countries, which account for nearly three-quarters of world trade. The big question at the moment is whether the industrial countries can solve their domestic macroeconomic and external imbalance problems. If they can, then the prospects for world economic growth and trade are improved. For example, if the United States reduces its budget and trade deficits, if Japan and West Germany stimulate their domestic economies enough to increase domestic growth and reduce their trade surpluses, and if the exchange rates of major currencies stabilize, then several things will happen that will favor the developing countries.

A fall in the U.S. budget deficit would lower interest rates, thus alleviating developing countries' external debt burden. It would also at least partially reverse the diversion of international capital flows to the United States and encourage foreign investment in the developing countries, which would thereby have access to more and cheaper capital for growth. If the decline in the U.S. budget deficit were to involve decreasing farm-export subsidies, the market for developing countries' agricultural exports would expand. A fall in the U.S. trade deficit would reduce protectionist pressures in the United States, thereby promoting trade growth. (Developing countries need not be hurt by a fall in the U.S. trade deficit if this is achieved by increased exports rather than reduced imports; even if U.S. imports fall, the slump is more likely to involve reduced imports from other developed countries whose currencies have appreciated than from developing countries whose currencies have mostly depreciated against the dollar.)

Reorientation of the Japanese and West German economies from export-led to domestic market-oriented growth would boost world trade, increasing their imports, including imports from developing countries, which would further benefit from faster world growth. Opening of the Japanese, and even the South Korean and Taiwanese markets, would also improve prospects for developing country exports.

Restoration of internal and external balance in the industrial countries and some of the NICs would have a favorable impact on world trade by stabilizing exchange rates. Currency shifts and interest-rate changes affect foreign investment, which has recently been declining from the United States and increasing from Japan as a result of the weak dollar and strong yen—a situation likely to continue into the 1990s. Foreign aid that comes from industrial countries' government budgets is obviously affected by how much and how government expenditures are cut (e.g., in the United States) or increased (e.g., in Japan and West Germany) and by the state of donor countries' external reserves. Thus, Japan—which has surplus external reserves—is increasing its aid to developing countries, while the United States is likely to continue reducing its foreign aid contributions until its twin deficits decline.

Of course, there is no guarantee that favorable developments will occur. If the industrial countries do not solve their internal and external balance problems, then the world may well be plagued with higher interest rates, slower growth of output and trade, and worsening protectionist barriers; under these conditions, developing countries would be worse off. As of early 1989, this had not happened; world economic performance bettered that predicted by earlier forecasts. Imbalances remain, but it seems safe to assume that world growth will continue to be respectable, though not necessarily at the high levels of the 1960s and 1970s. The International Monetary Fund's (IMF) April 1989 projection is that industrial countries' output will grow by about 3 percent in the medium term (through 1994), with developing countries growing at the higher rate of around 5 percent a year,[1] an improvement on earlier forecasts.

World Trade

Between 1980 and 1986, world trade grew by 18 percent in volume but by only 6 percent in dollar value. Mining exports declined in volume, while agricultural exports increased by about 8 percent, and manufactured exports grew by nearly 30 percent. Since most developing countries are predominantly exporters of mineral and agricultural products, they have been hurt by this relative performance. The dollar value of their share of world exports declined from 33.6 percent in 1980 to 24.6 percent in 1986, while their share of world imports declined from 28.7 percent to 25.2 percent.[2] In 1980, the industrial countries bought 29 percent of their imports from developing countries, and 66 percent from each other; in 1986, the comparable figures were 19 percent and 77 percent.[3] Strong growth of world trade and rising commodity prices in 1987[4] and 1988 prevented the developing countries' share from falling further.

But as world trade shifts increasingly away from merchandise items (especially raw materials)—in which developing countries arguably have a comparative advantage—toward manufactures and, especially, services[5]—in which they are unlikely to have a comparative advantage—developing countries' share of world trade may not improve. The exception is the export of manufactures: Developing countries' share of world trade in manufactured goods rose from 7 percent in the mid-1970s to 12.5 percent in 1985. In 1986, the value of their manufactured exports grew by 13 percent, and for the first time they earned more foreign exchange selling manufactured exports than fuels or nonfuel primary products.[6] Despite rising commodity prices in 1987 and 1988, the relative increase in developing countries' export of manufactures has continued.

The changing pattern of world trade has differing impacts on developing countries. Those that rely heavily on primary commodity exports suffered severely from slowly growing volumes and low and declining prices (until prices began to recover in 1987) and this may continue. But those developing countries that rely heavily on the export of manufactures are prospering. Most prominent among the latter are the Asian NICs, but export-manufacturing success is not limited to them. Manufactures now account for more than half the foreign exchange earnings of such large middle-income agrarian countries as the Philippines and Thailand, and are second only to oil as a foreign exchange earner for Mexico, Malaysia, and Indonesia. Manufactured exports are also increasingly important to the balance of payments in a range of other, very different, developing countries, including China, India, Bangladesh, Sri Lanka, Mauritius, Pakistan, Turkey, Morocco, Tunisia, Haiti, the Dominican Republic, and Colombia.

Increased protectionism in industrial countries is a major threat to developing countries' export, output, and income growth. Exports from developing countries are already subject to more trade barriers than are exports from other industrial countries. Agricultural products are both very heavily subsidized and more heavily protected than are manufactures in the industrial countries. Manufactured goods exported by developing countries (e.g., textiles, footwear) are also subject to more protection in the industrial countries than are manufactured goods predominately exported by other industrial countries.[7] Over time, both protection and subsidies have increased, especially on agricultural products. Trade preferences (mainly those under the Generalized System of Preferences [GSP]) for developing countries exist, but they remain limited and subject to ever more stringent eligibility criteria, including progressive graduation. As developing countries have moved toward more liberal exchange and trade regimes in recent years, developed countries have moved in the opposite direction.[8] This could deter further trade liberalization in the developing countries, by fueling nationalistic sentiments and bolstering the position of (mostly elite) interest groups who benefit from and favor continued domestic market protection.

Developing countries have a strong interest in several outcomes of the current eighth round of General Agreement on Tariffs and Trade (GATT) negotiations, which are expected to be prolonged and difficult but will set the stage for international trade relations in the 1990s. Together with industrialized agricultural exporters such as the United States, developing countries are pushing for liberalization of agricultural trade and the reduction or removal of agricultural production and export subsidies in developed countries such as Japan and European Community (EC) members. At the same time, a large bloc of developing countries, led by India and Brazil, is opposed to the liberalization of trade in services favored by the industrial countries, fearing that their own underdeveloped domestic service sectors will be unable to compete with industrial country enterprises in a free trade environment. Developing countries are also concerned that discussions on such issues as "safeguards," "intellectual property rights," and "graduation" from developing country status (and eligibility for trade preferences) could jeopardize their own future trade prospects. While some progress has been made, the GATT talks remain mostly stalled in 1989.

There are many special bilateral relationships between developing and industrial countries; for example, "free trade areas" have been proposed between the United States and such developing countries as Mexico and the members of the Association of Southeast Asian Nations (ASEAN), but for political reasons they are unlikely to be fully enacted. The United States already has its politically inspired and economically limited Caribbean Basin Initiative, meant to free up trade and capital flows with Caribbean countries, while the EC gives special trade preferences to its former ACP colonies (Africa, the Caribbean, and the Pacific) under the Lomé Convention. The United States has also been using its GSP program benefits and threats of selective trade restrictions to force trade policy changes in the Asian and Latin American NICs especially—including pressing them to open their domestic markets to U.S. goods and capital, to respect intellectual property and labor rights, and, in the case of the surplus countries, to revalue their currencies. As of January 1989, the four Asian NICs (South Korea, Taiwan, Hong Kong, and Singapore) have lost their U.S. GSP eligibility altogether. The United States has also imposed "voluntary export restraints" on certain products from South Korea and Brazil and is currently penalizing Brazil for closing its domestic market to U.S. computer software exports. Some developing countries (e.g., Vietnam, Nicaragua, South Africa) are subjected to various forms of politically inspired economic sanctions, including trade boycotts, by the United States.

If the GATT talks are successful, the importance of such bilateral policies should decline. The alternative to a more liberal world trading environment supervised by GATT is some system of "managed trade." While much would depend on its specific details, if such a system is implemented (which seems politically unlikely), it is apt to be to the detriment of the developing countries, since in a free market environment (and assuming the appropriate domestic conditions and policies) their competitiveness is likely to increase with time in both agricultural and manufactured goods markets. Any system of "managed trade" is also likely to be managed by, and in the interests of, the largest and most powerful trading nations, i.e., by the major industrial countries. Small, poor developing countries—and the smaller industrial countries as well—are unlikely to be included, since large numbers make efficient management difficult if not impossible. Proposals for "managed trade" have emanated, not surprisingly, mainly from the major trading nations whose international competitiveness and dominance of the world economy is being challenged by the industrialization of developing countries. The goal of most of these proposals is essentially to slow down or preempt market-induced changes that would involve a transfer of production and income from the industrial to the developing countries.

Finally, the future is likely to see an even greater shift of world trade flows from the Atlantic to the Pacific Ocean, including trade among the United States, Canada, Japan, China, other Asian countries, and Mexico. This is an ongoing response to demographic and economic shifts, with the center of gravity of the world economy increasingly shifting toward the populous and dynamic economies of the Asia-Pacific region especially. If Japan opens its domestic market, it will become an increasingly important export market for developing countries the world over, and particularly in Asia. Some who believe that the world may degenerate into regional trading blocs (particularly if GATT fails) even see Japan heading an increasingly trade-integrated Asia-Pacific region including China, the northeastern Asian NICs, and the Southeast Asian near-NICs, with some spillover into southern Asia. The EC would form a second bloc, and North America, possibly including Mexico, the third. Even if this does not happen, the rest of Latin America and, especially, Africa, may remain geographically and economically marginal to the main loci of world trade.

Currency Shifts

The biggest change in the world economy between 1985 and 1988 has been the change in exchange rates among the currencies of the major industrial countries, with the U.S. dollar depreciating by about 40 percent against the Japanese yen and the West German mark, and by a smaller fraction against other Western European currencies. The appreciation of the dollar earlier in the 1980s resulted in currency overvaluation and in balance-of-payments and external debt problems in the many developing countries that had pegged their currencies to the dollar. Many have since disengaged their currencies, thereby effectively devaluing, while those that remain tied to the dollar have depreciated with it. For example, between October 1983 and November 1986, the currencies of eight African nations depreciated against the dollar by between 57 and 98 percent;[9] between February 1985 and September 1986, the Mexican peso depreciated by 270 percent against the dollar;[10] and in August 1986, Indonesia devalued its currency by 45 percent. Oil-exporting Middle Eastern countries' currencies have stayed on par with, or about 10 percent below, the dollar,[11] while, under pressure from the United States, the currencies of South Korea and Taiwan have appreciated by nearly 40 percent against the dollar.

The majority of developing countries, whose currencies have depreciated with or against the dollar, are now more competitive in export markets, particularly in Japan and Western Europe. For many countries, this has translated into increased export earnings despite low price elasticities of exports. But it has not been an unmixed blessing: For some countries, export receipts have in fact declined with the terms of trade, while import bills have increased, limiting the improved competitiveness of exports dependent on imported inputs. Depreciating currencies also increase the domestic budgetary burden of external debt repayment (especially of yen-denominated debt), fuel domestic inflation, and reduce domestic real incomes, especially in very open economies. While the gains from currency depreciation are often only gradually realized, the costs are usually immediately felt, posing both political and economic problems.

Depreciation, however, also makes investment cheaper for foreigners and could encourage an inflow of capital if other conditions are right. For example, the massive and ongoing peso depreciation in Mexico has attracted U.S. and Japanese investment in its export-oriented border industries. At the same time, currency appreciation resulting in declining export competitiveness—a trend exacerbated by rising labor costs at home and loss of U.S. GSP privileges abroad—has led Taiwan and South Korea to relocate some of their simpler, labor intensive export industries to such neighboring developing countries as Thailand, Malaysia, and the Philippines, and even to Caribbean nations. It has also led Japan to relocate some of its manufacturing production to the Asian NICs, ASEAN nations, and Mexico, areas that because of the strong yen are now undercutting Japanese (and NIC) products in third country markets and making inroads into the Japanese home market as well. Within Asia, international competitiveness is shifting decisively from northeastern to Southeast Asia.[12]

In general, while some developing countries have benefited from recent world currency shifts, others have not. But all will stand to gain if wild fluctuations in exchange rates can be eliminated from the international monetary system, allowing for more rational long-term calculations of production possibilities, less frequent shifts in competitiveness, and less unpredictable balance-of-payments impacts.

Third World Debt

The ballooning external debt of developing countries and their inability to pay it have occupied center stage in concerns about development in the 1980s. Around 1983, debt-service payments began to exceed new borrowing, resulting in a net outflow of capital from the developing to the industrial countries. About half of the total outflow is principal repayment; the rest is interest. Overborrowing in the 1970s, high real interest rates in the 1980s, and wasteful and inefficient use of borrowed funds are to blame. Aggravated by the commodity-price slump and terms-of-trade decline of the 1980s, debt-service ratios increased, amounting to 47 percent of Brazil's and 50 percent of Mexico's export receipts in 1986, and as much as 70 percent of Argentina's.[13] The major debtor nations are middle- and upper-middle–income countries in Asia and Latin America that were able to borrow readily from commercial banks in the 1970s and early 1980s. The poorer African countries are mostly indebted to international development agencies and foreign governments.

The debt crisis was the major constraint on developing countries' growth in the 1980s, since large debt-service burdens limit their ability to import what they need for growth. Trade surpluses are required for debt repayments, but these have been difficult to earn, given falling commodity prices through most of the decade and rising protectionism in industrial countries. Since Mexico's debt crisis in 1982, debt renegotiations have been proceeding on a country-by-country basis and have involved a combination of measures—including refinancing with new loans, rescheduling of debt payments, lower interest rates, debt-equity swaps and other new financial instruments, the Morgan Guaranty Mexican debt-bond swap, and domestic fiscal and monetary reforms in debtor nations.

The results of these efforts have been mixed at best. Many debtor countries in Latin America and Africa have suspended or otherwise unilaterally limited interest as well as principal payments on their external debt, while Asian debtor nations, most of them much poorer than the Latin American countries, have continued to service their external debt and even to repay some principal. Even the major creditor banks—and, in 1989, the U.S. government—now recognize that defaults on some loans are probably inevitable. Default is particularly likely in the poorest countries (most of them in Africa), which cannot possibly repay their accumulated debts. There has been a partial shift away from the IMF type of austerity program, but "growing out of the problem" has not been successful either, despite improving commodity prices as world inflation built in the late 1980s. Long-term world market prospects for many commodities are weak, and most foreigners are reluctant to lend to, or invest in, Third World debtor nations.

In the meantime, many developing countries are responding to their debt problems by: liberalizing trade policies (to promote domestic efficiency and exports); privatizing state-owned enterprises (to reduce the burden of government budget subsidies);[14] and removing restrictions on foreign investment and welcoming it more enthusiastically (to obtain the foreign capital necessary for growth and debt repayment). All these policies face nationalistic objections, since they involve what many developing countries have become accustomed to viewing and abhorring as increased "dependence" on the industrial countries, though it is apt to differ more in kind than in degree from their present dependence on foreign commercial banks.

The issues raised by the debt-equity swaps pioneered by Chile suggest the complexity of the situation. A swap simultaneously relieves host governments of some debt, minimizes the creditor bank's loss on a dubious loan, provides foreign (or local) investors with cheap local currency, and injects new private capital into the economy; it may also attract back some domestic-flight capital. The problems are that creditor banks may not want to take the loss; investors may not want to invest or expand in such problem-ridden economies; nationalistic governments do not want to increase foreign ownership of their economies (a major reason why they preferred external debt to foreign investment in the 1970s); private investments may be merely subsidized, not increased, resulting in resource misallocation and eventual regeneration of outward payments (if the investors are foreign);

foreign investors may merely take over existing local enterprises, not create new production; the increase in the local money supply may be inflationary; and "round-tripping" may occur (e.g., if returning domestic flight capital is swapped cheaply for pesos only to be exchanged back into dollars on the black market). For all these reasons, while debt-equity swaps may be expected to grow, they are unlikely to account for a major proportion of current debt.

Foreign Investment and Aid

Because of the debt crisis—the unwillingess of creditors to lend, and the inability of debtors to absorb and service more debt—developing countries' external financing declined from $160 billion in 1981 to $68 billion in 1986, with the share of net private lending dropping from 57 percent of the total in 1981 to only 4 percent in 1986. The share of direct investment correspondingly increased, from 12 percent to 19 percent.[15] The United States has been the largest source of new foreign investment in developing countries, accounting for nearly half their stock, but is being surpassed by Japan. In investment flows to Asian developing countries, Japan surpassed the United States in the early 1980s and was itself surpassed by Taiwan, now ranking second, in 1989.[16] Investments in many commodities have declined in recent years (though disinvestment in oil is being reversed), while investments in manufactures have increased. Five countries—Brazil, Mexico, Singapore, South Africa, and Malaysia—accounted for almost half of the total stock of foreign investment in developing countries in 1986.[17] The ASEAN countries—Singapore, Malaysia, Thailand, the Philippines, and Indonesia—increased their share of total foreign investment in developing countries from a third in 1974 to more than 40 percent in 1984,[18] with 40 percent of the ASEAN total going to Singapore alone. Given the surge in Japanese and Taiwanese investment in these countries since 1987, their share has probably increased since then. In contrast, there has been disinvestment in most of Africa.

Because of their debt burdens and reduced capacity to borrow, many developing countries have become more welcoming to foreign investment in recent years—relaxing domestic ownership requirements, liberalizing trade, reducing bureaucratic regulations, and offering new fiscal incentives. Export-oriented investments are particularly sought after, because of their ability to earn the foreign exchange that alleviates the debt burden and permits continued growth. So far, in most countries these attempts to lure new foreign investment have not been very successful. Domestic political and economic conditions, including debt problems, remain discouraging in many countries, while internationally the U.S. stock and bond markets and fears of protectionism continue to divert and attract capital from the developing countries. The decline in the dollar has slowed, and in a few cases begun reversing, the offshore moves undertaken by U.S. industry in order to survive the strong dollar in the first half of the 1980s. There has recently been some corresponding increase in offshore investment in developing countries by Japanese, European, and Asian NIC firms whose home currencies have strengthened. But these, like new U.S. investments, tend to be concentrated in relatively few developing countries—primarily Mexico (which is attracting Japanese as well as U.S. manufacturing investment because of its much-depreciated currency and proximity to the United States), the Asian NICs (which are attracting both Japanese and U.S. investment because of their accumulated skills and infrastructure, as well as lower costs and growing home markets), and Southeast Asian near-NICs (attractive because of cheap but relatively skilled labor, relatively good infrastructure, political stability, access to GSP privileges, and strategic location in the world's fastest-growing and soon-to-be-largest regional market). China is also attracting considerable investment from other Asian countries, particularly from overseas Chinese (including Taiwanese) business interests.

Beyond these few countries, most foreign investment by industrial countries continues to go mainly to other industrial countries, often because of fears of being shut out of their markets by protectionism—as in the case of investment in Europe motivated by anticipated full market integration in 1992. Japan, for example, has for some years been investing more in North America and Western Europe than in its traditional Asian locations, so that by 1986, Japan's cumulative investments in the United States accounted for 30.2 percent of its worldwide foreign investments, followed by investment in Asia (23.3 percent), Latin America (18.7 percent), and Europe (13.2 percent).[19] Since 1986, Japanese investments in Asian developing countries have increased, and they will continue to increase, especially with the announcement of a new Japanese government Asian Industries Development plan to support private sector export promotion in China, Malaysia, Thailand, Indonesia, and the Philippines by providing financial, technical, and market assistance to export-manufacturing enterprises in these countries and by improving their access to the Japanese market. Still, this may be insufficient to increase the share of these countries in Japan's overseas investments relative to those of the United States, Western Europe, and the Asian NICs.[20] Overall, developing countries receive about one-quarter of the world's foreign direct investment.

In the long run, the amount of foreign investment going to developing countries will depend on what happens to trade patterns and policies, currency shifts, interest rates, and the prospects for commodity, manufactured, and service exports from the developing countries, as well as their internal economic and investment policies. Unless these underlying conditions change significantly, and favorably, foreign investment flows to all but a few developing countries are unlikely to increase dramatically. However, a significant increase may be expected in overseas investments by the Latin American and Asian NICs and their "Third World multinationals." Brazil and Hong Kong are already among the world's top 15 providers of direct investment abroad,[21] while both Taiwan and Singapore, rich in external reserves, are encouraging overseas investments by domestic firms.

As private lending has fallen precipitously, official loans and grants have risen from 31 percent of developing countries' external finance in 1981 to 77 percent in 1986, though in nominal terms this is only a small absolute increase.[22] In real terms, industrial country government aid to developing countries has been declining, and for political and budgetary reasons this situation is unlikely to be reversed soon, with the exception of an increase in Japan's overseas development assistance. For example, in May 1987, Japan announced that it would provide $20 billion of its foreign exchange earnings to debtor nations through a combination of untied export credits, increased contributions to multilateral development banks (MDBs), and loans jointly financed by government and private institutions. The Japanese government will also double its official aid to Asian developing countries that trade heavily with Japan to $8 billion a year by 1990.[23] While there is plenty of evidence to suggest that the net benefit of Japanese aid to developing countries may be limited by the many business strings typically attached to it,[24] the increased importance of Japan as an aid donor provides a sign of hope in an otherwise rather bleak foreign aid picture. Japanese aid will not only help to make up for declining real aid to developing countries from the United States and some other industrial countries, it may also stimulate more aid from the United States if the United States recognizes, as Japan clearly does, the importance of aid as an instrument that can open up foreign markets for donor country businesses, even without explicit "tying." The Asian NICs are also a potential source of aid to other developing countries: For example, Singapore has begun sending aid to the Philippines, and Taiwan is exploring aid-giving opportunities in a variety of countries, probably linked to its business and political interests.

Linking aid to donor countries' international business interests is a long-established practice that has its merits as a means of eliciting more aid flows to developing countries—but it also has its limitations. Relating aid to potential markets will mean a further concentration of aid in the more prosperous and promising developing countries, most of them in Asia and Latin America, that can deliver such a market, and a corresponding neglect of aid to the poorest and least developed countries, most of them in Africa. Yet, it is these poorest countries that need official assistance the most, on both humanitarian and developmental grounds, since they are the least likely to attract commercial lending and direct private investment. Aid to these countries—particularly if invested in infrastructure and human resource development—is necessary to enhance their attractiveness to and absorptive capacity for foreign private (equity or loan) capital that would not otherwise be forthcoming. But whether flows of commercial finance to developing countries can be increased in the 1990s depends on international trade, financial, and political developments that are by no means clear.

MICROECONOMIC DEVELOPMENTS

World Trade in Commodities

At the end of 1986, the world price of food and industrial raw materials, weighted by developing countries' exports, had declined in real terms by close to 30 percent since 1980, and by nearly 50 percent since 1954. Developing countries' raw material exports could buy, in 1986, only half the volume of manufactured imports that they did in 1974.[25] But commodity prices have been rising strongly since early 1987, largely because of heightened expectations of world inflation and continued respectable growth in developed and newly industrialized economies. Despite this—and for well-known reasons to do with low income elasticity of demand and high price elasticity of supply—structural conditions in world commodity markets are not favorable to developing country exports in the long run. With conservation, technological substitution, and taste changes in industrial countries reducing demand, and price responsiveness and technological innovation in developing countries increasing supply, relative prices have fluctuated around a declining trend. Interestingly, the more market-oriented that developing countries have become—the more they have dismantled agricultural marketing controls and removed policy distortions—the greater the risk of periodic oversupply and price collapses that may eventually discourage some market participation. In theory, price and income fluctuations can be managed on the national or international level (e.g., by hedging, buffer stock and crop insurance schemes, and international commodity agreements), but in practice this has not worked out well and there is no indication that it is more likely to in the future.

The major problem today is not periodic but rather chronic oversupply, which does discourage production, especially in food crops. The chief causes are agricultural protection and farm subsidies in the industrial countries—Japan, Western European nations, and the United States—that preserve a small but politically powerful and high-cost farm sector at the expense of both domestic consumers (and hence of industrial growth elsewhere in their economies) and, especially, vast numbers of impoverished Third World farmers who are or could be much more competitive in producing and exporting the same or substitutable crops at true market prices or scarcity values. The prospects for the continuation of this phenomenon of costly and regressive farm subsidies are uncertain, though the budget and hence political burden that they impose on developing countries could very rapidly become intolerable.

Technological innovation also makes possible continuously increasing agricultural productivity in both industrial and developing countries. In food production, the spread of green revolution technology in Asia and Latin America, together with the liberalization of agricultural policy in developing countries,[26] has turned such giants as India and, especially, China from food-deficit into at least marginally self-sufficient or food-surplus countries, exporting their surpluses to world markets in which they were major buyers just a few years before—though the Asia-wide drought and resultant shortages and high prices of food in 1987 show how much this success is still hostage to the vagaries of the weather. Still, technology has enabled even arid Saudi Arabia to grow twice as much wheat as it needs, and it may soon bring about a green revolution in Africa, despite serious ecological, political, infrastructural, and organizational constraints on that continent. Worldwide overproduction of food crops results in low food prices, farm incomes, and export receipts, and in increased farm indebtedness and government budget deficits. It also discourages food production in the developing countries, thereby threatening the adequacy of future food supplies and increasing both rural-urban migration and rural and urban unemployment.

Farmers in many developing countries have already diversified their market production, including export production, by shifting to higher-value foodstuffs and nonfood crops. In Southeast Asia, Central America, and the Caribbean, the shift has been to tropical (and even temperate) fruits, vegetables, flowers, and seafood, as well as marijuana, heroin, and cocaine. Thailand, the Philippines, and even the socialist countries of Burma and Vietnam have increased their shrimp exports (mostly to Japan) with the aid of technology and some capital imported from Taiwan. New crops grown in the highlands include strawberries for local hotels and the booming tourist trade, and potatoes for McDonald's french fries in the big cities. Meat and dairy production is expanding, mainly for home consumption. These countries are also capitalizing on the growth of the gourmet or exotic-foods market in Japan and Western countries, while some are benefiting from agricultural problems in competing developed countries. Brazil, for example, has been progressively taking over Florida's share of the orange juice market, following many years of frost damage and citrus-canker disease in Florida, and some Central American countries are following suit.[27]

While such diversification is admirable, its long-term success is by no means guaranteed. Import restrictions in the industrial countries remain a problem—for example, protective quotas have been imposed on Costa Rica's successful export of cut flowers to the United States; Florida orange growers have filed an antidumping suit against Brazil; and Japan still bans the import of bananas from the Philippines during the harvest season for domestic fruits. Japanese health inspection standards remain a major nontariff barrier for tropical food exports from other Asian countries. There is also the ever-present threat of oversupply, despite higher price and income elasticities of demand for the new foods. Innovative Asian or Latin American marketeers who develop a market for a new exotic food in the United States, for example, often find it quickly usurped by other developing countries and even U.S. suppliers. Exporting nongrain food crops also often involves greater dependence of developing country farmers on industrial country multinationals that either operate plantations or enter into contract relationships with independent farmers, supplying them with various inputs and credit in return for processing, packaging, and marketing their crop abroad (the higher value-added stages of production). While there are obvious benefits, many people argue that the relationship with multinationals also involves potential costs—including the risks of increased indebtedness for small farmers, vulnerability to price and other market manipulations by monopsonistic global firms with operations in many different competing countries, and the preempting by foreign firms of independent local processing and marketing activities that would increase the share of domestic value-added in the world price.

Market prospects for some nonfood agricultural products are not as bleak as they are for food products. Despite a long-term downward trend, prices of nonfood agricultural products recovered from their 1986 trough and by late 1987 were back at 1980 levels. A growing consumer preference for cotton, for example, increased demand and prices for this crop, while the spread of AIDS sharply increased demand for rubber for use in surgical gloves. Malaysia has developed epoxidized natural rubber, a composite that outperforms synthetic rubber and could replace it in vehicle tires. This could as much as double the world market for natural rubber, of which Malaysia is the largest producer, but there is already a growing global shortage of rubber. Because of acreage cutbacks during long years of low and declining prices, and because of the crop's long gestation period (seven years), supplies are not easily replenished. Malaysia is also intensively researching new processes and uses for palm oil, of which it is also the world's largest producer, but palm and other edible tropical-oil exports from developing countries are threatened by a consumer campaign in the United States against the use of saturated fats in processed foods, and by the imminent development of a no-calorie synthetic fat substitute. There is also the constant threat of oversupply, compounded by the ease with which technological innovators may be imitated by other countries. Domestic cost pressures from rising wages and acute labor shortages on plantations make Malaysia, the largest supplier of nonfood agricultural products among developing countries, particularly vulnerable to intensifying competition from lower-cost neighbors.

Of all the commodities exported by developing countries, metals are probably most vulnerable to declining demand from technological conservation, substitution, and the development of new composite materials. The amount of metals used per unit of manufacturing output has been falling fast. For example, between 1979 and 1985, while manufacturing output rose an average of 2.1 percent a year, world consumption of aluminum remained static, and world copper use fell because of the increasing substitution of fiber optics for copper wire in telecommunications.[28] Frequent price fluctuations are one factor encouraging consumers to switch from metals to nonmetallic manufactured substances such as various plastics, the supply of which is more readily controlled and prices therefore more stable. Metal producers also have to cope with oversupply, exacerbated by structural changes and government policy interventions. For example, country-by-country nationalization of the operations of large oligopolistic multinationals that once carefully controlled world supply and prices to maximize industry profits has resulted in a more competitive supply situation. Each individual country or producer (often a state mining enterprise) acts as a price-taker and seeks to maximize output for maximum national revenues, leading to worldwide oversupply and falling prices. Producer cartel attempts to raise prices have also resulted in increased output from nonmembers, including new entrants, thereby undercutting the cartel price through oversupply. Thus, Malaysia's attempt to push up the price of tin caused it to fall instead by nearly 60 percent between 1979 and 1986.

Current world excess capacity in metals production is likely to decline as the closing of old mines and smelters (e.g., for copper and aluminum) in developed countries such as the United States shift supply more toward the developing countries, where technological advancements in exploration and mining are making it increasingly possible to extract metals from previously difficult locations. But despite recent price increases, the generally dismal world market prospects for metals is a serious concern because many of the developing countries that export metals derive most of their foreign exchange earnings from a single metal (e.g., copper in Zaire and Zambia). Metals exporters, mainly in Africa, include some of the poorest countries in the world.

The price of oil, the leading fuel exported by developing countries, was raised dramatically by the Organization of Petroleum Exporting Countries (OPEC) beginning in 1973. After the "second oil shock," in 1981, oil prices slumped equally dramatically to about one-third their peak values by 1986. The cartel's success in raising the price of oil encouraged conservation and substitution on the demand side and increased production by nonmembers on the supply side, reducing OPEC's share of the world oil market and exerting downward pressure on the price. OPEC's failure to maintain cohesion among its members resulted in weakening observance of cartel quotas and undercutting of the cartel price, especially by Iran and Iraq, who needed their oil earnings to finance their war.

The oil price decline resulted in import savings and improved trade balances for oil-importing developing countries but caused huge revenue losses for oil-exporting countries and increased debt-service ratios for such heavily indebted nations as Mexico, Indonesia, and Nigeria. A heavy structural dependence on imports, permitted by many years of plentiful oil revenues, and heavy external borrowing for domestic industrialization based on assumptions of continued abundant oil earnings, resulted in severe balance-of-payments problems. In response, many oil-exporting countries have devalued or depreciated their currencies and are attempting to diversify into nonoil exports, including agricultural commodities and manufactures. Unaccustomed capital constraints and limited domestic skills are making this difficult for many. Indonesia is a rare example of success: It responded to declining oil revenues by currency devaluation, domestic austerity measures, economic reform (including trade, investment, and financial market liberalization), and promotion of nonoil exports, which have enabled it to sustain modest growth (3 to 5 percent) while attracting new foreign investment and increasing nonoil exports from 10 percent of foreign exchange earnings to 45 percent in 1988.

Oil prices began recovering in 1987, and the general belief is that the recent reduction in production capacity will result in oil shortages and high prices again in the 1990s. While this will help improve the situation for the oil-exporting countries, it will add to the burden of oil-importing countries, as it did in the 1970s. But the huge payments surpluses and external borrowing are unlikely to recur, in part because of the weakening of OPEC and the continued entry of new producers. Natural gas supplies, which are concentrated in oil-exporting countries, especially in the Middle East, but are also found in countries without oil, will in the 1990s continue to decline in the industrial countries and increase in the developing countries.

World Trade in Manufactures

Against the generally gloomy picture in commodities, manufactured exports are a bright spot. Developing countries that have specialized in the export of manufactures—mainly the Asian and Latin American NICs—continue to prosper handsomely and to make increasing inroads into industrial country markets for an ever-widening range of products. The less developed countries that have followed suit have almost all succeeded to some extent, at least in increasing the quantity and proportion of foreign exchange earnings derived from manufactured exports. They include a range of very different countries, from such large, populous, and poor countries as China, India, and Bangladesh, to such medium-sized, middle-income countries as Turkey, Thailand, and the Philippines, to such small, resource-poor island nations as Mauritius and the Dominican Republic. In almost all these countries, manufacturing for export has become the fastest-growing sector of the economy, though—especially for the larger countries—it typically remains small relative to agriculture and manufacturing for the domestic market. Export-manufacturing's contribution to the balance of payments is typically much greater than its contribution to total output or employment.

Developing countries have been increasing their share of both world industrial output and world manufactured exports since 1970. While light, labor intensive manufactures such as textiles, clothing, footwear, fashion accessories, toys, and sporting goods, and processed agricultural products such as food, rubber, and wood products remain the most typical and widespread exports, the range has increased to include more capital intensive goods such as iron and steel, chemicals, glass, petroleum products, transport equipment (cars, ships, and even planes), machinery and machine tools, electrical and electronic products, and professional and scientific equipment. Many of these capital intensive industries are set up or evolve to serve both domestic and foreign markets, allowing developing countries to enjoy the economies of scale that would not be possible if they were limited to their small domestic markets. The single most important manufactured export from developing countries is textile products, which account for 10 percent of all their exports and over 25 percent of their manufactured exports to industrial countries. In certain regions, mainly Mexico and eastern and Southeast Asia, electronics is also very important. For example, electronics products and components vie with petroleum products as the commodity-rich ASEAN group's primary export to the United States, followed by textiles and clothing, while the Asia-Pacific region generally (including Japan) is now both the world's largest source of, and the largest market for, electronics parts, components, and supplies.

Despite the fact that manufactured exports now have a long (more than 30 years) history of success, are fairly widespread in a variety of developing countries, and still enjoy faster-growing, less wildly fluctuating markets and more favorable terms of trade than do commodity exports, pessimism about long-run prospects has been common since the 1970s and persists despite the contradicting evidence. This largely reflects export-manufacturing's political unpopularity in industrial countries (which have been losing their world market shares in certain industries) and even in some of the developing countries (where domestic vested interests often oppose the liberal economic policies that must accompany export-manufacturing). I will briefly examine the reasons, related to the international economic environment, that are usually given for this pessimism and consider their validity.

Technological advancement is often considered to be disadvantageous to developing countries exporting manufactures, since it generally proceeds in a labor-saving direction. Thus, it has long been predicted that automation in such industries as textiles and electronics will result in comparative advantage shifting back to the industrial countries. In fact, high costs and risks have considerably slowed the diffusion of automated technology in industrial countries, while short product cycles, intense competitive-cost pressures, and market trends toward individually differentiated products have extended the life of labor intensive processes in high-tech and fad industries such as computer equipment, fashion garments, and toys—world manufacturing of which is now concentrated in Asian developing and newly industrialized economies. Even automated technologies frequently include intrinsically labor intensive processes or require some relatively labor intensive inputs that are best produced in low-wage developing countries, where they may attract the location of complementary capital intensive processes in order to benefit from economies of vertical integration and just-in-time delivery. "Deskilling" as a consequence of automation may also make more production processes feasible in developing countries, since machine operation substitutes for the operator skill they lack. These countries are also more likely to be able to offer the "flexible" labor willing to work the round-the-clock shifts necessary for the quick attainment of maximum volumes and rapid depreciation of expensive, capital intensive equipment.

More generally, advances in transport, communications, computers, and information technology have shrunk the world so that geographical distance is no longer a major handicap; it can be offset by good infrastructure, which many developing countries, especially the NICs, have developed. These countries have further expanded their technological capacity so that they increasingly possess relatively cheap supplies of skilled and experienced as well as unskilled labor. Some of the Asian NICs are now even in the position of offering cheap capital or direct capital assistance to capital intensive, high-tech companies, as well as providing training or training subsidies for skilled workers. Where technological change is rapid, developing countries can also benefit from the advantage of latecomers to industrialization in that they may immediately implement the latest technology without waiting for older equipment to be depreciated.

In short, technological advancement is at least as permissive as it is inhibiting of continued export manufacturing in developing countries. In particular, technological upgrading has helped the more developed NICs maintain their comparative advantage despite rising wages and appreciating currencies and has encouraged them to slough off some of their older, more labor intensive industries to lower-wage developing countries, often through the outward investments of "Third World multinationals." In the Asian region, for example, the relocation of labor intensive industry from South Korea, Taiwan, Hong Kong, and Singapore—in the process of their upgrading—has stimulated export-manufacturing in Thailand, the Philippines, Malaysia, Indonesia, China, and even Bangladesh, Sri Lanka, and Turkey.

Another common cause for pessimism about the future prospects of export-manufacturing in developing countries relates, as with commodities, to the fear of worldwide oversupply. It has been argued that as more and more developing countries are lured into manufacturing for the world market, competition among them will lead to overproduction, excess capacity, and falling prices. The entry of China and India into the market is particularly feared. In fact, nothing like this has yet happened, for many reasons.

Demand for manufactured goods is more price- and income-elastic than that for commodities and has been growing more rapidly than has income in industrial countries and in the world as a whole. Developing countries still account for only a small proportion of industrial country imports of manufactures, and for an even smaller proportion (less than 10 percent) of industrial country consumption of manufactures, most of it concentrated in only a few industries such as garments and footwear. From this small base, the scope for further market penetration, including displacement of huge ready markets, is enormous, even without considering the accelerating growth of developing country markets themselves. Thus, exports of manufactures from developing countries can grow more rapidly than demand for manufactures, which is itself still growing more rapidly than income. For example, in 1986 the volume of world trade in manufactures rose by only 3 percent (one of the worst performances in three decades, according to GATT, though still higher than total output growth), yet the value of developing country manufactured exports grew by 13 percent in the same year.[29]

The entry of more developing countries into particular export-manufacturing industries—usually textiles and garments—does not necessarily hurt older producers, who have the option of diversifying and are often keen to move up the industrial ladder. As incomes and costs rise in the NICs and they open their domestic markets, more opportunities arise for the developing countries to supply them with cheap manufactures. At the same time, the NICs remain much more attractive than the developing countries to many multinationals relocating production from industrial countries, especially in high-tech industries, because of their superior skills, infrastructure, efficiency, and supporting industries.

Not all developing countries at present want to or can embark on export-manufacturing on a scale large enough to "flood" world markets in particular product lines. Many of the countries beginning export-manufacturing are very small and have limited domestic capacity (e.g., the Caribbean islands and Mauritius). The larger countries, such as China and India, remain primarily domestic market-oriented and are interested in exporting manufactures mainly to earn the foreign exchange necessary to invest in their potentially huge domestic markets. They are unlikely to end up as "export platforms" only and bring with their increased supply also their increased demand for manufactures on the world market. Most of the low-wage countries also remain relatively inefficient, with the result that they do not pose a major competitive threat to more established exporters, while their policymaking elites still tend to favor import protection for domestic market monopolies and a low-waged, underemployed labor force, over the more democratic impacts (lower consumer costs, higher employment) of export-manufacturing.

In short, domestic supply-side limitations in developing countries remain a greater constraint to the expansion of manufacturing for export than do prospects for world market demand, which remain good for those countries that do succeed in establishing export-manufacturing industries. If these supply-side limitations are eased by political changes in the future, then concerns about excess capacity may become more valid; but even so this would depend on the rate of growth of demand. As the recent experience of the Asian NICs shows, incomes, demand, and imports all increase in developing countries as they advance up the industrial ladder.

The major demand-side constraint is not imposed by the world market, but rather by politics—specifically, protectionist trade policy in the industrial countries. Current trade policy in industrial countries already discriminates against developing countries, most notably through the Multi-Fiber Arrangement (MFA), which regulates world trade in textiles and textile products—the most important export-manufacturing industry in developing countries—outside GATT rules. There has also been a growing use of voluntary export restraints and other nontariff barriers against specific products from individual countries. Protectionism is certainly a major problem, especially for the NICs who have been its chief targets so far, but it is also a complex phenomenon, and complete pessimism about its spread and its effects may not be warranted.

For one thing, protectionism against some countries benefits others and helps to spread export-manufacturing among more countries. Examples include textile quotas against Hong Kong, and voluntary export restraints and other import restrictions against Japan, South Korea, and Taiwan—all of which have encouraged firms from these countries to relocate to other developing countries in Asia and Latin America, creating opportunities for the latter to penetrate industrial country markets. For example, the present boom in South Korean automobile exports owes much to the voluntary export restraint on Japanese car exports to the United States.

Protectionism also remains less severe against developing countries' manufactured exports than against their agricultural exports to industrial countries,[30] and this is likely to continue. There is a much larger number and wider range of manufactures; it takes time to identify import damage and to undertake the formal procedures, including political lobbying, necessary to obtain import protection—during which time many of the import-impacted companies may be forced to shut down or move out; rural-based farm sectors generally have more political clout, disproportionate to the numbers they employ, than do urban-based industries in developed countries (particularly Japan); unity is more difficult to achieve in manufacturing, where national companies may be highly competitive with and distrustful of one another, and capital and labor may have different interests—e.g., capital can meet import competition from developing countries by relocating to those countries, but labor, which is often weakly organized, cannot; protection against industrial inputs will be opposed by their industrial consumers, pitting capital in one sector against capital in another; there is usually a dominant preference for free trade among policymaking elites in industrial countries that are free enterprise–market economies; governments are sometimes hesitant to take policy actions that raise the prices of manufactured goods to consumers; and GATT regulates international trade in manufactures but not in agricultural commodities. Those developing countries whose manufactured exports benefit multinationals in the industrial countries also have a powerful ally against protectionism in their export markets, as in the case of the Mexican border industries.

Affected countries can, within limits, adjust to protectionism. For example, protectionism encourages them to diversify their export markets and their industrial production, shifting from protected to unprotected products and upgrading into more sophisticated, newer industries that tend to have growing markets and to be less inclined toward protectionism. Import tariffs or surcharges can be a stimulus to reducing costs in order to remain competitive, while quotas can be filled with higher-value products or avoided by shifting to products not covered by a quota, as has been the case under the MFA. Protectionism is also generally ineffective in improving the competitiveness and viability of protected industrial country industries. Although developing countries so far have been too weak to retaliate against discriminatory trade restrictions, their capacity to do so is growing with the size and purchasing power of their domestic markets.

Thus, while protectionism remains the major threat to developing countries' continued export of manufactures, this is not sufficient completely to condemn the prospects for such exports in the future. Protectionism has not so far undermined the growth of its major target countries—Japan and the Asian NICs—and is itself not a market parameter but a policy variable that can be changed and is likely to continue meeting at least some resistance within the industrial countries themselves.

Recent events in the world economy have in fact improved the immediate prospects for expanded export-manufacturing in developing countries. These events—including the appreciation of the yen and of European and Asian NIC currencies, and the depreciation of most developing country currencies even against the dollar—have increased the competitiveness of developing countries' manufactured exports against exports from established countries in world markets. If adjustment of the major industrial economies and Asian NICs to the changing world environment proceeds as desired—i.e., with stimulation of the Japanese and West German economies, and the opening of the Japanese, South Korean, and Taiwanese domestic markets to more foreign imports—the demand for the developing countries' manufactured exports will increase even further.

World Trade in Services

In addition to commodities and manufactures, developing countries' exports of services are also affected by the world environment. Workers' remittances have declined sharply since the early 1980s because of the slump in oil prices and in Middle East construction and other economic activity relying heavily on imported labor. Countries for which labor exports to the Middle East have been important include South Korea, Thailand, the Philippines, Indonesia, Bangladesh, India, Pakistan, and Egypt. Even with the recovery of oil prices, the completion of major infrastructural construction projects in the Middle East makes substantial rehiring of foreign workers unlikely. Elsewhere, high unemployment in Western Europe has slowed the flow of migrant workers from the Mediterranean, while the passage of a new U.S. immigration law that penalizes employers for employing illegal foreign workers will reduce and perhaps even reverse the flow of Mexican migrant labor. There has also been some retrenchment of foreign workers from neighboring black African nations in South Africa as a result of that country's economic woes. On the other hand, government-controlled labor exports are becoming more and more common for China and Vietnam, while workers from Thailand and the Philippines are increasingly finding work—often illegally—in the booming, labor-short economies of Japan and the Asian NICs.

Tourism earnings have remained relatively stable on the whole, and very much dependent on supply-side conditions, especially political conditions, in individual countries. Countries with depreciated currencies should become more competitive, and an increase in visitors from Japan and Western Europe may be expected because of their stronger currencies. There are regional variations; for example, tourism has declined in the Middle East and North Africa because of concerns about terrorism but has increased in the Caribbean, which is fortunately situated close to the United States. Tourism is booming in Asia as rising incomes have led to a huge increase (25 percent in 1988 alone) in intra-Asian tourist travel, especially by travelers from Japan and the NICs, resulting in extreme pressures on existing capacity. This will probably continue.

But for most other developing countries, the longer-run prospects for increased foreign exchange receipts from tourism are not particularly bright, especially for the many that lack local attractions or are far from the richer countries from which most tourists hail. This is the case, for example, for Africa (with the exception of Kenya), where the AIDS threat poses a further problem for tourism. Tourism is partially dependent on income growth in the industrial countries, is competitive among developing countries (and between developing and industrial countries), and tends to favor the more developed of these countries because of its relative capital intensity and need for expensive infrastructural support. Tourism in China, for example, is limited not by demand but by domestic capacity. In general, except for small island nations with few other resources, tourism is not likely to be a growth market.

Few developing countries are involved in exports of transportation services, which tend to be dominated by the industrial countries, are regulated by international or regional cartels, and often subject to protectionist restrictions in the industrial countries. Several developing countries are involved in shipping, but this is a competitive sector that suffers from world excess capacity. In general, transportation is a very capital intensive sector that few developing countries can enter successfully. The exceptions here are once again the Asian NICs and their neighboring Southeast Asian countries, which run highly successful international airlines that, with a combination of more modern fleets, better service, and lower fares (resulting in part from lower labor costs), have been outcompeting the airlines of older industrial countries. There is also scope for some developing countries to develop roles as regional transportation and communications centers, as Singapore, the busiest seaport in the world, already is for Southeast Asia. Some of the small South Pacific islands are trying to develop as naval bases for superpower military fleets.

Two service exports that have been increasing their share of world trade are investment income and consultancy services, including financial, technical, and business services. These are areas the industrial countries have traditionally dominated and are seeking to liberalize in the current GATT round. Most developing countries run deficits in these services, which could worsen if there is liberalization. However, there are prospects for at least some countries' increasing their exports of these services. The Asian NICs, for example, have been increasing their overseas investments and can expect to receive increased investment income in the future. They are also becoming important sellers of technology to less developed countries, for whom their technology is arguably more "appropriate" in scale, sophistication, and costs.

Hong Kong and Singapore are struggling to become world financial centers, but their prospects are limited by political uncertainty surrounding Hong Kong's incorporation into China in 1997, by Singapore's relatively small domestic (and even regional) market, and by intense worldwide competition. For example, in the Asia-Pacific region, which is expected to experience a boom in demand for financial services, the two city-states are likely to be overshadowed by both Tokyo and Sydney. However, both are likely to retain a regional role, as are the Cayman Islands and other Caribbean offshore financial centers and tax havens, and Turkey. South Pacific countries such as Vanuatu are also attempting to develop as tax havens and offshore financial centers but are likely to be less successful because of their remoteness and small size.

Low wages combined with improved education in some developing countries are increasing their ability to export manual and "brain" services, aided by technological advancements in communications and information technology. At the low end, Barbados and South Korea already perform labor intensive data-entry and processing operations for U.S. multinationals, while at the high end, computer scientists and engineers in the Asian NICs and India are beginning to perform skill intensive research and design functions and to develop software for high-tech multinationals in the industrial countries. This comparative advantage is likely to grow, and protectionism is much more difficult and unlikely in these "brain services" than it is in manufacturing.

In general, because of domestic skill and infrastructural constraints, only a few developing countries and NICs, mainly in Asia, are likely to develop significant service exports in the next decade, and these exports will remain smaller than their commodity and manufacturing exports. A partial exception is labor exports from the poorer Asian countries to their richer neighbors and beyond.

CONCLUSION

For a long time it has been fashionable—especially among noneconomists and in the developing countries themselves—to view the international economy as essentially unfavorable to the developing countries; even to see it as a constraint on their development and a major cause of inequality, both between developing and developed countries, and within developing countries. Participation of developing countries in the world economy has thus been denigrated.

This is puzzling, because the historical evidence is so completely different. First, those developing countries most integrated into the world economy (say, the Asian NICs and the countries of Southeast Asia), the most export-oriented, and the most dependent on the world market are also the most successful by any indicator of development: output and employment growth; income distribution; real and relative wage growth; mass living standards; and social indicators such as health status, educational attainment, infant mortality, female labor force participation, and so on. Those developing countries most marginal and least integrated into the world economy—say, in sub-Saharan Africa—have been the least successful on all counts. Within Southeast Asia, the contrast between the outward-oriented ASEAN countries and their socialist neighbors (Burma, Vietnam, Laos, and Kampuchea), which share similar colonial histories and resource endowments, is particularly striking—though the difference in domestic economic systems may have more to do with this since the socialist countries are at least as externally dependent as the capitalist ASEAN countries.

Second, those opposed to integration in the world economy often posit self-sufficiency as a desirable alternate goal, even though all the developed countries are heavily integrated into the world economy, with the smaller developed countries of Western Europe especially being much more export-oriented than are South Korea and Taiwan, for example. Self-sufficiency, even in a large, rich country such as the United States, has been decreasing rather than increasing. As self-sufficiency has declined, incomes and living standards (even in the United States) have risen. For both developed and developing countries, as participation in the world economy increases, so does domestic income, including incomes of farmers and of the urban working class. This partially explains the eagerness of many socialist developing countries—including China and Vietnam—to expand their participation in the world economy as a means of building socialism. Furthermore, only those developing countries that heavily participate in the world economy, especially in export-manufacturing, have any hope of narrowing the income gap with industrial countries or even overtaking some of them.

Third, no country—not even the United States or, at the other extreme, China—has the option of not participating in the world economy. This is particularly true of developing countries simply because they are small, poor, and not industrialized, and therefore do not, and in many cases never can, make all of their own needs, including basic subsistence needs. The relevant question really is the *terms* under which developing countries participate in the world economy—what they sell, what they buy, under what rules, and affected by what policies. Even where the world economy is likely to be unfavorable for some developing countries—especially the poorest of them—this does not imply that they should not participate in it, since nonparticipation is likely to be even worse (as the example of Burma's long period of virtual but progressively undermined autarky suggests).

I have outlined the features of the changing world economy that will affect developing countries in the 1990s. They include macroeconomic developments in the industrial countries, world trade patterns and policies, currency shifts, and international capital flows, including foreign investment, aid, and Third World debt. These developments are, of course, interrelated and difficult to predict with any certainty, given their dependence on political as well as market forces. My conclusion is an evasive one: that the world economy will "muddle through" without major calamities or boons for the developing countries. At the microeconomic level, I have suggested that the world market prospects for developing countries' commodity exports are likely to continue to be fairly poor and unstable in the 1990s, despite current and occasional price booms in particular commodities. Market prospects for manufactured exports are much better, though hardly excellent, with prospects for service exports lying somewhere in between. All these markets will be heavily conditioned by decisions on international trading rules, and by government policies in both the developed and developing countries. Because of different indigenous conditions, individual developing countries will have differing capacities to take advantage of favorable market prospects and to avoid or manage unfavorable ones, leading to greater differentiation among them. In particular, the Asian NICs are likely to join the lower ranks of the developed countries in the 1990s,[31] while the ASEAN countries rise to become full-fledged NICs, narrowing the gap that separates them from the developed countries but vastly increasing the gap dividing them from other developing countries.

If both the macroeconomic and microeconomic developments are favorable—and they are linked—many developing countries will be able to grow out of their current debt problems and to attract more external capital resources—both investment and loans—to finance their development. Official development assistance will become less necessary, though arguably more readily available, given healthier budgets and trade balances in the developed countries. On the other hand, if developments in the world economy are unfavorable, debt problems and slow growth will persist and official development assistance will become more necessary, though probably less available. With the increasing importance of Japan as a key player in a more decentralized world economy, and as a major trading partner, creditor, and foreign investor in developing countries, the role of official and private external finance in these countries' development may be set to undergo a subtle change, something that the United States must decide how to respond to in the 1990s. In particular, the United States may face conflict between the currently favored political goals of foreign aid, which direct aid largely to countries of "strategic foreign policy interest" (e.g., Pakistan, Egypt, the Philippines), and the more economically self-interested aid linked to the donor's international business interests, which is more characteristic of Japan and, increasingly, Taiwan.

NOTES

1. *IMF Survey* (3 April 1989).
2. IMF, *Direction of Trade Statistics Yearbook, 1987,* cited in *IMF Survey* (27 July 1987): 226.
3. Provisional estimates by GATT, provided in *The Economist* (4 April 1987): 104.
4. *IMF Survey* (25 July 1988): 241.
5. Between 1970 and 1985, the share of invisibles in world exports rose from 29 to 32 percent, while that of merchandise exports fell from 71 to 67.8 percent. Within the invisibles account, the share of investment income (accruing mostly to industrial countries) rose from 7 to 13 percent of all current account earnings, while that of transport and travel fell, and those of transfers (workers' remittances and government grants—important to many developing countries) and other invisibles (including financial services, consultancy, and royalties) were unchanged. IMF data cited in *The Economist* (14 March 1987): 98.
6. GATT report cited in *IMF Survey* (6 April 1987): 109.
7. For a brief survey of industrial-country protection and its impact on developing-country exports, see World Bank, *World Development Report 1985* (New York: Oxford University Press, 1985), pp. 37–41.
8. *IMF Survey* (27 July 1987).
9. *The Economist* (1 November 1986): 65.
10. *Ibid.* (11 October 1986): 79.
11. *Ibid.* (21 February 1987): 69.

12. See, for example, *Far Eastern Economic Review* (1 May 1989): 76–81.
13. *The Economist* (7 March 1987).
14. Note that in most countries privatization is unlikely to proceed very far or fast because of political and economic constraints, including vested bureaucratic interests, a lack of local private capital and managerial expertise, and fear of dependence on foreign capital and minority ethnic business groups.
15. IMF data, cited in *The Economist* (9 May 1987): 100.
16. In 1988, Taiwan invested some $2.1 billion in Thailand alone, and more than $500 million each in Malaysia and the Philippines. *The Economist* (25 March 1989): 79.
17. *Ibid.* (20 June 1987): 71.
18. *Ibid.* (25 October 1986): 72.
19. Ministry of Finance, Tokyo, data cited in *Asiaweek* (7 June 1987): 59.
20. *Ibid.*
21. *The Economist* (20 June 1987): 71.
22. *Ibid.* (9 May 1987): 100.
23. *Wall Street Journal,* 22 May 1987.
24. See, for example, *Business Week* (1 December 1986): 47.
25. UNCTAD data, cited in *The Economist* (22 November 1986): 107.
26. This involves returns to market pricing, private-enterprise and market distribution systems, and improved government agricultural management.
27. *The Economist* (14 February 1987): 60.
28. *Ibid.* (18 April 1987): 65.
29. *IMF Survey* (16 April 1987): 109.
30. For example, in 1983, 29 percent of developing countries' agricultural exports to industrial countries were affected by nontariff barriers, while the ratio for manufactured exports was 18 percent.
31. Per capita incomes in Hong Kong and Singapore already exceed those in such developed countries as Spain, Portugal, Ireland, and New Zealand.

THREE

Development and Global Environmental Change

WILLIAM U. CHANDLER

Human activities have reached a scale capable of altering the biosphere, a fact that places new demands on development policy. Signs of global environmental change have already become evident, particularly in the atmosphere. An unexpected "hole" found in the earth's ozone layer may portend a global ozone reduction that would expose all life to dangerous levels of ultraviolet radiation. Greenhouse gases such as carbon dioxide (CO_2) rapidly accumulating in the atmosphere threaten to warm the earth's climate, thus flooding coastal cities and shifting rainfall patterns. Acid rain carried by winds across international boundaries has damaged large areas of forest in Western Europe. Global environmental change may, as these problems indicate, undo decades of material progress and deny development to many of the planet's 5 billion people.[1]

The emergence of global environmental change adds urgency to appeals for "sustainable development." Sustainable development will require integrating environment and development policies, meaning that activities formerly guided by purely economic criteria will now have to satisfy conservation criteria as well. Economic criteria traditionally represent efficiency and require only that investments be good ones in terms of present value. Development can be sustainable, however, only if investments are good *and* do not undermine the environmental foundations of economies.

At least three major forces associated with economic development shape global environmental change: (1) energy use; (2) tropical deforestation; and (3) health and population growth. Energy use directly embodies the conflict between environment and development. Energy sustains modern societies; it not only reduces drudgery and makes inhospitable climates habitable, it substitutes for scarce resources. Energy permits the replacement of, for example, copper with aluminum, wood with iron, iron with ceramics. It is absolutely essential for industry, for transportation—in short, for development. But energy use, more than any other human activity, exacerbates the CO_2 greenhouse problem, acid rain, and so on. Energy productivity for economic growth will thus be a priority in any scenario of sustainable development.

Tropical deforestation represents a stark conflict. Logging, agricultural expansion, and urban growth contribute to the destruction of forests. Deforestation undermines development by destroying watersheds, reducing fuel and material availability, destroying species, and affecting global climate.

All environmental problems are driven fundamentally by population growth. Each of the 86 million people added to the population every year will consume additional energy, driving up CO_2 emissions. Each will require metals, wood, and chemicals, thus increasing pressure on energy supplies, forests, and environmental sinks (which must absorb the toxic wastes of industrial processes). Many of these people will be unable to find viable farmland and will thus push out onto marginal land, increasing soil erosion and deforestation rates.

But population growth is, in a sense, a symptom of underdevelopment. Its causes include not only lack of family planning services, but also the parental desire to have a sufficient number of children to assure that some will survive to help with the hard work of development and to provide for parents in their old age. Environmental diseases attributable to underdevelopment dramatically increase the numbers of children who die.

The decade ahead in development policy offers an irretrievable opportunity to ameliorate these problems, to integrate economic and environmental policies. Beyond that time, environmental stresses may cause disruptive climatic surprises and economic discontinuities. The reconsideration of development priorities requires a vision of goals that satisfy growing human needs while protecting the biosphere. And it requires a theory of change, a clear concept of how policies affect human behavior and natural resources.

GLOBAL ENVIRONMENTAL CHANGE

Atmospheric Change

If earth were an apple, the atmosphere would be no thicker than the peel; the bulk of gases forming earth's climate and sustaining life is only 36 kilometers deep.[2] This thinness makes it vulnerable to human pollution, and in ways scientists do not fully understand.

If the ozone layer of the atmosphere were condensed to a liquid, it would be no thicker than the sole of a shoe. Yet, it is vital to life on earth because it protects plants and animals from destructive ultraviolet radiation. An ozone "hole" over Antarctica has intensified scientific concern because no one knows how it formed. October ozone levels over Antarctica have been reduced by about 50 percent over the last two decades.[3] This "hole," a reduced concentration of ozone gas, appears each October and lasts for a month. Scientists believe that chlorine from chlorofluorocarbons (CFCs)—used in refrigerators and aerosol cans—destroys the ozone, with other pollutants such as nitrogen compounds from engine exhaust or fertilizers also contributing to its breakdown.[4] U.S. Environmental Protection Agency analysts have projected 800,000 additional cancer deaths in the United States alone over the next 88 years as a consequence of ozone destruction.[5] Costly crop damage would also arise from increased ultraviolet light intensity.

Air emissions such as CO_2 may affect development by affecting the global climate.[6] The National Research Council (NRC) has concluded that human-induced climate change—the "greenhouse effect"—is a likely prospect over the next century.[7] Earth's atmosphere, NRC estimates, will warm by 1.5 to 4.5 degrees Celsius, disrupting rainfall patterns and raising sea levels. The effect on low-lying nations such as Bangladesh and the Maldives could be catastrophic. Farmers will be forced to make expensive adjustments in irrigation and plant varieties, adjustments that will be much more difficult in developing nations. Large development projects may have their useful lives cut short. The question is no longer whether human beings will alter the earth's climate, but by how much. Development policies will in part determine the answer to this question.

Gaseous emissions from both agriculture and energy use exacerbate this greenhouse effect, but CO_2 is the most important trace gas. This by-product of the combustion of fossil fuel is accumulating rapidly in the atmosphere, where it absorbs reflected light and emits infrared radiation toward the ground, thus warming the atmosphere. Fossil-fuel combustion produces over 5 billion tons of carbon emissions per year, half of which remain in the atmosphere. Since 1960, the global concentration of CO_2 gas has increased from 316 to almost 350 parts per million (see Figure 3.1).[8] Most climatologists expect rapid climatic change to commence within the next two decades.[9]

Evidence is also mounting that non-CO_2 greenhouse gases such as methane may cause atmospheric change equal in magnitude to that projected for CO_2 (see Table 3.1).[10] CFCs and other chemicals that interact to destroy ozone also contribute to the greenhouse effect. Accumulating methane, for example, could seriously destabilize atmospheric chemistry because it neutralizes the main mechanism available for removing human pollutants. Technically speaking, methane destroys hydroxyl radicals that would otherwise remove nitrous oxide, acid rain–causing sulfur and nitrogen compounds, and unburned hydrocarbons. Methane is produced in anaerobic processes, including the decay of submerged material in rice paddies and the digestion of food in the stomachs of ruminants.

How the Third World develops will vitally affect emission rates for

Figure 3.1 Atmospheric CO_2 Concentration

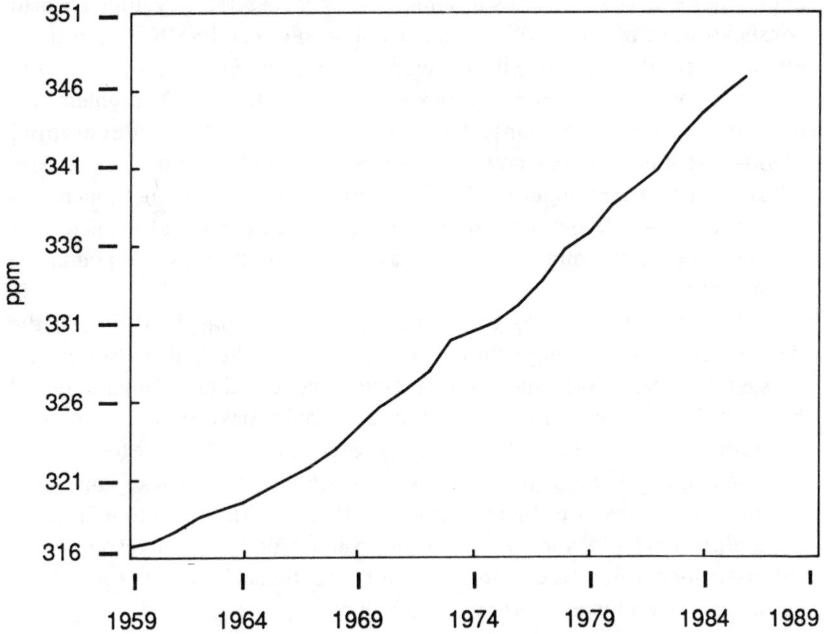

Source: C. D. Keeling, Scripps Institute of Oceanography, unpublished data.

Table 3.1 Anthropogenic Gases and the Greenhouse Effect

Constituent	Estimated Current Rate of Increase (% per year)	Effect of Doubling on Temperature (degrees Celsius)	Residence Time in Atmosphere (% per year)
Carbon dioxide	0.2–2.3	0.5	na[a]
Carbon monoxide	0	1–2[b]	3
Tropospheric ozone	0.9–1.1	—[c]	na
Nitrous oxide	0.3–1.1	0.2	150
CFC-11	0.1	5.0	75
CFC-12	0.02	5.0	110
Methane	0.3–1.4	1.0	7–11

Sources: Based on Jae Edmonds and Gregg Marland, "The Energy Connection to Global Climate Change: Gaseous Emissions" (Institute for Energy Analysis, 1986, mimeo); NASA, Present State of Knowledge of the Upper Atmosphere (Washington: NASA, 1986); and T. F. Malone and J. G. Roederer, eds., Global Change (London: Cambridge University Press and the International Council of Scientific Unions, 1985).

Notes: a. Estimates may be misleading because CO_2 is cycled in about two years but is not removed from the deep ocean for perhaps 500 years.
b. One source reports "no trend" in CO accumulation.
c. Measures of total column ozone indicate a depletion rate ranging from –0.2 to –5.0 percent per year, with most reduction coming in the stratosphere.

CFCs, CO_2, and other greenhouse gases—and thus will affect people everywhere. It is sometimes assumed that because the developed world consumes most of the world's resources, it should therefore be the focus of efficiency efforts. But while the developing world can justifiably lay claim to a greater share of resources, it does not follow that the CO_2 problem, for example, is a problem only for developed nations. The developing world—excluding China—now adds as much CO_2 to the atmosphere as does Western Europe (see Figure 3.2). To the extent that development increases wealth, it will—without a conscious effort—increase demand for activities that produce carbon and other trace gas emissions and thus compound the global problem.

Moreover, the curves of emissions are still sharply rising in the developing world, though they have declined in the United States and Western Europe. Development, on the other hand, could bring environmental benefits. Investments in capital equipment could make the economies of developing countries more energy efficient and therefore more environmentally benign. Investments in agriculture could make land more productive per hectare, thereby limiting the climatic impacts of rapidly expanding land use and deforestation. Such reductions in resource-use intensity per unit of economic output will increase the potential for sustainable development (as implied in Figure 3.3).

Deforestation and Development

Tropical deforestation raises global concerns. Forest-cutting annually injects from 1 to 2.6 billion tons of carbon into the atmosphere, equal to one-fifth to one-half that contributed by fossil-fuel combustion.[11] Moreover, as rain forests disappear, so too will many plant and animal species. Their loss may have implications for all countries because half of all pharmaceuticals were discovered in nature, including curare, quinine, and reserpine.[12]

Forest-cutting and other land-use changes arise with growing demand for food and fiber, lumber, land for cities, and firewood for fuel.[13] Globally, forests are being destroyed at a rate of about 0.6 percent per year, but high reforestation rates in the developed world mask very high rates of deforestation in the developing countries (see Table 3.2). Tropical forest–cutting occurs at rates higher than 3 percent per year in Costa Rica, Nepal, Nigeria, the Ivory Coast, and Paraguay. And though the percentages are lower, tens and even hundreds of millions of hectares are cut each year in Brazil, India, Indonesia, Papua New Guinea, Peru, and elsewhere.[14] The ratio of forest-cutting to replacement is 5 to 1 in Asia, 10 to 1 in South America, and 20 to 1 in Africa. The area of rainforest will, at these rates, be reduced by 12 percent by the end of the century.[15]

Deforestation and related land-use changes also promote soil erosion (which reduces land productivity), reduce water supply, increase flooding, and may affect local climatic conditions. They reduce the availability of

Figure 3.2 Fossil-Energy Carbon Emissions, 1986

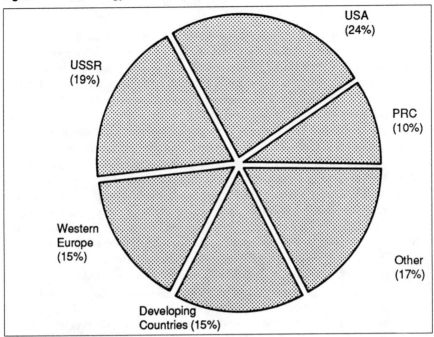

Figure 3.3 Carbon Emissions by Region, 1950–1984

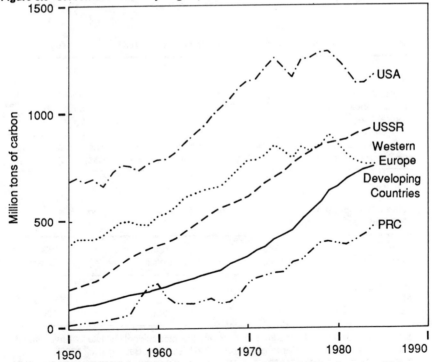

Source for both figures: R. M. Rotty, Institute for Energy Analysis, Oak Ridge Associated Universities, based on unpublished UN data.

fuelwood supplies and building materials. Fuelwood shortages, in particular, reduce development productivity by requiring long, time-consuming treks for firewood, and by making hygienic cooking and washing difficult. Hundreds of millions of people are already affected by the fuelwood crisis (see Table 3.3), which diminishes both land and labor productivity, and in turn diminishes development potential.

Another major forest problem is energy-related acid rain, which in some areas has extensively damaged forests, causing economic as well as environmental damage. In the Federal Republic of Germany, for example, over half of the forest area has been seriously affected by acid rain, and *Waldsterben,* or forest death, has become a household word.[16] Because coal resources are plentiful in many countries, including China, acid rain may undercut other development goals. Reforestation efforts to enhance wood and fuel supplies could be defeated by acid rain–induced damage to young trees.

The risks of failing to act on global change are high. As George Woodwell, director of the Woods Hole Research Center, has said:

> The issue is unquestionably one of the most urgent topics for the agenda of the councils of nations. It strikes at the core of the question of the continued habitability of the Earth at the very moment that the human population is passing 5 billion on its unplanned and uncontrolled upward path. It has a potential for disruption of the human enterprise over a few decades that rivals the chaos of war.[17]

Table 3.2 Annual Deforestation Rates, by Region, 1981–1985

Region	Area (ha)	Rate (%)
Tropical America	5,611,000	0.63
Tropical Africa	3,676,000	0.52
Tropical Asia	2,016,000	0.60

Source: Based on World Resources Institute and the International Institute for Environment and Development, *World Resources Report 1986* (New York: Basic Books, 1986).

Table 3.3 Populations Affected by Fuelwood Shortages, by Region, 1980 and 2000 (millions of persons)

Region	1980 Acute Scarcity	1980 Deficit	2000 Deficit
Latin America	9	152	50
Africa	49	131	175
Asia	39	288	239

Source: Based on World Resources Institute and the International Institute for Environment and Development, *World Resources Report 1986* (New York: Basic Books, 1986).

ENVIRONMENT, DISEASE, AND POPULATION GROWTH

The main causes of early death in the developing world are environmental diseases, though they may not often be categorized as such. This fact, and the higher priority that analysts and observers sometimes place on other environmental problems, recalls the aphorism that "the most common form of human stupidity is forgetting what one is trying to accomplish."[18] Because the goal of development is to improve the lot of people, special attention must be paid to sickness and early death.

Indeed, satisfying basic needs may be a prerequisite for solving that most fundamental environmental problem, population growth. High infant mortality directly contributes to high population growth rates. Parents who desire a certain number of children tend to have "extra" children in order to assure survival of a family of the desired size. Reductions in infant mortality increase parents' confidence that the desired number will survive despite their having smaller families. This behavioral change directly reduces the birth rate.

In addition, childhood and tropical diseases such as malaria and schistosomiasis hinder the hard work of development by sapping the energy of children and adults alike. Afflicted women, especially, have less energy for agricultural work, and so incomes and nutrition levels may be reduced. Similarly, sick children have less energy for learning and so may be stunted intellectually as well as physically.

Altogether, preventable diseases kill some 17 million children worldwide each year, causing a full third of all annual mortality. Ninety-eight percent of these deaths, moreover, occur in Third World countries.[19] Childhood disease each year kills as many people as would a limited nuclear war. But, unlike nuclear war, this annual toll is certain to occur—unless development intervenes.

Health problems can be ranked for priority by comparing the magnitude and risk of their consequences. Using this guide, the first priority for world health would be dealing with diarrhea (see Table 3.4). This humble disease is the largest single cause of premature death—death before age 65—in the world, claiming the lives of some 5 million each year.[20] Simple measles kills half as many. Tropical diseases take more than a million lives each year and make hundreds of millions sick (See Table 3.5).

Many people raise the deep question of whether a population explosion would accompany a successful campaign to combat infant mortality—and whether it would leave developing nations worse off than with high rates of infant and child death. To be sure, Africa in particular is experiencing unsupportable population growth. The growth of human numbers in Africa has wiped out or diminished gains in per capita availability of food on that continent (see Figure 3.4). Desertification and famine both contribute to and result from such imbalances.[21] Extrapolating current African trends in

Figure 3.4 Grain Production per Capita in Africa, 1960–1985

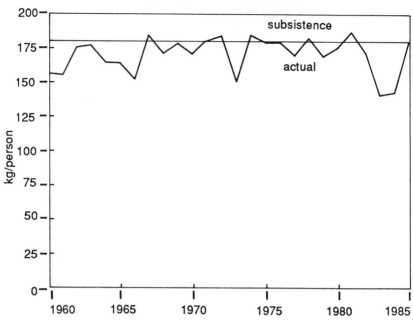

Source: Lester R. Brown and Edward C. Wolf, "Reversing Africa's Decline," *Worldwatch*, *Paper* 65 (Washington, D.C.: Worldwatch Institute, June 1985).

Table 3.4 Neglected Causes of Premature Death

Cause	Millions of Deaths/Year	Total Deaths (%)
Diarrhea	5	10
Pneumonia	4	8
Low birth weight	3	6
Measles	2	4
Smoking	2	4
Malaria	1	2

Sources: World Health Organization; UNICEF; and William U. Chandler, *Banishing Tobacco* (Washington, D.C.: Worldwatch Institute, 1986).

Table 3.5 Tropical Diseases and Their Consequences

Disease	Millions of Persons Afflicted	Deaths (%/year)
Malaria	300	>1
Elephantiasis[a]	270	na
Leishmaniasis	200	na
Schistosomiasis	200	.5–1.0[b]
Intestinal parasites	1,000	—

Sources: World Health Organization data bank; Tineke Boddé, "Biotechnology in the Third World," *BioScience* (October 1982); U.S. Congress Office of Technology Assessment, *Status of Biomedical Research and Related Technology for Tropical Diseases* (Washington, D.C.: U.S. Government Printing Office, 1985); and William U. Chandler, *Improving World Health: A Least-Cost Strategy* (Washington, D.C.: Worldwatch Institute, 1984).

Notes: a. All *Filariasis* infection.
b. Estimated for late 1970s.

population and food, according to the United Nations' Food and Agriculture Organization (FAO), yields "a doomsday scenario."[22]

But the United Nations Childrens' Fund (UNICEF), among others, has discovered that sharp reductions in child deaths lead to reductions in population growth.[23] Indeed, many techniques for reducing infant mortality—such as encouraging birth spacing and breast-feeding—require too much time for most developing nations to allow health improvements alone to halt population growth. The latter may be so burdensome that it will undercut the former. Family planning programs are necessary complements to primary health care innovations.

DEVELOPMENT FOR CONSERVATION

A vision of development must be matched with a theory of how to set world society on a course of energy, forest, and land conservation. Conservation ultimately requires setting limits on certain activities: For example, ozone-depleting CFCs may have to be banned; fossil-fuel use may have to be limited—somehow; forest-cutting may have to be restricted. Development policy can itself be fashioned to push back these limits by making resource use more efficient. Combining donor assistance—funds for energy-efficiency investments, technical help with reforestation, child survival efforts—with economic reform for efficiency in developing nations could critically reduce the energy, forest, and land resources needed to improve standards of living.

Development for conservation will require three elements: (1) strengthening economic signals about the value of resources; (2) protecting and restocking renewable resources; and (3) reducing environmental sources of disease, including childhood and tropical diseases. The first element suggests that pricing natural resources to reflect both their replacement costs and their environmental impacts is essential. The second suggests that conservation criteria must set limits on consumption that do not exceed sustainable yields or destroy the natural resource base of the global economy. The third element suggests that basic human needs underlie the drive for development, and that satisfying health and family planning needs is a prerequisite to sustainable development. These elements call for new directions in development policy in the energy, agricultural, and health sectors of developing economies.

Efficient Energy Use

Energy use—because it produces CO_2 and other greenhouse gases—represents the most important climatic concern. Nonfossil energy sources do not at present offer cost-effective alternatives, but detailed studies show that the world has barely cut into the potential for cost-effective energy conservation. By slowly adopting existing measures—technology for 50-

mile-per-gallon cars, continuous casting for energy-efficient steel-making, high-efficiency industrial motors—the world could cut the energy intensity of the global economy in half over the next 35 years. Slow energy growth would permit a shift of energy use per capita from the developed to the developing world without sacrificing living standards or development potential. Indeed, progress in development may be impossible otherwise.

The global conservation potential can be illustrated in energy portraits of a small number of nations. Some 15 countries, containing about 65 percent of the world's population, are responsible for about 80 percent of all fossil and electric energy use. Among these are developing countries such as Brazil, China, and India—nations that have a legitimate claim to a larger share of energy resources. On the other hand, developing country economies do rank among the world's least efficient in terms of energy used per unit of economic output. China, for example, uses twice as much energy per unit of economic output as does the United States, and four times that of Japan or Western Europe. Still, an effort in the United States to raise automobile fuel economy to 40 miles per gallon would save as much energy as Brazil now consumes. So would a commitment in the Soviet Union to produce steel as efficiently as do the Japanese.[24]

Industry accounts for two-thirds of Third World commercial energy consumption. Steel-manufacturing alone absorbs about 6 percent of total world commercial energy use. Yet, steel-manufacturing is grossly inefficient in several of the world's major producing nations. No steel-making nations are less efficient than India and China, with the Soviet Union following closely (see Figure 3.5). These nations plan major increases in steel-making.

Steel-making can be made more energy-efficient both by improving existing facilities and by switching to better furnaces. An assessment of investments available to the U.S. steel industry suggests the lucrative potential of conservation the world over. Upgrading conventional furnaces yields high average rates of return: 25 percent per year for continuous casting; 31 percent for waste-heat recovery; and 43 percent for more efficient electric motors. Switching to the electric arc "recycling" furnace can yield a 57 percent rate of return. In one study of U.S. industry, physicist Marc Ross of the University of Michigan estimated that investments such as these could cut the energy required per ton of steel by a third by the year 2000.[25]

China and India also still rely heavily on the open-hearth furnace and take little advantage of heat-recovery opportunities. Developing countries overall could save at least 10 percent of the energy they use in existing steel facilities by spending only $2 billion to $4 billion on conservation retrofits, according to a World Bank study. This investment would pay for itself in energy savings in just one year.[26]

Chemical-processing is the world's fastest-growing industry. Typical energy-efficiency investments by the chemicals industry in electric pumps, heat-recovery devices, and cogeneration offer rates of return of 43, 15, and 18

Figure 3.5 Energy Use in Steel Manufacturing, 1980

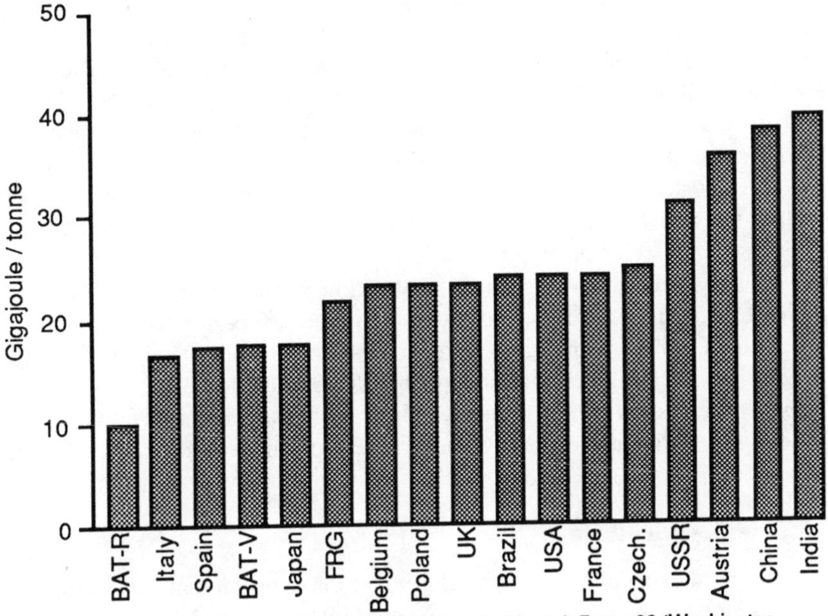

Source: Willam U. Chandler, "Energy Productivity," Worldwatch Paper 63 (Washington, D.C.: Worldwatch Institute, January 1985), p. 101.
Note: BAT-R: Best Available Technology—Recycling; BAT-V: Best Available Technology—Virgin Ore.

percent per year, respectively.[27]

Electric industrial motors consume a remarkable 40 percent of all electricity used in Brazil. One expert suggests that by investing in more efficient motors and motor-speed controls, Brazil could avoid building 10,000 megawatts of power plants by the year 2000—over 17 percent of projected new demand for generating capacity in that country. That heavily indebted nation could thus avoid the need to borrow some $20 billion to $30 billion.[28]

The key question is how to change energy-wasting behavior to energy-conserving behavior. Energy-price increases have stimulated more conservation than any other factor—witness the doubling of energy-efficiency improvement rates following the two petroleum price hikes of the 1970s. The United States now uses about 30 percent less energy per dollar of GNP than it would have if policies had not changed. Energy price increases probably caused two-thirds of this conservation response, with the remaining third attributable to a variety of government measures such as automobile fuel-economy standards.[29]

Much of the world's commercial energy use occurs in countries lacking realistic pricing mechanisms. Without decentralization—a move away from central planning and toward enterprise autonomy and competition—and economic reform, sustainable development will remain elusive. But markets alone will not solve the climate-energy problem. There remains the problem of market failure and the fact that market-induced rates of energy-efficiency probably will not be sufficient to avoid climate change.[30] Regulatory policies can provide a minimum level of efficiency where markets fail or do not exist. Obvious targets for minimum performance standards are automobiles, furnaces, water heaters, air conditioners, and heat pumps. This approach will not work well for industry, however, because industry uses thousands of processes and scores of "appliances."

The world faces two sharply contrasting visions of its energy future. One, based on past trends, indicates that global energy demand will more than double by the year 2025. The other, based on an understanding of energy economics and engineering, shows how demand could be held to a much smaller increase, stretching nonrenewable energy supplies and facilitating the use of renewable resources. Both visions have claim to validity. The one that comes to pass will depend on conscious development choices.

Efficient Agriculture

Agricultural production can critically affect the consumption and disruption of resources such as water, forests, and air. Soil erosion and deforestation can result from low agricultural productivity if new, marginal lands are pressed into production to make up for lost potential. Such expansions contribute to desertification. Efficiency is consequently an essential ingredient of agricultural sustainability. Unfortunately, many developing nations still lag dramatically in land productivity (see Table 3.6).

Post-Mao China has provided a rare and vast laboratory for testing the economic and environmental benefits of decentralization in agriculture. The shift to market incentives in China boosted grain output by a third between 1978 and 1985, and provided marked improvements in the per capita availability of food. Significantly, this growth was achieved along with a decline in water and pesticide use and a 4 percent reduction in cultivated area, as highly erodable land was taken out of production. The increases in output and efficiency translated into higher rural income, which has grown as much since 1978 as in the previous 30 years.[31]

In the West, resource efficiency is undermined by heavy farm-production subsidies, including trade barriers and direct budgetary expenditures. Misallocation of resources in this way undermines economic sustainability. When the efficiency of resource use declines, real costs go up. Governments often compound the problem by protecting consumers from rising food prices with further subsidies, which can drive budgets into deficit and economies into decline. When supports exceed world market levels, they interfere with trade, stimulate environmentally disruptive overproduction, and waste money. These distortions have political motivations that may well be worthy,

Table 3.6 Productivity in Grain Production, Selected Countries, 1984

Country	Labor Productivity (tonnes/worker)	Land Productivity (tonnes/ha)
United States	160.3	4.4
United Kingdom	57.3	6.6
France	34.2	6.0
Hungary	23.6	5.4
Soviet Union	8.5	1.4
Yugoslavia	5.2	4.2
Mexico	2.6	2.6
Japan	2.1	4.1
Philippines	1.1	1.4
Egypt	4.0	4.0
China	1.1	3.3
India	1.3	1.3

Source: U.S. Department of Agriculture, Economic Research Service data printouts.

but they are environmentally and economically unsustainable, and they undermine leadership in development reform.

Healthy Populations

Experience in China and Sri Lanka indicates that infant mortality can be reduced to industrial country levels despite very low per capita income. These nations have provided clean water supplies, promoted sanitation, and made available low-cost primary health care. More important, they have made a commitment to female literacy, which in general is the most important factor in child survival.[32]

Achieving the goal of reduced infant mortality will not suffice without complementary development and population planning programs.[33] Family planning must be provided in parallel with primary health care if either is to succeed. Fortunately, experience suggests this may be possible. In Jamkhed, India, the practice of family planning increased from 10 to 50 percent of families in the community when a primary health care clinic was installed. In Miraj, India, a similar project raised family planning participation from one-third to nine-tenths of families. Moreover, as demonstrated in China, Sri Lanka, Korea, Costa Rica, and Singapore, reduced infant mortality reduces the incentive to give birth to more children than a couple really wants.[34]

The United States, which has seen an explosion of development in the biotechnical sciences, may uniquely offer the potential to control debilitating tropical diseases. Vaccines for malaria, schistosomiasis, and leishmaniasis, for example, would be of inestimable value for the developing world.

Although a vaccine for malaria may be available within a decade, most trends in commercial biotechnology suggest that vaccines for tropical diseases will be slow in coming. Producing new drugs is an expensive and risky business venture. Developing and testing a new vaccine for market can take over seven years and cost more than $70 million. Commercial firms are naturally more likely to sponsor research for drugs with lucrative markets. Thus, the diseases of affluence take precedence over the diseases of poverty. Publicly sponsored scientific research could take up this worthy effort in the absence of commercial development. But U.S. scientific and development agencies have not come close to exploiting the potential bioscience offers for improving the human condition in the Third World.[35]

CONCLUSION

The prospect of global environmental change raises development assistance and development reform to a new level of urgency. Unguided development carries the potential to alter catastrophically the earth's climate by producing greenhouse gases from energy use and deforestation. Inefficiency and population growth fundamentally drive these problems, but development assistance, by providing the capital, skills, and conditions necessary for efficient resource use, could push back the constraints that limit improvements in the human condition. This means that the old character of the conflict between environment and development has changed forever. No longer is the claim valid that "developing countries cannot afford environmental protection." Moreover, the United States, like all nations, now has an environmental stake in the development policies of all other nations. The implication is that the United States will have to revise its approach to development assistance. That is, it will be forced to consider environmental impacts in its selection of projects, reconsider its priorities, and shift funds into efforts to make development "sustainable." These efforts must include assistance in structural reforms designed to reduce economic and resource waste simultaneously.

Markets alone cannot accomplish all that is needed, but to a large degree they offer a self-administering check on resource waste: The resource user pays for inefficiency. Government control of the production and prices of resource intensive goods and services has led to excessive consumption and unnecessary environmental degradation.[36] Market failure and overexploitation have also degraded the global environment. Governments must set boundaries on unsustainable rates of consumption.

In summary, six priorities arise: (1) energy efficiency can be improved worldwide, and a rate of at least 2 percent per year is possible; (2) infant mortality can be cut to Chinese levels throughout the developing world; (3) population growth rates can be dramatically reduced by coupling family planning services with primary health care; (4) small-scale agriculture, the primary economic activity of the developing world, can be significantly improved with decentralized incentives and financing; (5) deforestation can be halted and fuelwood needs satisfied; and (6) nations can cooperate to begin controlling industrial emissions of CFCs, methane, and other specific threats to global climate.

Each of these goals is possible; each is urgent. Some require U.S. funds; some its technical expertise and scientific resources. But the policies requiring adjustments of resource use most importantly require U.S. leadership, for U.S. inefficiency, waste, and pollution will undercut efforts to eliminate them elsewhere in the world.

NOTES

1. National Aeronautics and Space Administration, *Present State of Knowledge of the Upper Atmosphere, an Assessment Report* (Washington, D.C.: NASA, 1986); Alan S. Miller and Irving M. Mintzer, "The Sky *Is* the Limit" (World Resources Institute, November 1986); U.S. Department of Energy, *Detecting the Climatic Effects of Increasing Carbon Dioxide* (Springfield, VA: National Technical Information Service, December 1985).

2. The beginning of this section draws on the author's op-ed piece, "The Hole in the Ozone," published in the *Baltimore Sun* in April 1986.

3. F. Sherwood Rowland, University of California at Irvine, as cited in World Resources Institute and International Institute for Environment and Development, *World Resources Report 1987* (New York: Basic Books, 1987); David Lindley, "Ozone Hole Deeper Than Ever," *Nature* (8 October 1987).

4. NASA, *Present State of Knowledge of the Upper Atmosphere;* Robert T. Watson, F. Sherwook Rowland, and John Gille, "Ozone Trends Panel Press Conference," NASA, Washington, D.C., 15 March 1988.

5. Estimate attributed to a draft U.S. Environmental Protection Agency report in "Cancer Rise Linked to Thinning Ozone," by Philip Shabecoff, *New York Times,* 5 November 1986, and in "United States Floats Proposal to Help Prevent Global Ozone Depletion," by Mark Crawford, *Science* (21 November 1986).

6. World Commission on Environment and Development, *Our Common Future* (Oxford: Oxford University Press, 1987).

7. National Research Council, *Changing Climate* (Washington, D.C.: National Academy Press, 1983). To understand global change, the International Council of Scientific Unions in 1983 called for an International Geosphere-Biosphere Program; see T. F. Malone and J. G. Roederer, *Global Change* (Cambridge: Cambridge University Press and the International Council of Scientific Unions, 1985). This call was followed by similar ones from the U.S. NRC and by NASA; see National Research Council, *Global Change in the Geosphere-Biosphere: Initial Priorities for an IGBP* (Washington, D.C.: National Academy Press,

1986), and Earth Systems Science Committee, NASA Advisory Council, "Earth System Science: A Program for Global Change—Overview" (Washington, D.C.: NASA May 1986).

8. These data come from actual measurements in Hawaii and the South Pole, and show close agreement; data compiled by the Scripps Institution of Oceanography and the U.S. National Oceanic and Atmospheric Administration.

9. National Research Council, *Changing Climate* (Washington, D.C.: National Academy Press, 1983). CO_2's greenhouse effect is simple; it is a strong absorber of electromagnetic energy in the band of 13–18 microns. As a result, radiance from the earth's surface at a temperature above about 220 degrees Kelvin is blocked, and the heat retained. A great uncertainty for the CO_2 greenhouse effect is the linkage of climatically important mechanisms with the oceans. Only about half the emitted carbon has remained in the atmosphere. The oceans remove CO_2 from the atmosphere, store heat, transport heat, interact with ice, and provide a source of water vapor. They also contain an enormous sink for CO_2 in the form of clathrates, which if heated could release prodigious quantities of carbon. For a recent summary of expected climatic responses, see Jill Jaeger *et al.*, "Developing Policies for Responding to Climatic Change," final draft (Beijer Institute, February 1988).

10. Malone and Roederer, *Global Change.*

11. R. A. Houghton *et al.*, "The Flux of Carbon from Terrestrial Ecosystems to the Atmosphere in 1980 Due to Changes in Land Use: Geographic Distribution of the Global Flux," *Tellus* (February–April 1987).

12. World Resources Institute and International Institute for Environment and Development, *World Resources Report 1986* (New York: Basic Books, 1986).

13. *Ibid.*

14. *Ibid.*

15. Lester R. Brown *et al.*, *State of the World 1986* (New York: W. W. Norton, 1986).

16. Sandra Postel, *Altering the Earth's Chemistry: Assessing the Risks* (Washington, D.C.: Worldwatch Institute, 1986).

17. George M. Woodwell, "Forests and Climate: Surprises in Store," *Oceanus* (Winter 1986–1987).

18. Graham T. Allison, Albert Carnesale, and Joseph S. Nye, eds., *Hawks, Doves, and Owls: An Agenda for Avoiding Nuclear War* (New York: W. W. Norton, 1985).

19. William U. Chandler, *Investing in Children* (Washington, D.C.: Worldwatch Institute, 1984).

20. William U. Chandler, *Improving World Health: A Least-Cost Strategy* (Washington, D.C.: Worldwatch Institute, 1984); William U. Chandler, "Child Health, Education, and Development," *Prospects* 17, no. 3 (1986).

21. See, generally, Lester Brown *et al.*, *State of the World 1984, State of the World 1985, State of the World 1986,* and *State of the World 1987,* all published by W. W. Norton, New York.

22. Southern African Development Coordination Conference, *SADCC, Agriculture Toward 2000* (Rome: Food and Agriculture Organization, 1984).

23. UNICEF, *State of the World's Children 1986* (New York: Cambridge University Press, 1986).

24. William U. Chandler, *"Energy Productivity: Key to Economic Progress and*

Environmental Protection," Worldwatch Paper 63 (Washington, D.C.: Worldwatch Institute, 1985); William U. Chandler, *The Changing Role of the Market in National Economies, Worldwatch Paper* 72 (Washington, D.C.: Worldwatch Institute, 1986).

25. Marc Ross, "Industrial Energy Conservation," *Natural Resources Journal* (April 1984).

26. World Bank, *Energy Efficiency in the Steel Industry, with an Emphasis on Developing Countries* (Washington, D.C.: World Bank, 1984).

27. Office of Technology Assessment, *Industrial Energy Use* (Washington, D.C.: U.S. Government Printing Office, June 1983).

28. Howard Geller, "The Potential for Electricity Conservation in Brazil" (Washington, D.C.: American Council for an Energy-Efficient Economy, 1984). Similar opportunities exist in cement- and paper-manufacturing.

29. Eric Hirst *et al.,* "U.S. Energy Consumption: What Happened and Why," in *Annual Review of Energy* (Palo Alto, CA: Annual Reviews, 1983).

30. See Jae Edmonds and John Reilly, *Global Energy* (New York: Cambridge University Press, 1986).

31. Chandler, *Changing Role of the Market.*

32. Chandler, *Improving World Health;* Chandler, *Investing in Children;* and UNICEF, *State of the World's Children 1985.*

33. Chandler, *Investing in Children.*

34. Rashid Faruqee and Ethna Johnson, "Health, Nutrition, and Family Planning in India: A Survey of Experiments and Special Projects," World Bank Working Paper No. 507 (Washington, D.C., February 1982); Ruth Sidel, *Women and Child Care in China* (Baltimore, MD: Penguin Books, 1974); W. Henry Mosley, "Will Primary Health Care Reduce Infant and Child Mortality? A Critique of Some Current Strategies, with Special Reference to Africa and Asia," Report of the Ford Foundation to the 1984 United Nations International Conference on Population; "Findings of the World Fertility Survey on Trends, Differentials, and Determinants of Mortality in Developing Countries," prepared by the secretary of the World Fertility Survey for the 1984 International Conference on Population, 3 May 1983; R. G. Whitehead, ed., *Maternal Diet, Breast-Feeding Capacity, and Lactational Infertility* (Tokyo: The United Nations University, 1983); Chandler, *Improving World Health;* UNICEF, *State of the World's Children 1986.*

35. See Chandler, *Improving World Health;* U.S. Congress Office of Technology Assessment, *Assessment of Technologies for Determining Cancer Risks From the Environment* (Washington, D.C.: U.S. Government Printing Office, 1981); *Diet, Nutrition, and Cancer* (Washington, D.C.: National Academy of Sciences, 1982); Richard Doll and Richard Peto, "Quantitative Estimates of Avoidable Risks of Cancer in the United States Today," *Journal of the National Cancer Institute* (November 1981); B. N. Ames, "Dietary Carcinogens and Anti-carcinogens," *Science* (23 September 1983); and John Cairns, "The Treatment of Diseases and the War against Cancer," *Scientific American* (November 1985).

36. Chandler, *Changing Role of the Market.*

FOUR

Social, Economic, and Political Trends in the Developing World

JOHN STOVER

U.S. development cooperation with developing countries has undergone major changes in focus and approach since the 1950s. These changes have been the result of several factors, the most important of which are:

- Changes in understanding of how the development process works and what role development cooperation can play;
- Changes in perceptions of the role development cooperation can play in advancing U.S. political interests; and
- Changes in social, economic, and political situations in developing countries.

As we approach the 1990s, it is appropriate to consider how these conditions will shape the nature of assistance in the next decade. This chapter discusses two themes: (1) the evolving needs of the developing countries in the changing circumstances of the 1990s; and (2) the U.S. national interest in finding new patterns of development cooperation. The chapter describes the important social, economic, and political trends taking place in developing countries that will shape the context for development cooperation. It does not attempt to provide forecasts of economic or social indicators but rather to describe the broad forces for change in the developing world. Many of these forces will, in the 1990s, lead to a different environment for development cooperation from that existing in the 1970s or 1980s.

DEMOGRAPHY

One of the key determinants of conditions in developing countries is the growth and distribution of population. Most of the developing world experienced relatively slow rates of population growth until the 1940s and 1950s. Until that time, birth and death rates had both been high; since then, death rates have been reduced dramatically in many countries. The result has been higher and higher population growth rates as death rates dropped and birth rates remained high.

Family planning programs were introduced by some developing countries partially in response to these rising growth rates and partially to provide couples with the ability to obtain their desired family size and to attain the maternal and child health benefits of lower fertility and child spacing. These programs were adopted in the late 1960s and 1970s by many Asian countries, somewhat later by many Latin American countries, and are just now being considered by a number of African countries. In 1965, just 15 countries, mostly in Asia, had policies favoring lower population growth. By 1975, the number had increased to 31; today, 64 countries favor lower population growth, including 27 in Africa.

Population growth has a high degree of momentum. Changes in fertility and mortality tend to take place slowly and regularly. The 20-year lag between the time a woman is born and the time she enters into her main reproductive years means that, even when fertility does change rapidly, population growth rates are slow to respond. For this reason, the major demographic trends of the 1990s can be described with a greater degree of confidence than is possible for economic or social trends.

Figure 4.1 shows the number of people expected to be living in developing countries in 1990 and 2000 in major areas of the developing world. (Throughout this chapter, the figures for "Asia" or the "rest of Asia" exclude China.) Even excluding China and India, Asia will remain the most populous region of the developing world; India alone has more people than Africa, the Middle East, or Latin America. Figure 4.2 shows that Asia, the most populous region because of rapid growth in the past, will continue to be the fastest-growing region in terms of numbers of people, adding twice as many as sub-Saharan Africa and almost seven times as many as Latin America.

From the perspective of development needs, the rate of population growth is just as important as absolute growth; in some cases it is more important. Figure 4.3 shows that Africa and the Middle East will have far higher growth rates than will India or the rest of Asia. Their high growth rates have resulted from reductions in mortality that have not yet been matched by reductions in birth rates, whereas in Asia birth rates have been reduced considerably in countries such as India, Indonesia, Thailand, and Malaysia.

Fertility rates (the average number of live births per woman) have actually risen in some African countries, such as Kenya. The rise has been a result of the breakdown of traditional customs such as breast-feeding and postpartum abstinence that historically have served to limit fertility.

Table 4.1 shows the total fertility rate for individual developing countries. It shows clearly that in most African countries women average six or more births, while in Asia and Latin America the average is less than five. The high fertility rates in Africa have several consequences: (1) rapid population growth will continue into the 1990s; (2) the large number of births will mean that the African population will be composed of a relatively large number of young children; (3) the health problems associated with high fertility (high infant and maternal mortality and morbidity) will continue to be major development problems.

Figure 4.4 illustrates the position of a number of countries in the transition from high to low birth rates. The figure displays the crude birth rate (the number of births per thousand population) and it shows a clear distinction between those that have not yet begun the transition to lower rates (mostly African, plus a few Asian and Latin American countries) and those that are experiencing declines in birth rate (mostly Asian and Latin American countries).

Development cooperation efforts to provide family planning services were concentrated in Asia and Latin America during the 1960s and 1970s. Now that these programs are reaching maturity in many of these countries, they are characterized by a declining reliance on foreign donors to support family planning programs and a diverse mix of program types, including greater participation by the private sector in the provision of family planning services.

The family planning programs of the 1960s and 1970s had a major impact on fertility in many of the countries in Asia and Latin America. For all of Latin America, the total fertility rate fell from almost six in the early 1960s to about four by the early 1980s. Population growth rates dropped from about 2.8 to 2.3 percent per year during the same period. In some cases the change was extremely rapid: In Mexico, contraceptive use tripled from 1974 to 1979, and fertility fell by 30 percent; in Asia, the total fertility rate declined from 5.7 in the early 1960s to 3.5 by the early 1980s. In spite of these successes, future declines in fertility will not be automatic. Family planning programs need to improve access to services, particularly among the poor and rural populations, and improve the quality of follow-up services in order to reduce the remaining gap between desired and actual family size.

The major challenge in implementing new population programs is shifting to Africa. Several African countries have adopted population policies recently, including Nigeria, Zaire, and Liberia. Others are beginning to discuss, for the first time, the role that population programs can play in their development programs.

Clearly, there is an important role that development cooperation can play in helping these countries to develop and implement population programs. Figure 4.5 shows an estimate of public family planning expenditures by region during the 1990s. Even though there will be many more users of

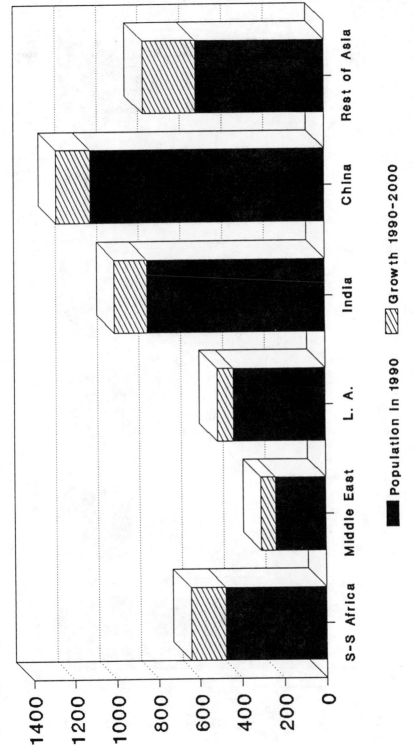

Figure 4.1 Total Expected Population of Developing Regions, 1990 and 2000 (in billions)

Population In 1990   Growth 1990-2000

Source: Based on information in *World Development Report 1988* (New York: Oxford University Press, 1988).

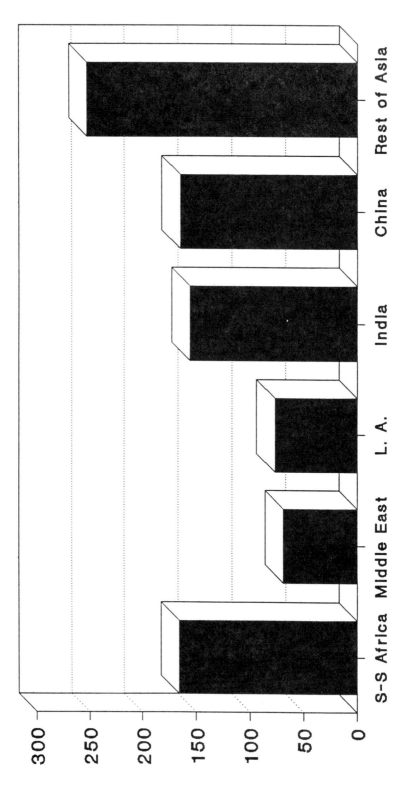

Figure 4.2 Growth of Population, 1990 to 2000 (in millions)

Source: Based on information in *World Development Report 1988* (New York: Oxford University Press, 1988).

Figure 4.3 Rate of Population Growth, 1988 to 2000 (annual percentage)

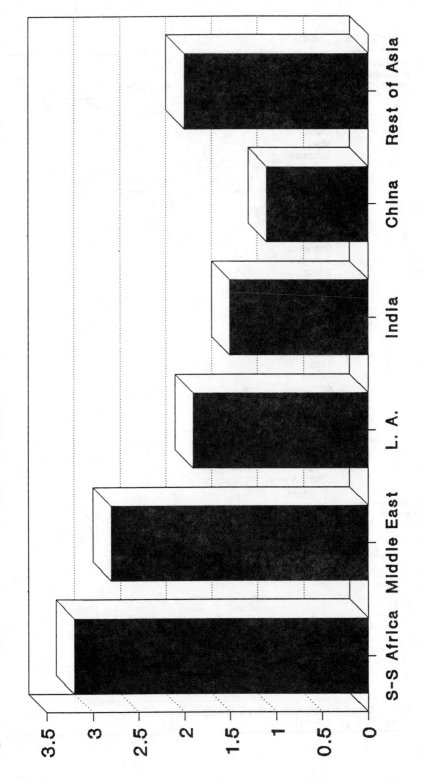

Source: Based on information in *World Population Prospects 1988* (New York: United Nations Department of International Economic and Social Affairs, 1989).

Table 4.1 Total Fertility Rate

Average Number of Children per Woman	Africa	Latin America	Middle East	Asia
7–8	Rwanda Kenya Malawi Niger Tanzania		Jordan	
6–7	Liberia Uganda Nigeria Zambia Somalia Cameroon Botswana Senegal Sudan Burkina Faso Madagascar Sierra Leone Burundi Côte d'Ivoire Benin Mali Togo Ghana Zimbabwe Congo Mauritania Zaire Guinea	Honduras Bolivia	Yemen Arab Republic Syria	Nepal Pakistan
5–6	Lesotho Chad Central African Republic	Guatemala Nicaragua El Salvador		Bangladesh Papua New Guinea
4–5		Ecuador Haiti Mexico Peru Dominican Republic Paraguay	Morocco Egypt Tunisia	India Philippines Indonesia
3–4		Brazil Colombia Costa Rica Jamaica Panama		Malaysia Thailand Sri Lanka
2–3	Mauritius	Uruguay Chile		

Source: Based on information in *World Development Report* (New York: Oxford University Press, 1986), pp. 230–231.

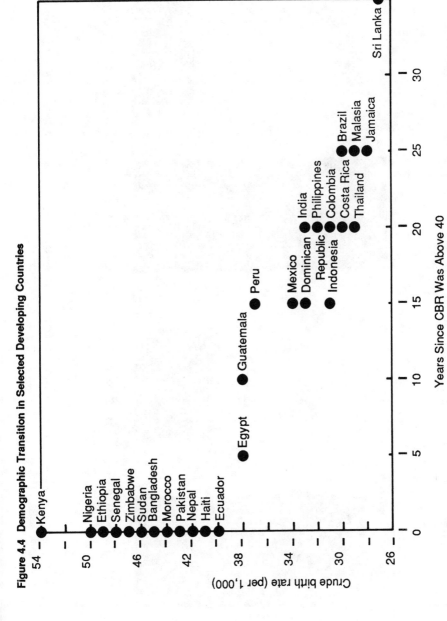

Figure 4.4 Demographic Transition in Selected Developing Countries

Source: Based on information in *World Population Prospects: Estimates and Projections as Assessed in 1984* (New York: United Nations, 1986).

Figure 4.5 Public Expenditures for Family Planning Requirements for 1990–2000 (billions of 1980 dollars)

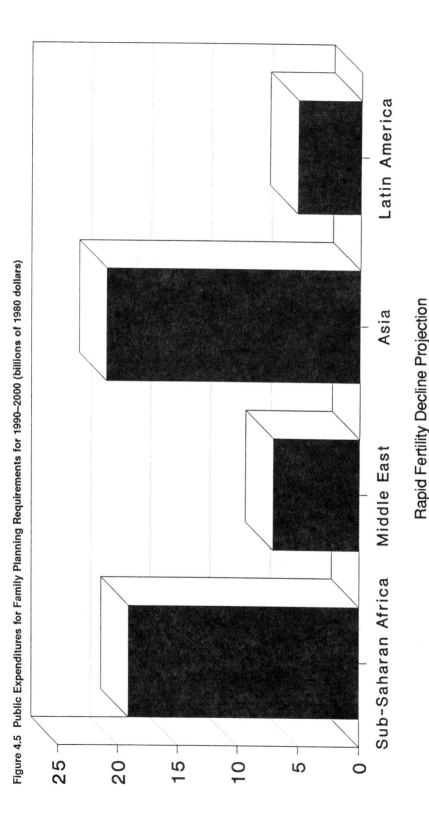

Rapid Fertility Decline Projection

Source: Based on information in Bulatao, Rodolfo A., *Expenditures on Population Programs in Developing Regions.* World Bank Staff Working Paper No. 679 (Washington, D.C.: World Bank, 1984).

family planning in Asia and Latin America than in Africa, those more mature programs have greater private sector participation. They are also more willing and able to cover some of the public costs from their own resources. In Africa, on the other hand, the beginning of widespread programs in many countries will require a significant amount of foreign assistance, especially in the early stages. This assistance will be needed not only in the provision of commodities but also in the design and implementation of programs that effectively reach the majority of the population with information programs and a complete range of family planning services.

LABOR FORCE AND ECONOMY

Rapid population growth during the 1970s and 1980s has created large young populations in most developing countries—people who will be reaching labor force age during the next two decades and looking for jobs. The creation of large quantities of new jobs for these young people may be beyond the capabilities of many economies. Table 4.2 shows expected annual labor force growth rates for a number of developing countries from 1980 to 2000; most will be experiencing growth rates above 2.5 percent per year, and many will have rates of 3 to 4 percent.

The challenge is serious: The current failure of most economies to create productive jobs is evidenced by the large numbers of underemployed workers in the developing world. The International Labor Office estimates place underemployment as high as 20 to 40 percent of labor in some countries. Thus, the future challenge of providing jobs for young people entering the labor force will be compounded by the backlog of existing underemployment.

This employment challenge has been a major factor in leading a number of countries to adopt population programs in order to slow the relentless climb of new job requirements. However, there is a lag of 15 to 20 years from the time that birth rates begin to fall until the effect is seen in fewer labor force entrants. For those countries that began their programs in the 1980s, the benefits in labor force growth will not appear until after the year 2000.

This problem has political as well as economic ramifications. If jobs are not available for young people, the potential for political turmoil may be heightened. Coupled with rapid urbanization, joblessness could lead to increased crime and political disturbances.

Although the developing world has experienced some impressively high rates of economic growth during the last three decades, these growth rates are not enough to eliminate poverty even if continued through the next decade. The World Bank classifies low-income countries as those that have GNP per capita levels of less than $450. There were 39 countries in this category in 1985. If each country in this group continued to grow at the same rate as the average annual growth rates it experienced for the period 1965–1984, then

Table 4.2 Labor-Force Growth Rate, 1980–2000 (percent per year)

	Africa	Latin America	Middle East	Asia
4–5			Jordan	
3.5–4	Ghana Kenya	Nicaragua	Syria	
3–3.5	Côte d'Ivoire Tanzania Nigeria Niger Cameroon	El Salvador Mexico Paraguay Dominican Republic Ecuador	Morocco	Papua New Guinea
2.5–3	Madagascar Sudan Malawi Liberia Zaire Benin Senegal Burundi	Guatemala Colombia Costa Rica Jamaica	Tunisia Egypt	Pakistan Nepal Philippines
2–2.5	Mali Central African Republic Chad Lesotho Mauritania	Brazil Haiti Chile		Bangladesh Sri Lanka Indonesia India
1.5–2	Sierra Leone Guinea Burkina Faso			Thailand
0–1		Uruguay		

Source: Based on information in *World Development Report 1986* (New York: Oxford University Press, 1986), pp. 238–239.

only six countries out of the 39 would graduate to the status of lower-middle-income countries: Rwanda, China, Kenya, Sri Lanka, Sudan, and Pakistan.

For the 39 countries in the lower-middle-income group (GNP per capita between $450 and $1,700) only nine would graduate to the upper-middle-income group under this assumption: Botswana, Congo, Ecuador, Turkey, Paraguay, Tunisia, Colombia, Jordan, and Syria. None of the developing countries in the upper-middle-income group (GNP per capita between $1,700 and $4,400) would graduate to more developed status during this period. Thus, in this sense, the 1990s will look much like the 1980s.

HEALTH

Development cooperation programs since 1950 have had a major impact on the health status of people living in the developing world. Figure 4.6 shows the increase since 1950 in life expectancy at birth in all regions of the developing world. These improvements have been realized through the implementation of effective sanitation programs, improvements in nutrition in many parts of the world, the provision of basic health services to more and more people, and the eradication or control of a number of key diseases.

The major factor in the improvement in life expectancy has been a reduction in infant mortality rates, shown in Figure 4.7. The reduction began before 1950 for all regions except sub-Saharan Africa and has continued steadily through the 1960s, 1970s, and 1980s. The improvement in infant and child mortality rates has been aided by vaccination and immunization programs and, most recently, by oral rehydration therapy. If these trends continue, infant mortality rates will decline to as low as 40 infant deaths per 1,000 live births in Latin America and the Middle East, and somewhat higher in Asia and sub-Saharan Africa. In the industrialized countries today, infant mortality rates are typically around 12; therefore, considerable progress remains to be made in the developing world.

Until a few years ago, these trends toward improving life expectancy and infant mortality were generally expected to continue through the 1990s. Now, however, the looming threat from AIDS requires a reassessment of these projections. The World Health Organization (WHO) recently estimated that 5 to 10 million people are currently infected with the HIV virus. The most seriously affected areas are in central Africa, though AIDS is also spreading rapidly in large metropolitan areas in Latin America such as Mexico City and Rio de Janeiro.

Statistics on AIDS are very uncertain. We do not really know how many people are infected, nor do we know what percentage of infected people will develop the full disease. Transmission patterns are also not well understood yet. Work on a vaccine is being conducted at an intensive pace, but the prospects for an early breakthrough are hampered by the changing nature of

Figure 4.6 Life Expectancy at Birth, 1950 to 2000

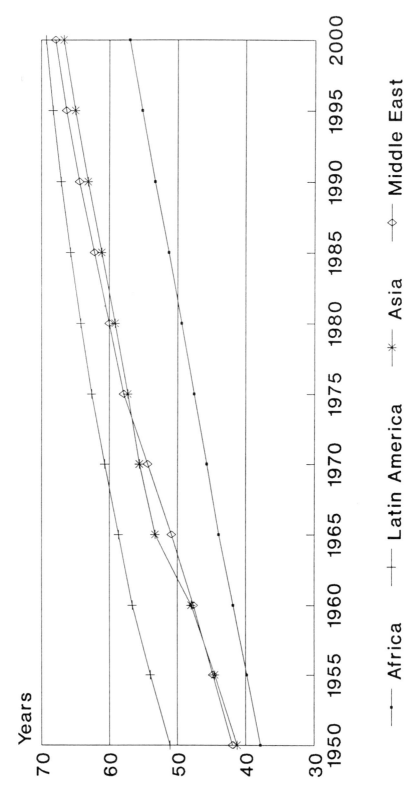

Years

Source: Based on information in *World Population Prospects: Estimates and Projections as Assessed in 1984* (New York: United Nations, 1986).

— Africa   — Latin America   — Asia   — Middle East

Figure 4.7 Infant Mortality Rate, 1950 to 2000 (per 1,000 live births)

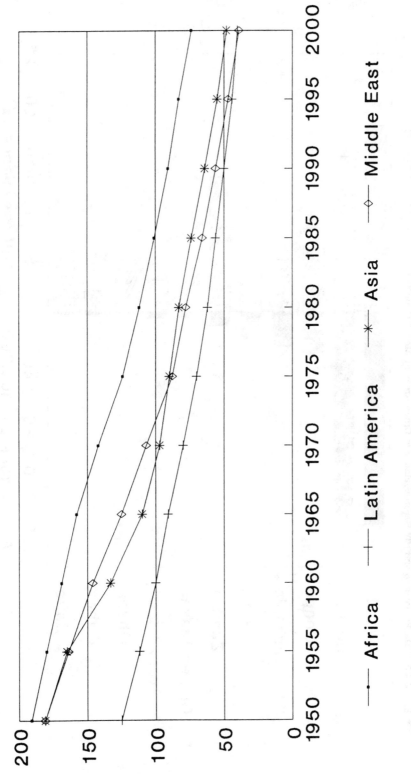

Source: Based on information in *World Population Prospects: Estimates and Projections as Assessed in 1984* (New York: United Nations, 1986).

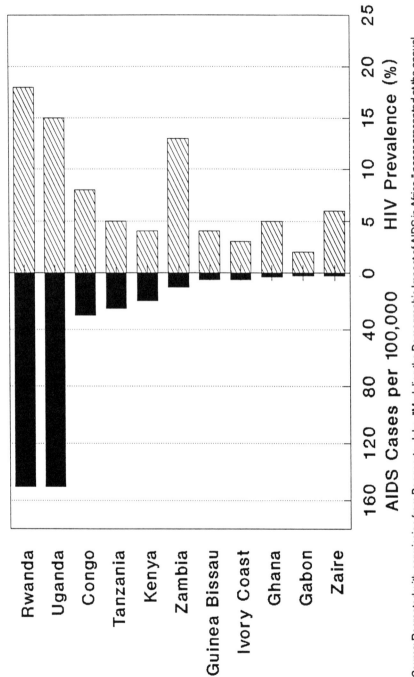

Figure 4.8 AIDS Prevalence and HIV Seroprevalence in Urban Areas in African Countries

Source: Recreated with permission from Bongaarts, John, "Modeling the Demographic Impact of AIDS in Africa," paper presented at the annual meeting of the American Association for the Advancement of Science, Boston, February 11–15, 1988.

Figure 4.9 Effects of AIDS on Population Growth Rates (percentage after 25 years)

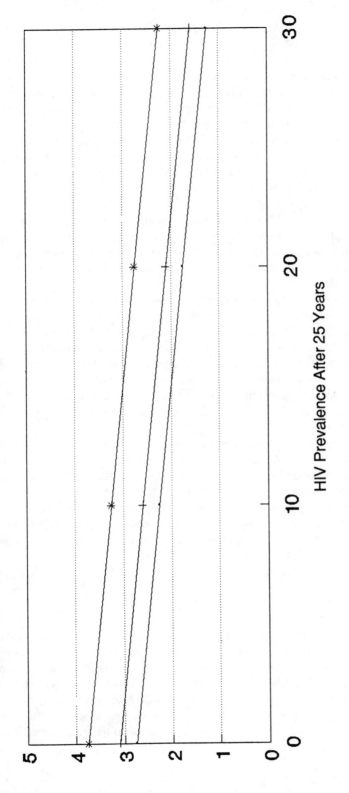

HIV Prevalence After 25 Years

Initial Population Growth Rate ⎯⎯ 2.5 % ⎯+⎯ 3.0 % ⎯*⎯ 3.5 %

Source: Recreated with permission from Bongaarts, John, "Modeling the Demographic Impact of AIDS in Africa," paper presented at the annual meeting of the American Association for the Advancement of Science, Boston, February 11–15, 1988.

the virus.

AIDS seems to have hit central Africa hardest. It has now spread to some 30 African countries, but the most seriously affected appear to be Uganda, Rwanda, Burundi, Tanzania, Zaire, Zambia, and Zimbabwe. In Uganda, the number of people with AIDS may be doubling every four to six months. The Ministry of Health has said that if present rates continue, more than half of all sexually active Ugandans may be infected by the year 2000. Today, possibly 15 to 25 percent of the adult population of central Africa may be infected. Figure 4.8 illustrates the extent of the problem in urban Africa. Figure 4.9 shows the impact on population growth rates of different levels of AIDS epidemics.

The nature of AIDS creates severe development problems beyond the pain and suffering of the victims and their families. Most areas of Africa are not equipped to provide the intensive care that is provided in industrialized countries. The cost of treating 10 AIDS patients in the United States may be as much as the entire budget of a large hospital in Zaire.

AIDS is contracted chiefly by adults between the ages of 19 and 40 and by newborn babies with infected mothers. It is also concentrated in urban areas. Thus, high AIDS mortality rates would seriously affect the group of young, educated professionals that nations are counting on to lead their development efforts in the next several decades. The Harvard Institute of International Development has estimated that the loss of skilled workers in the copper-mining industry in Zaire could lead to a loss of 8 percent of GNP by 1995, a loss larger than the amount of international assistance received by Zaire.

It may be that once we understand the disease better and develop ways to educate people and, ultimately, to prevent it, the overall impact will be no more than that of any other major disease. On the other hand, it could be devastating. There is the real potential for this to become the major development challenge of the 1990s, requiring the use of most of the available development resources to fight AIDS and to preserve life where we can, leaving few resources for other programs that are intended to improve the quality of life that exists today.

URBANIZATION

The population of the developing world is becoming increasingly urban. Figure 4.10 shows the trends since 1950 in the percentage of the population that lives in urban areas, projected to the year 2000. All four regions show increasing urbanization, with the highest levels in Latin America and the Middle East. In fact, urbanization has increased so rapidly in these two regions that more than half the population already lives in urban areas. Half the population of the world as a whole is expected to live in urban areas by the year 2000, and, by 2015, half the population of the developing world will live in urban areas.

The countries with the fastest-growing urban populations are shown in Table 4.3. As this chart shows, the most rapid urban growth is found in Africa, where rates reach 7 to 8 percent per year. At these rates, the urban population will increase by 100 to 115 percent during the 1990s.

Urbanization brings a mixed blessing to developing countries. On the positive side, cities of a certain size are necessary to achieve the economies of scale and critical mass that are necessary for some types of production (e.g., steel mills, automobile production plants) and for the economic provision of some kinds of services (modern hospital care, international financial and trading services). The modernization of individual attitudes and practices that comes with urbanization often plays an important role in development by affecting attitudes about, for example, education, family size, and national identity.

On the negative side, rapid urbanization also creates numerous problems that may be beyond the capabilities of developing economies to solve, including increased requirements for urban infrastructure (housing, water, electricity, sewage, transportation) and the creation of modern sector jobs. There may also be serious problems related to pollution and crime. Most urban experts agree that the benefits of increasing city size continue only until a level of 1 or 2 million people; beyond that, there are few additional benefits but an increasing number of problems to solve. As the developing world urbanizes rapidly, the focus of development cooperation may have to shift more toward urban problems.

One of the special problems that will be emerging is the rapid increase in megacities. In 1950, there were only two cities with populations larger than 10 million—New York and London. By 1975, there were seven, the former two and Los Angeles, Mexico City, São Paulo, Shanghai, and Tokyo. By 2000, there will be 26 cities with over 10 million inhabitants. Most of these will be in the developing world, as shown in Table 4.4. Mexico City and São Paulo are both expected to have over 20 million people by the year 2000. The list of cities of over 15 million will include Rio de Janeiro, Bombay, Calcutta, Jakarta, and Cairo. If we consider cities of over 5 million, there will be 58 by the year 2000, and again most will be in the developing world.

We are just now beginning to have experience with cities this large. What special problems might be created by cities of over 20 million in developing countries? Will they truly function as single cities providing the benefits of urban living to all residents, or will they break down and function as a conglomeration of separate enclaves providing exclusive urban advantages for a privileged few, and fewer and fewer services for the disadvantaged masses? Will they serve as breeding grounds for political turmoil or will they offer a quick path to development? Will the problems of pollution, congestion, and lack of services begin to outweigh the benefits of

Figure 4.10 Percentage of Population In Urban Areas, 1950 to 2000

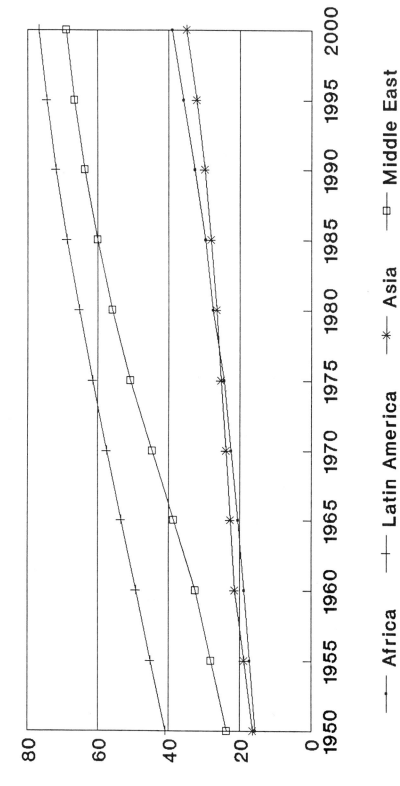

—•— Africa   —+— Latin America   —*— Asia   —□— Middle East

Source: Based on information in *World Population Prospects: Estimates and Projections as Assessed in 1984* (New York: United Nations, 1986).

Table 4.3 Urban Growth Rate, 1990–2000 (percent per year)

	Africa	Latin America	Middle East	Asia
7–8	Burundi Tanzania Rwanda Kenya			
6–7	Malawi Swaziland Uganda Burkina Faso Botswana Niger Lesotho		Yemen	Nepal Bhutan
5–6	Madagascar Benin Côte d'Ivoire Zimbabwe Mauritania Gambia Togo Nigeria Chad Zambia Guinea		Algeria	Bangladesh
4–5	Liberia Zaire Cameroon Guinea-Bissau Congo Mali Sudan Somalia Ghana Senegal	Honduras Bolivia Guatemala Nicaragua	Jordan	Papua New Guinea Pakistan India
3–4		Haiti Paraguay Ecuador El Salvador Costa Rica Guyana Dominican Republic	Morocco Egypt	Thailand Indonesia Philippines Malaysia Burma
2–3		Peru Suriname Panama Venezuela Mexico Brazil Jamaica Colombia	Tunisia	Sri Lanka
0–2		Chile Argentina Uruguay		

Source: World Population Prospects 1988 (New York: United Nations, Department of International Economic and Social Affairs, 1989).

Table 4.4 Urban Agglomerations in Developing Countries with Populations Greater than 5 Million by 2000

City	Population in 2000 (millions)
Mexico City	26
São Paulo	24
Calcutta	17
Bombay	16
Shanghai	14
Buenos Aires	14
Teheran	14
Seoul	14
Rio de Janiero	13
Jakarta	13
Delhi	13
Karachi	12
Cairo	11
Manila	11
Dhaka	11
Bangkok	11
Beijing	11
Tianjin	9
Lima	9
Madras	8
Bangalore	8
Lagos	8
Bogotá	7
Baghdad	7
Lahore	6
Pusan	6
Shenyang	5
Santiago	5
Caracas	5
Belo Horizonte	5
Ahmedabad	5
Hyderabad	5
Kinshasa	5
Algiers	5

Source: The Prospects of World Urbanization. Rev. 1984–1985 (New York: United Nations, 1987).

better education and higher wages that have traditionally drawn rural migrants? These and other questions will increasingly occupy the attention of planners and policymakers during the 1990s.

AGRICULTURE

The growing urban populations will place an increased burden on agricultural systems to provide food. During the 1970s and 1980s this challenge was not well met. As Figure 4.11 shows, increases in per capita output from 1974–1976 to 1982–1984 averaged only about 2 to 4 percent (or 0.2 to 0.5 percent per year). In sub-Saharan Africa, population growth outstripped food production, leading to a decline in per capita production of 8 percent. There were some successes, however. India increased per capita production by 10 percent during this period.

The lack of more rapid increases in agricultural production led to increasing needs for food from external sources. Figure 4.12 illustrates cereal imports in 1974 and in 1986. The developing countries classified as upper-middle-income by the World Bank led the way in cereal imports because of larger demand associated with higher incomes and because they were able to pay for imports.

Figure 4.13 shows the situation for food aid in 1974/75 and 1985/86. The largest share of food aid went to the low-income and lower-middle-income groups. Since the populations of these countries are still growing quite rapidly, even larger quantities of food aid may be required in the 1990s unless agricultural production can be stimulated to grow faster than it has in the past.

Growth in agricultural output historically has resulted from increases in the amount of land under cultivation. Now, however, most of the suitable land is already being cultivated. In fact, in many countries, agriculture has expanded onto land unsuitable for cultivation, resulting in low yields and environmental damage, especially deforestation and erosion.

Future growth in agricultural production will depend on increasing yields on the current land base. New high-yielding varieties of many crops have helped to increase yields dramatically in some cases over the last 20 years, but more work needs to be done in this area, especially to produce new varieties of crops that are the staples in Africa. In addition, more intensive use of fertilizer, pesticides, insecticides, and irrigation will be required. This will generate increased needs for improved farm-management practices and wider availability of credit facilities.

There is an additional link between urbanization and agricultural production that is a particular problem in some countries: the loss of agricultural land to urban expansion. Figure 4.14 illustrates this problem in Egypt. The upper circle is a processed Landsat satellite photograph showing

Figure 4.11 Food Production per Capita (percentage change 1974–1976 to 1982–1984)

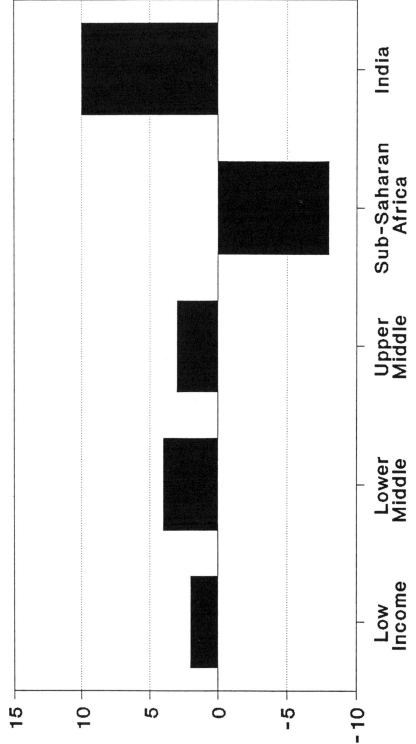

Source: Based on information in *World Development Report 1988* (New York: Oxford University Press, 1988).

Figure 4.12 Cereal Imports, 1974 and 1986 (in million tonnes)

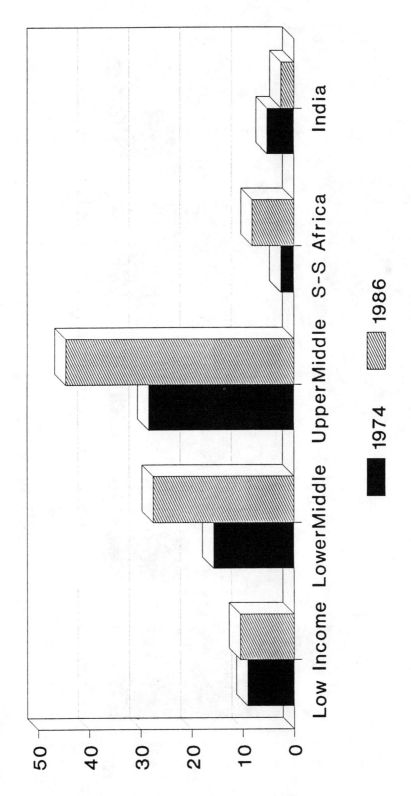

Source: Based on information in *World Development Report 1988* (New York: Oxford University Press, 1988).

Figure 4.13 Food Aid in Cereals, 1974/75 and 1985/86 (in million tonnes)

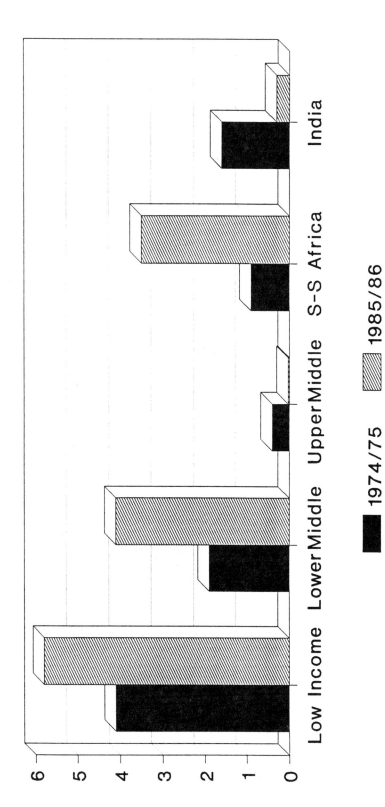

Low Income   Lower Middle   Upper Middle   S-S Africa   India

■ 1974/75   ▨ 1985/86

Source: Based on information in *World Development Report 1988* (New York: Oxford University Press, 1988).

Figure 4.14 Spread of Urbanization in Tanta, Egypt, 1972–2000 (10-kilometer radius)

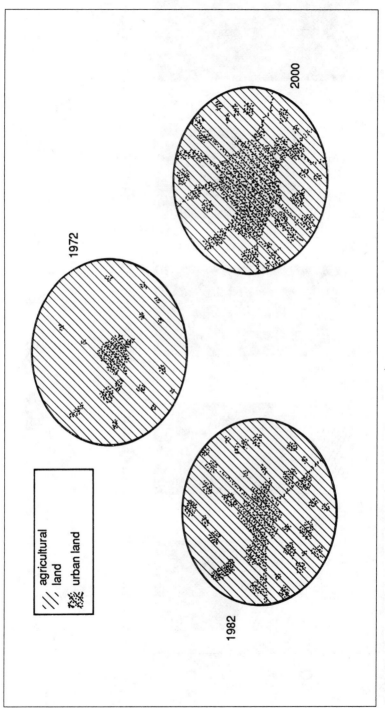

Source: The Futures Group: satellite studies. Printed with permission.

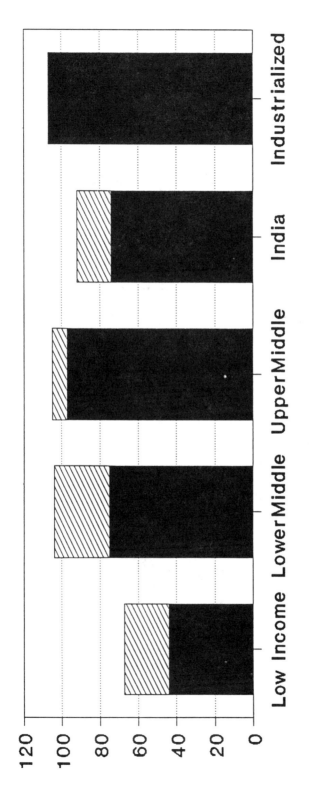

Figure 4.15 Primary Enrollment Rates, 1965 and 1985 (percentage of age group)

Low Income   Lower Middle   Upper Middle   India   Industrialized

■ 1965   ▨ 1985

Source: Based on information in *World Development Report 1988* (New York: Oxford University Press, 1988).

urban (dark shading) and agricultural land in a 10-kilometer radius around the Egyptian delta city of Tanta in 1972. By 1982, the urban area had tripled, resulting in a loss of good agricultural land. A projection to the year 2000 shows that the area will be almost 50 percent urban by that time. Thus, urban expansion may cause the loss of good agricultural land at the same time that it increases the demand for food in urban areas.

EDUCATION

Improvements in primary education have been remarkable during the last two decades. Figure 4.15 shows the primary enrollment rates for 1965 and 1985. Even in the low-income countries, enrollment rates are approaching 80 percent. Among the most impressive gains are the improvements from 1960 to 1985 achieved by Nepal (from 10 to 79), Zaire (from 60 to 98), Tanzania (from 25 to 72), Madagascar (from 52 to 100), Kenya (from 47 to 94), Zambia (from 42 to 100), Papua New Guinea (from 32 to 65), and Nigeria (from 36 to 92). (Enrolment rates may exceed 100 percent of the primary school age group if many underage and overage children are enrolled.) During the 1990s, those countries that have not yet achieved universal primary enrolment will be striving to do so. Female enrolment has traditionally lagged male enrolment, but the gap is closing rapidly in many countries.

The gains in enrolment rates have resulted in high financial burdens for many developing countries. The combination of increasing enrollment rates and increasing numbers of school-age children have forced many developing countries to allocate large portions of government budgets to education. While the industrialized countries spend an average of 5 percent of their central-government expenditures on education, many developing countries spend much more: Kenya, about 20 percent; Bolivia, 24 percent; Papua New Guinea, 18 percent; Ecuador, 30 percent; the Côte d'Ivoire, 16 percent. In some countries, such as Papua New Guinea, the goal of universal primary education has been temporarily abandoned because of high costs. In others, efforts are being made to provide the funds no matter what the cost.

The emphasis will probably be shifting during the 1990s from increasing enrolment rates to improving the quality of primary education. There is a need to make primary education more relevant to local situations. There is also a need for increased vocational training after primary school.

Secondary enrolment rates have also increased during the last two decades, though at a slower pace and from a much lower base. With primary enrolment rates near 100 percent for many countries, the focus is likely to shift to increases in secondary and vocational education. The challenge will be to provide relevant education at enrolment rates that are balanced to the needs of the economy. Several countries, such as Egypt, have already experienced the problems that can come from graduating more secondary and university students than the economy can absorb. The result is often pressure to provide government jobs even if the pay is low and there is nothing for the new employees to do. On the other hand, a well-trained labor force is essential for continued economic growth. The challenge is to balance the aspiration of students with the requirements of the economy, both in numbers of graduates and the specialties they pursue.

POLITICS AND GOVERNMENT

Political trends certainly play a major role in setting the climate for development cooperation. The 1980s have seen a number of political trends that have profoundly affected development efforts, among them:

- *Military regimes yielding to democratic governments in Latin America:* Among the countries where military was replaced by democratic governance are Argentina, Bolivia, Brazil, El Salvador, Honduras, Peru, and Uruguay. During the 1960s and 1970s the trend was in the opposite direction, so there is no guarantee that the current trend will continue through the 1990s. However, it does mean that the decade is likely to start with a predominance of democratic or partially democratic governments in place.
- *Peaceful change in leadership in many African countries:* There have been many violent regime changes in Africa during the last two decades. However, one striking fact of the 1980s has been that peaceful changes of regime have taken place in many countries. Examples of independence leaders who were peacefully succeeded include Ahidjo of Cameroon, Senghor of Senegal, Kenyatta of Kenya, and Nyerere of Tanzania.
- *The rise of Moslem fundamentalism:* In the Middle East, Afghanistan, the Philippines, Pakistan, and other countries, the trend toward Moslem fundamentalism has had a major impact on political and, in many cases, development conditions. One example is the institution of Moslem banking laws in Pakistan.
- *The fall of several powerful individuals:* A powerful leader can not only control the political climate in his country but often closely control the development agenda as well, often by setting the development philosophy that will be followed. The 1980s saw the fall of a number of individuals who had been a part of the development process for a long period. Examples include Indira Gandhi in India, Anwar Sadat in Egypt, Ferdinand Marcos in the Philippines, and Jean-Claude Duvalier in Haiti.

As we look to the 1990s, it is impossible to predict the political trends that will shape the climate for development. However, some forces that do appear likely are:

- *A continuation of the influence of Moslem thought on the politics and development philosophies of many countries with large Moslem populations.*
- *A continued struggle to complete the process of nation-building in Africa:* Although some countries have been able to maintain political stability and smooth governmental transitions, others have been beset by frequent coups or civil wars. These problems are likely to continue to influence development efforts, at least during the first part of the decade.
- *The emergence of new leaders in countries that have experienced long periods of unchanging leadership:* On the basis of age alone, we can expect to see major changes. Among the current leaders who are now relatively old, or who will be by the year 2000, are Castro (Cuba), Houphouet-Boigny (Côte d'Ivoire), Lee (Singapore), Kaunda (Zambia), Mobutu (Zaire), and Suharto (Indonesia).
- *Some countries will be plagued by political turmoil while others will remain relatively stable:* The effectiveness of development efforts is often severely affected when political turmoil causes delays in programs and rapid shifts in policy. Among the countries that now appear to have a high likelihood of political turmoil during the 1990s are Bolivia, Chile, Colombia, Ecuador, Egypt, El Salvador, Guatemala, Guinea, Haiti, Nicaragua, Nigeria, Peru, the Philippines, Sri Lanka, Sudan, Zaire, and Zambia.

WILD CARDS

In addition to the demographic, social, and political trends that will shape the world context for development cooperation, there may well be a number of additional events with important implications. A few of these are listed below; they are termed "wild cards" since none of them are certain to happen, but each could profoundly affect future development efforts. Among the potential technological and organizational wild cards for the 1990s are:

Biotechnology. This is one of the hot new fields in science that offer major benefits to developing countries. The use of genetic engineering techniques to unravel the secrets of disease and create custom-designed organisms offers tremendous promise if used wisely. The impacts on health are just being felt in the industrialized world. In the developing world, the most promising possibility appears to be the creation of vaccines against widespread diseases. Most of the activity now focuses on developing a vaccine for malaria, and field trials are being planned for Thailand and Papua New Guinea. If the development of a malaria vaccine succeeds, the search will expand to other diseases that have so far eluded our efforts at containment. Biotechnology also offers great promise in the field of agriculture, where the focus is on altering the genetic make up of crops or animals to provide new benefits. Among the possibilities are the transfer of nitrogen-fixing capabilities to corn or wheat, improving disease resistance in almost any crop, tailoring specific crops to local growing conditions, improving the protein content of cereal crops, and producing high-yielding varieties of cattle and fish.

Microcomputers. The spread of inexpensive, fast, and powerful microcomputers may create a kind of second industrial revolution. It has already transformed the work place in the industrialized world and is beginning to affect activities in the developing world as well. The real impact in the developing world will result from new applications of this technology, which might include the use of expert systems and artificial intelligence as well as the use of automatic control systems for small units that were previously uneconomical, such as the control of microhydroelectric generators. The potential in education and training applications is enormous.

Space communications. The use of satellite transmission to provide inexpensive communications to any part of a country could have major implications for communications and education in developing countries. For example, it could change the way school classes are conducted by allowing the country's best teachers to teach every student in the country for several hours each day through transmission from the capital city to television sets in classrooms throughout the countryside. We have not yet begun to explore how improved communications between urban and rural centers might affect such things as the urban bias in development programs or rural to urban migration.

Robotics. The use of robots in manufacturing is having far-reaching effects in the industrialized world today. Many of the most versatile robots can be programmed to perform a wide variety of assembly and testing tasks. There is a vigorous debate raging among economists and technologists about the long-term impact of such changes. Will robots replace human beings on the production line and in the office and thereby cause massive unemployment? Or will the use of robots result in massive increases in worker productivity and lead to greater incomes and rapidly expanding new markets, much as the introduction of machines did during the industrial revolution?

Superconductivity. Superconducting materials are those that can conduct electricity with no resistance, leading to no loss of power and no associated heat build-up. Before 1987, the only materials that were superconducting needed to be cooled to near absolute zero, requiring elaborate equipment to maintain such low temperatures. Recently, however, progress has been explosive in the search to find materials that are superconducting at higher temperatures. Now there is hope that we may soon discover materials that are superconducting at room temperatures. If this becomes a reality, it could mean inexpensive transmission of electricity throughout rural areas in developing countries. Among the other potential applications are magnetically levitated trains, practical electric cars, and more efficient and cheaper small electrical devices of all kinds.

In addition to the technology wild cards there are other forces for change that may affect the decade of the 1990s. Two of these are:

Privatization. Privatization is currently one of the fads in development. It is being widely talked about, and privatization schemes are being developed and implemented widely. So far, however, most schemes have not gone very far, because some governments are concentrating on selling off only the unprofitable operations that no one really wants. If privatization were implemented in a sweeping fashion so that governments retained only those functions that must be performed by a central authority, it would have a major impact on economic development and the ways in which development cooperation is carried out. However, this seems unlikely to occur in the present context.

Millennialism. The end of the 1990s will be marked by the beginning of the next millennium. The coming of the year 1000 created the occasion for all kinds of religious and cult movements to flourish. Given the vast scope of world communications today, there is certainly the possibility for similar occurrences on a global scale as we approach the year 2000. We can only speculate whether these movements, if they occur, will take the form of religious revivalism, new forms of religion or personal philosophies, or new movements for or against technology, humanism, sex, natural foods, education, or space travel.

FIVE

Financing Development in the 1990s

PERCY S. MISTRY

Economic development has been financed, one way or another, since time began. The requisite resources have, in the main, been *internally* generated, with cross-border *external* financing assuming importance after the era of discovery and colonization by European empires in the sixteenth century. From then up to the early twentieth century virtually all such financing was private. Public support for private initiative was limited to grants of sanction by sovereigns whose imperial treasuries grew adept in exacting a share of spoils. (Their successors now grapple with the opposite problem, attempting to rein in the intended "transfer of real resources" from rich to poor countries, which Bretton Woods adopted as a more reasonable goal for global prosperity and development.) No demands were made on public exchequers in developed nations to finance less developed countries (LDCs) until the emergence of the Bretton Woods regime. Until then, such tax revenues as were used to finance development derived principally from levies in overseas dominions, mainly from excise levies on trade. The massive disruption of the world economy and its financial system between the two world wars created an aberrant situation in which government-to-government financing played a significant interim role, only to collapse in the aftermath of recession. That period saw the United States displacing Europe as the primary source of capital.

The Bretton Woods Agreement brought with it an unprecedented period of imagination, intellectual leadership, and institutional innovation in financing global development. It successfully introduced enlightened public intervention in global affairs, with extraordinary results in the form of an explosion in world trade and sustained expansion of the global economy for nearly three decades, but post-Bretton Woods turbulence has culminated in confusion, with a weary treadmill effect. In an era of contrary ideology, it has gone unnoticed that "development" prospered when the official financial system worked well and came apart when the private sector got too heavily involved. What has happened during the 1980s raises some fundamental issues about the future of development financing. These issues are related, perversely enough, to the larger issue of growing disillusionment with public intervention.

This brief historical excursion underlines an important point: The post-Bretton Woods development-financing regime, relying extensively on official institutions supported by public revenues, constitutes a sharp departure from practices that had evolved over the preceding two and a half centuries. It is perhaps because contemporary development financing through foreign aid is relatively young, somewhat forced, and quite different from previous patterns of "natural evolution" that it has been dogged by controversy, though that controversy is not, as often thought, the product of reactionary forces that have ushered in a number of conservative governments. It has been evident even in the most benign and liberal of times.

The winds of disaffection with public interventionism (which swept simultaneously through several developed countries) brought changes that exacerbated a crisis that had already been in the making where development finance was concerned. The quality of recent debate about the value of external development financing, for instance in the United States during the first Reagan administration, was immeasurably impoverished, with ideological fervor and innate prejudice, reinforced by anecdotal evidence, replacing thoughtful argument and intellectual honesty. Sweeping remedial actions were consequently based on biases falsely invoking "taxpayer concerns" rather than upon a reasoned assessment of needs and priorities. With more experience, and some embarrassment at the wreckage wrought, the second Reagan administration made awkward attempts at damage containment. Unfortunately, they did not go far enough. Squeezed in a budget vice of its own making, the administration had severely limited room for maneuver.

The last 40-odd years have seen gross flows of about $600 billion to $700 billion (1985 dollars) funneled from developed into developing countries through public vehicles, and over $500 billion through private ones. A large proportion of the latter figure does not represent a resource transfer in the common sense of the term. It reflects an accumulation of capitalized interest obligations. Impressive though these total figures seem, they are hardly a commendable reflection on global achievement looked at in annualized terms. An aggregated 40-year perspective obscures the immense changes that took place during that period, especially the roller-coaster movements in the rates of growth in development finance. After a promising start, the gap between rich and poor countries is not narrowing, as intended, but widening—at a disconcerting rate. How much of the aggregate amounts provided to finance development have been recycled back into donor countries without any "real transfer" being effected is not clear. It is unlikely that real net flows could have exceeded more than 35 percent of gross amounts from official sources; moreover, the last five years have seen *reverse* net flows totaling about $150 billion in debt service and a further $200 billion or so by way of capital flight.

The results of government-to-government largesse as well as purely commercial lending to developing countries (too much of which is wrongly counted as assistance) have been found lacking by increasingly skeptical publics. Regrettably, public perspectives are often warped by exaggerated perceptions of waste and of the amount of external financing actually provided to the Third World. Continual sensationalizing of failure and downplaying of success in development has resulted in conditioning popular opinion, especially in the United States, to view development assistance through a distorted lens. The general public is largely unaware that expenditure of the aid dollar has been scrutinized and evaluated more thoroughly than has any other form of public expenditure, often to wasteful and self-defeating excess. The challenge of the 1990s will be to revive and restore a wider public mandate in support of development assistance in the United States, as has already happened in Europe and Japan.

In that connection, three things are striking: First, Africa apart, foreign aid has constituted a relatively small proportion (on average less than 5 percent) of total resources applied to development; second, overall progress in developing countries reflects better performance in the utilization of resources, over a greatly compressed time span, than was the case in developed countries at a similar point in their evolution; and third, in comparison with any other type of public expenditure program, whether social security, defense, infrastructure development, or space exploration, aid programs have generally been more honestly managed, productive, and effective.

Although predominant for nearly three decades after Bretton Woods, the role of official agencies in financing development was dwarfed between 1974 and 1981 by the forceful entry of private commercial institutions into the development-financing arena. That era ended abruptly in 1982, leaving in its wake a legacy of development unwound. Multilateral and bilateral agencies are being called upon once again to assume a larger, more appropriate role in financing development. But they are being asked to do so with a debilitating shortage of resources in a radically changed environment of political and financial risk. Development on two out of three continents has been derailed by debt. In too many countries, some about to cross the development threshold, a lethal combination of reckless borrowing, loose lending, and poor economic management has resulted in economic implosion. In Africa, nature intervened to abet these same factors at a particularly unpropitious time.

The abrupt reversals of the 1980s have resulted in two decades of growth, saving, investment, and steady gains in per capita living standards being lost in large parts of the South. What remains is an intractably large portfolio of relatively poor quality that the next phase of development financing inherits as a starting point. With the exception of the Philippines, Asia has so far escaped these traumatic vicissitudes. But misplaced pressure to graduate very-low-income Asian countries—especially India and China—from concessional funds, forcing them to rely more heavily on private borrowing, indicates that even tough lessons are easily unlearned.

In an ideological climate that equates "private" with good and "public" with ineffective, it seems to have escaped notice that this disastrous consequence has resulted from private banks displacing official intermediaries in providing the bulk of development finance in the 1970s. The private sector (in this instance, commercial banks) engaged in an inherently risky activity on an unprecedented scale. Its analysis of risk was inadequate, and the necessary experience and expertise to undertake this type of lending in large magnitudes were missing. Those shortcomings were abetted by a negligent policy posture on the part of governments that did not do enough to support and enlarge the official system's capacity to play a balanced role in petrodollar recycling. Since 1982, the world of development finance has lurched along, flashing every warning sign that foundation-shoring and change are urgently needed. These signs are being ignored. Dangerous symptoms are confronted by trenchant reluctance to treat them seriously. The notion that crisis prevention is better than cure has not yet permeated the consciousness of policymakers bent on repeating past mistakes. Changing that mindset is the principal challenge of the decade ahead.

It is clear that the challenges of development financing in the next decade will be hostage to what has already happened. How well the system responds to them depends on how well it applies the lessons of the past. What does experience suggest? Perhaps the following:

1. Global security and stability demand that poor countries advance, one way or another. Retrogression, even for short periods, is in no one's interests. The issue, therefore, is whether rich countries help, hinder, or do nothing at all. Domestic savings already account for over 95 percent of development finance on average across all developing countries. In the 1990s, that proportion may be increased but not by much; improvements will occur only at the margin. External assistance will therefore remain a crucial component of development financing at the margin.

2. Debate about the relative merits of public agencies versus the private sector as the principal vehicle for development financing is sterile. The choice is not a simple binary one. The experience of four decades indicates clearly that the roles of the public and the private sector are inherently complementary, and both are indispensable. Neither can substitute for the

other (except when each strays into areas where the other has comparative advantage). Both have weaknesses and strengths. Institutional capacities of individual agents in both public and private systems have serious flaws that need to be remedied. The real issue is one of defining the respective roles and achieving an appropriate balance between public and private agencies in financing development.

3. Public development financing through multilateral and bilateral agencies has lost its way. Too many of these agencies have become inward-looking, concerned about self-perpetuation at the expense of other agencies and their collective clientele. These tendencies reflect signs of tired middle age. They do not require the official system to be weakened or scrapped. What they demand is redirection, rationalization, and reinvigoration. On the multilateral front, agencies have multiplied much too rapidly, with overlapping, confused mandates and unclear divisions of labor. They compete wastefully for administrative and lending resources from a shrinking pool fed by too few donor countries. Bilateral agencies have had their efforts distracted and diverted by pressures to meet a diversity of domestic political, military, and commercial interests, all of which impinge on each other in a confused and often contradictory manner.

4. In the business of development financing, the clock simply cannot be turned back. The economic, financial, industrial, trade, and security regimes that exist today are global, not national. Their global nature might be partial and imperfect; sovereign governments might resent the implied loss of control; domestic political imperatives might, anachronistically, demand a contrary pretense. Nonetheless, the risks and costs of being guided by narrow nationalistic perspectives are now too great at every level. The Third World is too large a part of the global system to be ignored or treated peripherally by the First. Development finance is both a crucial mechanism and lubricant for better articulation between them.

5. The developing world is not a monolith but increasingly diverse. Despite important individual differences among developing countries, in the donor countries, attitudes, policies, institutions, and programs aimed at financing development continue to be influenced by a generalized view of the Third World shaped in the 1950s and changed little since. The challenge of the 1990s will be to recognize crucial differences in external financing needs and to shape tailored programs of assistance, along with suitably diverse financial facilities.

6. The globe is being sliced, orange-like, into geographically distinct North-South blocs, with Latin America (and the Caribbean) becoming largely a U.S.-Canadian concern; Africa a European concern; and eastern Asia a Japanese and Australian concern. Segmentation into zones of influence might be useful in shaping bilateral policy. It is distinctly detrimental either in establishing the priorities of, or in managing, the multilateral system.

IMPLICATIONS FOR THE FUTURE

Distilled from these lessons of experience, the directions that recommend themselves for the next decade include the following:

1.   Donor governments urgently need to explicate more clearly focused objectives in providing foreign aid, especially bilateral aid. These objectives need to be defined in the context of more "holistic" evaluations of political, security, and economic relationships between a donor country (most importantly the United States—simply because its own approach and priorities provide a benchmark for others) and countries in the developing world. No donor country, however large, can have a serious or practical development-financing policy toward the Third World at large or even toward a large portion of it. Any attempt in that direction can only result in resource dissipation.

2.   The continued dissipation of the three major international financial and trade institutions (the World Bank, the IMF, and GATT) needs to be swiftly reversed by strong collective action. Their institutional capabilities need to be restored, their global mandates made more distinct and clear. It is essential that the U.S. administration and Congress acknowledge the clear interests of the United States and its partners in having these institutions function well. Commitments by the major donor governments to strengthen these institutions must be linked to their further rationalization and operating effectiveness. (The recent reorganization of the World Bank has become an unfortunate example of how wrong these efforts can go and demonstrates the need for decisive, experienced leadership, along with fundamental change in the attitudes of management and executive boards in these institutions, all of which are sclerotic, with bureaucratic preoccupations and management ineptitude of proportions resulting in a serious loss of credibility—not least within their own staffs! It would be a tragedy if, when vested with renewed support and faith, these institutions proved unable to rise to the occasion.)

3.   Greater synergy needs to be achieved between public and private resources in financing development in the 1990s. The involvement of the private sector in providing debt and equity financing needs to be approached on a different, more durable basis than that of the 1970s. (Efforts, on the part of multilateral and bilateral aid agencies, toward achieving such leverage between their own resources and those of the private sector in the 1980s have proved fitful. An effective modus vivendi remains elusive. Vehicles such as cofinancing have proved desultory, as has experience with investment-guarantee mechanisms. Even efforts of institutions such as the International Finance Corporation, the World Bank's private sector appendage, have been but a drop in the bucket. The corporation seems to be permanently inhibited by structural flaws, which need to be reexamined. Unfortunately, these same flaws are now being replicated in other similar

appendages to the regional banks. Completely new and different approaches will therefore need to be tried, with the public agencies attempting to address the concerns, and compensate for the limitations, of the private sector, rather than the opposite.)

4.   The "portfolio risk" of development financing needs to be spread more broadly than it is now, across many more long-term financial institutions operating in global capital markets. (The most debilitating characteristic of the Third World debt crisis—one that has severely impeded its earlier resolution—is not that the debt burden is so large but that the risk of default is so heavily concentrated in a few large money-center banks. That concentration initially threatened the stability of the entire global banking system. Today, the systemic threat has receded. Foresightedness, prudent regulation, and more conducive banking legislation, along with fortuitous movements in exchange rates, have resulted in the banking systems of continental Europe and Japan being virtually immunized against prospects of default by developing countries. But the domestic banking systems of the United States and United Kingdom remain vulnerable to sudden loss of equity capital should defaults occur. The stock market collapse of October 1987 notwithstanding, there is considerable scope for restructuring present LDC debt at more realistic market values, to securetize it, and to spread it out in capital markets to meet the different yield/risk preferences of different investors. It is interesting in this regard that while outstanding LDC debt on their balance sheets of major U.S. banks amounts to nearly 80 percent of their equity capital, it amounts to less than 7 percent of the total pool of savings available in world capital markets.)

With the benefit of lessons learned in hindsight, and a glimpse of the principles that should guide action in the future, the following sections deal in much greater detail with specific observations and recommendations on what might be done to bolster the bilateral financing system, the multilateral system, the role of the private sector, and the involvement of the Eastern bloc in providing finance for development.

BILATERAL DEVELOPMENT FINANCING

Trends in Bilateral ODA, 1950–1986

Large-scale official development assistance (ODA) began with the most original and successful government-to-government program of foreign aid yet devised—the Marshall Plan. Between 1948 and 1953, the United States provided $13.6 billion (nominal dollars probably equivalent to well over $100 billion in 1985 dollars) in commodity grants to facilitate European reconstruction. Counterpart funds from commodity sales financed investments that enabled Europe to register a 40 percent increase in industrial production over those five years. Despite the Marshall Plan's success in engendering European recovery, and the predominance of the United States as the world's largest (and only) creditor, the Point Four program designed in 1951 for developing countries provided only technical assistance. Capital flows to these countries were left primarily for private sources to finance until 1957, when the United States set up the Development Loan Fund. Several European countries (the United Kingdom, France, and Germany being foremost) followed suit with bilateral ODA programs of their own. These programs expanded rapidly at first, stabilized in the 1960s, and were joined at intervals by new donors. As a result, step increases in ODA occurred at five-year intervals up to 1980. Japanese entry into the donors' club was the major event of the 1960s. The late 1960s and early 1970s saw smaller European countries and Canada emerge as significant donors, swiftly followed by Arab-OPEC countries in the latter part of the decade when generous proportions of windfall gains from oil revenues were provided as official aid. The 1980s saw real declines in ODA for the first time since Bretton Woods.

Between 1950 and 1965, total ODA (bilateral and multilateral) grew by 3 percent annually in real terms. Virtually all of that growth was in bilateral aid on concessional terms. Since then, ODA growth has been characterized by several sharp movements in the amount provided, the proportionate shares of different donors, the shares channeled through bilateral and multilateral routes, and the proportionate share of concessional assistance in total flows. By 1965, total annual ODA provided by the 17 members of the Development Assistance Committee (DAC) had reached a level of about $6.5 billion. Of that amount, $4 billion (over 60 percent) was provided by the United States alone. Bilateral aid accounted for $4.5 billion. In 1965, Japan provided less than $245 million, and Germany about $445 million in total ODA, while France and the United Kingdom provided $752 million and $472 million, respectively. Canada accounted for less than $100 million in that year. In 1965, only two OPEC donors (Kuwait and Saudi Arabia) had bilateral programs of any significance, with total official (concessional) aid from these countries amounting to less than $350 million, of which most was bilateral.

The next five years saw little change in the total DAC-ODA. Between 1965 and 1970, it rose to just under $7 billion, with the bilateral share accounting for about $5.1 billion. But major shifts in relative donor contributions began to show: The amount provided by the United States dropped sharply, to less than $3.2 billion in 1970; Japan and Germany increased their contributions to $460 million and $600 million, respectively; France's ODA increased significantly to $970 million (though contributions to its overseas departments and territories have always plagued assessments of France's "real" ODA) while the United Kingdom's increased only marginally to $500 million. In these five years, the dramatic increases were on the part of smaller donors. Canada, the Netherlands, and the Nordic countries registered threefold increases in ODA, while Italy's ODA doubled. Libya joined the Arab donor club, with Arab ODA rising to just under $400 million in that year.

The 1970–1975 period was, in sharp contrast, characterized by dramatic change. Total DAC-ODA nearly doubled (in current/nominal dollars, of course) to just under $14 billion while total OPEC-ODA increased by over 15 times, to $6.3 billion. Bilateral channels remained dominant but slipped in share, accounting for $10 billion of the total DAC-ODA flow and for $5.1 billion of OPEC-ODA. Again, however, the United States' position as dominant DAC donor continued to slide in share. In dollar amounts, its 1975 aid climbed back to just over the 1965 level ($4.16 billion) while almost all the other donors registered spectacular increases. Japanese ODA increased nearly threefold in these five years, to $1.15 billion; German, by about the same multiple, to nearly $1.7 billion. France more than doubled its ODA level, to $2.1 billion in 1975; and the United Kingdom just less than doubled its contribution, to over $900 million. The smaller donors continued to outperform their larger counterparts, with the Dutch contribution more than tripling and the Nordics actually quintupling their 1970 levels, while Canada's increased around 2.6 times. In OPEC, almost all members became donors by 1975, with the United Arab Emirates emerging as the second largest in that group and Iran taking a prominent place.

Galloping inflation ate heavily into real values between 1975 and 1980, when DAC-ODA again doubled in nominal terms, to nearly $27.3 billion, with OPEC-ODA registering a near 50 percent increase, to $9.6 billion. In this period, the United States' share of DAC-ODA kept declining though the rate slowed somewhat. In 1980, U.S.-ODA was over $7.1 billion (because of extraordinary lumpiness caused by a delay in the previous year's appropriations; a properly adjusted figure for the year would have been closer to $6 billion had 1979 not resulted in an unusual downward interruption). Through this period, Japan again tripled its ODA to $3.35 billion, while Germany more than doubled it, to nearly $3.6 billion—as did France ($4.16 billion) and the United Kingdom ($1.9 billion). Collectively, the smaller donors also doubled their ODA levels during this period, marking the emergence of some stability in the overall pattern of DAC burden-sharing. In OPEC, changes in the Iranian regime resulted in a sharp reversal, with Iran's ODA contribution becoming negative. Kuwait reasserted itself as OPEC's second largest ODA donor. In 1980, DAC channeled about $18 billion dollars of ODA bilaterally, and OPEC about $8 billion.

The halcyon decade of the 1970s came to an abrupt end. Between 1980 and 1985, total ODA fluctuated around the 1980 level in nominal dollars and declined in real terms. Whereas between 1950 and 1965, ODA increased at a rate of about 3 percent annually in real terms and between 1970 and 1980 at a real rate of about 5 percent, it fell at a real rate of around 2.5 percent annually until 1986, when it finally revived. The principal cause of the decline has been in OPEC-ODA, which, because of falling oil revenues, was $3.5 billion in 1985 (less than half its 1980 level). DAC-ODA grew marginally in nominal terms to about $30 billion in 1985 (but increased sharply to $37 billion in 1986). In the 1980–1985 period of stagnation, U.S.-ODA grew to $9.4 billion in 1985, while the ODA contributions of all other DAC donors stagnated or fell substantially. The reversal of exchange-rate parities in the 1980s accounted largely for the dollar declines in the ODA contributions of non-U.S. donors; in local currencies their aid efforts still registered substantial percentage increases. This, however, can be seen as a restoration of balance lost in the 1970s, when a large part of the dollar increase in other donors' ODA was also derived from exchange-rate movements in their favor rather than by their aid effort. Exchange rates have again reversed since 1985, and significant increases in DAC-ODA recovery through much higher non-U.S. contributions are becoming apparent—despite being constrained, as they usually are, by increasingly arcane and irrelevant burden-sharing concerns. Stagnation in total ODA between 1980 and 1985 was accompanied by a shift in favor of bilateral ODA. About $27 billion in DAC-ODA was channeled bilaterally in 1986. There was also a drastic cutback by OPEC sources in their contributions to multilateral agencies in that year.

The Current Situation and Its Impact on Recipients

Real declines in bilateral ODA in the 1980s (despite the exchange rate-induced rise in 1986) constituted double jeopardy for the low-income countries in Africa; and, because of the need to divert more scarce resources in their direction, a further blow fell indirectly on low-income Asia as well. Impressive increases in the 1970s notwithstanding, bilateral ODA grew at a much slower rate than other sources of external capital—in particular, private flows (associated with the commodity boom) and nonconcessional official financing both through export credit and multilateral agencies. These other sources of external capital have virtually dried up for low-income African countries. Although they have increased somewhat for the two creditworthy low-income Asian "giants," other smaller Asian low-income countries suffer from the African syndrome.

ODA flows are critical for the small low-income countries of Africa and Asia (as they are for Haiti, Bolivia, the Caribbean islands, and Guyana in the Western Hemisphere). In 1981 and 1982, ODA flows accounted for 82 percent of the total net capital receipts of low-income countries, and (along with nongovernmental organization flows) for nearly 95 percent of such receipts in 1985. Bilateral ODA flows, despite increasing dramatically in the aggregate through the 1970s, had actually declined very rapidly as a proportion of total inflows for the low-income countries. Although the falling share of bilateral ODA in the 1970s was offset by increases in multilateral ODA to low income countries, the 1980s saw retrenchment in multilateral ODA flows to these countries as well. While 1986 has seen a very sharp reversal of these trends, the durability of this shift is somewhat uncertain and depends very heavily on the United State' fulfilling its multilateral commitments.

What does this trajectory of ODA effort and particularly of bilateral assistance suggest? What are the pointers for the future? Broadly, the following observations come to mind:

1.   The dollar-based indicator for measuring the relative ODA efforts of various DAC donors is not useful in detecting marginal shifts, only in discerning major directional changes. Nor does the indicator adequately reflect the extent to which ODA efforts respond to the impact of exchange-rate movements on recipients' financing needs. At times of major exchange-rate movements, the dollar indicator invariably exaggerates or understates the relative efforts of dollar over against nondollar donors.

2.   In the 1950–1970 period, bilateral assistance (and total ODA) substituted to a large extent for the relative absence of private and nonconcessional capital flows to developing countries. In the 1970s, however, ODA flows grew rapidly but yet much more slowly than other external flows. Strangely, they seemed to become more misdirected by the influence of extraneous concerns—i.e., factors other than those that would govern the financing of sound economic development per se. That is to say, increasingly scarce concessional resources actually flowed from low- to high-income recipients even though the latter could avail themselves of other forms of financing, while the former could do so only at great jeopardy to their fragile economic structures.

3.   From 1980 to 1985, ODA stagnated at precisely the time that other flows also declined or reversed. This coincidence exacerbated rather than compensated for the financing shortfalls of ODA recipients, especially low-income ones. In 1986, this situation changed abruptly.

4.   Large fiscal deficits (experienced by almost all Organization for Economic Cooperation and Development [OECD] and OPEC governments in the 1980s), the dramatic fall in oil revenues, and the reversal of exchange-rate parities between 1980 and 1985 have combined to increase, rather than decrease, "pork-barrel" political pressures in the deployment of shrinking bilateral aid budgets (despite the attempt to maintain bilaterally controlled flows through offsetting reductions in multilateral contributions). As a result, the basic humanitarian, poverty-alleviating, capital-forming objectives of bilateral aid programs have become secondary and later tertiary to political, military, commercial, and special interest concerns.

5.   Private voluntary flows in donor countries—most of all the United States—are picking up to fill the moral void left by misdirected public programs. These flows focus on precisely the humanitarian, people-to-people concerns that seem to have disappeared from the vision of governments.

6.   A number of small, increasingly wealthy countries (in particular

three Asian NICs—Singapore, Hong Kong, and Taiwan) are *not* participating in the ODA system, unlike Finland, New Zealand, or most recently South Korea, when they reached a similar stage of development.

Taken together, these observations support the hypothesis that in the 1980s, donors' ODA efforts—with a few notable exceptions—have shifted from being "demand-driven" (i.e., recipient-need–focused) to being "supply-influenced." The bilateral aid budget is now much more a reflection of uneasy compromises made in ill-disguised efforts to reconcile the interests of various domestic constituencies in donor countries who have their own self-centered reasons for keeping bilateral aid programs going. When these motivations result in resource misuse, the economic failures of recipients are bewailed instead as the main reason for the continuing failure of potpourri programs—resulting in widespread public pressure to reduce them further. Ignorance of cause, coupled with disinformation about effect, has been more responsible for withering public support for aid in the United States than has any actual antipathy toward helping the less fortunate. Worse still, in potential donor countries, the view that official aid is a worthless pursuit has taken hold even before they have developed any experience with it.

The time for fundamental change is long overdue. If bilateral assistance in financing development is to be restored to earlier levels of utility and promise, then a clear-cut sense of priorities, along with a rigorously imposed "truth in packaging" self-discipline, is urgently needed. Perhaps nowhere is a change in commitment and strategic approach more needed than in the United States. Despite sustained relative diminution over the last 20 years—from over 60 percent of the total DAC-ODA effort to less than 30 percent in 1986—the United States remains the world's largest single donor. It would be no exaggeration to assert that the sense of drift and purposelessness (in actually helping recipients) that has come to characterize bilateral assistance is due in no small measure to the absence of a rudder in the U. S. bilateral assistance vessel.

The rest of the OECD world, for good or bad, still takes its cue from the United States no matter how hard other donors—the smaller ones in particular—try to emphasize other priorities and more useful alternatives. But even the voice of these donors (the aid "beacons" in a directionless environment) is weakened when their limited programs reflect their own political and commercial biases just as much as do those of the larger donors. When the United States goes adrift, it is impossible to expect the bilateral programs of the United Kingdom, France, and OPEC to adopt sensible allocation criteria outside of political considerations and historical or commercial ties. What is remarkable is that in spite of much bilateral misdirection the programs of countries such as Japan and Italy are taking a turn for the better in their orientation and in a reduction of their traditional proclivity for directing their bilateral aid programs toward immediate commercial gain.

In restoring both honesty and direction in U.S. bilateral assistance, it is not necessary to invent anything new. It would suffice for starters to return to the values and vision of old—perhaps with a little less unbridled optimism, a few more realistic assumptions and expectations, a mellow understanding of lessons learned (in other words, wisdom), and considerably greater patience in waiting for the fruits of success to materialize. Development financing is not an instantly gratifying activity. If the experience of the last 40 years has taught donors that development is not achieved simply by throwing money at it (an argument that never seems to apply as rigorously when it comes to value-for-money in other areas of public expenditure), the same experience is instructive in revealing that an absence of money does not help to achieve development either.

U.S. BILATERAL AID—WHAT IS WRONG?

It is perhaps useful to flag a few reasons the U.S. bilateral aid program seems to be adrift:

Stripped of security/military assistance and of other political aid, less than $2 billion out of a visible U.S. foreign aid budget of $13 billion can really be considered development financing in any meaningful sense. That the U.S. share of total DAC bilateral (and multilateral) ODA should have diminished gradually, reflecting the ascendancy of other major world economies (in particular Europe and Japan), was only proper. That the U.S. share was as high as 62 percent as late as 1965 was remarkable; that it should be as low as 29 percent in 1986 is totally unjustifiable.

In percentage of donor GNP, U.S. aid has fallen from the top in 1965, when its aid accounted for .58 percent of GNP, to near the bottom of the OECD league in 1985, when the percentage was less than .21 percent. By comparison, the average DAC ratio for all members was .48 percent in 1965 and .35 percent in 1985. It is a sad reflection of present-day reality that in total burden-sharing to maintain a "global order" the U.S. preference is to take on the defense expenditure burden rather than the aid expenditure burden—which is only one-twentieth the size of the former. (It should not, however, go unremarked that in bearing a "trade" burden, by way of more open access to its market for developing countries, the United States has played a disproportionately larger role as well. This particular burden, however, is one that the United States will find itself increasingly unable to shoulder with the same domestic political tolerance as in the past.)

To make matters worse, even within a smaller than appropriate U.S.-ODA envelope, the allocation of its bilateral aid is horribly skewed: About 40 percent goes to Egypt and Israel and a further 47 percent to middle-income developing countries in Latin America and Asia. Only 11 percent is allocated to low-income countries. In this particular respect, the United States presents itself as by far the worst of all donors, with its net bilateral flows to low-income countries having dropped from .26 percent of GNP in 1965 (or 45 percent of all its aid) to less than .03 percent in 1985.

U.S. bilateral assistance to the two largest low-income countries—India and China—is negligible. In net terms, capital flows on bilateral account with India are now negative; with China they hardly exist.

Apart from the Middle East (which increasingly includes Pakistan), most of the remaining U.S. aid is concentrated regionally in Central and Latin America and in the Philippines and (to a lesser extent) Indonesia and Thailand. It has modest presence relative to other donors in low-income Africa—clearly the region most desperately in need of concessional bilateral assistance. In other words, the U.S. bilateral aid program almost gives credence to the popular canard about the United States' alleged proclivity for dealing only with despots, dictators, and military regimes with right-wing biases. Its bilateral aid program has shown a distressing inability to foster the democratic and humanitarian values the United States stands for.

Assistance to low-income countries is heavily concentrated in food aid, which helps the United States perhaps more than it does recipient countries. U.S. leadership in areas such as population, nutrition, health, education, and sanitation has been replaced by an ideological emphasis on private sector development.

In short, after 1965 the United States went badly wrong in its perspectives on bilateral assistance. Before then, it did almost everything right, setting standards for the world to emulate. Since then, a peculiar political dynamic assumed primacy. That the Vietnam experience bent the United States' mind out of shape in aid policy would be an interesting but not very useful speculation. The points adumbrated above suggest that present trends in U.S. bilateral assistance are not sustainable. They need to be altered by the Bush administration if the United States is to regain international respect and credibility as a leader in development assistance. Grudging the dependence of its client states hardly fits the United States' image of itself as an aid donor. USAID certainly has the institutional capability to accomplish far more, with far greater effect, than the continual political constraints on it permit. That those capacities are being wasted is a grave loss to the United States and to developing countries increasingly convinced of the need to shift their policies in directions that the United States has been advocating so hard for so long.

The World Bank/IMF Task Force on Concessional Flows (TFCF) established the relatively unambitious target of trying to achieve real growth rates of 2 to 3 percent in concessional ODA flows throughout the next decade. It also recommended a redirection of flows toward low-income countries and restoration of better balance between the proportions of multilateral and bilateral assistance provided by donor countries. Total bilateral DAC-ODA in 1987 was around $28 billion in grants and concessional loans, of which the U.S. share was about $7.5 billion. The development component of that amount was barely $1.5 billion—about 20 percent—the rest being military, security, and political support. The United States' serious budget constraints argue for urgent improvement in the quantitative and qualitative dimensions of U.S. bilateral aid, though political influences have worked in the opposite direction. What is urgently needed is a reorientation of priorities. The Bush administration should aim to double the development component to about $3 billion in 1990 and should continue increasing that component to around $5 billion within four years, with an ultimate target of 75 percent of the total bilateral aid budget by the new millennium. The overall bilateral aid budget should be permitted to grow at rates recommended by the TFCF (2 to 3 percent real or 6 to 7 percent nominal) from around $8 billion in 1988 to $12 billion by 1995 (in nominal dollars). Even with these levels of growth, the U.S. share of total DAC-ODA is unlikely to rise in the first half of the next decade, and its ODA-to-GNP ratios will remain abysmally low.

OFFICIALLY SUPPORTED BILATERAL EXPORT CREDITS

Elements in aid budgets that aim primarily at achieving immediate commercial advantage for the donor rather than the recipient ought not to be classified as aid. This criticism is not meant to imply that such elements are inherently inappropriate. They clearly are not. What is inappropriate is the effort to disguise and misrepresent as development assistance what is in effect an export subsidy to domestic manufacturers or service providers. Apart from confusing the issue, this practice can result in diminishing broad public support for budgetary appropriations that transparently serve the interests of particular domestic business groups in the short run. Export credits have now become an essential element in the global trading regime. Insofar as competition among industrial countries to subsidize export sales lowers the overall financial cost of capital imports for developing countries, export credits are helpful. But they are not aid and should not be dressed as such. More often than not, the financial subsidy is overriden by much higher prices of goods being exported than would have obtained if the goods were purchased through international competitive bidding, so that the "aid" element of such export subsidies is quite difficult to justify.

From an average of under $8 billion from 1970 to 1972, gross disbursements of export credits from all DAC countries reached a peak of over $36 billion in 1981, and declined thereafter to less than $27 billion in 1985. In net disbursement terms, the picture was even more telling: Rising from a $2.8 billion average in 1970–1972, net credits peaked at $18.4 billion in 1981, then declined to $7 billion in 1986. During this period, the officially funded component of net export credits was relatively stable, fluctuating from a low 1970–1972 average of $.8 billion to a peak of $2.7 billion in 1982 (declining to under $2 billion in 1985). Since 1980, however, the amount has varied in the $2 billion to $2.7 billion range. Much greater volatility has been apparent in the privately funded component of net export credits, which rose from a 1970–1972 base of $1.9 billion to a peak of $15 billion in 1981, and fell off sharply to around $4 billion by 1985 and to less than $2 billion in 1986.

As a percentage of net developing country external capital receipts, export credits were a remarkably stable 12 to 15 percent of the total between 1970 and 1981 but then fell sharply to below 7 percent in 1985 and below 2.5 percent in 1986. The post-1981 decline (a direct reflection of the debt crisis) was caused both by sharp cuts in developing country investment programs and by an even greater withdrawal by the main export-credit agencies as a result of sudden high operating losses. The falloff was particularly sharp for the low-income African countries when disbursements of new medium- and long-term export credits dropped to $250 million in 1985, less than a fifth of the 1980 level. Although export credits were concentrated mainly in the more advanced, middle-to-high-income developing countries (which until 1981 got over 60 percent of the total net flow), a surprisingly large (net) share—90 percent—now goes to low-income countries, mainly for project finance. These net figures, however, obscure the pattern of gross flows (owing to much larger repayments from middle-income countries), which in 1985 still showed middle-income countries getting 70 percent of gross export-credit disbursements. In the 1980–1985 crisis period, however, there is considerable evidence that short-term export credits have been used in an undiscriminating fashion and have tended to exacerbate rather than improve external liability management.

The 1979–1983 period of recession for the industrial world saw increasing resort to "mixed credits." Larger amounts of bilateral aid were used in connection with export financing, a practice previously resorted to on any significant scale mainly by France. Data are crude, but mixed credits were roughly estimated to have risen from less than $250 million in 1975 (mainly France) to $10 billion to $12 billion for 1981–1983, with the amount of bilateral ODA diverted amounting to about 25 to 30 percent of ODA. Of total mixed credits, France accounted for 45 percent, with a mercantilist government in the United Kingdom pushing its share up to 23 percent; Italy and Japan followed with 9 percent each. ODA diversion for commercial purposes has diminished the development impact of bilateral programs. It has focused aid on inappropriate, capital and import intensive projects, in countries least able to afford their operating costs. Mixed credits have also resulted in shifting bilateral ODA away from low-income to high- and middle-income developing countries where export opportunities are highest and competition among industrial countries the keenest.

The U.S. posture of frowning on diverting scarce bilateral concessional funds toward associated export financing is entirely correct and needs to be maintained. But, quite apart from its aid budget and connected with the flow of market-sourced funding to finance development, the United States should, through a reorientation of its existing commerce and trade budgets, focus more on developing and regaining export markets in developing countries. Two problems need to be overcome. First, U.S. banks are probably the worst-positioned among banks from industrial countries as a whole to take on more developing country credit risk; therefore, their proclivity to expand lending to support U.S. exports to LDCs is constrained. Second, external indebtedness compels those developing countries with which the United States has traditionally had the strongest trade links to export more to the United States than they import from it, thus exacerbating the U.S. trade deficit.

Nevertheless, the United States' own troubled trade circumstances call for action to redress the situation in ways beneficial to developing countries as well. The first step may well be to expand substantially the capital base of the U.S. Export-Import Bank (EX-IM) and, along with the other bureaus of the Commerce Department, to mount an aggressive export drive focusing primarily on creditworthy developing countries and NICs—primarily in Asia. In developing this regional export market (left by default to Japan and Europe), the United States should focus on having the bank utilize sophisticated financing techniques in international capital markets rather than relying on domestic U.S. banking sources for funding. Note-issuance facilities and revolving underwriting facilities aimed at financing U.S. exports to countries such as India, China, South Korea, Turkey, and the ASEAN (sans Philippines for now) nations could be undertaken, using the liquidity available in Asian and European capital markets. Initially, securing the most competitive terms on such facilities may require full or partial U.S. guarantees as a sweetener to increase the quality and marketability of these financial instruments in global secondary markets. Apart from capital-market sources, negotiated arrangements with Japanese banks may also be possible to facilitate the financing of U.S. exports to developing countries.

This effort is only likely to be sustainable, and developmentally worthwhile, if the U.S. exports being financed are priced to be internationally competitive. To achieve that goal, the United States might consider targeting specific export industries as do the Japanese, providing direct assistance to sharpen their export capabilities. By international standards these capabilities are woeful, paradoxically in a nation known for its marketing abilities. Possibilities would (in addition to aviation and computer equipment) include telecommunications, composite materials, and sophisticated road transportation equipment—areas in which the United States might benefit from longer-term market footholds. This effort, focused on eastern and southern Asia alone, with public funding for expanded EX-IM operations of around $1 billion in equity capital up front, could result in expanding U.S. exports to those markets by $10 billion to $20 billion per year by 1995.

In its traditional export markets of Latin America, the United States' export losses (and its ability to recover them) are related directly to unwinding the excessive burdens of chronic indebtedness. If the current debt strategy is pursued to its illogical limit, there is little that can be done for anyone's benefit in trade terms. The export-market potential of this region, along with an increasingly urgent need to revive the United States' export engine, calls for more imaginative structural solutions to the debt crisis, which would restore the creditworthiness and external purchasing power of heavily indebted countries much faster than might otherwise be the case.

MULTILATERAL DEVELOPMENT FINANCING

Perhaps the most significant contribution of the Bretton Woods era will prove to be the advent of successful official multilateral financing of global development. The foundations for this remarkable, unprecedented enterprise, which imaginatively combined official capital support with enormous leverage capacity in mobilizing market resources, were laid in 1947. But it was not until 1968—when the McNamara presidency began at the World Bank—that the latent power of the vehicles available was unleashed. Multilateral development financing is very much, therefore, a phenomenon of the last two decades.

The United States was largely responsible for building the extant multilateral edifice. In recent years, it has been equally responsible for undermining it. Its actions seem to be born out of a reflex to the idea that multilateral institutions are too large and out of its direct, unilateral control.

Mindless negativism toward multilaterals characterized the 1981–1984 regime at the U.S. Treasury, as the first Reagan administration repeated—with greater enthusiasm—all the errors of the first Nixon administration in its crude efforts to bring these institutions to heel. Fortunately, the second Reagan administration tried to reverse and limit the damage, attempting with more responsibility and thoughtfulness to redirect multilaterals to serve U.S. interests better. But its actions may have been to little and too late.

Now the Bush administration has a special responsibility for leading the effort to revitalize and redirect multilateral institutions. It would be a unique evolutionary step if this administration were to take hold of the idea that these institutions can best serve U.S. interests be serving global interests first, not the other way around.

The multilateral development financing system now embraces the following distinct components:

1. *IMF and the World Bank* (with its various affiliates): These Bretton Woods twins still remain the centerpieces of the system and account for by far the bulk (over 70 percent) of the gross resource flows multilaterally intermediated, both ODA (concessional) and market-based.

2. *Regional development banks*: These are primarily the three World Bank clones in the African, Asian, and Latin American regions, but also smaller subregional institutions.

3. *Regional club institutions*: Donors serve particular regions; the largest and most influential are the European Development Fund (EDF) and the European Investment Bank (EIB), but there also the Arab, Islamic, and OPEC-based institutions.

4. *UN system*: This system includes a plethora of specialized institutions catering to special sectoral demands in population, child care, health, agriculture, industry, development programs, education, science and culture, and so on. Related to, but not part of this system, are organizations such as the International Labor Organization and new hybrids such as the International Fund for Agricultural Development (IFAD).

With rapid growth and institutional proliferation this four-pillared multilateral system has become somewhat confused and characterized by increasing problems of role definition, unclear mandates, unnecessary duplication of effort, and a collective burden of egregiously high, yet escalating, administrative expenditures. At the same time, the net transfers of real resources to developing countries actually taking place through these agencies have declined precipitously and are turning negative. As lending institutions mature and their portfolios stabilize, the proportion of net transfers relative to gross and net disbursements diminishes rapidly and eventually becomes negative when its borrowers reach a stage of development that no longer necessitates continued borrowing. But it is disconcerting that these institutions—particularly the World Bank—are no longer making positive net transfers at a time when their developing country members have been transferring, in net terms, real resources equivalent to an average of $25 billion to $30 billion annually to the private financial system of the industrial world for the last five years!

Past Growth and Performance

Between 1948 and 1968, the multilateral system and the largest driving force in it—the World Bank—developed quite slowly. Over a 20-year period (the first five of which were devoted largely to financing European reconstruction), the World Bank's gross lending had barely reached a level of

$1 billion annually, with net disbursements being under $400 million in 1970. Very few of the IMF's larger financial operations till then had a developing country focus either; net IMF purchases by developing countries were $.3 billion in 1970. The three regional development banks were nascent operators at the time, having been established only in the 1959–1966 period. The International Development Association (IDA), the World Bank's concessional window, was established in 1960, with the International Finance Corporation—its private sector arm—having come into being five years earlier. Their individual annual operating (commitment) levels had barely reached $400 million and $100 million respectively by the late 1960s. Resources flowing through the UN system and the European and OPEC funding mechanisms were also relatively small—in the range of $200 million (disbursements) annually.

These nominally diminutive flows from the official multilateral system—concessional and nonconcessional—provided less than 5 percent of net resource flows to developing countries in 1960, and less than 9 percent in 1970. By comparison, total official flows (mainly from bilateral sources) accounted for 65 percent of all net external capital flows to developing countries in 1970, diminishing to 50 percent by 1960. For the low-income countries, the proportion was a much higher 78 percent in 1970.

The 1970s saw an explosion in multilateral financing of development. Its relatively tranquil, almost somnambulistic, rate of growth till then began to seem like an aberration. Of total net external resource receipts by developing countries, multilateral flows grew from $1.8 billion in 1970 ($1.1 billion concessional) to $12.7 billion in 1980 ($7.8 billion concessional) and nearly $16 billion in 1985 (of which $7 billion was concessional). Over the same period, net IMF purchases by developing countries grew from $.3 billion in 1970 to $2.6 billion in 1980, peaking at $14 billion in 1985. Multilateral flows thus accounted for under 9 percent of total developing country receipts in 1970, nearly 13 percent in 1980, and over 20 percent in 1985.

Despite these comparatively phenomenal rates of increase, even multilateral financing was dwarfed by private flows to developing countries, especially in long-term commercial bank lending, which grew from $3 billion in 1970 to $23 billion in 1980, and to $36 billion in 1983. Over the same period, direct investment flows increased from $3.7 billion in 1970 to peak at $17.2 billion in 1981 before collapsing to $7.6 billion in 1985. These figures have to be judged against the highly inflationary circumstances of the 1970s and early 1980s. Seemingly large nominal growth rates hide the fact that real growth rates in resource flows to developing countries, though quite substantial, were much lower.

Although virtually every source of multilateral finance expanded rapidly in the 1970s and early 1980s, none did so quite as fast as the World Bank and its affiliates. Net disbursements of the International Bank for Reconstruction and Development (IBRD) and IDA grew from about $500 million in 1970 to over $7.5 billion in 1983 (and over $10 billion in 1986). Net transfers, however, have tapered off from a peak of just under $6 billion (IBRD and IDA) in 1984 to about $3 billion in 1986/87 (almost all transfers being from IDA, with IBRD net transfers approaching zero). Between 1970 and 1983, net disbursements (concessional and nonconcessional) of the three major regional banks grew from $300 million to about $2.5 billion; those of the EC and the EIB from $200 million to $1.7 billion; those of the UN system from $300 million to $2.6 billion (largely because of growth in the United Nations Development Program [UNDP] and the World Food Program); and finally those of the OPEC multilateral sources from zero to $300 million.

Since 1983, growth in almost all sources of multilateral finance has leveled off or has declined substantially (e.g., OPEC), especially in net resource-transfer terms. What was particularly noteworthy in the period from 1970 to 1983 was the substantial growth in multilateral flows of ODA, which increased as a proportion of total ODA from less than 6 percent in 1965 to 15 percent in 1970/71 and 32 percent in 1977/78 before falling back to 28 percent in 1982/83, around which its share has since remained.

What does the Future Hold?

Entering the 1990s, the multilateral system is hopelessly undercapitalized to meet the various demands being made upon it. This is particularly true of the World Bank, whose ability to finance global development in the 1990s is perhaps more vulnerable now than ever before regarding both the financial structure of its nonconcessional (IBRD) component and the uninterrupted availability of concessional funds (through IDA and an increasing amount of associated concessional cofinancing). Although, owing to its statutory limits, the bank has previously approached the limits of lending capacity, these limitations have invariably been removed at the eleventh hour by shareholder agreement to augment the bank's capital base either through selective or general capital increases. Such increases have always raised contentious shareholder debate, with the United States generally being the main holdout.

After the need for a third General Capital Increase (GCI) was mooted in 1984, it took over three years for the United States finally to agree with other shareholders that such an increase was needed. Had exchange-rate movements not suddenly restricted the bank's "headroom" for further lending and had the bank not been the only remaining vehicle for funding Secretary of State James Baker's debt strategy of muddling on without any clear sense of destination, the United States would probably have procrastinated even further. However, it is not just the unavailability of capital that threatens to act as a brake on bank lending in the 1990s. Now that a GCI has been approved by the administration and by Congress, it is deteriorating portfolio quality that threatens the viability of the bank's role as the most effective public intermediary between private capital markets and developing countries.

As noted earlier, the last four years have witnessed the World Bank's putting an increasing share of its portfolio at greater risk in the heavily indebted countries. As of 30 June 1987, just over 50 percent of its total loans (disbursed and undisbursed) were accounted for by 17 of these countries, which also accounted for just under 47 percent of its disbursed and outstanding portfolio. At the same time, both the number of countries and the amounts in serious (even if not yet protracted) arrears to the bank are growing at a worrying rate. This latter phenomenon was, until recently, unknown. With continued weakening of the net disbursement/net transfer role played by the bank, protracted arrears are likely soon to get worse before they get better.

Yet, with deteriorating portfolio quality, growing arrears, and diminishing capital ratios, the bank is under pressure from the U.S. Treasury to put out a larger quantity of funds to heavily indebted countries at a faster rate each time a critical rescheduling is being negotiated or due payment date arrives. The amounts of money the bank has put into these countries (particularly the five big debtors—Argentina, Brazil, Mexico, Nigeria, and the Philippines) places it on an increasingly untenable treadmill. Like commercial banks in previous years, the World Bank must now either keep lending larger and larger amounts to pay itself back or risk default along with permanent damage to its preferred-creditor status and triple-A credit rating. When the bank must keep lending to protect its own financial integrity—and indebted borrowers are increasingly aware that it must—there is little cause for borrowers to deliver on policy reform, or anything else for that matter.

Expanded multilateral bank financing was one of the three crucial components in the Baker Plan, with the World Bank assigned the largest role. It was provided unreservedly, while the other two components did not materialize. As a result, the bank now finds itself alone trying to bridge the annual external financing shortfalls of debtor countries—but in doing so it is building financial bridges to nowhere. The commercial banks are on a firm, unshakable path toward reducing their outstanding portfolios in the heavily indebted countries. The IMF, too, is being repaid more in principal and interest than it is recycling. Both these outcomes are possible largely because the bank is still pumping money in. The question is: How will the World Bank eventually be bailed out? Certainly not with the GCI—which unfortunately is being seen even by the bank's management as a panacea to a series of pressing financial problems. If a larger capital base is used as a springboard from which to increase financing to heavily indebted countries, without reductions in their other debt burdens, the GCI could prove detrimental rather than advantageous to the bank in the long run.

A $75 billion GCI has just become effective for the bank. It would have made more sense to split that amount between a capital increase for the bank proper (of about $50 billion) and a separate, smaller capital base (of about $25 billion) set aside to fund a debt-restructuring facility. The capital increase has improved the bank's capital ratios and enables it to lend more, but it will not serve to improve the quality of its loan portfolio unless an associated facility permits the bank to engineer the restructuring and write-down of clearly impaired, nonperforming commercial loans owed by its borrowers, thus improving their creditworthiness. Unless commercial debt can be wound down to tractable levels over the next five to 10 years, the bank should definitely not be providing additional loans to heavily indebted countries on its own balance sheet. It should instead provide restructuring facilities that permit the release of an equivalent (or greater) amount of usable resources for development through carefully engineered reductions in debt service and in outstanding debt. Without this approach, not only will the bank's ability to help heavily indebted countries be impaired, but it may not be able to do much for other borrowers either, because of capital preemption and loss of credit standing.

The Need for a Debt-Reduction Facility

Calls for a solution to the Third World debt problem are converging on the creation of a debt-restructuring facility. Ideas along these lines have been put forward since 1983 and refined considerably along the way. That it is urgent to move beyond the Baker Plan is accepted almost universally. It is clear that previous debt strategies have failed in one critical respect: While they have bought time for creditors to shore up their balance sheets, they have debilitated the economic capacity of debtor countries to a point where sustaining present approaches is no longer viable. The time bought for the financial system has not been as well used by the U.S. banking community as it has by other banking systems. One key element in the Baker strategy, requiring commercial banks to keep lending funds to countries demonstrably unable to repay, has been missing from the outset. Consequently the second element—i.e., swift adjustment in borrowing countries— has not materialized either, primarily because programs have been grossly underfunded but also because after six years of debt fatigue the political will to keep inflicting pain on domestic populations has withered.

Contrary to the views of U.S. policymakers, the reticence shown by commercial banks to get further enmired is entirely right and proper. No bank management can justify such an absurd course of action to its shareholders. Nor should it be asked to by any authority, particularly after three years of involuntary lending have only served to worsen the situation. The administration's belated response is to acknowledge that debt reduction must now be an important consideration in future action on the debt front, yet its prescriptions for achieving that goal are woefully weak and inadequate. Options and menus left entirely up to the private banks to experiment with are no substitute for a publicly funded special initiative to bolster the system where the market has clearly failed. The Brady initiative, clumsily unveiled in March 1989, has the hallmarks of yet another desultory, halfhearted approach that risks the financial integrity of the World Bank and IMF without achieving a material change in the prospects of debtors.

A debt-reduction facility (DRF) is now even more urgently needed. The essential features of such a facility would comprise the following:

1. The DRF would employ the same concepts of "callable" leverage as are used in the capital bases of the MDBs.
2. The DRF would in addition provide for much greater "statutory" leverage in having a significantly higher than 1:1 gearing ratio for authorized capital to outstanding loans.
3. The DRF would not need to raise cash resources from the marketplace in the same way the MDBs do; its operations would be confined to a "paper exchange," with the DRF "buying" a large portion of the syndicated loan claims of commercial banks against LDCs and "selling" to them instead its own DRF bonds—long-term (20 years) with a bullet maturity and priced at a premium over the respective equivalent Treasury issues of countries in which the banks were domiciled.
4. The "purchase" of commercial bank loans would be at a negotiated market-based discount, which would be passed on in its entirety to the borrowers by the DRF.
5. In purchasing the claims of commercial creditors, the DRF would, in turn, convert these claims into long-term (20–30-year) bonds, issued by indebted governments, yielding a coupon rate sufficient to provide the DRF with an operating spread over the interest it had to pay on its own paper.
6. The DRF would clearly not attempt to take over all LDC debt now held by commercial banks. It would offer to take up no more than 25 to 40 percent (a higher proportion in smaller debtors) of the total outstanding private debt of any one debtor. In doing so, it would operate with (one hopes) improved policy reform/conditionality approaches and objectives adopted by the World Bank (and IMF) to encourage adherence by borrowers to fiscal and monetary discipline in reducing their internal and external imbalances.

Reactions to this proposal (and its several recent variants) have ranged from the cautiously supportive (especially on the part of LDC authorities and European and Japanese bankers) to the strongly opposed, if not derisive (from the United States). Objections range from the difficulty of adopting "grandiose" and "global" solutions using taxpayers' money in a constrained political environment to excessively belabored (and false) claims of difficulty with technical aspects. In fact, the DRF is not any more "grandiose" a solution to the debt problem than is a GCI and could easily have been dealt with as part of the World Bank capitalization package. Nor is it a commercial bank bailout. The banks are likely to take heavy write-downs, which will need to be charged off over time. Nor will a DRF prevent case-by-case problem-solving; it will enhance it.

In that connection it should be noted that the present painful rescheduling negotiations are hardly unique to each situation, as is often alleged; features negotiated in one deal invariably spill over to the next one. Moreover, a properly functioning DRF is likely to support the development of wider, more efficient secondary markets in LDC paper. DRF bonds themselves, partially credit-enhanced as they are, will be marketable instruments. Depending on interest-rate movements and improved growth prospects in heavily indebted countries (resulting from a more durable solution to the debt drag), DRF bondholders may even realize capital gains on these instruments that could offset their initial discounted write-downs. Moreover, the LDC bonds held by the DRF are more than likely, in many cases, to be attractive to investors at some point before maturity unless one simply writes off any prospect of the more advanced heavily indebted countries improving their circumstances over the next 20 years. If that were the case, additional lending in large amounts by the World Bank is hardly advisable!

Opposition to the DRF proposal suggests that the real obstacle is not disagreement about whether it is the appropriate solution, but the absence of political will to go beyond half measures. There persists a dogged unwillingness to move away decisively from a debt strategy to which previous administrations have committed themselves—even though the evidence is overwhelming that a radical departure is neccesary because matters are getting worse, and time is running out. The Bush administration, without the encumbrance of previous baggage, should act to create a DRF swiftly, before the onset of increasingly likely political reactions in debtor countries tips the debt crisis totally out of the control of extant abilities to contain it, and such an eventuality seriously impairs the financial foundations of the World Bank and consequently of the official multilateral system.

Concessional Multilateral Finance

In addition to expanding the capital base of IBRD, there remains continual doubt and concern about the flow of regular funding for IDA—the World Bank's concessional window. IDA remains the central pillar of multilateral ODA, accounting for nearly 40 to 50 percent of such flows. From a peak commitment level of over U.S. $3.8 billion in 1980, IDA's commitments dropped sharply to $2.7 billion in 1982 and have averaged about $3.2 billion between 1983 and 1987. Net IDA disbursements, in the meantime, have leveled off at just under $3 billion in the last three years. Since IDA-6 was negotiated, the institution has been bedeviled by complex pro rata burden-sharing arrangements governing release of donor resources. These arrangements have resulted in linking the commitment (not disbursement) capability of IDA to the vicissitudes of appropriations sanctioned by the U.S.

Congress and have made IDA operations singularly vulnerable to domestic political influences of little relevance to its primary business.

The uncertainties and administrative difficulties caused by this linkage are, however, trivial when compared with the damage it has done, indirectly, to the integrity of IDA. Efforts to work around it have resulted in compromising the multilateral essence of IDA by necessitating successive "special arrangements" (first the Special Fund, then the FY84 Account, then the Special Facility for Africa). Such arrangements have undoubtedly helped in loosening the purse strings of some donors and capturing some available budgetary resources. But other donors were unwilling to provide funds directly to IDA because of an anachronistic preoccupation with arcane, irrelevant principles of burden-sharing, whose application has been invariably vitiated by movements in exchange rates. Unfortunately, such "special" arrangements have become a feature of every replenishment since IDA-5.

It was perhaps in dealing with the legislative schedule for obtaining IDA-6 appropriations that the most damage was inflicted on multilateralism by the first Reagan administration. The devastating impact of its lack of concern for honoring IDA-6 obligations on the schedule negotiated by the previous U.S. administration was compounded by its obdurate stance in negotiating an IDA-7 replenishment that was far too low (from any vantage point). Appeals to the White House from the State Department and the National Security Council (NSC), not to mention European and major Third World heads of state, urging reconsideration of the Treasury's indefensible hard line were unthinkingly disregarded.

The second Reagan administration attempted to undo some of the earlier damage with support for a much larger IDA-8 replenishment—$12.4 billion instead of the $9 billion for IDA-7. The irony is that exchange-rate reversals have resulted in annual SDR commitments for IDA-8 (SDRs are IDA's unit of account) below those for IDA-7. Fortunately, despite the United States' present budgetary constraints, Congress has since appropriated nearly the full amount for IDA-8 in the subsequent fiscal years. It must continue to do so. If it does not, appropriations wrangles over IDA could again result in derailing IDA with the same problems as occurred with IDA-6.

The Bush administration must grapple immediately with putting in place a framework for negotiating the next (IDA-9) replenishment. Its basic policy commitment should be toward increasing (by 3 percent) annual IDA flows in real terms, which would imply supporting an annual average level of around SDR 4 billion per annum. Moreover, the administration should insist on a replenishment period for its entire tenure, to avoid recurring appropriation battles. This would imply an IDA-9 replenishment of SDR 16 billion for the four-year period between 1989 and 1992. Instead of equal annual commitment levels, these should be tapered upwards (from say a level of SDR 3.5 billion in 1989, rising to SDR 5 billion in 1992). Such a commitment profile would avoid sharp increases in appropriation levels, such as occurred between IDA-5 and IDA-6 and again between IDA-7 and IDA-8 that fostered congressional resistance.

The Regional Development Banks

Comprising mainly the African (AfDB), Asian (ADB), and Inter-American Development Banks (IDB), the regionals also include smaller subregional institutions such as the Caribbean and South Pacific development banks. While the large regionals have grown in (relative rather than absolute) competence and strength, the subregionals have been weakened and brought to the verge of insolvency. Modeled as World Bank clones, these institutions—especially the big three—have developed distinct personalities and characteristics. Their growing financial capacity and relative operational competence (especially in the cases of the IDB and ADB) raises a fundamental question for the future: What is the appropriate division of labor between these banks and the World Bank in their respective regions through the 1990s and beyond? To the extent that they differ significantly from the World Bank, it is mainly in the politics of internal decisionmaking. Those politics, in recent times, have certainly impeded the course of smooth institutional growth and development, nowhere more so than in the IDB. In this instance, a critically needed capital increase was long delayed because of the unwillingness of borrowing regionals to concede de facto veto powers to the United States on the bank's lending decisions.

Together, the three large regionals account for a larger volume of net nonconcessional transfers than does the World Bank (IBRD) at the present (about $1.4 billion versus zero), though their combined concessional transfers are at about half the level of IDA's (i.e., $1.5 billion versus $3 billion). They are significant sources of net funding for developing countries; however, they, too, are likely to provide diminishing net transfers—or, in the case of IDB, negative net transfers—because artifical constraints on their capital have reduced levels of commitment to well below levels that reflect genuine borrower demand for long-term development financing. At present, they are also considerably cheaper sources of finance than is the World Bank. They enjoy the same credit standing as does the World Bank on capital markets but are likely to suffer a downgrading if the World Bank's credit standing is affected, regardless of differences in their individual financial circumstances.

In that sense (despite strenuous attempts on their part to develop distinct identities), these institutions constitute a linked MDB network as far as both borrowers and financial markets are concerned. That they retain separate identities is helpful both in raising private capital from global markets and in sharing portfolio risk. With increasingly shaky management capabilities being exhibited throughout the system, it is wise to continue spreading decisionmaking responsibilities across separate MDB managements rather than concentrating responsibility monolithically. Moreover, opportunities must continue to be provided for different institutions to be receptive to and experiment with different ideas and approaches to development financing—especially in regions with substantially different characteristics and needs. From the borrowers' viewpoints, the regional banks, while generally considered less technically proficient in an all-round sense than is the World Bank, are regarded as being easier to deal with and far more attuned to borrower needs.

In the 1990s, the regionals should be encouraged by the donor community—and particularly by the United States, which plays perhaps the single most significant role in shaping the policies and directions of all these institutions—to develop a larger role relative to the World Bank (i.e., their commitment levels should be permitted to expand at a faster rate) and a more distinct flavor in their operational orientation. Instead of operating at levels of around 25 percent of World Bank lending levels, the ADB and IDB banks should be lending at about half the levels of the World Bank by the mid-1990s. The African Development Bank's pace of growth will continue to be restricted by the pace of development of its internal lending and management capabilities.

The first order of business for the United States—in order to shore up the foundations for multilateral financing—is to establish a multilateral debt-restructuring facility. When that is done, the agenda for the donor community and the United States in the 1990s should turn toward strengthening the regional institutions. That agenda should be focused on the following:

1.   *For the IDB*: build on recently completed negotiations for a capital increase with a substantially augmented low-interest component to finance development in the Caribbean, Central America, and Bolivia; expand the bank's role in regional capital markets; foster a more symbiotic relationship with the Caribbean Development Bank; and, finally, abolish IDB's separate private sector affiliate, creating instead a third window within the institution that would enable it to make equity investments and commercially oriented loans.

2.   *For the ADB*: increase the capital base again in the mid-1990s and negotiate the next ADF replenishment at a level of about $6 billion to $8 billion to enlarge and shift the focus of concessional financing for low-income Asia through ADF rather than IDA; encourage the ADB to play a more aggressive role in mobilizing resources from regional capital markets in Asia and Australia; bring about greater linkage between these markets and the domestic markets of the larger, more advanced Asian countries; permit Japan to overtake the United States in assuming the single largest shareholding of ADB and to provide a substantially larger share of ADF and ADB capital funding. Finally, thought might also be given to relocating ADB from Manila to a less vulnerable environment, possibly in a nonborrowing

member country with a developed capital market, in order to better attract and retain high-caliber staff.

3. *For the AfDB*: concentrate on building up, with help from IBRD and EIB, the technical and broader institutional capacities of the AfDB before considering further expansion of its resources; focus on key sectors in which AfDB might develop a comparative advantage in project lending over the next five to 10 years.

4. *Aim to double*, in real terms, present levels of net disbursements (concessional and nonconcessional) to borrowing countries from the three regional institutions by the end of the next decade.

Other Regional Institutions

In addition to the major regional MDBs, in all of which the United States has a vital and constructive role, there are a number of "regionals" defined by the composition of the donors rather than by the location of borrowers. The largest and most influential of these is the European regional system (in which the United States plays no part) whose financial capacity and contribution—especially in Africa—far outstrip its institutional strength. The main pillars of the European system comprise the (concessional) European Development Fund—which is now a larger provider of concessional funds to Africa than is IDA—and the European Investment Bank (nonconcessional), whose development-financing activities remain peripheral to its main task of financing industrial and infrastructure investment within the EC.

Both these institutions could (and should) be encouraged to play a more closely interlinked role with the multilateral system, especially with the World Bank and the African Development Bank. The EDF could significantly augment its own effectiveness and leverage in Africa and other Lomé Convention countries by such association, as could the EIB in North Africa, the Middle East, and Eastern Europe. It should be a matter of priority for the United States to leverage its own scarce bilateral and multilateral contributions to the maximum by having the multilaterals it supports engage these European institutions in a much closer working relationship in these three specific regions. The nexus of relationships, however, requires the United States to experiment with adopting a posture with which it has little familiarity, i.e., that of a junior partner, with the Europeans and the multilaterals taking the lead—a relationship that might gradually evolve in Asia as well, with Japan being encouraged to assume a more appropriate leadership posture. If the United States is to tailor its role in keeping with its reduced resource circumstances, it has little choice but to adapt its political profile (especially in institutions and regions where other OECD partners have greater financial capability and commitment) in commensurate fashion.

The other significant source of regional funding comprises Arab OPEC states that are principal shareholders of several subregional development-financing institutions in the Middle East and North Africa (the Arab Fund for

Economic Development, the Islamic Development Bank, etc.) These institutions have waned somewhat in the 1980s as petrodollar revenues have declined, and their sponsors have correspondingly reduced levels of capital support. That unfortunate (and unnecessary) eventuality has imperiled institutions that have developed considerable potential and whose participation in development financing—especially in a troubled region—can make a crucial difference. These institutions need to be refueled and their capacities strengthened gradually instead of being left totally vulnerable to movements in spot oil prices. As for the United States, the issue for Arab donors is less one of affordability than of priority. Even in their significantly reduced circumstances, they can easily afford to maintain capital support for these institutions without the precipitous declines witnessed over the last five years.

The U.S. agenda as far as these particular institutions and their sponsors (over whom it retains significant leverage) are concerned should be to convince them to maintain past levels of capital support as part of the contribution that oil-rich (and by now liquid asset–rich) Gulf states make toward the maintenance of a secure, prosperous global system. These states benefit greatly from the existence of such a system, and it is in their interest to help defray the various costs of maintaining and strengthening it in whatever way they can. Protestations of Arab donors that their aid programs are pure generosity—and cannot, therefore, be taken for granted— because, unlike other donors, they derive no procurement benefits from their ODA need to be rebutted and put to rest permanently. These "holier than thou" invocations have little justification in fact, given the significant amounts of financing needed by developing countries to pay for oil imports and the egregious overall imbalances in payments between oil-rich states and the developing world, even with reduced oil prices!

If politically driven OPEC aid to countries in the Middle East—which, as was observed earlier, in the view of Arab donors is an essential response to misdirection of a large part of U.S.-ODA—is excluded, the ODA contributions of Arab donors flowing to developing countries outside the Middle East are relatively low. U.S. and OECD policy should be aimed at exerting political leverage in restoring OPEC-ODA levels to somewhere between the peak levels of 1980–1981 and the current desultory ones. It should also aim at redirecting a greater proportion of OPEC-ODA through multilateral channels and toward lower-income countries. Clearly, none of this can be done credibly without significant changes in the United States' own foreign assistance policies and priorities and without its voice being supported by other major donors—European and Japanese.

The UN System

A substantial number of UN and independent specialized agencies are engaged peripherally or directly in the business of providing external finance for development or emergency relief—almost always on grant terms. The more easily recognizable ones—UNDP, UNFPA, UNICEF, UNESCO, ILO, WFP, WHO, FAO, UNIDO, UNCTAD, to name but a few—play a large and extremely useful role in their respective sectors of specialization. From a net disbursement level of less than $400 million in 1970, UN agency–channeled assistance rose to nearly $2.7 billion in 1983 and to $3.3 billion in 1987.

The vast array of agencies in the UN system leads to neither efficiency nor effectiveness in providing external development finance. Institutional proliferation imposes a serious budgetary burden on donors, too much of which goes into defraying unnecessarily duplicated administrative costs. It imposes an equally onerous burden on the overstretched administrative capabilities of recipient governments in dealing with so many agencies. At the risk of oversimplification, one possibility that should be considered in the 1990s is for institutions within the UN system dealing with development assistance to be rationalized into a few specialized organizations with separate, streamlined administrative structures. If a successful program of rationalization and administrative reform were undertaken, budget support should be maintained by the United States and other contributors at current levels in real terms, resulting in net levels of assistance flowing from the UN system increasing in the 1990s, from around $4 billion at the beginning of the decade to around $6 billion (in constant dollars) by its end.

Once institutional rationalization and better-directed focus is achieved, UN agencies should consider ways in which the more advanced developing countries, while remaining recipients of higher-level technology and assistance, can become significant contributors in providing development assistance (primarily technical) to poorer countries, especially in sub-Saharan Africa and low-income Asia. Providing the United States and other OECD countries are willing to exert sufficient muscle to overcome the initial hostility and resistance of other blocs, there is no good reason why such an outcome should remain elusive for too long.

Finally, not slotting neatly into any other categories, the future of newly created institutions such as IFAD—intended to provide a model for cooperation between OECD and OPEC donors—that have run into serious funding problems needs to be urgently reconsidered. In the circumstances of the 1990s, it is difficult to see the raison d' être for separate institutions such as these being perpetuated. A model experimented with in good faith has not worked out very well. It is time, therefore, to ask whether IFAD should not be unwound as a separate institution and its financial obligations and claims folded into either IDA or into the FAO structure.

PRIVATE EXTERNAL DEVELOPMENT FINANCING

External Financing from Market Sources

From a relatively low profile in the 1950s and 1960s, external development financing from private market sources took a quantum leap in the 1970s.

Global commercial banks became major financers of development especially in the middle-income developing countries, whose creditworthiness and prospects seemed at the time to be almost unlimited. Such financing has since collapsed in the 1980s with the onset of the debt crisis. There have also been significant shifts in the nature of financing provided by private sources over the last four decades. The emphasis was almost exclusively on direct foreign (equity) investment (DFI) between 1950 and 1969. In those two formative decades there was relatively little commercial debt financing (except for short-term trade financing or privately funded export credits). In the 1970s, the "syndicated Eurocurrency loan" dominated as the primary vehicle for development financing from commercial sources. DFI increased substantially in nominal dollar terms during the same decade, but its value in real terms and its proportionate share in financing development declined dramatically. In the 1980s, private flows from all sources (except voluntary sources) declined very sharply. The signs now emerging suggest clearly that capital markets are likely to play a much larger role than are commercial banks in providing both debt and equity (i.e., portfolio rather than direct) flows to developing countries in the 1990s. In short, one full cycle has been turned in the last 40 years, with capital markets reemerging as the dominant force in development financing.

The foregoing chronology is a bit misleading in one important respect: It obscures the crucial indirect financing role that private capital markets have played throughout the last four decades (and the last two in particular). It is often overlooked that private capital markets have provided the liquidity (i.e., the actual money) for financing development under cover of the security provided by the major MDBs. These institutions raise between 80 and 95 percent of their nonconcessional lendable resources from private capital markets (in 1986–1987, gross borrowings of the four MDBs amounted to over $25 billion in global capital markets, though net borrowings probably amounted to less than $12 billion) against the guarantee of their paid-in and callable capital. Between 1960 and 1987, a crude estimate of gross amounts provided by private bond markets to the MDBs would be about $100 billion current dollars. This would amount to nearly $200 billion in 1985-equivalent dollars. (These and other developments have been cogently described and carefully analysed in the World Bank's 1985 *World Development Report*, titled "International Capital and Economic Development.")

A quick reprise of the relative and absolute role played by private sources in financing development is captured in numbers below:

1950–1969: External financing for development was dominated by official aid flows, channeled bilaterally by larger donors—primarily, the United States. ODA grew at a real rate of around 3 percent from less than $500 million in the early 1950s to $6.5 billion in 1965. It accounted for nearly 60 percent of total net flows. In that period, commercial lending was confined exclusively to short-term trade credits, averaging perhaps less than $300 million in outstandings at any time up to 1965. In net terms, such lending accounted for about 2 percent of total flows to developing countries in 1960, with that share increasing to 15 percent by 1969, when bank lending amounted to nearly $3 billion. Total DFI in all developing countries averaged around $500 million annually in the late 1950s and about $800 million in the early 1960s, rising to $1.2 billion annually in 1965 through 1969. It accounted for 23 percent of total net flows to developing countries in 1960 but less than 17 percent in 1970.

1970–1979: The share of ODA in total net flows to LDCs declined to about 45 percent in 1970 and to 40 percent in 1979, though the dollar volume rose from $7 billion to $32 billion. Nonconcessional ODA, however, increased to 5 percent in 1970 and 11 percent of the total in 1979 ($11 billion). In this period, commercial bank (long-term) lending expanded dramatically in volume (from $3 billion to $23 billion) and share (from 15 to 22 percent in 1980) in net flows. Gross flows of commercial bank lending, however, showed an even more remarkable rise, with annual syndicated Eurocurrency credits to developing countries, for instance, rising from less than $1 billion in 1970 to $49 billion in 1979/80. In this decade, DFI diminished, in proportional terms, even further, from 17 percent of net flows in 1970 to barely 8 percent in 1980, despite the fact that it averaged $2.8 billion annually between 1970 and 1974 and $6.6 billion between 1975 and 1979. This increase in nominal values notwithstanding, DFI hardly grew in real terms at all: More than 50 percent of the incremental DFI was in the form of reinvested earnings rather than new cross-border flows. As noted earlier, in tandem with commercial bank lending, export credits grew from less than $3 billion annually in 1970 (net) to $17 billion in 1980, with the share of such credits in total net flows rising from 5 to over 13 percent in the decade. Total net resource flows to developing countries during this decade grew fivefold, from less than $20 billion in 1970 to over $100 billion in 1979, $128 billion in 1980, and $140 billion in 1981.

1980–1986: The financial flow boom for developing countries ended in 1981. Since then, there has been a dramatic and sustained decline in all financial flows to developing countries. In nominal dollars, total net flows to developing countries recovered marginally, from a 1985 nadir to $84.7 billion in 1986. In real terms, however, this increase was illusory. Adjusted (to 1985 dollars) for prices and exchange rates, OECD estimates suggest that total flows to developing countries continued to decline, from $82.3 billion in 1985 to an equivalent $69.7 billion in 1986. DAC-ODA flows showed a sharp nominal increase but only a marginal improvement in real, exchange-adjusted terms. Total ODA continued to suffer a real decline. Whether the DAC-ODA figures portend a sustainable change in trend remains to be seen. From a level of $37.2 billion in 1981 (under 27 percent of total net flows), ODA, after declining to $33.4 billion in 1983 (when it accounted for 34 percent of net flows), has risen to $44.1 billion in 1986 (or over 52 percent of total net flows to developing countries). In the same period, long- and short-term commercial bank lending has declined from a peak of $52 billion in 1981 (over a 37 percent share) to barely $5 billion (long and short term) in 1986 (or under 6 percent of total net flows). Export credits, too, have collapsed in net terms, as indicated earlier, while DFI stagnated and later declined from an average of $13 billion between 1981 and 1983 to $10 billion between 1984 and 1986. International bond-lending, however, has recovered somewhat. From negligible levels, developing countries issued bonds for $1.5 billion in 1980/81, rising to $5 billion in 1982, collapsing completely thereafter to below an average of $1 billion for 1983/84 before recovering to an average $3.7 billion for 1985/86.

These overall changes need to be viewed carefully in the context of four key factors: (1) the uncertain financial conditions that have prevailed in global equity markets since the crash of October 1987; (2) the persistent fragility of the U.S. banking system's aggregate balance sheet despite massively increased loan-loss provisions on LDC debt portfolios; (3) the growing and urgent problem of the United States' own indebtedness (both internal and external), with accompanying uncertainty about exchange and interest rates; and (4) the pressures on multinational direct investors in an increasingly uncertain environment where attention is focused on acquisition and merger activity within the developed world. Under these circumstances, it is dangerous and irresponsible to gamble on maintaining minimum desired levels of net external resource flows to developing countries largely through private market sources in the immediate future, especially if such reliance is in the absence of public underpinning for the security of such flows.

Present capital market conditions are likely to persist into the early 1990s. The U.S. private financial sector at large is neither financially inclined nor sufficiently motivated to assume the risks either of net additional lending to, or large incremental equity investments in, the Third World, particularly when domestic economic circumstances and confidence are uncertain, and the United States' demands on its own and other capital markets are straining their capacities.

Implications for Private Solutions to the Debt Problem

These realities have profound implications that argue for further change in the debt strategy being pursued by the U.S. Treasury. One of the key design flaws in constructing the Baker Plan was ill-considered reliance on further lending by the commercial banking system. Already at grave risk, it was still expected to "do its part" in reversing negative net transfers through substantially enlarged relending. From a banking point of view that would have been neither wise nor desirable in protecting the interests of shareholders, depositors, or, indeed, developing country borrowers. That commercial banks did not respond with money or enthusiasm was a much-belated sign of good sense returning in the wake of prudence abandoned. Bankers saw clearly what policymakers refused to acknowledge—that this was no longer a problem of liquidity but of more fundamental structural proportions.

Furthermore, it makes little sense to keep LDC portfolio risk concentrated in the banking system. Indeed, the extant risks of residual LDC debt balances held by commercial banks need to be diffused more widely through the financial system—i.e., in capital markets at large, through a process of discounting and securing in the form of more amenable and tractable financial instruments. The task of shifting the risk of 30 to 50 percent of the outstanding stock of LDC debt onto capital markets (about the proportion that should be shifted over the next five years) is likely to preempt and dampen the enthusiasm of the marketplace to add significantly to present LDC indebtedness with new flows. At the margin, there will always be some appetite for taking on the risk of new LDC credits that are not considered overborrowed. But a wounded and volatile marketplace is showing signs of wariness—even for Indian and Korean paper—at times of stress. Institutions willing to take on more creditworthy LDC paper will most likely do so after unloading their less creditworthy LDC loan assets.

The dilemma confronting the international community is to reconcile the conflicting objectives of private creditors intent on receiving interest payments while reducing extant exposure, and debtor countries striving to stem and reverse massive outward transfer of resources from their own economies so that internal investment and growth can be revived. After six years of negative net transfers, it is painfully clear that the key objective for the development-financing community must now be again to achieve positive net transfers of resources to developing countries through the next decade. This can no longer be achieved prudently through additional lending to heavily indebted countries—from either the commercial or official multilateral banking systems. The only choice open, as observed earlier, is to restructure outstanding levels of debt in a manner that enables positive net transfers to be achieved through significant reductions of debt service and of outstanding levels of debt.

Reducing now unmanageable levels of Third World debt will involve both the financial engineering approaches being tried out in converting debt into equity with a view to recapturing lost asset value at some future date, and more structured approaches to reducing contractual obligations to reflect more realistic market-determined values of these risky assets. The former approach alone (e.g., an expanded menu of options and exit bonds) is unlikely to make more than an insignificant dent in the overall problem, especially when the problem keeps growing at the inexorable rate of $80 billion to $100 billion each year (as the difference between "contractually obligated" and "actually paid" debt service is added relentlessly to the outstanding amount).

Therefore, the first conclusion emerging from a quick analysis of trends is that some form of debt restructuring is a sine qua non for stabilizing the regime of private external financing for development. Second, at least through the first half of the 1990s, capital from private sources must be backed by the callable capital guarantees of the larger multilateral institutions, whose capital ratios need to be strengthened and their activities carefully redirected to avert, in some countries, a sudden escalation of portfolio risk caused by lending for purposes that these institutions are not now well equipped to handle. Substantial capital increases for the World Bank and, in quick succession, for the other MDBs are necessary to expand their ability to intermediate market resources and to keep these institutions from getting themselves into significant negative net disbursements and net transfer situations with their borrowers collectively. Third, the strident emphasis on restoring DFI (i.e., equity investment) to levels of the 1960s and beyond needs to be muted because it is achieving an effect opposite to intent.

There is clearly much greater scope for expanded DFI through debt conversion than is now being exploited. However, debt conversion is unlikely to bring additional foreign investment flows and may, in fact, even detract from additionality. Nonetheless, structured properly, such conversions will release resources currently devoted to debt service, but the scope for debt conversion is limited in the case of DFI.

There is definitely much more scope for applying debt-for-equity conversions to portfolio foreign investment in developing countries, but even in this respect there are limiting constraints that cannot be overlooked or wished away, including, inter alia: the relative backwardness, inefficiency, and small size of local capital markets (at least compared to what the international investor is accustomed to in trading in global market centers); the ease with which these markets can be manipulated by a few large individual or institutional players; the paucity of good, well-run publicly listed companies that would warrant capital market listing; and the adjustment pressures being exerted on indebted countries, by official agencies, to keep devaluing their currencies.

More concentrated effort in capital market development and more efficient linkage to regional markets will alleviate these constraints but not in the short term. For instance, the behavior of authorities in regulating the Hong Kong market during the October 1987 crash, as well as market collapses in Mexico and Korea, cast a temporary pall on what seemed to be looming as a promising opportunity to lure more portfolio investors into developing country markets. Matters have improved since but not decisively. Moreover, the underlying problems that influence the attitudes of foreign investors on the one hand, and developing country governments on the other, are not likely to evaporate simply because wishful words are thrown at them.

The process is likely to be long and slow despite arduous attempts to "buy" policy reforms in the direction of greater openness. To the extent that developing country governments feel compelled by external agents to act in ways they are not convinced will yield fruitful results, progress toward significant expansion in foreign investment flows is likely to be hesitant and nondurable. Meaningful change in attitudes is likely to be achieved more through direct exchanges between private sector entities in developed and developing countries than through the offices of governments, multilateral agencies, or multilateral insurance mechanisms. It is doubtful that the recently launched Mulitilateral Investment Guarantee Agency will achieve very much in unblocking DFI flows. Even with innovative arrangements developed by the International Finance Corporation over two years ago there have been virtually no takers!

Reliance on Domestic Finance

In the final analysis, developing countries face two unpalatable realities. First, budget constraints in developed countries will limit the expansion of official financial flows, whether concessional or otherwise. Second, the current set of circumstances is as likely to retard as to accelerate private financial flows in an environment of perceived higher risk. The combination of these two considerations must lead developing countries—except the poorest—to lessen reliance on external finance and increase both the quantity and use-efficiency of domestic savings.

Achieving this outcome depends on the rate of institutional development and policy change in domestic financial sectors that are the principal determinants of efficiency both in resource mobilization and allocation and on changing, perhaps radically, the balance between public and private investment and expenditure in developing countries. This is especially urgent in the face of clear evidence that the public sector has generally failed to perform satisfactorily in the business of running productive enterprises and equally persuasive evidence that a rich reservoir of private energies and resources in developing countries is not yet being fully tapped.

The focus of intellectual effort in laying the groundwork for the 1990s needs to be shifted from unrealistic navel-gazing focused on how to achieve increases in foreign aid to more careful consideration of how to improve upon the mobilization of internal resources, coupled with more intelligent use of all resources used to finance development. There is an equally urgent need to focus on how external assistance can be redirected to helping with increased mobilization and better use of domestic savings—in particular, private savings—in Africa and Latin America. In Asia, domestic savings rates are already high. There is little scope for increasing them much further without unproductively stifling growth in consumption. Effort in Asia, therefore, needs to be focused on better use of savings than on increasing the quantity per se. Apart from reliance on general policy change, much more could be done in the areas of institutional development (particularly in developing long-term savings institutions such as insurance companies and pension funds) and in increasing the efficiency of financial intermediation through the application of better financial controls and techniques in extant domestic banking systems. Service infrastructure in the accounting, auditing, and legal areas needs to be substantially and swiftly improved as well. The "hardware" focus of development financing in earlier decades and the "policy reform" focus of the 1980s need to be augmented in the 1990s with increased emphasis on services and management.

The United States' policy priorities for encouraging private flows in the 1990s should include:

1. Backing off from futile emphasis on massive relending by commercial banks;
2. More forthrightly supporting officially underpinned debt restructuring;
3. Shifting a part of the burden of commercial bank–held LDC debt onto capital markets through secured financial instruments;
4. Significantly expanding export-credit guaranteed lending to LDCs on longer maturities than are traditionally provided;
5. Expanding the role of MDBs in intermediating larger flows of private finance from capital markets, including specific measures such as doubling the extant capital base of the system, encouraging MDBs to concentrate on lending for projects and sector investments in the more credit worthy countries, supporting commitment levels that would result in achieving and maintaining positive net transfers to debtor countries through their own balance sheets, and encouraging them to "manage" the restructuring of external commercial debt in such countries;
6. Promoting wider application of debt-for-equity swaps, putting more emphasis on capital market development, and encouraging portfolio foreign investment in developing countries;
7. Abandoning high-pressure tactics for public divestiture and privatization—but encouraging and supporting such programs through agencies such as the World Bank when governments themselves are convinced that the fiscal and economic benefits of privatization are likely to prove far more durable than ideological rhetoric, which has been counterproductive;
8. Encouraging expansion of foreign private sector involvement in utility and infrastructural investments through greater use of "build-own-operate" and "build-own-transfer" financing techniques now being tested by the more innovative European merchant bankers—in this connection, the United States should require MDBs and export-credit agencies to review and revise those operating policies and procedures that might impede wider use of these techniques; and
9. Reorienting bilateral aid programs to focus more clearly on assisting recipient governments to mobilize and use domestic resources more effectively.

Private Voluntary Sources

One of the "constants" in net external resource flows to developing countries is the contribution of private voluntary and nongovernmental organizations, such as Oxfam, the Red Cross, CARE, World Vision, and Live-Aid, that raise the bulk of their funding from voluntary charitable contributions. The total contribution of these entities is significantly understated because the statistics available usually exclude the value of services provided by their volunteers in both donating and receiving countries. From a level of just under $1 billion in 1970 (excluding the matching contributions often provided by official bilateral agencies, which are counted as part of official ODA), private voluntary contributions (in money alone) have grown steadily to levels of $1.3 billion in 1975, $2.3 billion in 1980, and nearly $3 billion in 1986. Concentrating initially on relief and emergency operations, the private voluntary sector has been putting increasing emphasis on tackling grasroots development problems and programs.

INVOLVING THE SECOND WORLD

No prospective glimpse into the next decade is well served by excluding peripheral vision. OECD statistics provide regular vignettes of Council for Mutual Economic Assistance (CMEA)–financed ODA tinged with skepticism about what the "aid" content of these ODA contributions actually is. More recent evidence indicates a creeping increase in CMEA-ODA coupled with a genuine interest on the part of CMEA—and the Soviet Union in particular—to join the world community in managing both its own and global economic affairs. The present Soviet regime appears, prima facie, to offer an unprecedented opportunity for the world community. The question is whether the world community—and, most important, the United States—is willing to take the large risk of calling the USSR's hand—if indeed, as the more hardened skeptics suspect, it is playing one. There is a clear danger that premature and ill-prepared entry by the Eastern bloc into the world monetary, trading, and financial regime might result in constipating the global system. It could, were entry permitted, also render the troika of key multilateral institutions (GATT, the IMF, and the World Bank) ineffectual and impotent—much the same thing that large sections of U.S. and Western opinion believe has happened to the UN system with the voting combination of the Second and Third worlds.

Whether that danger is greater than that of perpetuation of the status quo is the question that U.S. policy must address as one of the key issues of the 1990s. Are the United States and other members of OECD so weak, so divided, so threatened by prospective collusion by the Second and Third worlds against their economic and security interests as to shun the opportunity of expanding global membership in multilateral institutions to accommodate the "prodigals"? Or are conditions such that, with painstaking effort and considerable future frustration, CMEA entry into the global regime can actually be made to result in reducing tensions and anxieties by capitalizing on the interest of CMEA members to put their economies in shape rather than indulge in continued global adventurism?

These questions have no easy answers. After 40 years of living with the alternative, however, the attractiveness of a step toward a more promising future has its own compelling dynamic. Serious questions were raised about the implications of China's entry into the membership of global economic institutions. The experience so far has been mutually rewarding and satisfactory. Moreover, Hungary, Poland, and Romania are already members of the IMF and the World Bank. But Soviet entry raises issues quite different from those of China's or the smaller Eastern bloc countries' entry. The USSR is not a poor, underdeveloped economy that requires concessional lending and across-the-board development assistance. Its entry into the global system will require a major change in the size and composition of the quota of the IMF, the capital of IBRD, and the size of IDA. It will probably seek to displace Japan as the second-ranking power in the World Bank— a position that Japan has achieved with considerable effort and after overcoming considerable (totally unnecessary) resistance. (Japan is anxious to achieve the same rank in the IMF.) As a donor member, the USSR may still need (perhaps more so than did Saudi Arabia) continuing technical assistance from the World Bank and possible standby assistance from the IMF. The sheer number of technical difficulties in negotiating its entry have not even begun to be identified.

None of these considerations, however, pose insuperable obstacles. The main impediment is the unwillingness of the Group of 7 nations to take a political decision welcoming Soviet entry into the global monetary system. That decision would be of equal if not greater historical significance than the Nixonian era decision to establish relationships with China. Soviet overtures have, so far, been hastily but decisively rebuffed. U.S. policymaking on such a crucial issue requires a more thoughtful, deliberative response. The unfolding of events along their present trajectory may well require President Bush to consider Soviet and enlarged Eastern bloc entry into the world economic and monetary institutions on appropriate terms.

The costs and benefits of Soviet entry into the multilateral system need to be urgently thought through in strategic terms from the viewpoint of the United States and that of Europe and Japan, as well as of the developing world, in particular the littoral giants—China and India. In benefits to the institutions concerned, Soviet entry in the near term could be a substantial boon. In the case of the World Bank, Soviet entry would result in additional capital of $18 billion, of which nearly $2 billion would be in cash (but a much smaller proportion in convertible currency). These figures exclude the effects on entry of the three other members of CMEA who are not yet members of the World Bank or the IMF. Similarly, if the Soviet Union were to attempt to secure second status in IDA on a cumulative basis (an expensive proposition), the addition to IDA's resources would be quite substantial. With total replenishments from IDA-1–8 amounting to over $55 billion, a Soviet share of, say, 20 percent would result in additional resources of well over $11 billion. Even on a marginal basis, assuming it were to participate from IDA-9 onwards, the cost to the Soviet Union would be in the range of $2 billion to $3 billion (were it to take on a higher share than does Japan). Hence, entry to these institutions is likely to involve a fairly substantial cash cost in gold and convertible currency. Willingness to meet those obligations would pose an interesting test of Soviet intent

CONCLUSION

This chapter has attempted to review extant sources of external financing for development, extrapolating from experience and gauging prospects for the future. In doing so, it focuses on changes in U.S. policies—bilateral, multilateral, and vis-à-vis the private sector—that are necessary to avoid paralysis and achieve greater effectiveness without necessarily increasing the budgetary burden. The position taken by the United States is critical, not just for the United States but because U.S. policy drives the entire system—however hard other participants strive to avoid being hostage to the shifts in the United States' posture with its quadrennial changes in administration.

External development financing in the 1990s must carry with it the baggage of unwinding a large amount of outstanding debt—mostly private but also public (in Africa)—that imposes a severe drag on development. Both the amounts of financing needed in the 1990s and institutional reengineering must be considered in the context of that unfortunate legacy.

Bilateral development-financing programs are now confused compromises among vested interests in donor countries with conflicting and incompatible objectives. They need to be straightened out, especially in times when shortages in the quantity of resources must be compensated by improvements in the quality of aid programs. Bilateral aid has shifted from being driven by recipient needs to being a hostage of the donor's "supply interests." This situation must be reversed.

Multilateral institutions have proliferated extensively. Their collective administrative costs now exceed the (net) transfer of real resources that these institutions were set up to achieve. This state of affairs calls into question their raison d'être and begs urgent selective rationalization accompanied by an expansion of the capital and operations of core institutions. GATT, the IMF, and the World Bank, in particular, need to be strengthened.

Public resources need to be used to leverage private financing imaginatively, especially at a time when budgetary resources are tight in the public sector and private proclivities are to reduce rather than expand profiles in development financing.

On the Bilateral Front

The U.S. bilateral aid program is grossly misdirected. As a possible consequence, it has also resulted in the skewed distribution of the bilateral programs of other donors, most notably OPEC. The following five-point program could restore credibility to U.S. bilateral aid. First, "truth in packaging"—i.e., include only genuine development assistance expenditures in the aid budget and put other items elsewhere. Second, Egypt's and Israel's components in the aid budget, absorbing 40 percent of the United States' bilateral ODA, have become entitlement programs; their share should be reduced over five years to 20 percent. Third, the United States should increase its share of bilateral aid to the least developed countries from 15 to 40 percent by 1995, concentrating primarily on humanitarian and social sector lending. Fourth, the U.S. aid program should incorporate a suitably tailored component for India and China, building up to 20 percent of the program by 1995. Fifth, "political" aid to Latin America should be reduced and targeted at the interface of achieving greater leverage with private capital. Such a program would enable the United States to live within a genuine aid budget of $10 billion in 1990 (less than 1 percent of the total U.S. government budget and considerably less than the UN target of .7 percent of GNP), rising nominally by 5 to 6 percent each year.

Budgetary resources should be applied (but not from aid allocations) to expand the capital base and operating capacity of the U.S. Export-Import Bank.

On the Multilateral Front

The IMF has, after dealing with the effects of successive oil shocks, the debt crisis, and a collapse of commodity prices, gone (through the back door) into the business of development financing. Both the IMF and the World Bank are focusing on structural adjustment lending, and the fund is competing with IDA for contributions .to its own adjustment facilities. The wisdom of the fund's becoming permanently involved in development financing is questionable. The United States should reverse itself on support for SAF and get the fund to focus more on establishing the framework of a more durable post–Bretton Woods monetary regime.

The World Bank is suffering from an identity crisis, caught between the IMF on the one hand and increasingly capable regional MDBs on the other. Its role in the 1990s needs to be more clearly defined, with better conceptualized divisions of labor. The bank is today a hesitant, unsure institution focusing increasingly on activities it has demonstrated no particular competence in handling—i.e., structural adjustment lending. It shows no signs of developing the same disciplined approach to SAL operations that it has developed in the context of its project lending. Part of the bank's problem lies in earlier U.S. hostility toward fast-disbursing lending, followed later by a U.S. policy volte-face requiring the bank to play an unduly aggressive "money-spraying" role in debtor countries, as part of a flawed debt strategy. This measure has coincided with an ill-concealed proclivity to exercise unilateral control over the affairs of the institution at a time when the United States must depend increasingly on other donors to provide the financial support the bank needs. With excessive attention on Latin America and Africa, the bank is becoming less and less relevant to other quality borrowers, especially in Asia, which represent its more "natural" market.

Present U.S. policy is leading the bank into loading much more risk on its financial structure than circumstances warrant, with the prospect of further deterioration in its financial standing and creditworthiness. To avert such risk, a debt-restructuring facility urgently needs to be established to permit the bank to assist heavily indebted countries through reductions in their outstanding debt and debt service rather than through additional lending on its own balance sheet.

On the concessional side, the bank (IDA) has taken bold initiatives in sub-Saharan Africa based on expectations of IDA availabilities in the amounts negotiated under IDA-8. Congress has acted on the first two instalments under IDA-8, appropriating nearly the full amount. The same wisdom needs to be exercised for the next instalment and for IDA-9 so as not to compromise further the bank's credibility and effectiveness and thus diminish prospects for achieving key U.S. policy objectives in Africa.

The United States needs to act swiftly in defining more clearly the roles it expects the regional MDBs to play, especially vis-à-vis the World Bank, and to bolster their capital bases. Regional MDBs should not be encouraged to engage in policy-based lending, for which their decisionmaking processes are not well suited. The United States should consider permitting Japan to assume a clear position as the largest shareholder in the Asian Development Bank, provided it offers commensurate financial support.

As a matter of policy, the United States should encourage the World Bank and the African Development Bank to develop much closer operational linkages with European multilateral institutions, especially in the context of their activities in Africa, the Middle East, and Eastern Europe. In the same vein, the United States should exert some political leverage over OPEC donors in bolstering their levels of ODA support and the quality of their assistance, but it can hardly do so before making radical changes in its own policies and programs.

Encouraging Private Finance

Private sources are unlikely to be aggressive financers of development in the early 1990s, especially in the face of unfolding circumstances in international banking and capital markets. U.S. policy should focus on using private markets to restructure and secure the extant overhang of LDC debt rather than look to markets to provide significant amounts of additional development capital at their own risk. This argues in support of earlier suggestions for establishing a DRF and enlarging the capital base of the MDBs in efforts to leverage private capital with public resources.

Exhortation in favor of expanding DFI might be in danger of achieving a counterproductive outcome. DFI may well increase if the use of debt-for-equity swaps expands. However, such transactions are not likely to account for very large amounts of equity. Equally, progress toward public sector rationalization and privatization in developing countries is more likely to be achieved through quiet diplomacy than through overt U.S. pressure.

Constraints on official resources and dampened proclivities on the part of the external private sector to finance development will compel greater reliance on the more efficient mobilization and use of domestic resources (a problem the United States now shares with the developing world). External assistance needs to be focused more sharply on achieving this objective by focusing U.S. assistance on financial sector/capital market development in the Third World.

Gradually rising flows from private voluntary organizations pose a challenge and an opportunity for reorientation of the United States' official aid and for the construction of a more effective interface between people-to-people and government-to-government assistance. U.S. policy should focus on achieving greater symbiosis between private voluntary and official aid efforts, playing on the comparative strengths of each.

The Second World

Finally, a unique historic opportunity seems to be presenting itself to bring the Soviet Union and other Eastern bloc countries not yet members of the international financial institutions within the ambit of the free world's monetary, trading, and financial regime. U.S. policy for the 1990s must answer the question whether the time has not now come to engage these economies within a single global regime.

SIX

Accelerating Development in the Poorest Countries

PAUL STREETEN

THE CASE FOR COOPERATION

It is now evident that few of the early generalizations about "the Third World" or "development," and the recommendations based on them, can withstand close analysis and scrutiny; that different principles apply to different regions at different times under different circumstances. This chapter is devoted to exploring U.S. policy toward the poorest countries. These are in southern Asia, in sub-Saharan Africa, and—a few—in the Caribbean and Latin America. Even for this group of low-income countries few generalizations are possible, and policies have to be tailored to the special needs and opportunities of different countries and regions.

Although everyone now accepts the need for differentiation, there has also been an opposite tendency at work. We have learned that some of the problems of the developing countries are shared by all, and features that were thought initially to be applicable only to them have been found to apply also to the advanced countries. While analysis and policy have therefore become more differentiated, there has also been a reassertion of the unity of the subject, particularly if we remember that the now advanced countries once were also underdeveloped and poor, that some regions inside the advanced countries suffer problems similar to those of low-income countries, and that some very poor countries have achieved quite high incomes within a few decades.

In differentiating between the low-income and the middle-income developing countries, the first difference to be noted, at least for some of the poorest countries, is the basis of the case for U.S. cooperation and assistance. It is nowadays fashionable to base the case for international cooperation, including aid, on national self-interest. These countries, it is said, constitute important markets for U.S. exports, generate many jobs in the United States, and supply it with important raw materials, lower-cost imports, and opportunities for remunerative private investment. On the political plane, it is said that development makes for democracy and peace, and that aid helps the United States win friends, allies, and strategic support. Whatever the merit of these arguments, it is fairly clear that they would have to be radically modified for the lowest-income countries of Africa. If development aid were a form of U.S. export-sales promotion or U.S. employment program, it would be concentrated on the highest-income developing countries—the best markets and employment generators. It is true that NICs, such as South Korea and Taiwan, were very poor only 30 years ago (Taiwan, the United States' seventh largest trading partner, and enjoying a per capita income of $2,200, had a per capita income of only $100 in 1950), and some of the poor countries today may be relatively well off 30 years from now. But even 30 years is a long time if U.S. policymakers are interested in earning foreign exchange or creating jobs now.

There can, of course, be a national self-interest in developing some of the poorest countries that arises from causes other than U.S. exports and U.S. employment. Some of the low-income countries provide very important raw material imports to the United States; tungsten, tin, bauxite, manganese, and cobalt are metals of value to the U.S. economy of which the developing countries supply more than half. All natural rubber and cocoa are imported from developing countries. Food aid to very poor countries can usefully dispose of U.S. agricultural surpluses. Some of these countries may have strategic importance. But the principal argument for cooperating with the poorest countries is largely moral or humanitarian, or, if self-interested, based on a long-term view that a prosperous world is a better world for the United States. Enlightened long-term national self-interest may largely coincide with the humanitarian case: Every human being born into this world should be given the opportunity to develop his or her potential, and this makes for a better (as well as more productive) world community than one in which human talent is wasted and human misery persists.

The case for aid to, and cooperation with, India and other countries in the subcontintent is somewhat different. By whatever criteria, India is still one of the poorest countries in the world, though its development potential is high. It has an efficient administration, a high level of education and skills, and a reserve of entrepreneurship. It is now the world's seventh-largest industrial power and a large potential future market. Its plans and policies are well conceived, and it has achieved high savings rates. There can be no doubt that it has considerable absorptive capacity. It is the world's largest democracy and has strategic importance to the United States. Whether the criterion is strategic, the encouragement of democratic government, the promotion of self-help, good performance, the relief of the poor, meeting basic needs, or the activation of development potential, India should qualify for massive concessional aid. To drive India into the commercial capital markets may amount to preparing the ground for a Latin American type of debt crisis in a few years' time.

It can be argued that agricultural growth in the developing countries does not reduce but, on the contrary, increases agricultural exports from the United States. This is so for three reasons: (1) because the propensity to spend on food in developing countries is higher than is their additional food production; (2) because the switch to meat as people's incomes grow raises the demand for feedstuffs for cattle; and (3) because the growth of nonagricultural incomes, to which agricultural growth contributes, and which also occurs autonomously, gives rise to a higher demand for imported food. U.S. farmers therefore need not be afraid that helping poor countries to develop agriculture will undermine their earning opportunities, as long as their exports remain competitive. But these opportunities apply largely to middle-income countries, where the agricultural revolution has already taken place. It is mentioned here only to show that there is no need to fear that encouraging the poorest countries to develop their agriculture could in the future damage U.S. farmers.

ADAPTATION OF POLICIES

Not only is the case for cooperation and aid different for the poorest countries, but the prescriptions for policy are also in some respects different. Some of the tenets of current conventional wisdom about development policy have to be qualified for the poorest countries. It is important to bear these qualifications in mind not only for the policymakers in the developing countries, but also for the United States when it is imposing policy conditions on aid loans:

First, economic growth as measured by rising national income or national income per head, sometimes taken as a principal performance criterion, is not the top priority for very poor countries. (Some would say it should not be a top priority for any country.) If we adopt the metaphor of the "take-off into self-sustained growth," the task for the poorest countries is to lay the runway. Laying the institutional and human foundations for future growth is not immediately reflected in high growth figures. A curve relating growth of income per head to levels of income per head would show the shape of an elongated S. At both very low and very high levels, growth is relatively slow, while in middle-income countries the rate is higher. The indicators to seek in monitoring performance are then not so much growth of income per head as, for example, increases in life expectancy, reductions in mortality (especially infant mortality), and rises in literacy. Massive human investment in the early stages of development can pay high growth dividends later, as Japan, Israel, South Korea, and Taiwan have shown. The United States can contribute to this foundation-laying. A high priority should be attached to projects and programs for the social sectors, and within these to projects and programs specifically tailored to poor people. Not only will these raise the welfare of particularly deprived groups, but they will also contribute to raising production and productivity by improving human capital. Conventional infrastructure projects may also be indicated in some countries, though attention has to be paid to the correct type: small feeder roads from farms rather than four-lane highways; small local storage facilities rather than mammoth silos.

The poor countries, particularly in Africa today but also India in the past, are (and were) often berated for their low growth rates. But in addition to the need to lay the foundation, which makes future growth possible, poor countries have a large agricultural sector, and agricultural growth rarely exceeds 4 percent per year. When 80 percent of the labor force is in agriculture, and population grows by 2 or 3 percent, aggregate growth of income per head cannot be very rapid, even if industrial growth is very high, as it often is.

Second, in very poor countries lacking in technological, entrepreneurial, managerial, and administrative skills, the common prescription of minimal state activity, even if it were correct for middle-income countries, would not apply. Even though the state performs many activities badly, if there is no one else to carry them out, it must. Hence, the role of government intervention in very poor countries is inevitably different from that in richer countries. Clearly, even in low-income countries state intervention should be efficient and, in view of the scarcity of administrative resources, concentrated on priority areas. But to advocate that the state should withdraw from most activities would mean either that they would not get done at all or that they would be taken over by alien minorities organized in private monopolies.

Even in countries where the public sector should be shrunk, it is very important to maintain incentives for public servants to give their best. The present mood of state minimalism threatens to lead to actions that permit the best people to leave the public service so that only the deadwood remains, and then to underpay them, so that they become demoralized, open to corruption, and, in order to survive, have to take outside jobs.

Third, the common prescription of "outward-looking" trade policies has to be qualified. In presentations common today (such as the World Bank's *World Development Report 1987*), outward-looking trade strategies are cited as the cause of good growth, and inward-looking policies made responsible for slow growth. This argument has been criticized on several grounds: (1) trade strategy and economic performance may both be due to a third factor; (2) correlation does not indicate causality; and (3) causality may run from performance to trade policy.[1] For periods of world growth, the relationship is different from that for periods of stagnation. Moreover, a phase of inward orientation may be a necessary condition for a subsequent successful phase of outward orientation.

But a fundamental flaw in the report's statistical association between outward and inward orientation on the one hand and economic performance on the other is that it ignores the fact that the inward-looking and slowly growing countries are also the low-income countries. It could therefore be that their slow growth is the result of their low incomes rather than of their inward-looking trade policies. South Korea has clearly had a better growth record than has Zambia, but surely this cannot wholly or even largely be due to South Korea's outward-looking trade strategy. The low-income countries of Africa are not so much handicapped by the inward-looking character of their trade policies as by their low income levels, their lack of skills and infrastructure, and the instability of their import volume.[2] It could, of course, be argued that the instability of imports is itself a function of the absence of diversified exports and foreign exchange reserves, themselves the result of inward-looking trade policies. But this would be ignoring again the inevitably low levels of adaptability and flexibility in very poor countries.

Fourth, the widespread view that development can be speeded up by providing more money ("throwing money at the problem," as the current phrase goes) has to be modified for the poorest countries. While money can, of course, often help, the crucial bottlenecks are human attitudes and aptitudes, skills and motivation, which are essential to prevent the money from being wasted.

Fifth, the current obsession with "getting the prices right" has its uses in Africa, but it is important to remember that the right prices work only in conjunction with other measures, many of which are in the public domain. Without roads, the larger agricultural crops, stimulated by higher prices, cannot be brought to the market. Without research into appropriate seeds, the supply elasticity of agricultural crops is liable to be very low. Without credit institutions, farmers cannot get the money to buy the inputs. Without irrigation, arid land cannot produce much more. In some situations, "getting prices right" without such other measures can be either ineffective or counterproductive.

Sixth, there is an important difference in the way of dealing with the debt problem. Debt forgiveness for sub-Saharan Africa has three merits that do not apply to Latin America or other parts of the world with higher incomes:

1. The debts are much smaller in absolute terms, and write-off presents no danger to the financial and banking system.
2. Debts are largely owed to governments rather than private banks, and therefore forgiveness presents no threat to the banking system or to the debtor's creditworthiness, which is low anyhow.
3. For these and similar reasons, forgiveness is not likely to be regarded as a precedent by others, who would not demand similar treatment.

For these three reasons, debt forgiveness should be a high priority for the poorest countries.

The World Bank and the IMF have now come to see this difference and are advocating, for the poorest and weakest countries (such as Zambia, Bolivia, and, perhaps, Costa Rica), forgiveness of debt as a precondition for their resumption of economic growth. For the richer countries (e.g., Mexico, Brazil, and South Korea), additional lending and increased indebtedness can be a way of raising export earnings, reducing import requirements, and attracting additional capital, though some debt reduction will be necessary here, too. But for the poorest countries, solutions that increase indebtedness will not work. Of course, multilateral action is necessary or else one creditor's forgiveness just goes to pay off less lenient creditors instead of helping the country. But both World Bank President Barber B. Conable and IMF Managing Director Michel Camdessus have made attempts in this direction.

DEVELOPMENT AID

In the past, aid used to be considered as a gap-filling activity. Aid was thought to supplement either the domestic savings or the foreign exchange earnings of low-income countries, and accordingly to fill the resource gap or the foreign exchange gap. Today, this way of looking at aid has been replaced by a different view: External resources, properly used, add flexibility and adaptability to otherwise rigid and inflexible economies. It makes it possible to bring about less abruptly, and therefore at lower social costs, the many adjustments that development requires. External resources can also be used to bring about these adaptations with less damage to particularly vulnerable groups (e.g., the poor, the unemployed, children, and women) and to productive investment, the source of future growth. But, since aid can also be used to postpone or evade these adjustments, it is important to ensure that it is used efficiently.

At the same time, it has often been said that poor countries lack "absorptive capacity," by which has been meant their limited capacity to prepare, design, execute, and maintain aid projects and to formulate and implement development plans. But on closer analysis the notion of "absorptive capacity" dissolves into the question of the composition of aid, especially among technical assistance (including assistance in project preparation) and financial aid, project and program aid, and aid covering capital and recurrent costs. Aid donors can and should give technical assistance in project design, as well as in the execution, maintenance, and management of these projects.

Adjustment and adaptation are of the very essence of development: from subsistence to production for the market; from rural to urban; from agriculture to industry; from self-sufficiency to foreign trade; from exports of primary products to nontraditional manufactured goods, and so on. But more recently, a particular type of adjustment has been discussed to which aid can contribute, to wit, adjustment from a set of bad policies to better policies: from capital intensive to labor intensive development; from high-cost, capital intensive import substitution to labor intensive exports; from excessive emphasis on protected industry to agriculture for both export and domestic consumption. One may add adjustment to economic and social reforms, such as a land, tax, or administrative reform. In such situations, aid can be used both to tide a country over transitional economic difficulties and as compensation to overcome vested interests.

Such adaptability can be achieved by assisting in the development of four resources—management, institutions, technology, and human resources—but this section is concerned with improving methods of aid administration, and of improving the impact of finance on development, which can be done in ways that are not often discussed. I shall concentrate on relatively unexplored ways of raising the effectiveness of aid.

First, when macropolicy conditions are attached to aid loans, it should be done in ways socially and politically sensitive to local conditions. Externally imposed policy conditions can be counterproductive if they encourage the mobilization of opposition groups. One way of overcoming this difficulty is to have a decentralized aid administration. The local aid representatives are then in daily contact with the policymakers and understand their concerns and constraints, while keeping a low profile. Flown-in foreign missions, which stay for a brief period and think they know all the answers, can be ineffective or counterproductive. USAID is already considerably more decentralized than, say, the World Bank or the IMF, but further strengthening in this direction can yield high returns in the acceptability and soundness of policy proposals and the effectiveness of the policy dialog. The British Commonwealth Development Corporation began to be an effective aid agency when Lord Reith decentralized the staff to regional offices from which project proposals came to headquarters in London.

Decentralized local offices with long-term staff should not be on a national basis, except for very large countries, but on a transnational, regional, or subregional basis: for example, West Africa, East Africa, or the Caribbean. Only in this way can regional cooperation be encouraged, and malinvestment, in which one country diversifies into the export surpluses of another, be avoided.

A second reform points to the need not just to lend money, sometimes combined with technical assistance, but also to manage the projects, with a direct stake in their success. Now, aid agencies cease to take an interest in a project just when it becomes most important for them to maintain involvement. This applies partially to the way in which capital costs or (often) initial recurrent costs only are covered; when the project has to be continued and sustained, the foreign agency withdraws. But it also and mainly applies to continued supervision and management after the project has been put in place. The purpose of continuing management would not be to maximize profits (as in direct private foreign investment) but to maximize development. This means training local counterparts, to whose management the project is gradually turned over. In Africa, the problem is above all a shortage of managerial talent and entrepreneurial and technical skills. Technical assistance, advisors and experts, often hired for short periods without home-base backing and without career prospects, are no substitute for direct management and responsibility. Here again, the Commonwealth Development Corporation is a model worth studying. It is unique in that it is the only development agency that combines the task of lending with initial responsibility to manage its projects and enterprises efficiently, covering costs, and handing over to local people, when they are ready, both ownership and management.

The development of what in Britain was called the Paunch Corps and in the United States the International Executive Service Corps was initiated by David Rockefeller and William Paley. It is an imaginative beginning. Retired business executives make their services available to manage enterprises in Africa and to train local counterparts. The proposal here is that members of this corps should not act just as advisors but be fully responsible for the efficient running of their projects.

A principal objection voiced against the proposal that U.S. management should be involved is that it is neocolonialist and politically unacceptable. To meet this objection a high degree of sensitivity to local social, political, and cultural conditions is needed. It might also help if the corps of managers were recruited not from one group of nationals only but given a genuine international flavor. Managers' style of living should also not be too different from that of their future counterparts. In order to work out an acceptable salary structure without creating excessive differences between foreign executives and locals, a part of the remuneration could accrue in the home country of the foreign managers, while they were living modestly in the developing country. Retired executives might also be willing to provide their services for less than their market value in the United States. This proposal is intended only for some of the low-income countries of sub-Saharan Africa and not for the Indian subcontinent, which is already quite rich in managerial and entrepreneurial talent.

There are four other ways in which the quality and effectiveness of aid can be improved. First, project aid still has a bias for capital and foreign exchange expenditure, and against operating, recurrent, and local costs. A correction of this bias could help to make a given amount of aid more effective. Second, annual budgetary allocations (the present way of funding) interfere with the long-term expectations of a reliable, continuing flow of aid funds. Commitments should be made over longer periods, so that they can be confidently fitted into the development plans and strategies of recipient countries. Third, there is the much-discussed point of the need for coordination of different donors' efforts. In spite of some successes by consortia and consultative groups, the present uncoordinated system puts a heavy burden on the frail administrative base of poor recipients. Fourth, donors are often more interested in quick and visible successes than in helping to lay the institutional and educational foundations for future development, whose results are slow. This emphasis should be changed.

It would be a gross oversimplification, but with a kernel of truth, to say that southern Asia needs capital, Latin America needs trade, and Africa needs technical assistance. This section has argued that technical assistance, as dispensed now, is too short-term, without a proper career structure, and with inadequate home-base backing. The result is that it does not attract the best people. Dudley Seers once wrote an article titled "Why Visiting Economists Fail." The companion piece to this remains to be written: "Why Failed Economists Visit." To overcome these shortcomings, better ways of strengthening the institutional and human bases of poor economies have to be found.

Who should get aid? A cynic might say there are the needy and the speedy: The needy do not know how to use the aid (they lack "absorptive capacity"); the speedy do well without aid and do not need it. Therefore: no aid to anybody. The proper recipients are, of course, those with greatest potential to improve: those to whom the aid makes the greatest difference in the current value of the future discounted flow of welfare, properly weighted for poverty, discounted for time, and, for a bilateral donor, also weighted for political importance. In practice, this would mean supporting governments intent on embarking on a sensible set of policies with respect to economic growth and poverty eradication. Given sensible policies, the choice of aid projects becomes much less important. Even the best projects can be ruined by bad macroeconomic policies, and even quite unimaginative projects can be very useful if they free domestic funds for more imaginative uses. But it must be remembered that not only projects, but policies, too, are fungible. It is of no use to focus on single issues such as devaluation or the budget deficit. Nor is it sensible to impose the "correct" policies, even if known, as conditions for aid: They should emerge from a sensitive dialog between people fully acquainted with each other's problems.

VULNERABLE GROUPS

In our preoccupation with abstractions and statistics, we sometimes forget that development is for people: to give them the opportunity to develop their full potential. All too often in the process of development vulnerable groups shoulder the heaviest burden. Thus, in the transition from subsistence-oriented agriculture to commercial agriculture, women and children are sometimes hardest hit. In the transition from a traditional society, in which the extended family takes care of its unfortunate members, to a market society, in which the community has not yet taken on responsibility for the victims of the market, the fate of these victims can be cruel. The protection of these groups is needed mainly for their well-being, but also as a way of protecting the environment, of raising the productivity of the present and the future labor force, and of reducing population growth. The emphasis in the literature is laid on the productive and reproductive aspects of meeting basic needs, but it should never be forgotten that these are also ends in themselves.

The contribution of U.S. policy here can be the improvement of cooking facilities, so that women do not have to spend hours collecting firewood and denuding the thinning forests; the construction of water wells nearer homes, so that women do not need to spend long hours fetching water and have time to care for their children, to contribute to production, and to participate in the political process; and the strengthening of educational facilities for girls and women, which results not only in better home care but also in reducing desired family size and improving the impact of schooling by reducing dropout rates. Some of these issues come down to political representation. In some African countries, women are not represented on village councils; their needs are therefore not heard. Deforestation and desertification are as much the result of lack of empowerment of women as of ignorance or poverty.

But the best support for projects can be futile if the macropolicies are wrong. A resumption of higher growth and demand for imports by the industrialized countries, a reduction of protectionist barriers, and a lowering of interest rates on the debt would repair the damage that has been done to women, children, and the jobless in the poor countries. A change in the thrust of technology, which has been biased against women's activities in agriculture, would also help. Support for education that aims at producing an adaptable, flexible labor force, not the educated unemployed with excessive aspirations for employment, should be high on the agenda.

FOOD AID

Food aid, properly administered, can contribute to development and simultaneously draw on U.S. farmers' support. In the low-income countries, food aid can contribute to food security, and it can also play a part in programs with objectives other than food security, such as employment generation through rural public works or programs of improving nutrition.

There are at least seven criticisms that have been made of food aid other than emergency famine relief:

1. It reduces the pressure on recipient countries to carry out policy reforms, especially with respect to producer incentives and nutritional objectives.
2. It tends to depress domestic farm prices, to discourage domestic agricultural production, and to reduce the spread of production-

increasing agricultural technology.

3.   It is unreliable, because it depends on donors' surpluses. When needs are greatest (i.e., when prices are high), it tends to dry up. Thus, in the plentiful year 1970, annual food aid exceeded 12.5 million tons, whereas in the food crisis of 1973–1974, when the price of wheat rose by 50 percent, annual shipments fell to below 6 million tons. Not only the timing but also the country distribution serves the political, economic, and military interests of donor countries. Thus, in 1982 and 1983, Egypt received 18 percent of the food aid distributed by the Food Aid Convention. Moreover, since donors make their allocations in money, higher prices buy a smaller amount of grain.

4.   If administered through state agencies, food aid is said to reinforce state hegemony over people and not to reach the poor.

5.   It promotes an undesirable shift in consumption patterns away from staples and toward wheat and wheat flour.

6.   It disrupts international commercial channels.

7.   It leads to unfair burden-sharing between food-importing and food-exporting donors, if the price of food is overvalued.

The principal objection, that food aid discourages domestic agriculture by depressing prices, can be met by using the counterpart funds from the sale of the food at market-clearing prices to make deficiency payments to the farmers who would otherwise be injured, so that supply prices are restored to the level they would have attained without the food aid. (Even food distributed at no cost, say in schools, frees budgetary revenue if the government would otherwise have paid for it.) In this way, the amount by which expenditure on food aid reduces demand for domestic food is channeled back to the farmers, and incentives are fully restored. The reason why this obvious solution has not been adopted more frequently is the budgetary/political constraint: Financially straitened governments normally find other uses, of greater importance to them, for the collected revenue and cannot or do not wish to collect additional revenue.

Food aid can also be used to finance additional food consumed by construction workers on infrastructure projects for agriculture. Or, to avoid neglect of agriculture, food aid can be linked with other forms of agricultural assistance. Or, additionality of demand can be ensured by distributing the food or its money equivalent to the poorest households, who could otherwise not afford an adequate diet.

But the importance of the charge that food aid discourages farmers has been greatly reduced, if not entirely eliminated, by the fact that many developing countries have become substantial food buyers. (Only in low-income African countries is food aid increasing as a proportion of food imports.) In such a situation, the traditional roles of food aid and financial aid are reversed. Food aid, insofar as it replaces commercial purchases, becomes fully convertible foreign exchange, whereas financial aid often remains tied to procurement, commodities, or projects. It has, however, been argued that the free foreign exchange made available to governments presents an obstacle to fundamental reforms, such as devaluation of the exchange rate or investment and reforms in agriculture, which would raise food production. However, this is not an argument against food aid, but against all forms of intergovernmental aid. It can be used either to support or to delay reforms.

Food aid can be used either as balance-of-payments support or as budgetary support. The two extreme cases are: (1) where the food aid is wholly additional to commercial purchases and is sold by the government in open markets at market-clearing prices, yielding government revenue in the form of counterpart funds of the maximum amount; or (2) where the food aid wholly replaces commercial imports, and the foreign exchange saved is used to buy other imports, or more food, or to repay debt.

Historically, there are many instances of food aid that did not harm domestic food production. Forty percent of Marshall Plan aid consisted of food aid, yet European food production flourished, excessively. Similarly, South Korea, Israel, and India received large amounts of food aid without apparent long-term harm to their agriculture. It can be shown both analytically and historically that food aid can be given in ways that encourage domestic agriculture.

The charge of disruption of commercial sales is greatly reduced by the shrinking and now small role of food aid in total world food trade. If food aid wholly replaces commercial sales by the donor (the government pays the farmers what they otherwise would have earned), no disrupting effects on sales by other countries are suffered. Ensuring additionality—e.g., by linking it with job creation for poor people who spend a large portion of their income on food—also reduces the damage to commercial sales.

Additionality of supply is important in order to meet the charge that advanced countries that are commercial food importers are faced with higher prices than would prevail if, in the absence of food aid, the food had to be sold through commercial channels. The valuation of food aid has to be done in such a manner as to ensure fair burden-sharing between food-surplus donor countries and food-importing donor countries.

Another charge against food aid is that tastes depend, to some extent, on relative prices and food availabilities (and are not given exogenously, as is often assumed in economic analysis). A prolonged policy of finer grain imports changes tastes away from domestically produced foodstuffs and, it is alleged, increases dependency on foreign supplies. The situation has been described as analogous to drug addiction: Countries become "hooked" on certain grains. It should, however, be remembered that these changes in tastes have many causes, connected with development and urbanization, with commercial import policies, and with the growing value of time as incomes grow: Food aid is only one, possibly small, contributory cause.

One of the key questions in improving the role of food aid is, again, administrative capacity and the avoidance of corruption. What has been said above about the role of management, both in the private and in the public sector, also applies here.

The volume of food aid has been greatly reduced in the last 20 years; it has, however, increased since 1975. In the 1960s, it was as high as 17 million tons in some years. In 1973/74, cereal tonnage fell to 5.5 million tons. In 1976/77, it was 9 million tons and in 1984/85 rose to 10.4 million tons. The 1985/86 figure is higher because of emergency aid to sub-Saharan Africa. There has been an increasing proportion of noncereal food aid, not covered by these figures, especially EC aid in dairy products. The aid component of food aid has also increased, and more has gone to the poorest countries. Africa has benefited at the expense of Asia, and, within southern Asia, Bangladesh at the expense of India; project and emergency aid have replaced bilateral program aid.

At the same time, so-called subsistence crops such as sorghum, millet, yams, cassava, and bananas could be traded in local and even national markets, if they were not discriminated against. Low prices of subsidized grain, the import of which is encouraged by overvalued currencies, or grain that is supplied by food aid, discourage the production of these "poor man's crops" for the market. Although devaluation would encourage the production of export crops, the demand for the subsistence crops would also rise and would constitute an incentive to produce more. The precise amount would depend on the elasticities of substitution in supply and demand. Relatively little research is done on these crops, though there are some exceptions, such as sorghum in Maharashtra and the Sudan, and maize in Zimbabwe. The International Institute for Tropical Agriculture in Ibadan (Nigeria), which is part of the system set up by the Consultative Group for International Agricultural Research, specializes in research on roots and tubers. But more could be done for these crops, especially millet and sorghum. Even where research on food crops has been successful, African countries lack the indigenous research capacity to adopt and adapt the results, so that much expenditure on research has low yields.

Greater encouragement should be given to research on subsistence crops since they can be grown on marginal land, do not require sophisticated technology or complex skills, are ecologically benign, and frequently have great nutritional value. They can also be used to supplement the preferred cereals when these are in short supply, through additions to wheat flour or maize meal. But even if research in this area yielded good returns, there are limits to what can be expected. These crops, particularly roots and tubers, are bulky and expensive to transport. Storing and processing them is costly and often capital intensive.

PRIMARY EXPORTS

The low-income countries tend to be primary exporters of minerals and agricultural products. Concentration on one or a few of these commodities, and often also on their destination, tends to be high. As a result, the countries are vulnerable to price fluctuations and technical innovations that replace these products.

The commodity-price stabilization schemes propagated by the United Nations Conference on Trade and Development (UNCTAD) and others have not succeeded in getting accepted. The reasons are in part political, but in part a lack of a convincing analytical justification. In the past, the case for such schemes has been made on grounds of stabilizing incomes of producers or consumers, an argument that has been largely refuted. But the case is much stronger if it is made on grounds of macropolicy. Primary product exporters from developing countries show two characteristics. First, primary producers are largely price-takers, whereas the producers of manufactured products are price-makers: A fall in demand for manufactures leads directly to a reduction of output and a rise in unemployment, whereas a fall in the demand for primary products leads directly to a fall in their prices. Second, whereas the benefits from higher productivity in manufacturing are largely retained by the producers in the form of higher wages and profits, the benefits of technical progress in primary production are largely passed on to buyers in the form of lower prices.

Volatile primary product prices have, in the last 10 years, aggravated both inflation and unemployment; they have discouraged investment in the developing primary exporting countries and have disrupted the performance of low-income exporting countries. The collapse of primary product export prices has been a major contributory cause of the debt crisis. Stabilizing these prices eliminates an important source of inflationary impetus when demand is high, and a source of unemployment in advanced countries and of poverty in developing countries when demand is depressed by anti-inflationary policies. The case for buffer stocks is much stronger if it is based on such macroeconomic considerations. If the cause of stagflation in advanced industrial countries that use raw materials as inputs into their manufactured products were the unexpected large jumps and fluctuations in prices, the smoothing out of such fluctuations would reduce both inflation and unemployment. James Baker, in his speech to the IMF in September 1987, indicated some sympathy with this view.

In the longer run, the solution for the developing exporters lies in diversification out of primary products, the demand for which is declining. Here, the United States can set an example of taking a global view. All too often now, country A is advised to diversify out of crop X into crop Y, and country B is advised to diversify out of crop Y into X, when both X and Y are in global surplus.

TECHNOLOGY

Appropriate technology for the low-income countries is often lacking: technology appropriate to factor proportions (labor surplus and capital scarcity); to climate; to the small scale of production; to lower incomes, investment, and savings ratios; to soils; and to the social and cultural conditions. But even more research on such appropriate technologies—desirable though it is—is not enough. Since technology transfer implies not the movement of pieces of hardware from one country to another, but the transfer of knowledge from the brains of one set of people into the brains of another, there is always a need to build up indigenous technological capacity, particularly in agriculture. The dilemma in the early stages is that there can be a conflict between the need to build up this indigenous capacity, which implies some closing off from foreign influences, and the transfer of what is known abroad, which implies opening up to foreign influences. Closing the communication gap by opening up the country to foreign influences may widen the suitability gap and discourage the invention and adaptation of appropriate technologies, because such a closure increases dependence and reduces self-reliance, while closing the suitability gap may widen the communication gap.

But a judicious combination of policies can reduce both gaps simultaneously. A combined policy implies strengthening both local research institutions and those in advanced countries specifically concerned with appropriate technologies, encouragement of exchanges among developing countries, the creation of a bank that would pool international information on appropriate technologies, and assistance for strengthening the indigenous technological capacity in order to reduce dependence and build self-reliance. This is needed in any case, not only in order to make good use of foreign technology transferred (maintaining, running, repairing, and replacing it), but also in order to adapt foreign technology to local conditions, invent and innovate new appropriate local technologies, and ensure that the developing country knows what it is buying and gets better terms for the purchase of technology from foreigners.

PRIVATE FOREIGN INVESTMENT

Much has been written about the role of private foreign investment in development, both in its creative role as a package combining capital, management, marketing, and technology, and as a harbinger of exploitation.

Without wishing to defend or attack either the proposition that the Ford Motor Company is the nearest thing to the Ford Foundation, or, on the other hand, that private foreign investment is, if not the devil incarnate, the devil incorporated, some useful guidelines can be laid down.

First, it is clear that private foreign investment, to be successful, calls for complementary and supplementary action in the public sector. Roads, railways, ports, and airports; education and research, nutrition, and health measures for farmers and factory workers: all these are preconditions for productive and remunerative private investment, parts of the physical and social infrastructure normally provided by the public sector.

Second, the foreign firm should not replace but should encourage the growth of domestic enterprises. In particular, the small-scale family enterprises of the informal sector should be encouraged to produce inputs, components, spare parts, repairs, and ancillary services for the normally large, foreign firm. Such a symbiotic relationship calls for the removal of discrimination against the informal sector and for credit, information, market access, and institutions that assist the informal sector enterprises to thrive. In the past, relations between large (domestic and foreign) enterprises and small, informal sector firms have often been competitive, with the large firms getting public support. A change to greater complementarity has implications both for institutions (credit, information, marketing) and for policy. To give only one example, the conventional prescription that lower real wages make for higher employment may have to be revised, if higher wages in the organized sector induce firms to contract out labor intensive activities, previously done in-house, to the informal sector firms, where incomes are more flexible.

Third, thought should be given to institutional innovations that combine features of efficient large-scale private management with the objective of social responsibility. The nucleus estates of the Kulai Oil Palm project in Malaysia or the Kenya Tea Development Authority may serve as examples. The basic idea is to combine modern processing, marketing, credit, and extension services in a central enterprise with smallholders who grow the crops on their plots of land. This type of institution is particularly suited for agricultural projects, but similar forms can be explored for industrial firms, where production facilities calling for large capital expenditure are located in the central plant, and the manufacture of spare parts and components, items that can be produced labor intensively, and ancillary services such as packaging and transport, are grouped in small enterprises around the central firm. The institutional innovation applies both to the form of organization and to its financing. In principle, there is no reason why both private and public money should not be harnessed to this purpose. Treasury-appropriated funds could be used together with funds borrowed in the capital market by the U.S. Treasury, together with private investors' participation.

Although the ideological and political divide is still between the private and the public sector, a more relevant line can be drawn between small-scale enterprises, many in the informal sector, run by families with no or only a few employees, and the large institutions, comprising both large private firms and public sector institutions. The former harness the initiative, enterprise, and efforts of individuals and spread widely the benefits of growth. The latter are run along bureaucratic lines and, while having the merit of being socially accountable and more easily regulated, they also have the drawbacks of bureaucracies. Much has been written about the distortions caused by government interventions that give rise to "rent-seeking" or "directly unproductive profit-seeking activities." But these are not confined to government activity. In large private firms, exactly the same type of "rent-seeking" and "influence-seeking" is pursued at the cost of economic efficiency. The encouragement of genuinely private and free enterprise can have quite radical implications for developing countries.

Another important area of policy is the imaginative exploration of new legal and business institutions that combine the considerable merits of the transnational corporation (TNC) with the maximum beneficial impact on national policy objectives. This area comprises joint ventures (i.e., joint between private and public capital and between domestic and foreign capital), which go further than window dressing by giving the developing host country access to information and decisionmaking, and various provisions for divestment and gradual, agreed transfer of ownership and management from foreigners to the host country. Countries wishing to curb the power of large groups in their manufacturing sector may find investment reduced, and this may make it advisable to institute a "joint sector" in which public capital is combined with private national management with or without an equity stake, or public capital is combined with private international capital. Another possibility would be a management contract with a national or international investor.

Thought and action in this area have suffered from a poverty of the institutional imagination, which has lagged behind the advance of the scientific and technological imagination and the global vision of transnational firms. Discussions have turned partly on the ideological dispute between private and public enterprise, yet the real issues have little to do with ownership. Mixed companies can be devised that simultaneously harness private energy and initiative, yet are accountable to the public and carry out a social mandate, on the model of the already mentioned British Commonwealth Development Corporation. Equally arid has been the dispute over the virtues and vices of private foreign investment. Here again, the task should be to identify the positive contributions of foreign firms and the social costs they impose on the host country, to see how the former can be maximized or the latter minimized, and to provide for gradual, agreed transfer to national or regional ownership and management. There is a need for a legal and institutional framework in which social objectives not normally part of the firm's objectives can be achieved, while giving the firm an opportunity to earn profits by contributing efficient management, marketing, and technology.

The quantitative contribution of private foreign investment in the developing countries as a group, and particularly in the poorest countries (outside mining and plantations, where these have not been nationalized) is bound to remain small. But its qualitative roles as a center around which to cluster numerous small domestic enterprises and as a potential mobilizer of domestic enterprise remain to be explored.

There has been a good deal of experience in the growth of lending to very small and poor businesses. The Grameen Bank in Bangladesh was one of the first to venture on such lending, but the experience has been replicated in many other countries. One important lesson is that even without collateral, poor people tend to repay loans. Another is that, combined with some degree of training in bookkeeping and management, these loans have multiplier effects that create jobs for other poor people. They break the grip of the usurious moneylender and enable people to start businesses who could not have done so without these loans.

AN ILLUSTRATION OF A NEW FORM OF PARTNERSHIP FOR DEVELOPING COUNTRIES

The TNC clearly has an important part to play in assisting the progress of the developing countries. At the same time, a number of obstacles now stand in the way of its greater participation in the development process. New institutions and new procedures are needed to overcome these obstacles.

The obstacles are partially practical, arising from the difficulties of operating in countries with shortages of skilled manpower and basic utilities, and partially political. The latter include the sometimes ambivalent attitudes of the governments of developing countries and the resulting political risks faced by the TNC. The reluctance to welcome TNCs wholeheartedly has itself a number of causes: (1) the fear, whether justified or not, that the TNC may exploit its market power and deprive the country of valuable resources in general and, through remittance of profits abroad, aggravate balance-of-payments difficulties; (2) the fear that the TNC will form a foreign enclave whose activities will not benefit and may harm the rest of the economy; (3) political fears of foreign domination or interference that add fuel to economic fears of exploitation. The debt crisis has greatly reduced these fears, and many developing countries are now welcoming TNCs, but areas of friction remain.

Foreign enterprise has the capacity of bestowing great benefits on the economy of the host country. It can combine the provision of capital, a team of skilled people, and access to markets; it can transmit rapidly the latest products and technology to the host country; it can encourage the growth of a number of ancillary domestic enterprises; and it can reduce the economy's dependence on imports and increase its capacity to export.

The international community could help by investigating ways in which the fears of both overseas governments and private firms can be allayed and the advantages maximized. This could be done by devising a form of joint enterprise through which finance, skilled manpower, and training are provided in a way acceptable to the host governments and carrying sufficient profit to be attractive to the foreign firms.

One way of achieving this would be for a private firm to establish a joint enterprise with a local government or a government agency, such as a local development corporation. The foreign firm should put up not more than 49 percent of the capital, but enough to benefit when the enterprise succeeds and, of course, suffer if it fails. It should have a substantial minority interest, while the local government has the dominant interest. Such a holding would often be sufficient to secure a decisive role in management, but it might be possible to arrange in special circumstances that, in the initial phase, the foreign investor should hold a higher percentage of the equity, as long as the arrangement for eventual transfer to local ownership is clearly stated. The foreign firm might also provide some of the money on a fixed-interest basis or in the form of preference shares.

The equity interest of the foreign firm would be bought out by the local government at the end of a suitable prearranged period. This period could be 10 years, with provision each year after, say, seven years to extend for a further five years up to, say, 15 years or longer in the case of, for example, plantation enterprises. Various other forms of "rolling" continuation could be devised, such as a possible extension of another five years. Alternatively, the period could be longer, but there could be options at fixed points when either the local government could buy out or the firm sell out.

Managerial and technical staff would initially be provided almost exclusively by the foreign firm, perhaps under a management contract, but with the obligation to train local replacements within the specified period before buy-out. The rate of replacement could not be specified contractually, but the local government would be able to use its representation on the board to ensure that it went forward at a satisfactory pace.

Housing and community services should be provided by the local government or appropriate local statutory body set up for the purpose. In view of the relatively short period of ownership participation, the foreign firm's capital should be concentrated on productive activities.

The scheme would operate through a tripartite agreement among the parent government of the firm, the local government, and the private firm concerned. The parent and local governments would provide a guarantee against expropriation. The parent government (or the World Bank) might also provide aid funds in appropriate cases to enable the local government to finance its participation or, either directly or through one of the international financial institutions, to help finance housing or community services required for the project.

Procedures for assessing an appropriate value at the time of buy-out would have to be agreed upon in advance, as well as procedures for arbitration should disputes arise.

Advantages

Most of the advantages of private enterprise are preserved. The foreign firm brings in capital, together with technology, market access, and a team, possibly with local experience, and the overhead facilities and international experience the firm can provide are thus made available.

At the same time, the fears that local governments or public opinion may feel are removed. The opportunity for indefinitely exploiting a position of monopoly or oligopoly no longer exists. The fear of foreign ownership and domination is removed.

The TNC, on the other hand, acquires a guarantee against expropriation, combined with the incentive to enjoy a share in the profits. Clearly, it would still carry the commercial risks of failure, but political risks would be eliminated.

The buy-out arrangement after an agreed period releases capital and know-how. These very scarce resources can thus be used on a revolving basis for initiating and pioneering new ventures and are freed from maintaining a going concern, which can more easily be transferred to local shoulders. The "spread effects" of enterprise on the rest of the economy are thus increased.

Fields of Application

The scheme would be particularly suitable for large-scale agricultural enterprises and for countries with a small entrepreneurial and managerial class. If new enterprises were successfully established, existing ones might also be converted into this type. Regimes committed to replacing foreign by domestic economic activity might, instead of expropriating, be persuaded to work for the transformation of foreign-owned enterprises into the new type of joint venture.

If such a scheme were to be accepted by the parent governments, it would be desirable to present it as a form of transfer that combines adaptability to different circumstances with sufficient concreteness to have an appeal. It would need to be announced with a good deal of publicity, after careful preparation and consultation with selected host governments and TNCs.

THE TOTAL RELATIONSHIP

The aid relationship between the United States and poor countries has sometimes been isolated from other policies and presented as an indicator of international cooperation. Yet, a country can perform well on aid and undo, to some degree, any good done on this front by policies in other directions; and a country can do little for aid yet have a highly beneficial impact through its other policies. If international cooperation is taken seriously, the impact of *all* policies on the low-income countries should be one of the considerations entering into policy design. Trade is clearly important, particularly since most developing countries, if given the choice, prefer trade to aid. Agricultural, industrial, and regional policies, taxation relating to foreign investment, monetary, fiscal, and environmental policies all can have an important impact on low-income countries, even though this is not part of the design.

In the past, the combination of loose fiscal and tight monetary policies, adopted by the Reagan administration, was harmful to low-income countries. Although the large U.S. trade deficit encouraged exports from the developing countries, the high interest rates increased the debt burden, slowed down growth of demand in the United States, and induced other OECD countries to follow in order to avoid excessive capital flight. The harmful consequences of these effects outweighed any beneficial impact on import demand. Many times more important than any likely specific aid or trade concessions would be the resumption by the United States of higher growth with accompanying higher demand for imports, and lower interest rates, which would lighten the debt burden. In addition to economic policy, the thrust of foreign, strategic, and education policies also affect the developing countries.

If this argument of the total relationship is accepted, it might call for a revision of the organizational structure of development policy. Many countries have ministries of development whose task it is not just to dispense aid but to bring to bear on all policy decisions their impact on the developing countries. On the other hand, the danger of a separate department for international cooperation is that other departments may feel themselves freed from having to look after the development impact of their policies, and cooperation then may go by default. On balance, a strong department of cooperation, with cabinet rank, is probably necessary until everyone has become sensitized to the issues.

NOTES

1. See Hans Singer, "The World Development Report 1987 on the Blessings of 'Outward Orientation': A Necessary Correction," *The Journal of Development Studies* 24, no. 2 (January 1988): 232–236.
2. See Gerald K. Helleiner, "Outward Orientation, Import Instability and African Economic Growth: an Empirical Investigation," in *Theory and Reality in*

Development, ed. Sanjaya Lall and Frances Stewart (New York: Macmillan, 1986), pp. 139–153; and Singer, "Blessings of 'Outward Orientation.'" Also Michael Michaeli, "Exports and Growth: An Empirical Investigation," *Journal of Development Economics* 4, no. 1 (March 1977); David Wheeler, "Sources of Stagnation in Sub-Saharan Africa," *World Development* 12, no. 1 (January 1984); and R. M. Kavoussi, "International Trade and Economic Development: The Recent Experience of Developing Countries," *The Journal of Developing Areas* (April 1985): 379–392.

PART TWO

U.S. Interests and Capacities

SEVEN

U.S. Foreign Policy Interests in the Third World in the Years Ahead

CHARLES WILLIAM MAYNES

There is a paradox about U.S. relations with the Third World. The interests and sympathies of the most powerful figures of the U.S. foreign policy elite have long been directed almost exclusively toward Europe—no one who has ever served in the U.S. government can have any illusion on this score. Yet, since 1945, these same figures repeatedly and disastrously have accepted their greatest challenges in the Third World.

Here is another paradox: Presidential candidates risk a serious electoral setback if they display too much sympathy for the Third World. Being "soft" on the Third World has become almost a disqualification for the highest office in the land, yet once in office, presidents will find that their political popularity and even their political survival may depend to a very significant degree on the success or failure of their policies in the Third World.

Indeed, most postwar U.S. presidents have been driven from office or disgraced by their policies in the Third World. Harry S Truman decided not to run for reelection in part because of the domestic passions his decision to involve the United States militarily in Korea had unleashed. Lyndon B. Johnson withdrew from his reelection effort rather than face, in the next presidential campaign, the wrath of the anti–Vietnam War movement. The Iranian hostage crisis doomed Jimmy Carter's effort at reelection in 1980; and Ronald Reagan, who looked as though he might leave the White House able to claim that he had enhanced the powers of the presidency, left tarnished because of his arms-for-hostages policy toward the regime in Teheran.

Dwight D. Eisenhower besmirched his historical reputation through his administration's efforts to assassinate Patrice Lumumba and Fidel Castro. John F. Kennedy had his Bay of Pigs, and his administration continued the disgraceful efforts to eliminate Castro, even trying to enlist U.S. gangsters in the effort. Many of the excesses that finally drove Richard Nixon from office can be traced to his decision to conduct secret and illegal bombings of Cambodia.

Significantly, only one president escaped this troubling pattern—Gerald Ford. And he may be the exception only because his presidency was so truncated. Perhaps he did not have the time to repeat the mistakes his predecessors had made. The general rule thus applies: The Waterloo of U.S. presidents is found in the Third World.

Another paradox: there is no more cherished goal of the U.S. foreign policy elite than to reestablish a bipartisan foreign policy consensus in the country. Yet, that elite follows a policy toward the Third World that alienates or offends many of the groups—the churches and nonprofit developmental organizations—whose support is critical in trying to reach and educate the larger U.S. public. The postwar foreign policy consensus shattered in Vietnam was, after all, the result of a coalition between the iron-willed and the big-hearted. The former urged large defense budgets and committed anticommunism; they raised the clenched fist. The latter embraced developmental assistance and the policies of interdependence; they extended the helping hand. Each group tolerated the other; each made compromises it might have preferred to avoid. But the result was an uneasy consensus about the direction and content of U.S. foreign policy. As long as the U.S. economy was strong and the casualties were low, the consensus endured.

Clear direction in U.S. foreign policy, however, is now missing; and one major reason is that it is so hard to hold together either side of the earlier coalition, much less unite the two sides in a common consensus. Those favoring only the clenched fist find their ranks divided as the nature of the Soviet Union seems to be changing almost from one week to the next. Those favoring the helping hand harbor increasingly ambivalent attitudes toward the Third World. Should the United States help economically those who are opposed to it politically? Should it help those who are clearly becoming its competitors?

Unfortunately, current trends in U.S.–Third World relations may pose even greater difficulties for future administrations than current trends in U.S.-Soviet relations. For though the Soviet Union will remain a security threat to the United States, U.S.-Soviet relations over several decades have moved fitfully toward better understanding and greater cooperation. In the case of U.S. relations with many countries in the Third World, current trends seem to be moving in the direction of ever greater conflict—over markets, drugs, politics, and even religion.

Current trends aside, why is the Third World such a problem for the United States? The answer appears to be rooted in the United States' rather special history in dealing with Third World people in this hemisphere. After all, the North American colonies were settled by people who came as both conquerors and missionaries. The early settlers in New England and those who later pushed West found the American Indians a personal menace and a religious challenge. They tried both to destroy them and to convert them. The destructive tendencies, however, were stronger. It seemed as though one civilization could survive only by subjugating and destroying the other; some of the darkest chapters in U.S. history cover the treatment of the American Indians by the white settlers. In brief, the United States' earliest history with so-called Third World peoples was one of conquest and betrayal.

This history of conflict between whites and nonwhites found its way into U.S. literature and folklore. The United States in the nineteenth century developed a unique form of popular literature—the penny novel detailing terrifying tales of whites taken captive by savage Indians. Those looking for the roots of the extraordinary U.S. obsession with the fate of citizens taken captive by radical forces in the Middle East should look to this example of the nation's literature, which according to *The Cambridge History of American Literature* has no counterpart in any other Western country "in terms of vividness or in the bare statement of physical suffering and of mental torment."[1] The idea of "innocent Americans," in the hands of "savages" has been a powerful one for more than a hundred years.

The United States' experiences with other Third World peoples living in or brought to this continent only reinforced these early attitudes of suspicion and hostility. Central to the nation's development and progress have been cruel or hostile acts against both blacks and Mexicans that few contemporary citizens would attempt to justify. This is not to say that had the tables been turned, those who were history's victims would have been any more humane or magnanimous than were history's victors. But a cruel past inevitably leaves its painful scars and searing memories.

Yet, as mentioned, there is another side to the U.S. attitude. The original settlers came to this country to save as well as to subjugate. The first charter of the Virginia Company, which founded Jamestown in 1607, showed concern for the spiritual salvation of the natives. Article III of the charter called for efforts to propagate the Christian religion "to such people as yet live in Darkness and Miserable Ignorance of the true Knowledge and Worship of God." When the Virginia colonists established William and Mary College, once again the education of American Indians was to be a central purpose, though this proved not to be the case. The charter of Harvard College, secured in 1650, listed among the designs of the institution "the education of English and Indian youth of the country in knowledge and godliness."[2]

These attitudes persist to this day. In the U.S. character there appears to be a strong impulse to help those who live in "Darkness and Miserable Ignorance." It cannot be an accident that U.S. citizens have in both public and private life played such a key role in advancing and establishing the concept of international cooperation for the purpose of raising up regions of the world less fortunate than North America or Western Europe. Nor that again and again ordinary U.S. citizens have shown themselves willing to respond with generosity to others suffering from malnutrition or hunger. Yet, it probably also is not an accident that the people of the United States are acutely sensitive to criticism from Third World countries and have managed to demonize and make larger than life several Third World figures whose real influence in international affairs by no means justifies such high levels of U.S. attention.

In brief, the unusual history of U.S. racial relations has helped to foster ambivalent feelings toward the Third World, which range from guilt on the left to suspicion and hostility on the right. With such polarized feelings, it is difficult for any U.S. administration to maintain a balanced approach toward Third World countries. The tendency within the body politic has been and remains either to idealize or to demonize Third World countries, and these countries seem to repeat the pattern in reverse in their approach to the United States.

If the United States' difficulties with the Third World could be traced only to its own unique history, the issue of U.S.–Third World relations might be more manageable. For historical memories must fade, however slowly, from a nation's mind just as normal scars do from a person's body. Unfortunately, several new developments now reinforce the ambivalence of the past.

One involves the mounting costs—in lost blood, money, and pride—of U.S. involvement in the Third World. It is ironic that though postwar U.S. foreign policy has remained fixated on the Soviet threat, the Third World has, in fact, inflicted many more defeats or setbacks on the United States than has the Soviet Union. The list runs from Korea to Vietnam in the military field, from OPEC to the eastern Asian tigers in the marketplace, and from Cuba to Iran in the world of geopolitics.

In war, the United States since 1945 has lost more than 100,000 troops in combat to Third World armies. It is true that the United States was unable to prevail in Korea or Vietnam only because it was unwilling to use the full measure of force in its possession. But that truth is not fully reassuring, for the hard fact remains that in combat on equal terms, Third World armies met the U.S. military and neither withdrew nor surrendered. And indeed, the United States never really had the option of using the ultimate weapon—its nuclear arsenals. Any resort to nuclear weapons in Korea or Vietnam would have shattered the United States' alliances in Europe and convulsed its politics at home.

Even in minor skirmishes with Third World states, the United States has not fared well. Every recent administration seems to have suffered a humiliating setback at the hands of a militarily second- or even third-class developing country. The Ford administration sent the Marines ashore on a small Cambodian island to rescue some U.S. citizens held by the Cambodian government. More Marines were killed in the Mayaguez affair than civilians were saved, and the operation was launched after the Cambodian government had indicated its willingness to release the people it held. When the Carter administration embarked on the ill-fated effort to rescue the U.S. and

Canadian diplomats held hostage in Teheran, the result was eight dead servicemen, the resignation of the secretary of state, and an international humiliation of the United States.

The Reagan administration declared the presence of U.S. Marines in Lebanon to be in the vital interests of the country. It was forced to withdraw them after a single successful car-bomb attack on the Marine barracks in Beirut. The conquest of the tiny island of Grenada was at first touted as a brilliant military operation, which in part compensated for earlier reversals, but it is now known that this operation, though militarily successful, was logistically a disaster. Had the opponent been larger, the U.S. military would have suffered grievous losses.

Those in the U.S. foreign policy community who favor the "helping hand" are making a serious error if they do not understand that these setbacks at the hands of some Third World states color the citizenery's attitude toward all Third World states. After all, the very use of the term "Third World" inclines the people to believe that a defeat at the hands of one Third World state is in some sense a defeat at the hands of all of them. And, in addition, the fact that other Third World states have generally applauded these U.S. setbacks has not been lost on the average citizen. Few "men on the street" know what the Non-Aligned Movement or the Group of 77 is, but many of them know that in a showdown Third World states tend to support Cuba and Libya, not the United States.

The evolution of the United Nations has also profoundly affected U.S. attitudes toward the Third World. With its location in New York City, media capital of the world, the United Nations is not an irrelevant house of winds, as a majority of U.S. policymakers in recent years has either publicly asserted or privately believed. Its debates significantly shape the North-South agenda both at the elite level and within the U.S. body politic.

Regrettably, the three dominant issues at the United Nations all pose unique difficulties for the United States. Because of its special ties with Israel, the United States has been and will remain totally isolated on Middle East issues in the United Nations. Its extreme isolation probably can end only in the context of settlement arrangements that permit Palestinians self-determination leading to the creation of an independent state alongside Israel. On the issue of apartheid, the United States finds it difficult, because of its own troubled racial history, to forge a national consensus. Isolation on this issue will end only when there is majority rule in South Africa. Finally, the United States' commitment to free market principles is so single-minded—and not just in the Reagan administration—that U.S. delegations often find themselves a minority of one in discussions of North-South economic issues. Isolation on this issue probably will never end because the majority of UN members who are poor have a vested interest in continuing the pressure for concessions from the minority of UN members, including the United States, who are rich.

As a result of UN debates on these three key issues, the average U.S. citizen soon gains the impression that the Third World is more of a monolith than it really is. Unfortunately, it seems a monolith in almost predictable and regular opposition to the United States.

Certainly contributing to the strained relationship between the United States and the Third World are the very special attitudes that most people in the United States have toward development assistance. The very approach of most of them to those less fortunate than themselves seems to be at odds with the basic ideas underlying the concept of development assistance: They believe that neighbors deserve help if through no fault of their own they are in temporary trouble. Calls for disaster relief therefore receive an enormous response in the United States, usually greater than in any other country. But most people in the United States also believe that over the longer run people and nations fundamentally get what they deserve. The rich are rich because they have earned their wealth; the poor are poor because they have not tried hard enough. Franklin D. Roosevelt showed a profound understanding of the U.S. character when he defended his decision to "lend" Great Britain destroyers to continue the struggle against Nazi Germany. Even in those perilous circumstances, Roosevelt judged that the average U.S. citizen would not be willing to give Britain something for nothing, so he explained his decision to help Britain by comparing the U.S. action to the case of a man who lends his hose to a neighbor whose house is on fire. When the blaze is put out, the hose is returned. So would the destroyers be returned (even though after use in a war they might be somewhat the worse for wear—worse for wear than a garden hose used to extinguish a blaze).

The Marshall Plan was brilliantly successful not only because the Europeans were able to use the U.S. aid so effectively but also because, again, the situation conformed to U.S. preconceptions. A disaster, though human in cause, had struck Europe. The task was to lend a helping hand to an afflicted neighbor until he could stand on his own feet. That could happen fairly quickly; then he would cease to receive special treatment.

The initial U.S. approach to Third World distress also respected these traditional mores, and that may be one reason why foreign assistance was more popular then than now. There were still some areas in the world besides Europe in desperate need of reconstruction assistance, and administrations were able to persuade Congress to allocate funds to help these nations get back on their feet. Regarding the future, the U.S. emphasis was—appropriately, given popular attitudes—on technical assistance. Just as the poor at home were expected to make their way by themselves after they had been given a somewhat equal start in life through mass education, so the Third World could make its way in the world economy after it had received the necessary technical assistance, which would then permit it to enjoy an equal chance. The United States would do its modest share; the rest would be up to the Third World.

The experts soon realized that technical assistance was not enough. Large amounts of capital would also be required. The U.S. government approach to this problem was another brilliant effort to match foreign needs with domestic attitudes. The government embraced a theory that virtually guaranteed that the problem of development would soon go away. Walt Rostow's *Stages of Growth* became a bible for U.S. officials. It was one of the few books all young foreign service officers entering the Department of State in the early 1960s were required to read. The reason was obvious: It contained an easily grasped formula for success. It explained to U.S. voters why they could in good conscience engage in the unnatural act of giving their money away: They would not have to do it very long.

Meanwhile, powerful economic changes were altering this more optimistic view of the Third World's prospects within the United States. As some Third World countries seemed to founder economically, the popular perception shifted from a view that they were in need of help to a view that they were without hope. As a result, a new category of countries, known as the basket cases, was created. Perversely, as other Third World countries began to develop successfully, their image shifted from one of presenting a development challenge to the international community to one of presenting a commercial threat to the United States. Increasingly, the question—and it will be stronger if the U.S. economy continues to stumble—is why help foreigners, even if poor, and not help those at home when they are also in distress? After all, a significant number of U.S. residents live in crippling poverty. Many are losing their jobs to Third World countries. Skilled workers in many developing countries are now capable of mastering the same production techniques prevalent in developed countries, and they will accept lower wages. Why increase their advantage through aid programs designed to make them even more competitive?

These are questions hard to answer, particularly in a manner that will persuade more than a small circle of experts. Can such attitudes be changed among the general public? Or if we cannot change them, how do we work around them? Fortunately, there are several forces at work that, with luck and sensible public policy, might ameliorate this attitude toward the Third World.

First are changing racial attitudes inside the United States. It is painful for many people to face up to the contemporary impact that racial relationships inside the United States have had on the country's foreign policy. But there is an interaction between the two that the U.S. public should confront because the news is getting better. I, for one, recall a memorable afternoon in the late 1950s at Harvard College when I and three other impressionable young men met Eleanor Roosevelt, then at the college to dedicate a room in honor of her husband. She had asked to meet with representative students to inquire about their attitudes toward "America's coming revolution." When we four acted mystified, she explained that because all the British and French colonies in Africa were soon to acquire independence, it was only a matter of time before the United States' black population rose up to demand equal treatment: "There will be a revolution in this country because our Negroes will no longer tolerate the terrible treatment they receive from us when they see that colored people in Africa are finally free, and I want to know what you are going to do about the revolution when it comes."

If Eleanor Roosevelt was right, as I think she was, in believing that at times positive developments abroad have positive effects at home, then I would assert that a healing current can also flow in the other direction—already is flowing. Racial troubles on U.S. campuses and ethnic clashes on the streets of New York remind the U.S. public and the world that racial tensions in the country persist, but the mounting white vote totals for the Reverend Jesse Jackson suggest a larger trend of healthier racial attitudes among the general population. As a result, a significant U.S. diplomatic handicap is not ended but eased. Improvement in domestic relations is a steadily growing factor resulting in a better U.S. understanding of Third World peoples. The changing attitude of the U.S. people toward apartheid is an example of this constructive interplay between internal attitudes and external realities.

The emergence of Third World leaders whose policies or personalities are much more likely to appeal to the average U.S. citizen also reinforces more positive attitudes. In Latin America, the hero of the moment is a democratic president of Costa Rica, not some charismatic guerrilla leader fighting in the bush. In Asia, attention is focused on democratic leaders in Manila and Seoul, not on their communist counterparts in Vietnam or Cambodia. And in black Africa, Robert Mugabe has become the most discussed leader in the region because of his effort to forge a new nation in which both black and white can live without fear.

The Middle East is an exception to these generalizations. The moderate policies of the Egyptian government were beginning to have an impact on the U.S. consciousness toward the Moslem world, but then the Ayatollah Khomeini rose up, and most of the U.S. population began to confuse Iran, which is not Arab, with the rest of the Middle East. But even here there may be some grounds for hope. The radical wave that swept over Iran is unlikely to be reversed there, but it now seems much less likely than it did a few years ago that one government after another in the region will succumb to radical forces of a similar religious intensity. Iran itself seems to have internalized its revolution and is less active in exporting it.

Reinforcing these generally positive trends is another development that should have a beneficial effect on U.S attitudes toward the Third World. The heroic age in the developing world seems to be drawing to a close, except perhaps in the fundamentalist Moslem world. In the 1950s, the task of Third World leadership was liberation. In the 1960s and 1970s, it was political consolidation. To free a nation or create a nation, Third World leaders needed to unite their people against an enemy, usually identified as the imperialist West led by the United States. In the 1980s and 1990s, the task of leadership is economic survival and development under almost any formula that brings steady results. Increasingly, Third World leaders will be judged by the actual results of governance—the degree of economic development they gain and of political decency they permit.

The U.S. population, in turn, will be in a better position to assess these developments than it ever has been, in part because the United States for the first time in its history has developed a significant elite with experience in the Third World. More than ever before, U.S. citizens now travel and work in Third World countries. More than 120,000 volunteers have served in the Peace Corps since 1961; many of them returned to foreign policy or development assistance jobs in the U.S. government. The growing economic importance of Third World countries is luring the U.S. business community to the Third World in growing numbers. For the first time in history the foreign editors' jobs at the three national newspapers—the *New York Times,* the *Christian Science Monitor,* and the *Wall Street Journal*—are occupied by individuals who have spent the bulk of their professional career reporting in the Third World or had their only professional experience abroad in the Third World.

Meanwhile, Third World peoples are entering the United States in growing numbers both as students and immigrants. There are now 349,000 foreign students in U.S. universities, the overwhelming majority from the developing world. Although there is no guarantee that study in a foreign country will lead to favorable attitudes about that country's foreign policy, it seems incontestable that the links forged through this massive transnational educational effort will at least improve the ability of different cultures to communicate, and that over time the improved understanding that results will influence policy.

The ability of the United States to see the Third World through a less distorted focus may be especially important in the years ahead if, as many U.S. specialists on the Soviet Union suggest, Moscow begins to show greater hesitation in getting involved in new Third World adventures. It is difficult to predict how the Gorbachev revolution in domestic and foreign policy will unfold, but it seems probable that the Soviet Union will display less interest in becoming involved in the Third World in the coming decade than it has in the last 10 years. The reasons reflect both greater Soviet understanding of the realities there and less money to spend there. Several years before Gorbachev came to power, Soviet Third World analysts began suggesting in their writings that the politics and economics of developing countries were more complicated than Marxist theory allowed, and that the Soviet Union might find the costs of involvement outweighing the gains. With the rise of Gorbachev, such views seem to have moved from the pages of academic journals onto the pages of Politburo position papers. The issue of cost is particularly important when the Soviet Union is trying to marshal its resources for the purposes of domestic reform.

Insofar as there is a diminution in cold war competition in the Third World as well as a better U.S. understanding of Third World realities, the two superpowers may be able to agree to allow Third World countries greater breathing space to concentrate on the more pressing issues of economic development. It might even be possible for the superpowers to work out informal rules of disengagement from some areas of the Third World that in truth have little strategic value for either side—much of Africa, for example.

Nonetheless, in at least one respect, a respite in East-West competition in the Third World, if it occurs, will be a mixed blessing for administrations in Washington. Regrettably, the most effective argument of every administration in persuading Congress to be more forthcoming on North-South issues has been the contention that only in this way could the United States compete successfully with the Soviet Union in the Third World. It seems unlikely that any other argument will be as persuasive, at least in the short run, in persuading Congress to commit resources to the cause of Third World development or security.

Attitudes are important, but interests are even more so. If interests conflict too glaringly with attitudes, in time the latter will have to give way. What, then, can be said about concrete U.S. interests in the Third World over the term of the current administration? Will such interests, if they are well understood, permit Washington to build a political rationale for U.S. involvement in the Third World that is not so reliant on a continuation of the cold war?

POLITICAL INTERESTS

The aspect of North-South relations that will dominate U.S. policy toward the Third World in the years ahead is that the North is getting old while the South is becoming young. This contrast is important because in almost all societies the young are a wellspring of political turbulence and change. While the West continues to become grayer, many developing countries already face populations more than 50 percent below the age of 20. The coming years, therefore, are almost certainly going to be a period of tremendous political stress in the Third World. The children in the West Bank with rocks in their hands, or the children of the black townships of South Africa who have seized control of the streets, are the wave of the future.

How will the United States react to this prospect of sweeping political change? One response seems certain: The present administration will have to abandon, at least in its more sweeping dimensions, the counterrevolutionary crusade known as the Reagan Doctrine, which has been used to justify U.S. support for the anticommunist resistance movements in Afghanistan, Angola,

Kampuchea, and Nicaragua. Most U.S. adults agreed that the United States should support an aggressive policy to drive Soviet troops out of Afghanistan. (They may even harbor a similar attitude about the Vietnamese military presence in Cambodia.) But the Reagan administration was never able to develop the same consensus about its decision to support UNITA in Angola or the Contras in Nicaragua. Most U.S. citizens are not terribly enthusiastic about the regimes in Luanda and Managua, but they do not believe that they represent a threat to the United States, and they are unlikely to change their mind unless either regime provides the Soviet Union with military advantages clearly damaging to the United States. These attitudes might change if it could be demonstrated that the government of either Nicaragua or Angola were engaged in sending significant quantities of military supplies to an insurrection in neighboring states friendly to the United States, say Zaire or El Salvador. But the Reagan administration did not make that charge against Angola and was never able to intercept a single arms shipment from Nicaragua to El Salvador after the Nicaraguans said that they had stopped such shipments. At this point, therefore, the Reagan Doctrine seems likely to follow President Reagan into retirement. Certainly there is no natural disposition to seek out new countries to which the doctrine might be applied.

Yet, if the Bush administration is likely to abandon a sweeping policy of rollback or containment of radical forces in the Third World, it is also unlikely to remain indifferent to political change in the Third World. So long as some form of the superpower competition survives, and the United States lives in a world of nuclear weapons, every administration will worry that a conflict in one of the more obscure corners of the Third World may escalate into something much more serious, finally drawing in the nuclear powers.

Another reason that the United States cannot be indifferent to political developments in the Third World is that it also may be entering a new age of multilateralism. The international economy seems to be moving toward a major watershed in such different areas as money, trade, and debt settlement. The United States' eroding economic preeminence will, at some point, open the very difficult questions of leadership and voting rights in international financial institutions, on which the developing countries will have an important, even if not decisive, voice. In addition, Gorbachev's September 1987 statement on Soviet UN policy is a revolutionary document, opening up doors that had been shut for decades. The Bush administration will come under enormous pressure to put to the test of serious discussion such unprecedented Soviet proposals as an increase in the mandatory jurisdiction of the World Court, or a greater role in the world for UN mediation and peacekeeping, or a Soviet interest in participating in some of the international economic organizations.

A final U.S. interest in the political development of Third World countries concerns the issue of democracy. Although the United States can tolerate and even work with nondemocratic regimes that pose it no security threat, the Third World represents most of the world's people. Over the longer span of time, it is difficult to believe that the world's democracies will remain as open and tolerant as they now are if the rest of the world explicitly rejects their values. The United States is neither omnipotent nor omniscient. It cannot and should not attempt to impose its values on others. But it will betray its special heritage if this and future administrations do not display a special sympathy for those abroad who share the United States' moral values and political goals.

MILITARY INTERESTS

There has been a dramatic change in the military relationship between the United States and the Third World, though most political debates in the United States still do not reflect the shift. For a considerable while after World War II, Third World states played a key but inadequately appreciated role in Western defense: For much of the postwar period, U.S. bombers and missiles could not reach Soviet targets without the advantage of air or naval bases in countries bordering the Soviet Union. Many of these were in the Third World. U.S. efforts at targeting and verification also depended on bases located close to Soviet borders, but the advance of technology has considerably reduced the value of foreign bases for strategic purposes, wherever located. As rocket ranges have increased and submarines can roam more widely, the United States has responded by closing down bases from Ethiopia to Scotland: New technology is enabling the United States to depart voluntarily. Meanwhile, even those bases the United States retains seem of less value than in the past because of political restrictions that host countries increasingly place on their use. Turkey, for example, will not allow the United States to use its bases in that country in a Middle East conflict involving Israel, and the Philippines has stipulated that U.S. bases on its soil are never to be used to attack Vietnam. The Western Europeans—the British excluded—would not allow the U.S. military to use its bases in their countries to attack Libya.

It seems likely that U.S. bases in the Third World will become a declining asset to the United States unless the purpose is intervention in the Third World itself. And this purpose must be questioned, particularly if the cold war continues its fitful 30-year warming trend. Very few areas in the Third World raise by themselves serious security considerations for the United States; it is the presumption or fact of a Soviet role that transforms setbacks in the Third World into geopolitical crises for U.S. policymakers. An evolution of that role that would reduce U.S. fears would, in turn, call into question many U.S. military arrangements or security understandings in the Third World now regarded as vital.

Paradoxically, the Third World, while militarily less useful to the United States in a strategic sense, is much more dangerous to it in any regional conflict involving the armed forces of the United States. Third World states are developing their military capacity in ways that over the longer run will have profound implications for U.S. security interests: India is openly aspiring for naval supremacy in the Indian Ocean; Iran and Iraq seek a similar position in the Gulf; Brazil has become a major arms exporter. The slow but steady spread of nuclear weapons technology to such countries as Israel and Pakistan risks transforming virtually unsolvable regional conflicts into global catastrophes. States unable to develop nuclear weapons but facing what they regard as a supreme security threat are turning to chemical weapons; Syria is an example. It must be expected that these trends will continue. In the coming decade, the United States and other major powers will therefore have to answer two awkward questions: Are they willing to recognize some of the larger and militarily more significant Third World states as the hegemon in certain areas of the Third World? If they are not, what are they prepared to do?

During the Bush administration, the United States will have a strong interest in trying to build firebreaks between local conflicts in the Third World and the superpowers, to promote conventional arms control among Third World countries, and to strengthen prohibitions on the further proliferation of chemical and nuclear weapons. It will need to devise new, more accommodating policies toward the Third World states acquiring the capability to become major actors in key regions of the world and posing no meaningful security threat to the United States.

ECONOMIC INTERESTS

The United States' economic stake in the Third World is strong and growing. U.S. trade with the developing world now accounts for roughly 40 percent of U.S. exports and supplies roughly 40 percent of U.S. imports. More to the point, U.S. exports to developing countries have been growing much faster than have U.S. exports to developed countries. Until the recent debt crisis forced developing countries to cut back imports, the differential was as high as 33 percent. Moreover, it has been estimated that if Third World countries can resume their earlier growth patterns, they could account for as much as 50 percent of all U.S. exports by the year 2000.[3]

U.S. investment patterns have followed the trade patterns. During the 1970s, U.S. investment in the Third World (excluding investment in the oil industry) grew at a rate double that of U.S. investment in the industrialized world. So it seems incontestable that the United States has a major economic stake in the prosperity and growth of Third World countries. To date, however, U.S. policy has developed in disregard of these widely known facts.

For example, policy on Third World debt has not taken into account the devastating effect of the debt crisis on U.S. export markets in developing countries—a loss some estimate may have cost the United States as many as a million jobs. Changes in U.S. monetary policy have almost totally ignored the impact of exchange-rate changes on developing countries, even though some of these countries—namely, the oil producers—were in a position to take decisions equally damaging to U.S. economic interests and proceeded to do so.

The United States also depends on the Third World for the supply of many strategic commodities. In 1978, the United States imported 93 percent of its tin, 88 percent of its columbium, 56 percent of its aluminum, and 35 percent of its manganese from the developing world. In the reverse direction, the United States sends important commodities to the Third World. Every fifth acre in the United States produces for export to the developing world.[4]

Finally, many analysts in recent years have focused on the obvious relationship between the economic health of the U.S. banking community and the economic health of the developing countries, particularly in Latin America, to which the U.S. financial community has lent so much money. Even if country default no longer threatens the international financial structure to the degree it seemed in the early 1980s, it remains true that the debt of the developing world, now over $1 trillion, is an economic cancer that threatens the prosperity of all members of the international community.

Yet, the paradox is that these compelling economic facts notwithstanding, most of the U.S. population continue to regard the Third World as marginal to U.S. interests unless there is a danger of a communist takeover. Such responses can only be explained by ambivalent attitudes rooted in U.S. history.

GLOBAL AND MORAL ISSUES

A growing number of global issues are crowding their way onto the international agenda—AIDS, the ozone layer, the loss of the rain forest, and other natural disasters of a regional or global character. The United States has a strong and growing foreign policy interest in the successful management of these issues, which have both a global and moral character. Norman Myers, an environmental specialist, has pointed out that the tropical rain forests, which cover only 7 percent of the earth's land surface, harbor at least 40 percent of the world's species and that the North is dependent on the South for much of the germplasm that enables the North to maintain a productive agriculture. Yet developing countries, desperate for hard currency, are allowing these forests to be cut down in order to promote lumber exports to the industrialized world, which in the future will regret this irreplaceable loss.[5] The World Resources Institute in Washington has done fascinating work on the intersection of environmental issues and security questions. For example, U.S. demands for meat from Central America to feed the fast-food industry had the result of driving peasants from the land, as landowners decided to raise cattle instead of crops. The environment was also harmed as forests were cut down for even more grassland. The social basis for the revolution of the late 1970s was laid. In Central America, the world ended up with its first "hamburger war."

It is a major and growing foreign policy interest of the United States to work with the developing countries on these emerging issues. On some environmental issues time may be urgent. For that reason, environmental issues should have a much higher priority in the Bush administration, particularly since the Soviet Union has recently indicated its growing concern with this issue.

ACCOMPLISHING MORE WITH LESS

Are there some basic lessons about U.S. policy toward the Third World that one can draw from this examination of U.S. attitudes toward and U.S. interests in the Third World?

There seems to be no prospect of any significant improvement in the U.S. record on ODA for many years to come. With a budget crunch so severe that the United States is threatening to close down embassies and consulates to meet the Gramm-Rudman-Hollings targets, it seems highly unlikely that an effort to increase ODA will succeed. That being the case, priority must be on ways to get more out of the aid that the United States now delivers. Ways to accomplish this might include the following:

1.   The United States must adopt more exacting performance standards in distributing aid. Those states that accept the aid, adopt parallel policies that augment its effect, and achieve results should be rewarded with more aid. Those that do not take these steps should receive less. This approach requires that the Bush administration accord greater priority to developmental than to political considerations in allocating aid. In manning its aid programs, the United States should explore the economics of hiring only locals. After the enormous education effort of the last 40 years, it is no longer the case that all expertise is to be found in the North.

2.   The Bush administration must accord a much greater weight to multilateral aid efforts than has been given in the past. Japan is the treasure house of the 1980s, as OPEC was of the 1970s. To tap that treasure house most constructively, Japan must be accorded a much larger role in all international financial institutions. The United States should press the other major donors of the international development banks to study seriously the pros and cons of changing the gearing ratios for lending to see whether the

donor community can get more out of the money it contributes. The United States should try to reach an agreement with other OECD-DAC countries about regions in which major donors will take the lead in organizing international development efforts. The United States might select the Western Hemisphere and Southern Africa; European countries might concentrate on black Africa and the Middle East; the United Nations could address itself to countries that seem no one's priority. The advantages of this approach would be greater coherence in the international effort, and perhaps more money, as lead countries would feel that most of their money was going to an area that for historical or other reasons its citizens felt strongly about.

3.   The United States should consider announcing a date for phasing out all grant economic assistance. Thereafter, all bilateral projects should pay for themselves, even if the rate of interest is at times subsidized. Countries requiring grant aid on a quasi-permanent basis should receive it through multilateral channels so that the burden can be shared. Popular attitudes toward aid might change if the U.S. government could contend, with only a half a tongue in cheek, that at some clearly established future date all grant aid would end. This approach also has the advantage that it would force more rigorous planning among recipient governments.

4.   To counter the growing feeling among U.S. workers that the aid program helps foreign countries get a leg up on the United States in the field of international trade, the United States should orient its aid program away from projects that seem to have a direct commercial payoff and stress programs with common benefits or programs designed to eliminate development bottlenecks. Examples of common benefit programs might include projects to save the tropical rain forests; examples of eliminating bottlenecks might be measures to eradicate a dread disease or increase literacy. It is a fact well known to lobbyists for development assistance that Congress will still respond to programs that arguably have the effect of dealing with common problems or that help ordinary people compete fairly.

5.   The United States, which appears to have a special strength in science and technology, should put heavy stress on programs in this area. The goal would not be a greater sharing of U.S. technology but the creation of new technology of special relevance to the problems of development.

DEALING WITH TRADE AND MONEY

For the foreseeable future and for virtually all developing countries, the trade and monetary policies of the donor countries will be much more important than the amount and terms of aid. Therefore, it is vital that pressures be increased on the donor countries to conduct themselves responsibly. Ways this might be accomplished include the following:

1.   OECD might encourage all members, when adopting major trade and monetary measures, to agree to issue at the same time a statement that assesses the development impact of these measures on the developing

countries. Alternatively, the OECD might be empowered to issue such a statement unilaterally.

2. Bilateral retaliation over trade disputes makes no sense in a multilateral world. The end desired is to balance U.S. trade worldwide, not with a particular country. In this regard, it is very important that other developed countries open up their markets to manufactured and agricultural goods from the Third World. Currently, for example, Third World exports of manufactured goods flow disproportionately to the United States, which absorbs some 63 percent, while 23 percent go to EC countries and only 7 percent to Japan. The United States must step up the pressure on others (such as Japan) to establish a more constructive trade relationship with developing countries. It should raise such issues much more vigorously in the GATT and other international economic organizations. U.S. willingness to accord Japan a greater leadership role in international economic institutions might be conditioned on better Japanese performance in opening its markets to Third World countries.

ALTERING PERCEPTIONS

A major obstacle to North-South progress is a sense that the relationship is a zero-sum game: The North gives and the South receives. To counter that sense, the United States might explore the pros and cons of allowing international agencies to undertake programs among disadvantaged groups in this country. For example, could the UN high commissioner for refugees assist the United States more in the refugee field? Are there international agencies that could help the United States settle groups such as the Hmong, who are having difficulty adapting to life in the United States? Could the WHO assist the United States in the field of preventive medicine? It is not that the United States is incapable of undertaking these programs itself, but there is a need to build a greater sense of community between North and South and to reduce the belief in the United States that it never benefits except indirectly from programs of international cooperation.

But perceptions will never change until administrations work more actively to change them, and this means leadership at the presidential level. It is expected of every administration that the president early on will deliver a speech on East-West relations. There should be a similar expectation with respect to North-South relations.

Finally, in the security field, the Bush administration will need to help the international community to develop a more stable security system, which can reflect the new power realities, for Third World states. Worldwide containment is dead. Local conflicts now seem fueled by local causes more than ever before. The Iran-Iraq war or the conflict between Libya and Chad is probably a more relevant model of what lies ahead than was the Korean War, in which cold war overtures were clear from the first day. Yet, as the Iran-Iraq war has repeatedly demonstrated, there remains a constant danger of superpower involvement.

There seem to be three possible approaches for the United States during an era of more locally generated Third World conflicts. One involves a more careful identification of U.S. political priorities and calls for the United States to devote more of its attention to the Western Hemisphere and to Third World countries that are key to its security or welfare. The United States would take less interest in the political or economic fate of countries that do not fall into these categories. Another approach would be seriously to consider Gorbachev's revolutionary September 1987 statement regarding global security, with its extraordinary reversal of long-standing Soviet positions on collective security, UN peacekeeping, the role of international law, and the use of the Security Council. A final approach would call for the United States and the Soviet Union to work out rules of the road to guide their respective conduct in Third World countries. Since in diplomacy nations never wish to discard any potentially useful tool, all three approaches, in fact, should be pursued seriously.

CONCLUSION

The administration that took power in 1989 should not believe that in its term the outlook for U.S. policies in the Third World is likely to be bright, but over the longer run prospects need not be viewed as bleak. Counterproductive attitudes are steadily fading away. Concrete interests are major and growing. The fitful relaxation in the cold war is continuing. The ability of the U.S. citizenry to see Third World realities more clearly is growing. Policies adopted by the Bush administration can bring a brighter future even more quickly within our grasp.

NOTES

1. *The Cambridge History of American Literature* (New York: Macmillan, 1947), p. 6.
2. Oliver Wendell Elsbree, *The Rise of the Missionary Spirit in America* (Philadelphia: Porcupine Press, 1980), p. 13.
3. *Not Far Afield: U.S. Interests and the Global Environment* (Washington, D.C.: World Resources Institute, June 1987).
4. John W. Sewell and John A. Mathieson, *The Ties That Bind: U.S. Interests and Third World Development* (Washington, D.C.: Overseas Development Council, May 1982).
5. Norman Myers, "The Exhausted Earth," *Foreign Policy* 42 (Spring 1981).

EIGHT

Opportunities for U. S. Leadership in a New Development Partnership

JOSEPH C. WHEELER

In 1987, world aid reached some $48 billion.[1] Members of OECD's DAC provided about $41.5 billion net, with the United States providing about $8.9 billion net. For the United States this represents a 9 percent decrease in real terms from the 1986 level—a drop of $600 million in a year when Japan's aid increased in nominal dollar terms by about $1.8 billion, and France's increased by $1.4 billion.

In 1987, the U.S. GNP, at about $4.5 trillion, represented about 37 percent of total DAC member GNP of over $12 trillion. U.S. aid, which 25 years ago represented about 60 percent of DAC aid, now represents about 22 percent (see Figure 8.1). As a percentage of GNP, U.S. aid now represents less than half the proportion provided by other members of the DAC. By way of perspective, as a percentage of GNP, U.S. aid in Marshall Plan days represented over 2 percent of GNP, U.S. aid to developing countries in 1987 represented less than one-tenth that amount—.20 percent of GNP (see Figure 8.2). We estimate the rest of DAC, taken together, provided .43 percent of GNP in 1987.

Aid, of course, is only one factor affecting development; the primary responsibility is with the developing countries' governments and people. Development is also affected by such important factors as markets, growth rates in major industrial countries, and even the weather. It is, of course, difficult to give a weight to each of the factors. As a minimum, we can say that aid plays a significant role. It is worth considering what has been achieved in developing countries through the combination of factors since World War II.

More than a hundred countries have become independent and have made substantial progress in building their institutions and improving their conditions of life. For example, developing country adult literacy rates have increased from under 30 to over 60 percent; mortality rates for children under five have come down from levels in the 300 per thousand range to levels in the 100 to 200 per thousand range; life expectancy has gone up

Figure 8.1   Share of GNP and ODA

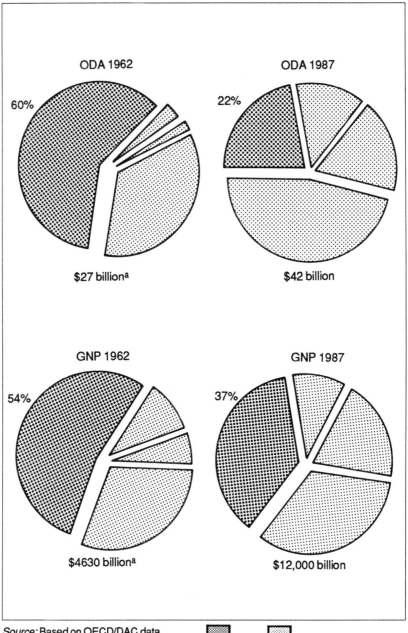

Source: Based on OECD/DAC data.
Note: a. At 1967 prices and exchange rates.

Figure 8.2 Net ODA from DAC Countries in 1987

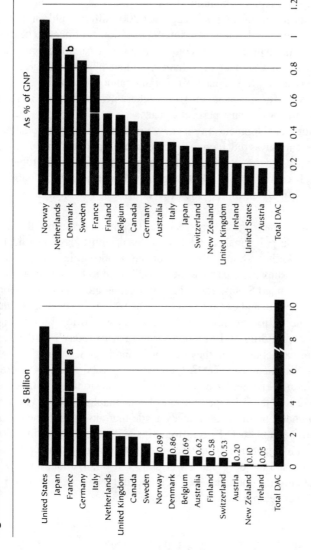

Source: Based on OECD figures.

Notes: a. France including DOM-TOM, 6.52; France excluding DOM-TOM, 4.2
b. France including DOM-TOM, .74; France excluding DOM-TOM, .51

from about 35 to nearly 60 years; and, in an extraordinary tour de force, Asia and Latin America have increased their agricultural production faster than their rapid rates of population growth.

Yet success breeds ambition and a sense of responsibility to achieve much more. Concerned U.S. citizens do not accept that developing country child mortality rates should remain 10 or in some cases 20 times those in developed countries. They cannot accept that 300 million children of school age are not in school, and that most primary education continues to be of very low quality. In this day of instant communication, it cannot be completely hidden from view that 15 percent of humanity does not get enough to eat to lead a fully productive life. Concerned people cannot accept the experience of the past 30 years in sub-Saharan Africa, where per capita food production has gone down by more than 1 percent a year.

Furthermore, development reveals new problems and creates others. The United States cannot avoid recognizing pressures humans are putting on natural resources nor the development of some environmental problems as global issues. It cannot ignore the implications of the expected doubling of world population. It cannot ignore the challenges of new diseases or spreading drug use.

Beyond these challenges, there are other factors that confront the United States. Even while policymakers necessarily deal with today's political and security concerns, they should not neglect the opportunities for improving long-term relationships with parts of the world bound to become increasingly important to the United States. These long-term strategic issues are important in political, economic, and commercial terms as well as in social and cultural terms. What the nation achieves in these areas will often be even more important to its children and grandchildren than to today's citizens. But today's citizens care about what they pass on to future generations.

While, as chairman of the DAC, I am expected to be primarily interested in the volume and efficiency of members' concessional assistance and, therefore, make that the principal subject of this chapter, it would be wrong for me not to underline the point already made that aid is only one of many instruments important to U.S. relationships with the developing world. Indeed, to mention just one issue, the rules governing commerce between OECD countries and the developing world are critical. Without markets, the day when developing countries can achieve independence from aid and sustainability in development will be postponed.

AREAS NEEDING U.S. LEADERSHIP IN THE 1990s

It would be reasonable for the United States now to consider increasing its aid effort to match the effort of other members of the DAC—that means moving from .20 percent of GNP in 1987 to something on the order of .43

percent of GNP, or, in today's terms, moving from $8.9 billion per annum to something on the order of $20 billion per annum. These proposed increases could be used to support a new partnership among donors and recipients in order dramatically to improve the lives of the billion people who live in dire poverty. The partnership should emphasize policies and programs that achieve both faster economic growth and access to resources and services for the sick, the illiterate, the jobless, the hungry. In a world that will add another billion to its population in the next dozen years or so, the task is daunting. But it is a task that has become a moral imperative now that experience tells us that the United States has the resources and know-how to succeed in it.

I have been vigorously told that the consideration of such an increase in aid by the United States would be entirely unreasonable—out of the question in today's world of huge budget deficits. But I want to emphasize that what I am suggesting is a matching of what the rest of OECD is already doing. Furthermore, mine is a strategic goal for the 1990s. One can only assume that the United States will be successful in its plans to deal with its budget and trade deficits in the next few years and be in a position to make the strategic shifts in priority that it perceives to be in its interest to make.

Where is U.S. leadership needed in this new development partnership in the 1990s? Each of us has a list. Mine is surely incomplete, but let me put it forward for consideration.

The Global Environment

No country is without environmental problems. Environmental issues need to be seen both in national terms and in broader regional and global terms. For some countries and for many population groups the issue is one of life and death. Needed natural resources may be disappearing by desertification, deforestation, salination of irrigated lands, or the pollution of fishing grounds. Sometimes these issues affect others. For example, countries contribute pollution to regional seas such as the Mediterranean or the Caribbean and to the oceans. Acid rain affects other countries' forests and lakes. We each contribute to the depletion of the ozone layer. As time goes on, our understanding of both national and global issues is expanding. It has become important to develop the institutions to monitor our fragile environment with more precision and to take remedial steps where they are needed. With a doubling of world population almost certain, and with rising incomes adding to the pressure, we are bound to need joint action to protect our life resources.

The United States has been a leader in environmental monitoring. It has made available its satellite technology to other parts of the world. Through the National Aeronautics and Space Administration, it has contributed to the development in Geneva and Nairobi of the United Nations Environment Programme (UNEP)-sponsored Global Resources Information Database. The United States has the technology and management skills to help countries create the institutions to make use of the rapidly expanding information being generated by a myriad of institutions around the globe.

When major environmental issues are identified, the United States should be a part of the effort to deal with them. For example, the job of sustaining tropical forests is big enough to require the expertise and funding of many donors. The U.S. aid program should be large enough to play a leadership role in this area.

There has been a move in recent years under the leadership of the International Union for the Conservation of Nature and Natural Resources toward the development of national conservation strategies. These strategies must be the products of developing countries themselves, which means that their very articulation is a process of institution-building. A national conservation strategy requires improved ability to collect the facts, as well as to analyze them, and improved systems for reflecting the analysis on a crosscutting basis within governments. The United States has already given support to some of these strategy development processes. While many donors can be involved, this seems to be an area where U.S. leadership would be particularly appropriate.

In another few decades, more than half of the people in the developing world will be living in cities, but a majority of these urban-dwellers are likely to be without water and sewerage, without electricity and gas, without trash collection, and to be living in jerrybuilt houses on land where their tenure rights have not been established.

The United States, over the past two decades, has played a leadership role in devising approaches to urban development that emphasize secure land tenure, self-help, cost recovery, low-cost systems, and the beginning of a self-sustaining urban development process. But the Housing Investment Guarantee Program that has taken the lead for USAID in devising such an approach can provide funds only at market interest rates, which are most applicable to advanced developing countries rather than to the poorer countries needing concessional aid. Is it not time for the United States to recognize that urban poverty is an increasing part of its challenge and be willing to make assistance in this field a mainstream part of the aid effort?

African Agriculture

For an aid veteran, perhaps the most discouraging statistics to come out each year are those depicting the deterioration of African per capita agricultural production. Africa's population has been increasing at 3 percent a year, while agricultural production has increased at less than 2 percent a year. Because this has continued over three decades, the problem has become appalling.

Yet, in Latin America and Asia, developing countries in general have pulled off one of the great success stories in development history—an increase in agricultural production faster than population growth rates and sustained over a period of time.

I remember the days in the late 1950s when I was assistant India desk officer at USAID and when some of the best talent of the U.S. agricultural community, involving a host of land grant institutions and supported with aid funding, were helping to build India's capacity for agricultural research, extension, and education. USAID built upon the pioneering contributions of the Rockefeller and Ford foundations and worked closely with them both in support of international research institutions and in application of the breakthrough varieties, especially in India. Some of the best talent of U.S. universities was involved. The United States, in those years, also provided enormous amounts of aid to India, but in the perspective of history, it is the U.S. contribution to the scientific breakthroughs and to the development of India's agriculture-related institutions that are best remembered.

Today, the United States continues to make a significant contribution to international agricultural research institutions that have fed new materials and new systems into national programs. Since new crop varieties know no boundaries, the benefits of this international research have come to U.S. farmers as well as to developing country farmers, repaying our investments manyfold. Thus, it is worrisome that funding constraints have led to lower levels of U.S. support for the international agricultural research centers.

In a number of cases the United States has given leadership to the development of national agricultural research strategies. For example, I was in Pakistan when the Pakistani government, with U.S. advice, articulated its strategy for the development of a national system. But today, U.S. aid levels are insufficient to continue to help national systems in very many places. Yet who can say that the United States is not almost unique in its capacity to share the genius of its systems of interrelated research, education, and extension? Would not a new and deepened partnership with the land grant universities in support of agricultural institution-building in Africa be right for the 1990s?

In recent years, the United States has turned more of its attention to the African problem. The international research system has been nudged to give higher priority to African issues. With encouragement from the United States and with the critical help of the World Bank, the donor community has supported a parallel mechanism—the Special Program for African Agricultural Research—for coordinating help in the development of national research systems in Africa. But we need to face the fact that this process is not getting off the ground nearly fast enough. In each African country, the effort needs leadership from a donor with the technical and institutional capacity to provide it. Africa and the donor community should jointly decide that efficient, effective national agricultural research systems should be put in place by the end of the 1990s. Strategies should be developed, and then project components of these strategies should be implemented. While the financing and much of the strategy can benefit from a joint donor approach, this is an area crying out for leadership. For the United States to play its appropriate role, USAID needs more funding for Africa.

There are other components of a successful agricultural strategy in Africa that need comparable attention. For example, in each Asian country, it has been critical to have a strategy for fertilizer as an overlay on the overall agricultural development strategy. Issues involving production and inputs, distribution systems, and prices had to be thought through, policies adopted, and projects implemented in order to ensure that adequate supplies of fertilizer got to the farmer. This is another area in which the United States, which took the lead in creating the International Fertilizer Development Center and which has worked with a number of countries on fertilizer strategies, has excellent experience to bring to bear. Recently in one West African country—Ghana—fertilizer arrived three months late. This tragedy, I suppose, was the fault of the country itself, but I have seen in the past an energetic U.S. aid mission help a country avoid such a failure. Yet what can a U.S. aid mission do with the very limited resources now at its command? Clearly, with U.S. aid levels for sub-Saharan Africa down radically from the level reached in 1985, the United States is in no position to play a significant leadership role in development in Ghana today.

Infrastructure is critical, particularly in high-potential agricultural areas. The agricultural revolution required in Africa, following the examples of Asia and Latin America, must be a high-tech revolution involving a stream of improved plant varieties, the utilization of adequate levels of nutrients, the development of small-scale irrigation where the potential exists, and, above all, a rapid increase in entrepreneurial services for the marketing and maintenance of farm inputs and products. This means rural roads, water supplies, electricity, communications, the development of sophisticated market towns, improved education, increased health services, and all the rest. Infrastructure will not be cheap, and most of it will have to be provided or paid for by the rural people themselves. Yet there can be no doubt about the need for a major infusion of outside funding to accelerate this process if Africa is to be successful in achieving its needed agricultural revolution over the next decade or two. While the United States holds no monopoly on the capacity to help in this area, it should make a substantial contribution.

Using Food Resources

The OECD countries have been examining their own agricultural policies and have discovered that they are putting nearly twice as much money into subsidizing their farmers as they are into assistance to the developing world. The United States alone in 1986 subsidized agriculture to the tune of more than $35 billion—more than three times its aid level. It is not yet clear how much political will has been gathered toward dealing with this problem, but the United States, at least, is on record that together the OECD nations should eliminate their subsidies systematically over the next decade. During this 10–year adjustment period, the incentives are in place for OECD countries together to produce more food than can be economically absorbed by the market.

Meanwhile, the U.S. PL-480 program resembles something of the proverbial camel, built and operated by a committee and representing many conflicting interests; it has not been well structured to support development efforts. The United States has responded magnificently in the provision of food for starving people, and in many cases it has financed a substantial part of required imports not related to famine on very concessional terms. But it seems, so far, to have found enormous difficulty in using food resources effectively for more direct development purposes. Program commitments tend to be made for only one to three years, when what are needed are sustained programs providing combinations of food and other forms of aid to support five-, ten-, or fifteen-year strategies for food security and agricultural growth. Supporting strategies by provision of food alone, in light of variable production levels, implies an on again–off again program depending on changing supply and demand factors, making it extremely difficult to plan an orderly development effort. Ways need to be found to separate decisions on food imports (which should vary in response to annual supply and demand factors for the country as a whole) and expenditures for development purposes (which need continuity in funding and management). It would help if legislation did not insist on use of food as payment in kind and instead permitted maximum use of private marketing systems.

Agriculture-led developing country growth will lead to increased total consumption of food, and in the end to increased international trade of agricultural goods. The 1987 report of the International Food Policy Research Institute cites research that indicates that the 16 developing countries with the fastest growth in food production have had an even faster growth rate in cereal imports. Other research, related to India, suggests that a combination of faster growth and improved income distribution would quickly increase demand for food. Food aid should not be limited to feeding starving people. It should also be used to create jobs and incomes, especially in rural areas, and in this way increase production and markets for food and other goods. There needs to be a new consensus that would put OECD farm surpluses on a coordinated basis behind strategies that achieve both food security and agriculture-led growth. This would lead to increased commercial markets. And who is in a better position than the United States to give leadership to such a strategy?

Support of Third World Private Communities:
New Roles for U.S. Private Voluntary Agencies

Over the past several years, the development community has discovered the new phenomenon of a burgeoning number of citizen-led private organizations involved in development in their own countries. Whether in Kenya or India, the Philippines or Ghana, the process of development is encouraging the creation of enormous numbers of self-help organizations. They plant trees, maintain farm water courses, support health clinics, run schools, and do many other things. Just as official development agencies are appreciating the increased capacity of developing country governments to run themselves, so are the DAC countries' nongovernmental organizations increasingly understanding that their role more and more will be in helping Third World private organizations. We are all becoming wholesalers rather than retailers.

Issues abound in this area. There are delicate relationships between Third World private organizations and their governments: Governments worry about uncoordinated interventions from outside groups; voluntary organizations can sponsor policies that conflict with those of governments or aid agencies. We should not pretend that it will be easy for all of the actors to work together, but the United States should not walk away from the opportunity for U.S. private organizations to play an increasingly significant role in helping to build these private or informal developing country vehicles of participation and development progress. The aid relationship with the voluntary community has evolved and grown over the last decade. The U.S. voluntary community has played critical roles—for example, in response to the African drought and in the support of many health systems. With this successful partnership, the United States now needs to move on to deal with rapidly evolving circumstances and opportunities in many developing countries.

The United States is known today, as it was earlier described by de Toqueville, as a society where people naturally join together in communities to help each other: to lead scout troops, to improve schools, or to campaign for a better policy or a new facility. U.S. citizens have unique experience in community involvement and in communications, with broad applicability for the development process. The U.S. voluntary community can lead in encouraging developing country groups to play similar roles.

Another area in which the United States is well respected is in its pioneering of the revolution in the role of women. Even if in the United States there is more to achieve in this area, it is respected elsewhere for what has so far happened. While women in development issues are now accepted as critical in many elements of the development process, implementation of these ideas can benefit from the participation of our voluntary groups.

Poverty in India, Brazil, and Elsewhere

Sixteen percent of the world's population lives in India. India contains well over one-third of the developing world's people living below the poverty line, eating too little to do a full day's work. In spite of internal cultural, language, and religious diversity, India has held together and operated within a democratic framework. Remarkably, India, because of careful fiscal management, is not one of the countries on the Treasury Department's list of the highly indebted countries. It now ranks about tenth in industrial production; yet most of the population is not fully integrated into the economic process. Only half of India's adults are literate, and a quarter of the girls lack a primary school education. The mortality of children under five years old is about 150 per 1,000, and more than 20 percent of the world's infant deaths occur in India. The unfinished job of meeting basic human needs is gigantic.

The donor community faces India with a certain quiet neglect. In 1970–1971, 12 members of the DAC counted India among their top three aid recipients, including six who gave more to India than to any other country. By 1985–1986, only seven DAC donors included India among their top three recipients. India receives on a net basis less than 1 percent of GNP from aid—about $2.60 per capita.

The United States provided very generous aid to India back in the 1950s and 1960s. Today, the United States is actually in a negative aid position there—receiving substantially more in repayments on earlier loans than it commits for new efforts. The United States, except through its IDA contributions, is no longer a significant player in the field of development in the country harboring the largest number of the poor. If the United States wishes to play a leadership role in the 1990s in dealing with the problems of mass poverty, it should look again at its priorities in the subcontinent. An aid administrator, faced with today's level of resources, cannot give India much help. The lack of U.S. leadership there also puts a damper on the efforts of others.

In India, success and failure coexist. India uses the highest technology, yet tradition dominates most of life. Thousands of experiments are going on, with dramatic successes, yet the application of results in many parts of the country is only beginning. India has enormous potential markets and is a potential source of a wide range of goods and services. Looked at over a 30- or 40-year perspective, we should certainly hope that India, when it becomes the world's most populous country early in the next century, can deal with its poverty problems, can effectively bring into its market economy those who are now outside, and can play a constructive political and commercial role internationally as an ever more important partner.

In view of India's unique position in the world, one wonders whether there is not room for an entirely new approach to working with that country in its campaign to reduce poverty. The donor community might indicate a willingness to triple gross aid from its present $2.5 billion level if India could put forward a proposal for a total government effort for accelerated activity affecting the poor. If provided as grants, such a tripling would increase net aid to $7 billion. By implementing such an approach, might the United States and other donors together be able to accelerate progress by the turn of the century on rural employment, agriculture-related infrastructure, literacy, health, nutrition, and some of the worst problems of India's burgeoning cities? Might the United States not provide additional assistance to India in such a way that U.S. foreign exchange would be sold to the private sector for its import needs, with the proceeds available to the Indian government for strengthening programs already in place to increase the number of children in school, to improve the quality of education, to increase the provision of health services, and to support infrastructure construction and other poverty-alleviating initiatives? Such an approach would both accelerate growth by strengthening the capacity of the productive sectors and directly attack poverty issues. The old-fashioned systems of aid micromanagement that may be applicable to less sophisticated societies surely could be replaced in the case of India by a new relationship in which India puts forward the program, and the donors respond in a way that recognizes that India is fully capable of running its poverty-related programs without donor involvement at the project level. (I am not suggesting a blank check or no review on how the funds are spent.)

The framework for such an approach is not really thinkable with today's aid levels. Increases would be required from the United States as well as from other donors. But if the United States were pulling on its aid oar with the same forcefulness as is the rest of the DAC, U.S. leadership in putting together such a new approach could become a serious possibility.

It seems that such an approach would have applicability in other situations. For example, the donor community came to feel that Brazil no longer needed concessional lending on a large scale. This was certainly justified on the basis of per capita income statistics and the extraordinary progress that Brazil had been able to achieve. Yet, the question of Brazil seldom comes up without mention of the vivid contrast between the dynamic industrial centers and the poor areas of the northeast. Furthermore, reality has left Brazil in the middle of a debt crisis that will certainly be a problem for the decade ahead, dragging down the priority Brazil can give to poverty alleviation. Is it out of the question to consider responding to a Brazilian initiative in which the problems of poverty in the northeast might be given a stepped-up priority in response to a donor willingness to provide foreign exchange that Brazil could well use in dealing with its overall development challenge? Again, U.S. leadership on such an idea is only thinkable if more resources are available.

One could imagine similar approaches having an applicability in other countries, including Indonesia, Nigeria, and Pakistan, not to mention smaller countries that might profit from such a less patronizing, less micromanaged system of assistance provided in such a way that significant progress in dealing with the problems of poverty might be realized. Also, some other DAC donors—led by Japan—have started providing significant assistance to China. The question of U.S. bilateral aid to China should certainly be considered in the years ahead in light of U.S. long-term interests.

Small-Enterprise Development

In the United States there is a broad consensus on the importance of the private sector in its own continuing development. One statistic that distinguishes the United States from many other countries is the one on employment creation, closely related to an environment in which small enterprises are encouraged by policy and by the provision of efficient facilities.

In its aid program, the United States has been a pioneer in helping developing countries improve conditions for the private sector, introducing modern banking techniques and supporting the creation of development banks. The aid program has extensive experience in agricultural credit and, in the school of hard experience, has learned what works and what does not. The United States has encouraged the provision of credit to women on equal terms with men. In its programs, it has sought to increase the availability of credit for new categories of people, often in the more remote parts of the developing countries. More recently, the United States has offered leadership in the policy debate regarding parastatals and the need for a combination of privatization and effective management.

But this process of improving the climate for the private sector and enhancing the credit facilities for it is often at an early stage. Today, the United States has only very limited funding to put behind its policies in this area and to support developing country leadership prepared to accept the wisdom that, step by step, has been accepted in the development debate.

U.S. leadership continues to be needed in this area. It is important that the United States stay in the game, offering its experience and helping to finance some of the facilities needed. While this is an area in which many donors have expertise and an area in which funding from many sources will be required, U.S. leadership continues to be needed.

Child Survival and Safe Motherhood

I have already said that the world has made magnificent strides in health, with developing country health standards improving dramatically over the past 40 years. But there is a long unfinished agenda: We know that many diseases can be avoided with low-cost inoculation programs and that the effects of diarrhea can be mitigated with oral rehydration; we know that iodine deficiency can be countered by iodizing salt; we are learning more about how to deal with other nutritional deficiencies, such as lack of vitamin A and iron; we know that rural health systems must be designed to be largely self-sustaining and less dependent on central government support. We know that poor people without modern health care spend large portions of limited income on traditional and often useless health expenditures, which means many health services could be financed by the users. With this knowledge, further dramatic progress is a matter of management and funding.

The United States traditionally has been a strong supporter of the WHO and UNICEF, and these organizations have done a good job, often with major funding from the United States and other aid programs, in giving leadership in the health area. Their efforts and our bilateral programs for the same purposes deserve continuing support. However, even though the United

States has tried to give priority to their efforts, U.S. contributions have been less than one would expect in light of its comparative economic size and historical concern with these issues. Just as one example, I understand that in 1989 Sweden is providing more to UNICEF than is the United States.

Quite aside from the impact of family planning on numbers, family planning is also the most important measure in reducing the number of deaths of women in pregnancy and childbirth. Some 500,000 women die in pregnancy and childbirth each year. The chance of dying having a child in developing countries is 100 times the chance in OECD countries. If mothers could control conception, avoiding pregnancy when too young or too old and avoiding having children too close together, the 500,000 figure could probably be halved. The United States was the leader in the population area and still provides the most significant financing. But there is a growing demand for services. A severalfold increase in population funding is needed. The United States could take the lead with the other donors in achieving such an increase if it could make an additional effort itself.

One new issue, that has come upon the world suddenly, deserves special attention. We read in the newspapers about a U.S. investment in AIDS research and education programs on the order of $2 billion. But AIDS is a problem of awful significance for many developing countries. We need to ask whether the balance of funding for AIDS might not appropriately swing a bit more toward the international programs. I do not pretend to know the right proportions for expenditures in this area. With the priority the United States quite rightly gives to AIDS because so many U.S. citizens have been affected by it, it seems that this should be one of the areas where the U.S. aid program should be playing a leadership role in the 1990s.

Drug Abuse

One of the most vexing and disheartening problems to arise over the past two decades has been drug abuse. The worst thing is that, at bottom, the United States really does not have a strategy it can confidently predict will work.

One thing we know: This is not an exclusively U.S. problem; this is a global problem. It involves producers in the hills of Thailand and Pakistan, Colombia and Bolivia, and many other countries. It involves traffickers from all countries. Drug use is now a major health problem in developing countries. This is a problem of personal attitudes and mass sociology. Solutions to the problems of drug production, trafficking, and use will certainly involve education, health, and enforcement programs, not to mention developing country agricultural programs.

The worldwide drug problem will not be dealt with successfully simply by setting up special offices and devoting a few million dollars to it. All countries need to seek a global strategy in the spirit of partnership. This is another area where U.S. resources sufficient to exercise imaginative leadership will be needed over the next decade.

Education

The hallmark of the U.S. development process has been devotion to universal educational opportunities. Education has been part of the United States' culture from the beginning, and families have made enormous personal sacrifices to be sure that the community had a teacher and that children could get to school. As U.S. development experts look at the astounding successes achieved by many fast growers of the twentieth century such as Japan, Korea, and Taiwan, they cannot help feeling that the high priority these countries give to education has been an important factor in their achievements.

Development in one field often has a positive impact on others, as in the interrelationships among education, population, health, nutrition, and agricultural production. But, of course, education is not simply a means to better health or increased productivity. It is a fundamental objective of the development process, the enabling factor that opens the individual to the world.

While education has always been one element of the U.S. aid program, only negligible resources are devoted to it. There are only a few countries where the U.S. aid program has taken education truly seriously over a long time. One of those is Jordan, where U.S. citizens worked with Jordanians across the board, from ministry management to curriculum development, from teacher training to the production of books and equipment, from primary school through university, but with the main focus on the development of a universal primary and secondary education system. The last time I looked at the figures, fully one-third of all Jordanian citizens were going to school, and the results are manifested in an economy led by its well-developed human resources and making record progress, measured by both economic growth and human resources development, in spite of a relatively limited natural resource endowment. The U.S. effort was made sensitively in full recognition that Jordan, in the end, had to develop its own education system reflecting its own history and values.

Today, the world has 300 million children of school age not in school. The education challenge for some countries is staggering. For example, the DAC countries, home to about 700 million people, have about 10 million children coming to school age each year. Sub-Saharan Africa, with less than 500 million people, has 20 million children coming to school age each year, and this number will increase to 30 million over the next generation. Africa is challenged to educate its children in a situation wherein (excluding Nigeria) per capita income averages about $350. The demand for education in Africa is such that whole families will go hungry to find the money to keep a child in school. But many do not make it.

Another problem is that the poorest are often not well represented in the power structure, and funding priorities frequently are assigned to the already better-off portions of the society. Aid can help bend priorities toward the poor.

Also fundamental are issues of decentralization and cost recovery. To universalize a service almost always requires the financial participation of the people who get the service. Education needs to be dealt with in strategic terms. By making only token contributions to the sector, the United States oftentimes inadvertently supports a distortion of priorities by encouraging the creation of institutions that are very costly to operate, thus taking money away from low-cost primary education.

Should donors as a group not be prepared to respond to developing country requests for help in the education sector? While most of the investment inevitably will be made by the developing country populations themselves, could not the donor community play a vital catalytic role by working with governments in the development of education sector strategies and then helping in the institution-building required for better curriculum development, textbook production, equipment provision, management, teacher training, and similar kinds of back-up services needed to make community and individual investments in education more efficient? Together, developing countries and donors ought to be able to turn around recent trends that suggest that the number of children not getting into school has been increasing. Should we not, over the next decade, get that 300 million figure down to 200 million or even 100 million?

Latin America and the Caribbean

As the final item on my list of 10 areas for U.S. leadership in the 1990s, I come to Latin America and the Caribbean. The progress made in this area over recent decades is well known; it shows up, for example, in statistics on education and health. In general, Latin America has been very successful in agricultural development. Further, the United States can be pleased that most Latin American and Caribbean countries have achieved democratic systems. But there are still poor countries such as Haiti and Bolivia, there are a number of countries with fairly high average incomes but large numbers of very poor people, and there are middle-income countries where oligarchic systems need to give way to broader-based social and economic systems. Social transformations cannot be simply bought and they cannot be managed from the outside. Yet, an aid process that has as an important objective the encouragement of modernizing forces can give them support. Universal education, land reform, and private sector development all can, over time, be helpful in achieving the transformation.

As in many areas of development, the broad goals are easier to articulate than the specific programs, and I do not pretend to have a blueprint. In any event, program content will have to capitalize on opportunities that may grow out of changing political facts. Latin America and the Caribbean are of critical importance to the United States. U.S. relationships with countries in these regions deepen as commercial relationships grow. It can only strengthen the United States' own security and economic opportunities to have neighbors further along in a broad-based development process. U.S. policy toward its neighbors has been marked by many initiatives, each of which has reflected awareness of the importance of area relationships. The lack of adequate aid on a sustained basis has not permitted the United States to see through many of the good programs it has so imaginatively initiated.

A NEW STYLE FOR THE 1990s

The first DAC chairman, Ambassador James W. Riddleberger, in his initial report on the activities of the members, described total official flows to developing countries. In 1960, the 10 members of the DAC provided about $4.7 billion, and the United States, with $2.8 billion, provided 59 percent. By 1980, there were 17 country members of the DAC providing a total of over $27 billion, with the United States providing about 26 percent. In 1987, the total, as indicated earlier, was about $41.5 billion from 18 country members, with the United States providing about 22 percent. Even if the United States were to more than double its aid to provide the same percentage of GNP as the rest of DAC provides, its share would be just over a third of the total. This reflects the underlying reality that U.S. economic growth rates have been exceeded by the rest of DAC. While the United States will still have by far the largest economy among the members, it will no longer dominate as it did in the 1950s. Even with higher aid levels, in any given developing country the United States is no longer likely to be the largest DAC donor, though it will have that role in a few. Also, the developing countries themselves have changed through the years. Their ability to manage and to assert their views is greatly improved over what it was two or three decades ago. Reflecting these fundamentals, a new style of leadership needs to be forged.

The style of the 1990s needs to change toward partnership—partnership with the recipient and partnership with fellow donors—both bilateral and multilateral. While in some countries or in some activities the United States will be the natural leader among the donors, in others it should be increasingly willing to accommodate itself to other donors' leadership. Agencies in and of developing countries should be encouraged to accept more of the programming and management responsibility. The new partnership needs to be implemented by new signals to staff, streamlined procedures (including sometimes streamlined legislation), and a new U.S. willingness to accept the methods and procedures of recipient governments or other donors. When the United States was the dominant donor almost everywhere and when developing countries were much weaker, it was natural for U.S. procedures and policies to be seen as the standard to which others could adjust. Now the situation is different. With its long experience and excellent professional staff overseas, the United States brings strong assets to this partnership-creating, consensus-building process. Good policies and procedures will be as important as ever, but a more participatory process for achieving them and more flexibility on the details will make it easier to put together the new diversity of funding sources into manageable packages of support.

The amounts required for restoring proportionality to U.S. participation in the OECD partnership for helping poorer countries in their economic development represent a shift of one-quarter of 1 percent of GNP, or 1 percent of the budget. While a healthy process of broader shouldering of responsibilities by our strengthened OECD partners is welcome, burden-sharing works both ways. The United States now makes less than half the effort of its OECD partners in the field of development. There is much to be done, and U.S. leadership continues to be needed and wanted.

NOTES

1. All aid data used in this article are from the OECD, which provides statistics on ODA in accordance with definitions agreed among the members of the DAC. The primary measure of burden-sharing among DAC members is the ratio of ODA to GNP.

NINE

Shaping a U.S. Approach to the 1990s: "Reading Reality Right"

COLIN I. BRADFORD, JR.

The enormous popularity of Paul Kennedy's book *The Rise and Fall of the Great Powers* in the United States is irksome to an economist! Since many economists have written about the competitive challenges to the United States, it is interesting that a historian should have seized such attention. Perhaps one of the reasons for this is that U.S. citizens are struck by a sense of historical inevitability surrounding the current pressures on the United States that have been intrinsic to great powers in the past. The question riveting us is, can we do anything to affect our destiny or are we victims of some law of nations that is akin to the law that says what goes up must come down? Are we a free people still in charge of our destiny or are we out of control? History perhaps can provide an answer that economics cannot.

The challenge to the United States is in fact multifaceted in nature and global in scope. Nonetheless, the rise of Japan, the entrance into the world trade system of the eastern Asian NICs, and the rapid growth of the next-tier NICs in Southeast Asia (Malaysia, Thailand, Indonesia, and the Philippines) has been the cutting edge of the broader challenge to the preeminence of the United States and has led to speculations about a shift in the center of gravity from the Atlantic to the Pacific, among other ruminations.

U.S. citizens are used to being in charge and to assuming that their values and beliefs will become universal values and beliefs. Yet, there has rarely been as deep a concern in the United States about its destiny and hegemony as there is today. As a result, questions about the future of the Pacific and the challenge to the United States are in the end questions about the United States itself. Carlos Fuentes, the Mexican writer, was one of several world figures asked by *Time* magazine, three years ago, what the United States does best. Fuentes replied, "What the U.S. does best is to understand itself. What it does worst is to understand others." The challenge that the United States faces today—particularly in the Pacific but also in the world at large—is that it can no longer understand itself and its destiny without understanding others. In Fuentes' terms, it cannot do what it does best until it learns what it does worst.

MISREADING SUCCESS ABROAD:
MARKETS AND STRATEGY IN THE PACIFIC

The fusion of inward-looking self-understanding and outward-looking projection of beliefs to the world worked as long as U.S. hegemony was clear. The rise of Japan and the eastern Asian NICs has been perceived in a U.S. perspective through this lens, so that there has been a transposition from self to other. On the surface, especially given U.S. occupation and involvement in Japan, Korea, and Taiwan, it seemed logical to assume that they were like the United States and succeeded because they adopted its path to progress. President Ronald Reagan reflected this view in his speech to the UN General Assembly in the fall of 1987:

> In the newly industrializing countries of the Pacific Rim, free markets in services and manufacturing as well as agriculture have led to a soaring of growth and living standards. . . . Those who advocate statist solutions to development should take note—the free market is the other path to development and *the one true path*. It is the people's path. And unlike many other paths, it leads somewhere. It works [Emphasis added].

U.S. development assistance policy and position within multilateral agencies have given priority to this single-formula view of development.

Economists have been quick to engage in a similar sort of transposition. Neoclassical economics tells us quite clearly and rigorously that opening an economy to trade through internal liberalization, making domestic prices for goods and factors of production be determined by competitive market forces, leads to efficient resource allocation and more rapid economic growth. Getting prices right puts an economy on a competitive footing to respond to external demand. As a result, dynamic export expansion and high economic growth are anticipated from outward-oriented, open economy policies. This is the theoretical line of argument.

In what one colleague has reportedly called an act of reflective narcissism, economists turned the theory-practice relationship around. Seeing highly dynamic export performance and GDP (gross domestic product) growth in the eastern Asian NICs, economists associated market-oriented policies with these phenomena. As a consequence, the NIC success stories were seen as vindications of free market trade regimes, development strategies, and macroeconomic adjustment policies when in fact different policies were being pursued in eastern Asia.

There is now a fairly widely accepted view of the eastern Asian NICs as having adopted strategy-led growth paths.[1] Instead of having adopted a static, comparative advantage view of their niche in the economic system, the NICs used a more aggressive, dynamic, comparative advantage approach, seizing opportunities to create niches and to acquire advantage. Their experience was less one of responsiveness to external demand than one of supply-driven increases in market shares through quite explicit export strategies. It was not a question of letting market forces work but of using market forces and policies internally and externally to create a dynamic economic growth pattern.

A key element in the eastern Asian NICs was a highly interactive relationship between the government and the private sector rather than exclusive reliance on one or the other. The stylized contrasts between the supposed inward-oriented, import-substituting, interventionist trade regimes of Latin America and the outward-oriented, export-led, free market regimes purportedly characteristic of eastern Asia were useful to the advocates of the new orthodoxy but not reflective of the real differences and similarities of these two regions.[2] The genius of the highly effective economic performance of economies in both regions was their ability to combine elements and catalyze interactions between sectors, altering the mix over time rather than making once-and-for-all categorical choices of policy regime. Strategy serves as the integrating force providing purposive direction and coherence to policy choice in contexts in which unexploited yields can be realized.

There is a parallel development in the management of global firms in which, because of the multiple markets, products, and subsidiaries composing these entities, there are opportunities to appropriate gains from the interrelationship of these elements. The essence of the management task of the global firm is strategy, wherein strategy is the web that exploits the potential connection of parts to the whole. The organizational configuration of the firm—the accounting, marketing, finance, production, and servicing functions of the firm—are shaped by the strategy. Maximizing results within rather than between the component entities of the global firm would forgo the yields derived from exploiting their potential interaction through an integrative strategy. Leaving resource allocation to atomistic firm behavior and markets ignores the potential gains from acquired comparative advantage through strategy-led development. Strategies are increasingly the key to competitiveness and dynamism both for global firms and national economies.

The insistence of U.S. theorizers that free enterprise, free markets, and free trade are "the one true path" is an ideological proposition that is increasingly at variance with the experience of other nations.[3] It not only misinterprets the ingredients of success of the NICs but creates a poor instrument to forge U.S. responses to challenges to its international competitiveness and to shape a U.S. approach to development strategies. If the challenge from the Pacific is one that is rooted in strategy-led development rather than free market–oriented economies, then a more appropriate response would be a competitive strategy for the United States rather than a mere push for more open markets abroad. A strategic approach defining U.S. foreign economic–policy goals, relating instruments to them, shaping private and public sector interactions in a dynamic rather than adversarial fashion, and focusing on the longer-term positioning of the U.S. economy in the world economy rather than on short-run maximizing would be more consistent with shaping a U.S. response to the world as it is.

Such an approach would engage the United States in the search for new formulae and policies appropriate to both the global context and its unique national characteristics in a way similar to the effort other nations are making. Forging a proactive strategy for the United States that builds on elements from the international environment and the internal institutional heritage shifts the U.S. role in the world in two ways: (1) it makes clear the interdependence of the United States and the rest of the world in a way that the hegemonic approach does not; and (2) it joins the United States with the quest of others for appropriate answers rather than places the United States in the presumptive position of articulating national values as if they have universal application. Intellectually, such a new approach would engage the United States in the world instead of continuing to feed expectations that U.S. power is measured only in terms of its capacity to prevail over the views of others.

ECONOMICS AND CULTURE:
WESTERN TRADITION VERSUS CULTURAL RELATIVISM

The difference between a hegemonic approach and an approach that might be called interdependent pluralism is connected to the debate in academic circles on Western traditions versus cultural relativism. U.S. attitudes about economics presume an objective neutrality to its beliefs that others do not share. In fact, the United States is hard put to realize that its position has ideological and political content.[4] Further, the United States seems totally insensitive to the fact that what fires passions abroad in economic policy debates is the fact that the central wellspring of economic strategy is the determination to maintain and enhance cultural uniqueness. Economic incentives are important, but they do not constitute a raison d'être.

Curiously, Allan Bloom, who in the debate on cultural relativism seems insensitive to the parochialism of Western traditions, is able to see what is missing from U.S. economic ideology: "Those interested in the free market do not seem to recognize . . . that their 'rational' system needs moral supplement. . . . So proponents of the free market should not be surprised when they see that what was once generally agreed upon *no longer compels belief.*"[5]

The debate concerning "great books" or the "canonization" of culture has a direct bearing on the problem of U.S. economic ideology. The issue is whether art, philosophy, and literature from foreign and minority cultures has equal standing as "civilization" with the Western tradition. Bloom, former U.S. secretary of education William Bennett, and French philosopher Alain Finkielkraut (among others) argue the defense of Western culture, while critics such as Henry Louis Gates, Jr., argue that there is a "tyrannical connection between the words humanity on one hand and the humanities on the other. . . . For the humanities as these have been taught in the West have embodied only the thought of the thinkers of the West and not the thought of the great cultures of the world." People from other cultural traditions were never "able to discover the reflection or representation of their images or hear the resonances of their cultural voices" in the teaching of literature, for example, Gates writes. As he points out, what might appear to be a purely academic exercise is in the end a political issue. "Isn't that what ideology is all about?" he asks rhetorically. "Making sectarian interests appear universal?"[6]

The new global context now makes economics and culture connected, not just analogous. "La transformation de notre univers familier en société pluriculturelle"[7] is a phenomenon that arises in large measure because of the globalization of economic forces. Whether this interpenetration of cultures through economic interdependence ultimately defines a more homogeneous or a more differentiated world is in part what the cultural debate is all about. The economic debate should be informed by it rather than isolated from it. The issue of whether there is variety or uniformity in the choice of economic policy regime is intimately connected with whether the world of the future will be more homogeneous or more differentiated. If the dominant view is that there is only one true path and that path means opening national economies to international markets and sublimating the role of the state, following that path will work against national cultural autonomy, differentiation, and pluralism.

The conflict between the United States and Brazil over informatics policies is illustrative of the convergence of economic and cultural choices and the differences between the United States and a NIC in approaches to the conjuncture. The United States has pressed Brazil to eliminate its protection of the Brazilian computer industry on grounds that it is more efficient for Brazil to import computers, software, and so on than it is to produce computers domestically, and that Brazil's policies violate principles of free trade on which the world economy is built. The Brazilian position is expressed by President Sarney:

> Our country knows that the 21st century will have moved beyond the division between poor and rich nations. The world will instead be divided between peoples condemned to cultural colonization and people who control technologies. No one should expect Brazil, with its riches, with its potential, with its determination, to be a second-rate country. We have a different vision of ourselves, and we expect the United States to share that vision.[8]

The United States needs to see that this "different vision of ourselves" has been at least as important in the export-oriented development paths adopted by the successful developing countries in harnessing instruments to objectives and in galvanizing society to the national strategy as has the adoption of market-oriented measures. Such an understanding is important not only for dealing with competitive pressures from the Pacific but also in reading accurately the meaning of economic reforms in the Soviet Union, China, and Eastern Europe, and in making policy toward developing countries.

MISREADING SOCIALIST REFORMS:
FROM REFLECTIVE NARCISSISM TO REFLECTIVE REALISM

There is a tendency in the United States to see economic reforms in socialist economies as conversions to the free market system instead of attempts to strengthen national economic regimes by incorporating useful reforms from capitalist economies. In what is otherwise a very positive review of Ed Hewett's excellent book, *Reforming the Soviet Economy*, V. L. Makarov, director of the Central Economic and Mathematical Institute of the Soviet Academy of Sciences, writes:

> Mr. Hewett, it seems to me, believes the best route of change for the Soviet economy is for us to copy the most effective ingredients of a free entrepreneurial system like that of the United States—especially by introducing competition into all markets, including capital and labor markets.
>
> Well, the Russian spirit is likely to produce something different. We are more accustomed to, and comfortable with, collective behavior than Americans. In a way our customs are closer to those of the Japanese. But I do not doubt that the economy that eventually emerges in the Soviet Union will be original, not identical to that of Japan or the United States, or anywhere else. Economics, after all, is a symbiosis of historical, religious, cultural and ethnic factors, not only of economic ones. The Russians, and the many other ethnic groups in the Soviet Union, have accumulated a great common cultural and intellectual potential that will distinctly shape the Soviet Union's role as it enters the world market.[9]

Essentially, the United States may again be transposing the paradigm of U.S. economic success onto the reform movement in the socialist bloc in the same way that the eastern Asian NICs have been seen to follow that paradigm in achieving dynamic export-oriented growth. Such a transposition in the case of the eastern Asian NICs may have made the United States grasp an oversimplified recipe for development strategy. But such a transposition in the case of the socialist economies may lead to an initial misinterpretation of their reform process, frustration at later stages when complete systemic transformation does not occur, and ultimately a political failure to bridge economic differences and achieve greater understanding between the socialist economies and the West. If a book as good as Ed Hewett's is open to criticism for analytical bias, it seems that there is a larger problem of national perception at issue and that U.S. decisionmakers are vulnerable to making major policy mistakes if the nation does not learn to "read reality right."

The curriculum issue in colleges and universities is, of course, related to national outlook. U.S. minds need to be more highly sensitized over the next decade to the biases in their perceptions by exposure to diverse approaches and paradigms from the national experience of other societies: Until we have stood in the shoes of the others, we cannot fully understand our own subjectivity. In this age, we cannot do what we do best until we learn what we do worst. Over the next decade, the United States must make the transition from reflective narcissism to reflective realism, in education, in economics, and in foreign policy.

CONCLUSION:
FROM HEGEMONY TO PLURALISTIC INTERDEPENDENCE

Identity comes first; economic choices follow. Designing effective development strategies will never be an act of pure economic technique and rationality. They must embody hopes, enhance identity, and inspire the spirit to "compel belief," gain support, and affect reality. The single-recipe approach is doomed to failure in an increasingly self-conscious world. Differentiating the U.S. approach to development strategies rather than standardizing it is an essential element for U.S. development cooperation to succeed in the 1990s.

Japan and the eastern Asian NICs were successful because they made a national commitment to compete globally, while the United States assumed that the free market system would keep it efficient and competitive. The lesson for the United States is to learn from the NIC experience rather than seeing its own likeness in it. This will help forge a more effective competitive strategy for the United States, provide a better prism through which to interpret events in the socialist bloc, and encourage a more effective approach to development cooperation.

The parochialism of U.S. beliefs and ideology are getting in the way of the transition to coping with the pressures of a competitive world, the shifts in the international security environment, and the increasing pluralism of the world community. For the United States to make an effective transition in its approach to global change, intellectual renovation must precede economic restructuring. Intellectual renovation requires interaction rather than imposition, and a genuine engagement with the diverse world, learning from it, adapting to it, seeking a new understanding of one's own identity and self-definition by involvement with other nations, systems, and cultures. The world of pluralistic interdependence is a more exciting and interesting one than is the unidimensional world of economic and ideological hegemony that is quickly disappearing.

NOTES

1. Frederic C. Deyo, ed., *The Political Economy of the New Industrialism* (Ithaca, NY: Cornell University Press, 1987); George C. Lodge and Ezra F. Vogel, *Ideology and National Competitiveness* (Boston: Harvard Business School Press, 1987); Bruce Scott and George Lodge, *U.S. Competitiveness in the World Economy* (Boston: Harvard Business School Press, 1985).
2. Colin I. Bradford, Jr., "Policy Interventions and Markets: Development Strategy Typologies and Policy Options in Latin America and East Asia," in *Development Strategies in Latin America and East Asia,* ed. Gary Gereffi (Princeton, NJ: Princeton University Press, 1989).
3. Colin I. Bradford, Jr., "East Asian 'Models': Myths and Lessons," in *Development Strategies Reconsidered,* ed. John P. Lewis and Valeriana Kalleb (New Brunswick, NJ: Transaction Books, 1986).
4. David Baldwin, *Economic Statecraft* (Princeton, NJ: Princeton University Press, 1985), pp. 44–46.
5. Allan Bloom, *The Closing of the American Mind* (New York: Simon and Schuster, 1987), pp. 209–210 (emphasis added).
6. *New York Times,* 29 May 1988.
7. Alain Finkielkraut, *La Défaite de la pensée* (Paris: Gallimard, 1987), p. 113.
8. José Sarney, "Brazil: A President's Story," *Foreign Affairs* 65, no. 1 (1986): 117.
9. V. L. Makarov, in *The New York Times Book Review,* 29 May 1988, p. 22.

TEN

Development Cooperation: Creating a Public Commitment

JOHN MAXWELL HAMILTON

While the science and practice of economic development have advanced steadily over the past four decades, one aspect of foreign aid has stayed the same: U.S. adults have remained uncertain about the meaning and purpose of assistance. Always there has been a sense that public support is tenuous. The Point Four program, the United States' first major effort to help developing nations, was at one time a single vote away from dying in Congress.[1] In recent years, the lack of enthusiasm for development assistance programs has been attributed to "aid fatigue." "The continued quest for a rationale for foreign aid is one of its distinguishing characteristics as an area of public policy," political scientist Samuel Huntington observed nearly 20 years ago. "It is a quest which has been passed through countless commissions, study groups, conferences, reports, and memoranda."[2]

This chapter examines U.S. attitudes toward foreign aid and argues that making the case for economic development assistance, whether bilateral or through multilateral banks, could become harder rather than easier in the future. The reasons for furthering development abroad have increased as a result of interdependence, but an unfamiliar interlinked world threatens many in the United States and could push them inward rather than outward. A compelling rationale for assistance is needed to overcome this possibility, a controlling concept that underpins and informs a practical program of economic cooperation with developing countries.

Aid legislation has come to symbolize the lack of purpose that permeates assistance programs. The current foreign aid statute lists at least 33 separate objectives, ranging from promoting cooperatives to protecting endangered species. Lacking a clear guiding rationale or unified national constituency, aid has been subject to numerous legislative amendments that have nothing to do with Third World economic development.[3]

The strategy of courting special interests has not produced a strong political base for assistance programs. Although these special interests win legislative victories from time to time, the aid program as a whole steadily loses ground. The size of the career USAID staff dropped 20 percent between 1981 and 1986. While this was not the largest decrease among federal agencies during the period and was offset by the use of consultants, it has been severe. USAID is one of the smaller federal agencies. It has less fat and relies heavily on its professional staff in the field to carry out its programs.[4] Meanwhile, funding for development assistance has dropped in real terms since the Marshall Plan for European economic recovery after World War II. Expressed in 1989 dollars, bilateral development assistance dropped from $8.9 billion in 1952 to only $2.3 billion in 1988.[5]

Foreign assistance funding in per capita terms today compares to aid levels at the beginning of the century, when aid was not considered an established government activity. Total U.S. nonmilitary assistance was .24 percent of GNP in 1986. Rough calculations show that in 1919 the United States gave .33 percent of its GNP to help other countries; in 1920 it gave .08 percent, and in 1921 .13 percent. Contributions in 1921 included $20 million worth of food from the U.S. Grain Corporation for Russian relief, $500,000 to transport grain to famine victims in China, and more than $73 million in U.S. Treasury loans to Belgium, Czechoslovakia, France, Greece, and Italy. These figures, culled from budgets during the period, are not complete. They do not include other assistance monies, for instance those given when the United States decided that $17 million of the $25 million Boxer Indemnity should be used to further Chinese education.[6]

The decline in foreign aid can be measured in another way. In anticipation of the 1988 presidential election, the Center for Excellence in Government examined the most important jobs for which the new president would make appointments just below the cabinet level. The job of aid administrator was not included among the 118 or so positions on the A list. Although hardly in a precise exercise, *U.S. News & World Report* recently assembled a picture of The "New American Establishment," including those who have replaced statesmen such as Dean Acheson and Averell Harriman, luminaries in the 1940s and 1950s. None of the new establishment had obvious connections with development assistance, while Acheson and Harriman were deeply involved in foreign aid.[7] Little wonder that a group of USAID mission directors meeting in Asia in 1987 sent a cable to Washington, lamenting that the foreign aid program is drifting, without a strong rationale that accords with national interests in their rapidly changing region.[8]

WHERE THE UNITED STATES HAS BEEN

The U.S. public's view on foreign assistance is difficult to measure precisely. But it is certain that the public does not rank foreign aid high on its list of priorities. Poet Archibald MacLeish, who headed President Roosevelt's wartime Office of Facts and Figures, reported to Roosevelt in 1942 that "four out of five people believe that this country should and will help to feed the hungry peoples of the world after the war is ended." That attitude has prevailed. A 1987 Overseas Development Council (ODC)–InterAction poll found that 89 percent of the U.S. public agreed (45 percent strongly) that "wherever people are hungry or poor, we ought to do what we can to help them." In the very same breath, however, the same public typically expresses another set of beliefs that run against foreign aid. In the ODC-InterAction poll, for instance, 84 percent agreed (60 percent strongly) that "we need to solve our own poverty problems in the United States before we turn attention to other countries."

The contradictions abound. A slim majority of respondents in the ODC-InterAction poll said it supports foreign aid. Another slim majority agreed that "we should give the Third World countries less aid and leave them alone so they can develop in their own ways." Sixty-two percent agreed that "aid programs get us too mixed up with other countries' affairs."[9]

A number of explanations help justify these different, apparently contradictory, responses. U.S. citizens have strong humanitarian impulses. When faced with mass starvation overseas, which can be solved quickly by shipments of food, they respond positively. Almost three-quarters of the respondents to the ODC-InterAction survey rated disaster relief a high priority. Long-range development programs, which require patience and produce complicated outcomes, are not so appealing to the U.S. public, which does not favor big government interventions. U.S. tradition presumes that government cannot succeed as well as individuals can.

But these factors alone do not explain why economic aid is held in such low esteem. The U.S. public does not oppose all government expenditures to the same degree. A Conference Board poll recently found that the majority *opposed* cutbacks in social security and veterans' benefits, but more than nine out of 10 supported cuts in foreign aid.[10]

The fact is that those who believe in government-supported foreign assistance simply have not made a convincing case that foreign aid is as important as government expenditures domestically. Foreign aid is seen, clearly, as foreign to U.S. interests.

For more than two hundred years arguments for foreign aid have rested on three legs, which might be described as ideological, humanitarian, and economic self-interest. But while three legs make for a sturdy stool, they have not effectively supported foreign assistance programs. Understanding why is crucial to convincing the public of the utility of economic cooperation with developing countries.

Ideological reasoning: The "ideological" leg argues that aid promotes U.S. values, particularly democracy. This rationale has implicitly promised to create the unswerving friendship of recipient countries and to enhance U.S. national security. The motive behind such assistance is as old as the Puritans and their self-appointed mission of redemptive activism. The Bay Colony, as John Winthrop professed, would be "as a city upon a hill. The eyes of all people are upon us."

The ideological rationale has been central to building public support since the very first days of post-World War II foreign assistance. In a Truman administration briefing of congressional leaders on the proposed Greco-Turkish aid program in 1947, Secretary of State George C. Marshall told the legislators about the humanitarian reasons for such assistance. Concerned that Marshall was having no impact on his audience, Undersecretary of State Dean Acheson leapt in with a discussion of the importance of stopping the spread of communism. "If you will say that to the Congress and the country," replied Senator Arthur Vandenberg, ranking Republican on the Foreign Relations Committee, "I will support you and I believe that most of its members will do the same."[11]

Such arguments continued in the intervening 40 years. As just one example, the Title IX amendment to the Foreign Assistance Act in 1966 called for USAID to assure "maximum participation in the task of economic development on the part of the people of developing countries, through the encouragement of democratic private and local government institutions."[12] In the 1980s, leaders have continued to describe the United States as "an anointed land" and to talk about aid promoting U.S. values.[13]

But as neatly as this rhetoric fits with U.S. tradition, the ideological arguments are fatally flawed. They have done more damage than good because they have built expectations that simply cannot be achieved. The ideological rationale presumes a consensus that does not exist on how U.S. values should be applied overseas. Although anticommunism was once a rallying point for U.S. voters of all political persuasions, that is no longer so. Whereas some viewed the 1970 Chilean election of Marxist Salvador Allende as democracy in action, others saw U.S. efforts to overthrow Allende's regime as striking a blow for free government.

Even if anticommunism still attracted wide support, the ideological rationale would promise more than it could deliver. This is because it cannot meet any of the standards set up in the popular mind for success. One test of success is whether a recipient country copies the United States' political system. But even two nations as apparently similar as the United States and Britain have major differences on laws as fundamental as freedom of speech. U.S. views on the role and rights of the individual are as different from the views of developing countries as the U.S. heritage of wide-open spaces is different from traditions of people working the same plot of land their ancestors tilled. Moreover, U.S. citizens from the beginning sought to stabilize a system that had equity built into it. The search for equity in many developing countries must produce dramatic upheaval.

Another test of success is that of winning political friends. Here again failure is certain. There is a contradiction between the goals of creating compliant allies and fostering strong democratic nations. Aid that seeks to make nations resistant to foreign Marxist influence and responsive to domestic sentiment cannot simultaneously make nations responsive to the U.S. political agenda and traditions. Yet the U.S. public has often assumed that this goal could be achieved and as a result has judged the effectiveness of foreign assistance by the way recipient nations vote in the United Nations.

Economic aid, of course, can have an impact on the political complexion of a nation. Development experts are right to think about economic assistance programs' creating greater economic equity. But economic aid is most effective at promoting economic development. As such, it can create economic partnerships. Promising more creates expectations that cannot be met and ultimately discredits assistance programs. "Public statements force the policymaker to work with the goals and expectations established by those statements because congressmen and various aid constituencies do not forget the rhetoric even if the official may want to," Robert Packenham has observed. "Thus, having 'sold' doctrines, officials may be 'stuck' with the consequences."[14]

Humanitarian reasoning: Looking back nostalgically, the U.S. public likes to remember the humanitarian aspects of the postwar recovery program that George Marshall outlined for Europe in his famous Harvard commencement address: a program "not directed against any country or doctrine but against hunger, poverty, desperation, and chaos." But whatever Marshall may have said at Harvard, he took a more practical line with Congress: "If we decide that the United States is unable or unwilling effectively to assist in the reconstruction of Europe, we must accept the consequences of its collapse into the dictatorships of police states. . . . There is no doubt in my mind that the whole world hangs in the balance." At the same time, President Harry S Truman, among other policymakers, recognized the economic importance to the United States of aiding Europeans. It is clear, one historian has noted, "that what defined the needs of 'European recovery' for Americans' purposes was an estimate of what would be required to maintain American exports at existing levels."[15]

A strong tradition of voluntary giving, as cultural historian Merle Curti observed in the 1950s, is "a significant facet in the American character."[16] Early private philanthropy supported projects overseas that have appeal today. Despite government concerns about the constitutionality of using government funds to promote economic progress at home or abroad, elected officials found ways in the nineteenth century of helping other peoples.

Still, as Marshall's pragmatism suggests, humanitarian reasons are not sufficient to mobilize political support for foreign assistance. While it is true that survey respondents most frequently articulate humanitarian reasons for supporting foreign assistance, humanitarian sentiment is not particularly strong. The ODC-InterAction poll, after all, showed that barely half of the respondents cited humanitarian reasons for assistance, and even that slim majority cannot be assured.[17] A 1985 poll on charitable behavior in the United States found that 51 percent disagreed that because U.S. adults are wealthy they have a special obligation to help the poor in other countries. Forty-seven percent agreed that the government had no special responsibility to spend money helping the poor in other countries. Only 40 percent disagreed.[18]

Several other factors contribute to the weakness of humanitarian arguments. First, charity is by definition something that is good to do, not something that is essential. This makes foreign assistance a lower priority than many domestic development programs. Polls show that one of the chief reasons given for opposing economic aid overseas is poverty in the United States. Second, humanitarianism, based as it is on feelings, responds quickly to crises but not so readily to fundamental development problems where solutions are not obvious or quickly achieved. It is easy to evoke humanitarian feelings for an emaciated mother and child on the edge of an African desert. But the lack of clean water or educational opportunities are not so easily photographed. Strong public support for assistance addressed to these long-term problems is possible only when people are intellectually engaged. Unless leaders want to limit aid to relief, they must face this problem.

Economic reasoning: As with other arguments for foreign assistance, economic gain has long served as an important argument for foreign assistance. Commercial considerations surfaced prominently in relief to earthquake victims in Venezuela in 1812. Secretary of State James Monroe told Alexander Scott, the man selected to administer the $50,000 aid program, "the real as well as ostensible object of your mission is to explain the mutual advantages of commerce with the United States, to promote liberal and stable regulations, and to transmit seasonable information on the subject."[19]

President Taft's "dollar diplomacy" in 1909 promised to help nations with natural wealth achieve "a measure of stability and the means of financial regeneration to enter upon an era of peace and prosperity, bringing profit and happiness to themselves and at the same time creating conditions sure to lead to a flourishing interchange with this country."[20] President Herbert Hoover articulated a similar vision: "The making of loans to foreign countries for productive purposes not only increases our direct exports but builds up the prosperity of foreign countries and is a blessing to both sides of the transaction."[21] The mission of missionaries was hospitable to U.S. commercial interests. Missionaries in Hawaii easily made the leap from preaching the gospel to becoming large plantation owners and government advisors. Far from being an enemy of commerce, the successful Christian missionary could argue that he was making good customers for U.S. manufacturers.[22]

This good-for-business approach offers an important departure point for creating practical reasons for fostering economic development overseas.

Unfortunately, the search for short-term economic payoffs has consistently obscured the long-term possibilities.

First, where U.S. policymakers and interest groups should see the value of market creation, they have instead fixed on tying assistance to immediate purchases of U.S. goods or insisted that the aid commodities travel on U.S. vessels. Such approaches have not convinced the public of the wisdom of development, for it is obvious that if foreign aid is good because the money is spent for U.S. goods and services, then it is even better if it is spent for U.S. goods and services to be used in the United States.

Second, those highlighting the economic benefits of development have typically fixed on trade, without recognizing that nonbusiness development pays economic *and* noneconomic dividends for both donor and recipient. Toward the close of the Reagan administration, a U.S. Chamber of Commerce task force drafted a statement of principles for assistance that had sensible things to say about the importance of fostering trade with developing countries. But the task force's seven-point summary was far more simplistic, recommending "that agencies implementing any program which draws on foreign assistance funds assess and report to Congress on the impact on U.S. trade flows of such programs."[23] That approach, which the chamber mistakenly calls new, ignores U.S. interests in environmental conservation or mutual interest in health and family planning programs overseas.

Third, and related, economic self-interest arguments have often sounded like aid programs for U.S. business rather than for the broad range of the U.S. public and, not surprisingly, have alienated those in the development community whose goal is to assist developing countries. Under these circumstances, it should not be surprising that so few U.S. citizens seem impressed with arguments that economic assistance is in their self-interest.[24]

Taken separately, each of these three rationales has distinct liabilities. Taken together, they confound support for aid all the more. The array of goals, competing with each other, are a recipe for bewilderment. They confuse the U.S. public, they confuse the people who carry out the program, and they confuse recipient nations.

Without dramatic change in the articulation of goals, this trend could get much worse in the 1990s. The U.S. system is going through a profound transition from relative self-sufficiency to permanent interdependence. That transformation creates possibilities for greater cooperation with developing countries and, at the same time, enhances the possibility that U.S. voters will ultimately decide to do less rather than more to assist the Third World.

WHERE THE UNITED STATES IS GOING

In speculating on the earthshaking events that could occur, futurists have noted that the earth's magnetic field periodically changes. Over the past 76 million years the poles have switched, according to some estimates, at least

171 times, so that compasses that pointed north start to point south. The next shift, expected around the year 4000, could have vast implications.[25]

But a political-economic shift, with equally profound implications, is already knocking the U.S. public's world figuratively off its axis. Global interdependence is transforming relationships between the once all-powerful North and once weak South. The implications for foreign assistance are potentially momentous and worrisome.

Nothing in its history prepares the United States for such a sweeping recalibration of foreign policy. From the early days of the republic, U.S. settlers rightly assumed that they could isolate themselves from the rest of the world. The United States was many days' sail from the Old World and an ocean away from Asia. Latin Americans posed no real security threat. Early residents of the United States shrank from the diplomatic practices of their European antecedents, who had learned how to jockey for position among the many nations they bordered. With plentiful resources on the East Coast and open western territory, the United States had every reason to think of itself as self-sufficient.

Merchandise trade provides a useful yardstick to measure the persistence of self-sufficiency. In 1929—a peak year for U.S. business—foreign trade, excluding services, was only 12.5 percent of U.S. GNP. From 1954 to 1963, it averaged 7.9 percent. This is much below trade activity in other countries. Trade was 38.1 percent of British GNP from 1924 to 1928; 51.3 percent of French GNP from 1919 to 1928; and 35.5 percent of Japanese GNP from 1918 to 1927.[26]

Only recently has change come—but it has come with blinding speed. From that 7.9 percent average between 1954 and 1963, trade has leapt to a commanding position in the U.S. economy. In 1980, total trade of goods and services amounted to 21 percent of GNP; in 1987, it was about 26 percent.

This increase is significant not only because overall transactions are increasing but because it has paralleled the evolution of a truly global economy. Although the U.S. public has thought of foreign affairs chiefly in terms of Europe, developing countries have come to make up a much larger share of the world market. In 1985, manufactured exports to the United States from the four eastern Asian NICs equaled three-fourths of the quantity of exports to the United States from the EC's 10 members. That same year, the United States imported more manufactured products from all developing countries than from Japan and the EC combined, and, until the Third World debt crisis began to bite in the early 1980s, exported substantially more to developing countries than to Japan and the EC combined. Even with Third World debt problems, as well as drought in Africa and generally low prices for many of the commodities that developing countries sell, about a third of U.S. manufacturing exports went to Latin America, the four Asian NICs, and other developing countries in 1985.

There is virtually no prospect for reversing this trend. Foreign companies have become the only suppliers of some products—for instance, compact-disc players. Corporate America, not just consumers, relies on imports. Imports of capital goods by U.S. businesses have increased 40 percent since 1985, according to a February 1988 article in the *Wall Street Journal*. Although foreign indebtedness has dominated the news about Third World countries, those nations hold the greatest prospect for growth. Thirty-nine of the 40 fastest-growing GNPs between 1973 and 1986 were in developing countries (see Figure 10.1).

Merchandise trade is only a fragment of a larger range of economic interdependencies reaching into every corner of U.S. society. In 1985, the United States not only became a net debtor for the first time since World War II, it also became the world's largest debtor. In 1987, for the first time in 29 years, the United States paid more to foreign investors than it gained from investments overseas. "More than two hundred years after the Declaration of Independence," Felix Rohatyn observed of this indebtedness, "the United States has lost its position as an independent power."[27]

The precipitous stock market drop on 19 October 1987 was a first in world history. Never before had average citizens in the United States and elsewhere followed stock market prices in other countries on a minute-by-minute basis and projected the impact of those fluctuations on their own securities markets. This was more than a vivid example of global finance. The workings of the global stock market demonstrated the enhanced power of communications facilities and showed that foreign commerce is not simply a matter of shipping food or steel abroad but of services that have themselves become "tradeable."

The spread of AIDS highlights the way health in one country or region has an impact on health in another; the dependence of U.S. farmers on genetic material from seeds grown in other parts of the world—and the danger that Third World genetic material can be lost as a result of environmental degradation—illustrates environmental interdependence. One of the chief concerns in U.S. schools—drugs—has its antecedents in developing countries, where poor farmers must grow coca to earn money to feed their families. Indeed, what U.S. residents wear, where they go for vacations, the music they dance to, and the exotic foods they have come increasingly to eat—all reveal proliferating connections to developing nations.[28]

For many people, the idea of interdependence is positive, potentially enriching their lives and culture and perhaps contributing to better world understanding and peace. But interdependence also presents challenges. These challenges are, paradoxically, so formidable that they could make the U.S. public less tolerant of others, rather than more outward-looking, and in the process make economic cooperation harder instead of easier.

Figure 10.1   GNP Real Growth Rate, 1973–1986 Annual Average

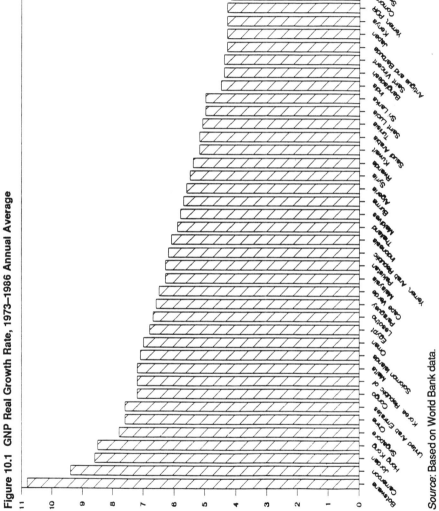

Source: Based on World Bank data.
Note: Does not include data for some centrally planned economies and Taiwan.

Without suggesting that this is a comprehensive list of factors, some concerns stemming from interdependence portend possible negative attitudes about foreign assistance.

Jobs

First and foremost in politicians' minds today is the issue of jobs. Although many U.S. workers recognize that developing countries offer promising markets, the dominant sentiment is one of fear about relatively low-paid Third World labor forces taking U.S. jobs, and with good reason. LDCs have become large importers of U.S.-grown food, but they have also become competitors in global food markets and are now exporting large amounts to the United States. Foreign manufacturing competition in the U.S. domestic market, a growing share of it from developing countries, has increased. In the early 1960s, only 25 percent of U.S. products faced such competition; more than 70 percent fought foreign competition in 1985. Put simply, imports have grown much faster than have exports since 1980.[29]

One of the most obvious solutions for competing with low wage rates in developing countries is to automate at home—that is, to eliminate human workers. While that may make sense for businesses, it is not good news for workers. As Peter Drucker has pointed out, "If a company, an industry or a country does not in the next quarter century sharply increase manufacturing production and at the same time sharply reduce the blue-collar work force, it cannot hope to remain competitive—or even to remain 'developed'."[30]

U.S. living standards are under pressure. Department of Labor statistics show that average weekly nonfarm earnings measured in constant 1977 dollars declined from $201.78 in 1972 to $168.28 in 1987. An increase in the number of families with two wage earners has helped many people keep up. But the gap between the wealthiest and the poorest is now larger than at any time since 1947, when such data where first collected. For the first time since the 1930s, the share of U.S. residents who own their own homes is dropping.[31]

It is hard to overestimate the impact of this trend. In any country, workers who lose their jobs or settle for lower-paying jobs become unhappy. But in the United States, more than in many other countries, jobs have played the central role in distributing wealth and have served as a way of siphoning off disenchantment. That is one reason why the left has never been strong in the United States. It is also the reason why political leaders are likely to favor quick fixes to save and create jobs at home, which could mean promoting government investments here and protecting workers from foreign competition.

Charity

The U.S. public's generosity continues to reveal itself on an international scale, a recent dramatic example being donations for victims of the African drought. Despite talk of a "me generation," a Gallup poll has found an increase in volunteerism.[32] This upsurge in volunteerism complements a view by some futurists of the advent of a new era. Daniel Yankelovich, for example, has speculated that in making changes to cope with new economic realities, U.S. citizens are developing a new social ethic in which people will "grow less preoccupied with themselves and look for closer ties with others."[33]

But are there grounds for being so confident? Much of the new volunteerism is a product of affluence. Many of the "New Volunteers," as described in a 1988 *Newsweek* article, are those who have prospered. Giving is a way of adding meaning to their lives. What will happen if affluence decreases? Moreover, recent volunteerism has been directed chiefly at local causes with which people can identify. Even in an age of interdependence it may be difficult to give people a real sense of involvement with citizens overseas, particularly if a "them-and-us" attitude continues to evolve. Yankelovich inadvertently identified the problem when he noted why a new social consciousness was necessary:

> We need new rules to encourage people to channel their creativity away from themselves and back into concrete tasks that need doing in the new era—creating new forms of energy, taming technology, investing in new industries, *creating new jobs, competing more effectively with the Japanese and Germans and Koreans* . . . creating community through caring for others.[34]

Other evidence suggests that a new social consciousness may not be taking shape at all. Per capita private U.S. contributions to development assistance dropped from $7.58 in 1970 to $5.63 in 1983, according to the OECD.[35] A 1987 study of collegiate freshmen by the Cooperative Institutional Research Program reported that 71.3 percent of those surveyed indicated that a key reason for going to college was "to make more money." In 1971, only 49.9 percent gave that response. In 1987, 39.4 percent considered "developing a meaningful philosophy of life" a very important goal. That was down from 82.9 percent in 1967. Last year, only 19.8 percent thought it essential or very important to participate in community action.[36]

Corporate leaders, who are more likely to have a global perspective as a result of their work, are not necessarily inclined to use their corporate assets to help developing countries. Many large businesses that once made contributions to social programs are backing away from such activity, according to the Conference Board. "Born and raised in depression and war, [earlier corporate executive officers (CEOs) held views] influenced by the harsh realities that they recalled; many developed a pronounced social interest. A new generation of CEOs faces different challenges. Fierce foreign and domestic competition are their daily fare. Often there is less time or interest for social concerns."[37]

Local International Constituencies

A trend toward grassroots international activism holds some promise for the development of an active constituency for economic cooperation with developing countries. Civil rights advances have strengthened blacks and other minority groups with natural foreign interests, and the Bureau of the Census reports that one out of every 10 babies born in the United States in 1986 had a foreign-born mother.[38] Chicano businesspeople have supported the idea of closer ties with Mexico and, according to reports, an agency within the Mexican government is pursuing plans to facilitate dialog with Mexicans in the United States.[39] Meanwhile, citizen groups and local governments have begun to speak out more loudly on international issues. In mid-1987, more than 110 cities and 21 countries passed nonbinding resolutions supporting a comprehensive nuclear test ban; 22 cities and two states told local police not to cooperate with the U.S. Immigration and Naturalization Service's efforts to deport immigrants from Latin America; more than 70 cities have begun divesting their assets in companies doing business in South Africa. Virtually every state has an overseas office for trade expansion to increase investment. Not long ago the city council of Davis, California, sent a 16-person fact-finding mission to evaluate U.S. policy toward Nicaragua.[40]

Yet, here too is cause for concern. Minority groups in this country can be expected to behave like any other group if they see their advances erode as a result of foreign competition. Furthermore, it is possible that immigrants will in the next decade find themselves on the defensive about their place in the United States and, therefore, less interested in international issues. However much immigrants enrich the United States, critics may be able to argue that foreign-born women and their families are a drain on the economy, putting strains on social services and encumbering "American" jobs. By one estimate, 5.5 million illegal aliens working for relatively low wages in the United States displace 3.5 million legal workers.[41] As much as U.S. citizens like to talk about being open to the disadvantaged from abroad, waves of nativism have swept across the United States before. Some already worry out loud about high-achieving Asian-Americans dominating academic awards in high schools. The Department of Justice reported a 62 percent increase in violence against Asians between 1985 and 1986. Seventy-one percent of respondents to the ODC-InterAction poll thought "the United States should limit the number of immigrants entering the country because they compete with Americans for jobs."[42]

Grassroots activism does not address the problem of creating new national institutions and initiating processes to cope with a more complex interdependent world—and it may actually hinder the search for solutions. As George Ball has noted, "Our political structure is totally inadequate for a world where technology has assured that capital flows move around without regard to national boundaries."[43] One obvious need is to find ways of working multilaterally, rather than unilaterally and bilaterally, as past periods of self-sufficiency permitted. Local efforts may at times make it more difficult for the country as a whole to cope. Does the country, for instance, get the best deal possible when two states compete for foreign investment? Does the growth of special interests permit leaders to define a coherent strategy in foreign policy?

The United States faces an unresolved dilemma: how to involve citizens while creating a more stable, coherent foreign policy than currently exists.

Global Awareness

Facts about interdependence swirl around the public. Routinely, the government issues reports that spotlight international connections: the annual summary of patents, which has shown growth in the number of foreigners applying for patent protection; the one-time 1988 study describing the Internal Revenue Service's problems monitoring the growing numbers of U.S. citizens working abroad. It is not unusual for *Variety*, the magazine of the entertainment industry, to feature front-page stories reporting that companies produce more films overseas, that the Brazilian record business is booming, and that the New York Latino Festival had grown from a $25,000 one-week event to a 26-day extravaganza involving over $1 million. Even the defrocking of Jimmy Swaggart had its international aspects when in the first days of the episode church leaders announced that the evangelist's television programs would still appear overseas.[44]

It would seem that U.S. citizens could not miss the overwhelming reality that domestic events are tied to events abroad. Yet, even as they talk more and more about "what a small world it is," evidence suggests that they often do not see that these connections converge on *their* lives. Two readership surveys conducted in conjunction with a Society of Professional Journalists' project to improve news coverage of developing countries illustrate the point. In both surveys, one conducted in Hattiesburg, Mississippi, and the other in Richmond, Virginia, readers were asked whether they agreed or disagreed that, with growing interdependence, "what happens in one country influences another country." In both cases, more than 80 percent of respondents agreed. But when asked whether political and social upheavals or economic growth in poorer countries affected Virginians or Mississippians, positive responses were more than 25 to 50 percentage points lower.[45]

The root of the problem is lack of education, which is sustained by the U.S. tradition that relegates foreign affairs far down the list. Shortcomings are only partially reflected in the inability of grade school students to locate the United States, let alone South Vietnam and Egypt, on a global map. Education does not impart specific practical knowledge to help students comprehend foreign connections. According to one study, 61 percent of U.S. business schools do not offer any international courses. According to a 1986 report of the Southern Governors Conference, the U.S. foreign service is the only one in the world that a person can enter without fluency in a foreign language. A National Science Foundation report has lamented that inadequate language training and inadequate study-abroad programs for faculty, students, and professionals have prevented U.S. engineers from learning about and using technological advances in other countries.[46]

The Southern Governors Conference's concerns about the state of international education is a positive sign. But improved education about the world is hardly assured. Sentiment for becoming involved overseas in any kind of activity, including military intervention, may have weakened in recent years. Pollster William Schneider has detected a shift in U.S. attitudes away from internationalism between 1974 and 1978.[47] Thomas L. Hughes, president of the Carnegie Endowment for International Peace, observed in 1986 that internationally minded organizations such as his "are compelled to operate in an American milieu less favorable than at any other time in [the endowment's] history; even in the 1920s, there was confidence that internationalists were riding the wave of the future."[48]

Resources and Power

The federal government lacks the financial resources it once had, a factor that is unlikely to change soon. The pressure on the budget is immense. For the first time in 50 years, liberal Democrats run for office on a platform of fiscal constraint as much as of spending for social programs. The issue is related to interdependence—for instance, the growing foreign trade deficit and dependence on foreign investment to finance the government budget deficit. And this interdependence makes it more difficult than in the past to increase spending on programs for international economic cooperation.

The challenge for the United States may go beyond money to power. In the years after World War II the United States was the undisputed world leader, not least in providing foreign assistance. Despite domestic ambivalence about foreign aid, the United States was the prime mover in the establishment of the IDA, the soft-loan window of the World Bank, and by far the largest bilateral donor. Although it is still powerful, the United States does not dominate in the same way today. Japan is now outdistancing the United States' foreign aid program in absolute dollar terms.[49] At this writing, it is uncertain how the United States will adjust to this shift in global power. One danger seen by some observers is that loss of power will prompt leaders to devote more precious resources to security-related assistance, rather than to development assistance.[50]

The above problems do not predict absolutely what will happen. It is quite possible that a backlash against immigrants will not materialize and that minorities will have a positive impact on U.S. aid to developing countries. It is also possible that the next years will witness a "greening" of the United States in which concern for others develops into a sense of global community. But even the most positive scenario will be tempered by negatives, including the reality of constrained government resources. It cannot be assumed that the old arguments will become more persuasive in the next decade than they have been in the past four.

WHAT CAN BE DONE

The question that faces the United States is not how it can maintain its extraordinary postwar leadership but how it should grow older gracefully, learning to share power and still make a difference. The development aid arena may prove a good test of the United States' ability to manage the much larger international challenges it faces. The specific question is how the United States can build a constituency to support economic assistance programs overseas.

Typically, the response to this question has been to advance campaigns for selling the idea of helping countries overseas. But more than Madison Avenue slogans are required, as public opinion analyst Burns Roper suggested more than a decade ago:

> To develop a public opinion that is positive toward foreign aid would require demonstrating that foreign aid, in addition to what it does for "them," does more for "us" than if the same money were spent at home. It would also require demonstration that the money does get to the right people in the right countries and, further, demonstration that it has gained us valuable allies.[51]

The United States needs a new rationale for economic cooperation with the South—a rationale that makes sense to the public and that responds to the world as it is today. It must articulate why U.S. citizens should care, which is to say it must be in the U.S. interest at the same time that it aims to address development needs overseas. It must be achievable. And it must be seen as of transcendent importance—something that *must* be done, not something that *could* be done.

The creation of a new rationale requires strong leadership both from government and nongovernment sectors. That leadership must be created, in large measure, by development advocates who speak in terms that clearly relate to and draw from voters' priorities. A program that truly resonates with the U.S. citizenery must become part of the normal political process of debate. Although a quick fix is necessary, the only workable answers will come through a long process that enables citizens to reckon their interests overseas—and to decide which of them can be addressed by programs for economic cooperation.

That said, three propositions would define the outlines of a new rationale for economic assistance: that it be (1) self-interested but not selfish; (2) modest but effective; and (3) part of a coherent whole.

1.   "Nations have no friends," Charles de Gaulle once said. "Nations have only interests." While that is true, it does not mean that self-interest cannot be mutual interest. The challenge in developing a new rationale for economic cooperation is to define a set of goals in the United States' interests and in the South's interests. Such a program can and should take the interests of the poor into account, but it must be tied to the urgent concerns of U.S. citizens. As James Russell Lowell observed in the last century, "The masses of any people, however intelligent, are very little moved by abstract principles of humanity and justice, until those principles are interpreted for them by the stinging commentary of some infringement upon their own rights."[52] It is true that more competition has arisen between the North and the South, but interdependence has also opened up the possibility of a much broader definition of mutual interest than in the past. The U.S. public has few commercial reasons for assisting Africa, for instance, where trade will remain modest for some time. But citizens do have other reasons; a common interest in protecting the environment is one. African land is under great strain. The erosion of soil and loss of forests is destroying valuable plants and animals and has an adverse impact on the global atmosphere. An aid program addressing these concerns must look particularly at the poorest in African countries who live on marginal, fragile lands.

2.   The United States must be realistic about what it can do if it hopes to effect substantial change. Any argument for assistance must recognize that financial resources will be limited and that the bilateral program must accordingly be limited in its scope. Spreading assistance over a wide number of sectors will diminish the effectiveness of individual programs and projects. Giving new direction to assistance requires difficult choices to establish priorities. Some development interventions, however important, must be left to others. This is not wholly negative. First, a short list of bilateral development objectives may be easier to explain to U.S. voters than is the shotgun approach that has characterized the program in the past. Second, a short list will allow the United States to concentrate on areas where it has a comparative advantage. One sector that immediately comes to mind is higher education. The United States has long been the world's classroom, something that has both helped developing countries and enriched U.S. educational institutions. Third, by pursuing activities that the United States can do well, development advocates will have a better opportunity to prove to the public that assistance works. Put another way, aid will address Roper's concern that aid is going to the right people. While such economic assistance may not create allies who will always do the United States' political bidding, it will create allies in trade and environmental issues, partnerships that are no less important.

3.   What is needed, above all, is a broad, new foreign policy designed to cope with interdependence. It will not be helpful to see Third World issues

apart from all of foreign policy or to promote developing country issues so vehemently that a new North-South perspective replaces the old East-West point of view. The goal is to find a way of acting on a more complex view of the world, fitting all the pieces together. This broad approach should apply to economic cooperation with developing countries. More than foreign aid is needed. Reduction of trade barriers and greater reliance on multilateral assistance activities are essential as well.[53] Better multilateral coordination, for instance, can promote more effective use of bilateral assistance. Many of the tasks that the United States cannot do alone with its limited resources—debt relief stands out—can be done together with other donors acting through ad hoc groups or through multilateral banking institutions. Just as Japan must learn to be more of a leader in assistance, not only financially but also intellectually, so must the United States learn to be more of a collaborator in its style.

SHAPING THE NEW AGENDA

The shaping a new agenda for economic cooperation with developing countries should be seen as a matter of process. Any number of schemes might foster such an approach, but two broad approaches are worth considering.

First is the need to create a mechanism to assess and manage interdependence. In the mid-1970s, a National Commission on Coping with Interdependence, organized by the Aspen Institute, projected the kind of government structures needed for the closely interlinked world taking shape. Believing that no government agency should see itself "preoccupied with purely 'domestic' issues," the commission suggested that the president's Domestic Council should become the Council on Interdependence.[54] A Council on Interdependence may be too much, too soon, but the proposal offers avenues for thinking about interdependence.

Specifically, the president could call on government departments and agencies to carry out an inventory of their foreign connections, looking especially at the ways foreign decisions affect the business of the bureau and its U.S. constituency. Virtually no part of government, however domestically oriented it might seem, would be exempt. Many agencies already recognize that they have some connections—for example, the Patent Office, as mentioned earlier—but this process would require government bureaus to look at the trends and the implications of the trends, not just to record the connections.

Such a review would have several benefits. It would force the government to examine the full range of its relations with the rest of the world. Just knowing what connections exist would improve policy analysis—including analysis of aid policies. Beyond that, the review could lead to government restructuring that might produce better and more creative management of foreign relations in the executive branch and the Congress. Finally, it would draw U.S. citizens' attention to the need to think internationally—and thereby contribute to the second important approach: education.

With good reason, the Commission on National Challenges in Higher Education in its January 1988 report stressed the need to gear education toward an interdependent world. Improvements in international education are often framed in terms of improving language skills and area studies, both of which are needed. But, as the commission report noted, international education must also reach into "professional schools, particularly those concerned with law, public policy and business."[55] Interdependence cuts across virtually every aspect of life—and across all classroom instruction that presumably prepares young people for life. Thus, art, biology, journalism, medicine, engineering, information services, and hotel management should also have international components.

There is no escaping the fact that government will have to shoulder much of the financial burden for improved education. Political leaders must understand that education is the single most important government expenditure. Even so, there is a role for nongovernment institutions. Corporations have during the past century funneled financial resources to universities to promote the development of new products and stimulate the education of professionals needed in the work place. This same kind of foresight must be directed at international aspects of education through endowments, scholarships, and funding for research. As a president who wants to improve education, George Bush should summon the heads of the largest corporations to his office and ask them to pledge resources for such international education. The government could help reach other business groups by working through business associations.

These approaches are not specific to the Third World. They would not succeed on a grand scale if they were. Nevertheless, there is scope for giving more support to what has come to be called "development education." To date, resources for development education have been much too scant. By far the largest development education underwriter in the United States is USAID, whose annual expenditures have reached a $3 million level. In per capita terms, total U.S. funding—which includes monies from a handful of philanthropic foundations—is far below levels in other industrialized countries. "If a government foundation in the United States were to make $47 million available annually in grants to citizen organizations and educators to increase the awareness of Americans about developing countries," one 1984 study calculated, "its per capita expenditure would correspond to that of Canada."[56] The figure would need to be three times higher to match per capita funding in Sweden or the Netherlands.

Much can go wrong in the implementation of these suggestions. Many leaders still believe that political goals should be the prime objective of development assistance.[57] In addition, the creation of a broad-based self-interest argument is threatened by the power of special interests, all of whom ardently support the idea of helping countries develop but plead most effectively for their own programs.

The features suggested in this chapter for a new rationale are open to criticism on two mutually exclusive grounds: (1) that it is naive to assume that aid will ever have salience beyond a small group of U.S. interests and elites; and (2) that the arguments suggested here are too crudely selfish to be persuasive.[58] But is it not more naive to assume that a stronger constituency will emerge if development experts muddle along with the anodyne arguments that have not convinced the public in the past? And is it not more selfish to assume that the great mass of U.S. citizens, who do not devote their lives to international affairs, should not be shown why it is in their interests to help people overseas?

Does it not make sense to pursue a modest proposal for economic assistance that builds on U.S. interests and the realities of what the United States can sustain financially, in exchange for a program of economic cooperation that makes real development sense overseas?

NOTES

1. Jonathan B. Bingham, *Shirt-Sleeve Diplomacy: Point Four in Action* (New York: John Day, 1954), p. 13.
2. Samuel P. Huntington, "Foreign Aid for What and for Whom," *Foreign Policy* 1 (Winter 1970–1971): 161.
3. For examples see John Maxwell Hamilton and John H. Sullivan, "Penny-Wise, Pork-Foolish," Outlook section, *Washington Post,* 13 September 1987.
4. *Washington Post,* 30 April 1986.
5. Stanley J. Heginbotham, revised by Larry Q. Nowels, "Foreign Aid: The Evolution of U.S. Programs" (Washington, D.C.: Congressional Research Service, 1988), p. 17. These figures exchange economic support funds.
6. John Maxwell Hamilton, "Foreign Aid: Mirror of American Culture," paper given at Michigan State University Symposium on U.S. Development Assistance: Retrospect and Prospects, 1 May 1986; Heginbotham, "Foreign Aid," pp. 22–23. The .24 percent includes economic support fund assistance, such as used to pay for base rights in the Philippines.
7. "The New American Establishment," *U.S. News & World Report,* 8 February 1988.
8. Cable, Bangkok to Washington, D.C., 11390, 8 March 1987.
9. Christine E. Contee, *What Americans Think: Views on Development and U.S.–Third World Relations: A Public Opinion Project of InterAction and the Overseas Development Council* (Washington, D.C., 1987), *passim;* John Morton Blum, *V Was for Victory* (New York: Harcourt Brace Jovanovich, 1976), p. 29.
10. *The Public View of Public Spending* (New York: Conference Board, February

1988).

11. Richard M. Freeland, *The Truman Doctrine and the Origins of McCarthyism* (New York: New York University Press, 1985), p. 96.

12. Robert A. Packenham, *Liberal America and the Third World* (Princeton, NJ: Princeton University Press, 1973), p. 100.

13. *National Security Strategy of the United States* (Washington, D.C.: White House, 1987), p. 6; Charles W. Kegley, Jr., and Eugene R. Wittkopf, "Beyond Reagan: The Future of American Foreign Policy," *Korean Journal of International Studies* 28 (Spring 1987): 110.

14. Packenham, *Liberal America and The Third World*, p. xx. Talk of democratization has also been confusing to the South. For an interesting discussion see Javier Gonzalo Alcalde, *The Idea of Third World Development: Emerging Perspectives in the United States and Britain, 1900–1950* (Lanham, MD: University Press of America, 1987), p. 213.

15. Freeland, *Truman Doctrine and the Origins of McCarthyism*, p. 165.

16. Merle Curti, "American Philanthropy and the National Character," *American Quarterly* 10 (1958): 437.

17. Contee, *What Americans Think*, p. 24.

18. Virginia Ann Hodgkinson and Murray S. Weitzman, *The Charitable Behavior of Americans: A National Survey* (New York: Rockefeller Brothers Fund, 1986), pp. 48–49.

19. Harold A. Bierck, Jr., "The First Instance of U.S. Foreign Aid: Venezuelan Relief in 1812," *Inter-American Economic Affairs* 9 (Summer 1955): 47–59.

20. Alcalde, *Idea of Third World Development*, p. 6.

21. Charles A. Beard and Mary R. Beard, *America in Midpassage* (New York: Macmillan, 1939), p. 94.

22. Richard W. Van Alstyne, *The Rising American Empire* (New York: Oxford University Press, 1960), p. 129.

23. Chamber of Commerce Trade and Aid Working Group, "Trade & Aid: A New Foreign Assistance Focus," 15 June 1987 (emphasis added).

24. Contee, *What Americans Think*, p. 24.

25. Isaac Asimov, *A Choice of Catastrophes* (London: Hutchinson, 1980), pp. 219–225.

26. Trade data are found in Peter J. Katzenstein, "International Interdependence: Some Long-Term Trends and Recent Changes," *International Organization* 29 (Autumn 1975): 1032; *United States Trade: Performance in 1985 and Outlook* (Washington, D.C.: Department of Commerce, 1966), pp. 5, 27–37; David Wessel, *Wall Street Journal,* 9 February 1988.

27. Felix Rohatyn, "Restoring American Independence," *New York Review of Books,* 8 February 1988, p. 8.

28. For a more detailed discussion of different ways interdependence manifests itself in the lives of U.S. citizens, see John Maxwell Hamilton, *Main Street America and the Third World* (Cabin John, MD: Seven Locks Press, 1986).

29. James R. Donald, "World and U.S. Agricultural Outlook" (Washington, D.C.: USDA, 1 December 1987), p. 11; Pat Choate and J. K. Linger, *The High-Flex Society: Shaping America's Economic Future* (New York: Knopf, 1986), p. 53.

30. Peter F. Drucker, "The Changed World Economy," *Foreign Affairs* 64 (Spring 1986): 777.

31. John Meehan, *International Herald Tribune,* 20–21 February 1988; *The Forgotten Half: Non-College Youth in America* (Washington, D.C.: William T. Grant Foundation Commission on Work, Family and Citizenship, 1988), p. 20.

32. "The New Volunteerism," *Newsweek* (8 February 1988): 42–43.

33. Daniel Yankelovich, *New Rules: Searching for Self-Fulfillment in a World Turned Upside Down* (New York: Random House, 1981), pp. 246–248, 261.

34. *Ibid.,* p. 264 (emphasis added).

35. Private contributions are from *OECD Development Cooperation 1984 Review* and *1975 Review.*

36. Alexander W. Astin, *et al., The American Freshman: National Norms for Fall 1987* (Los Angeles: Higher Education Research Institute, 1987), p. 7.

37. Anne Klepper, *Corporation Contributions Outlook* Bulletin No. 204 (New York: Conference Board Research, 1987), p. 3.

38. *Fertility of American Women: June 1986* (Washington, D.C.: Government Printing Office, 1986).

39. Rodolfo O. de la Garza, "Chicanos and U.S. Foreign Policy: The Future of Chicano-Mexican Relations," *Western Political Quarterly* 33 (December 1980): 571–582; Dianna Solis and Alfredo Corchado, *Wall Street Journal,* 4 January 1988.

40. Michael H. Shuman, "Dateline Main Street: Local Foreign Policies," *Foreign Policy* 65 (Winter 1986–1987): 154–174; Peter Spiro, "Get States and Cities off Foreign-Policy Stage," *Wall Street Journal,* 24 September 1986; Jeff Aberbach, *Davis Enterprise,* 24 May 1984; John Pomfret, AP dispatch in Rochester, NY, *Democrat and Chronicle,* 28 June 1987.

41. Choate and Linger, *High-Flex Society,* p. 37.

42. *Wall Street Journal,* 7 April 1989; Contee, *What Americans Think,* p. 20.

43. *New York Times,* 24 January 1988.

44. *Variety,* 20 August 1986.

45. John Mauro, "Readers Care," appendix, in Hamilton, *Main Street America and the Third World.*

46. *Wall Street Journal,* 30 June 1987; Tom Peters, *U.S. News & World Report,* 3 March 1986; *Washington Post,* 22 November 1986; National Academy of Engineering, *Strengthening U.S. Engineering through International Cooperation: Some Recommendations for Action* (Washington, D.C.: National Academy of Engineering, 1987), p. 6.

47. William Schneider, "Conservatism, Not Interventionism: Trends in Foreign Policy Opinion, 1974–1982," in *Eagle Defiant: United States Foreign Policy in the 1980s,* ed. Kenneth A. Oye, Robert J. Lieber, and Donald Rothchild (Boston: Little, Brown, 1983), p. 45.

48. Thomas L. Hughes, "The Twilight of Internationalism," *Foreign Policy* 61 (Winter, 1985–1986): 25–48.

49. Nancy G. Morrison, *The Price of Success: Japan Pressed to Boost Third World Aid* (Washington, D.C.: Bretton Woods Committee, 1988).

50. Robert O. Keohane and Joseph S. Nye, Jr., *"Power and Interdependence* Revisited," *International Organization* 41 (August 1987): 725–726.

51. Burns Roper, "The Limits of Public Support," *Annals of the American Academy of Political and Social Science* 442 (March 1979): 45.

52. James Russell Lowell "Abraham Lincoln," in *Harvard Classics: Essays (English*

and American) 28 (New York: Colliers, 1910), p. 447.

53. For a useful discussion, see John W. Sewell and Christine E. Contee, "Foreign Aid and Gramm-Rudman," *Foreign Affairs* 65 (Summer 1987): 1015–1036.

54. Adam Yarmolinsky, "Organizing for Interdependence: The Role of Government," Interdependence Series No. 5 (Aspen, CO: Aspen Institute for Humanistic Studies, 1976).

55. Commission on National Challenges in Higher Education, *Memorandum to the 41st President of the United States* (Washington, D.C.: American Council on Education, 1988), p. 1.

56. Lynn Randels, *Overcoming Isolation through Development Education: Lessons for the United States from Canada, Sweden, and the Netherlands* (Washington, D.C.: Global Education Fund Project, 1984), pp. 3–4.

57. For examples of this point of view, see Richard Nixon, "6 Ways to Compete with the U.S.S.R.," *New York Times Magazine,* 13 March 1988, p. 28; Samuel P. Huntington, "Coping With the Lippmann Gap," *Foreign Affairs* 66 (America and the World Edition, 1987–1988): 469; Nicholas Eberstadt, *Foreign AID and American Purpose* (Washington, D.C.: American Enterprise Institute, 1988), *passim.*

58. Everett Carll Ladd, "American Opinion on Issues of Foreign Assistance" (mimeographed, n.d.), p. 83.

PART THREE

Implementing
U.S. Development
Cooperation Activities

ELEVEN

U.S. Coordination of Economic and Development Cooperation Policies

MAURICE J. WILLIAMS

Coordination within or among governments essentially is a process of consultation among parties concerned with a common objective. It is a process that is applied for different purposes: For example, it may occur at various stages in the identification of problems, in collection and analysis of information to illuminate alternative approaches, and in agreement on specific policy responses; it may prove useful for the formulation of program proposals, for mobilizing the necessary financial and organizational support, and for building understanding for implementation. Thus, coordination can take place at the level of problem-solving and policy formation, as well as at the level of program execution.

Coordination also is a means for ensuring coherence among similar or related programs, or among agencies concerned. It can serve as a means of communication and education, or of control.

However, coordination arrangements cannot meaningfully be discussed without a prior understanding of the central policy objectives being served. It is also true that coordination arrangements within the U.S. government tend to be most highly elaborated in areas of central policy concern. But, are the central policy concerns of the United States for the 1990s likely to be the same as those of the past decade? If major changes are likely to take place, how would they affect the organizational and coordinating structures of government?

CHANGING CIRCUMSTANCES
AND ECONOMIC POLICY COORDINATION

Since the early 1970s, strategic thinkers and planners have concluded that there has been an acceleration of change toward an interdependent world economy and a lessening of U.S. dominance relative to other centers of industrial production. It is alleged that these trends require greater coordination of economic policies both within and among national governments for more effective management of the world economy.

There also has been growing concern with a range of functional problems that reflect increased interdependence and a need for concerted action among nations. These problems are predominantly but not wholly economic, encompassing also world population growth, poverty, environmental degradation, natural resource depletion, control of infectious diseases, drug and narcotic abuse, and security of international travel. Means for addressing these issues often call into question the effectiveness of existing governmental arrangements.

A report issued by the ODC in 1977 foresaw a possible "shift in relative emphasis in international politics from the traditional politico-military security to the interdependence issues," and a consequent need for restructuring the U.S. government in order to deal more effectively with them.[1]

Much has been written about the emerging problems of interdependence, of the profound changes caused by continuous economic growth over the past 40 years, of the effects of the technological revolution, of the transition to postindustrial modes of production, of integrated financial markets, of multinational enterprises, and of the expansion of international trade.

Yet the phenomenon of economic interdependence and its evolving effects on national institutions and policies is not well understood. While some believe that new institutional arrangements are necessary for management of the growing interdependence among nations, for the most part the vision of change has remained partial and selective; existing political structures have perpetuated national concern with traditional diplomatic and military issues.

Recognition of interdependence by the advanced industrial countries and of its implications for national economic policies initially arose from the necessity for a collective response to the oil shocks of the 1970s, and to the ensuing demands by developing countries for a new international economic order. The events led to annual summit meetings among the seven advanced industrial countries. Until recently, these summit meetings and consultations for their preparation were the main new institutional response for the management of economic interdependence.

Since the mid-1980s, there has been an intensification of informal economic policy consultation among the seven industrial countries on a number of increasingly serious problems affecting their economies and the level of world economic activity. These include the persistent imbalances of the trade deficits and surpluses among several of the leading countries, the rise of protectionist trade measures, destabilizing fluctuations of exchange rates, and the debt and insolvency of many developing countries.

While a conceptual framework for managing global interdependence has yet to emerge, some new principles of economic cooperation appear to have gained acceptance at least among the industrial countries: economic prosperity for North America, Europe, and Japan is closely interlinked; inflation is best contained at relatively lower and stable levels of economic growth; and a flexible system of consultation is vital in order to ensure sufficient "harmonization" of the national economic policies of the leading countries for maintenance of the main equilibriums affecting their economic well-being.

The approach of the industrial countries has favored pragmatic solutions that deal mainly with the problem of economic interdependence among themselves. Other countries are expected to adjust to the resulting policy orientations.

For developing countries, interdependence in the 1980s has meant adjustment to lower levels of economic growth and world trade as well as the management of their external debt problems. Despite an unprecedented effort under way in international and financial agencies to influence economic policy changes in many developing nations, economic prospects for much of the developing world in the years ahead are gloomy.

Most international organizations have now been marginalized in terms of the broader problems affecting the world economy. For example, the United Nations is looked to by the major countries only for necessary but limited tasks, in areas such as human rights, environmental concerns, refugees, famine relief, and—more recently—for Security Council assistance in settlement of regional disputes. The Bretton Woods institutions have focused on enhancing the capacity of developing countries to pay and grow out of their debts.

Thus, changing world circumstances have brought recognition of a much closer economic interdependence among the key industrial countries, an interdependence that will require their foreign and domestic economic policies to be more coordinated than they have been in the past. In particular, the large imbalance-of-trade-and-payments deficit of the United States, its dependence on international borrowing, and the external surpluses of Japan and the Federal Republic of Germany will demand greater attention by the U.S. government to foreign economic–policy issues.

Much less understood is how far the resolution of the trade problems and large imbalances among the advanced industrial countries is dependent on the economic health of developing regions. In particular, the best means for the United States to reduce its large external trade deficit is by expansion of markets in Third World countries—which account for one-third of U.S. exports. These markets have been constrained by the overly heavy burden of debt repayments that have dampened their prospects of economic growth. The industrial countries are now receiving some $30 billion annually more in repayments on past loans than developing countries are receiving in new capital.

During the past year, a number of leaders of industrial countries have come to the conclusion that lightening the burden of Third World debt would, in a manner similar to the effects of tax reductions in industrial countries, stimulate growth of investment, production, and trade, and actually enhance debt-repayment capabilities over time. For example, it is estimated that a 30 percent reduction in developing country debt servicing—selectively applied—would stimulate $50 billion to $100 billion in increased industrial country exports to Third World markets, and that the United States would be the principal beneficiary, given current foreign exchange and market conditions.

Imperatives of U.S. Foreign Economic Policy in the 1990s

The growing economic strength of other key industrial countries, dramatized by the United States' dependence on them for the financing of its large trade deficit and high external debt, will require the closest attention of the U.S. government to economic security concerns in the management of its foreign and domestic economic policies. Economic security is now the first-line U.S. defense. The government must retain both the confidence and cooperation of the other key industrial countries to avoid a sharp fall in the dollar and a contraction of international finance and trade that could tip the U.S. and world economies into deep recession.

Adjustment of the U.S. trade imbalance—short of recession—depends on concerted action to expand developing country markets. This heightened economic interdependence means that the United States will have to adjust its economic and development cooperation policies in a framework of concerted action with other key governments. Hence, close cooperation between the Congress and the Bush administration, and improved coordination, will be imperative.

The administration and Congress will face four major international economic issues:

1. By the early 1990s, the foreign debt of the United States will have risen to $1 trillion. This debt build-up must be slowed down and reversed. But even while this is being done, several hundred billion dollars of external financing will be necessary to cover the continuing deficit in foreign trade and interest payments.
2. U.S. economic policies must be oriented to improving the international trade and competitive position of the United States.
3. Improving the trade balance of the United States will depend heavily on both improved coordination of the major industrial countries' policies concerning their trade and foreign exchange regimes and on adopting means for dealing more effectively with the financial needs and debt problems of developing countries. U.S. policy requires a more differentiated approach to developing countries about trade, finance, and aid issues.

4. A number of the global interdependence issues—the environment, drugs, AIDS, and degrading poverty—are becoming increasingly serious and will require greater attention on the development agenda.

Coordination of Development Cooperation

The overwhelming concentration of U.S. policy in recent years on military and geopolitical issues has meant that many of the economic problems of the Third World have not engaged priority attention. Rather, the countries of the Third World have been seen as a zone for strategic and military competition between the United States and the Soviet Union, as well as areas of economic, cultural, and ideological rivalry.

This competition has taken the form of support for friendly Third World governments through military and economic assistance, efforts to destabilize countries in the opposite camp, and direct and indirect support for parties opposed in internal domestic conflicts. The intensification of East-West rivalry in developing regions has brought about a substantial redirection of U.S. economic cooperation policies toward military and security objectives.

Of the $13 billion of U.S. budget authority for foreign aid in 1987, almost $9 billion was for military and security assistance. In contrast, the USAID administered only about $2 billion for strictly development objectives. This does not include PL-480 food assistance, which added another $1 billion. Given their heavy emphasis on the military and security purposes of foreign aid, the Reagan and Bush administrations have been better organized to achieve coordination in this area than to focus on critical foreign economic and development problems.

Coordination of foreign assistance by the Department of State. The principal vehicle for overall coordination of foreign aid programs has been a process, organized by the undersecretary of state for security assistance, science, and technology, focusing upon annual aid budgets. The process is initiated by the secretary of state, who provides general program guidance to the relevant agencies that outline strategic objectives and funding targets for each area of the globe.

Objectives and targets of the review process cover all foreign aid—military assistance, foreign military sales, economic support funds, development assistance, PL-480, and contribution to multilateral agencies. Objectives for U.S. bilateral programs are defined on a country-by-country basis. Appeals for modifications to the funding guidance are dealt with by the undersecretary and, if necessary, by the secretary of state, who may consult with the secretary of defense.

On the basis of the funding targets, interagency country reviews for military assistance, foreign military sales, and economic support funds are conducted under the direction of the State Department's Bureau of Politico-Military Affairs. Parallel reviews for development assistance, PL-480, and economic support funds are conducted by USAID. Participating agencies in these reviews include those relevant to the process, principally the departments of Defense, Treasury, and Agriculture, and the Office of Management and Budget (OMB). The results of these reviews are checked for overall coherence and consistency with the initial policy guidance by the undersecretary of state.

While development considerations are said to be part of the State Department's reviews "to the maximum extent feasible"—particularly for economic support funds—descriptions of the review process by those directly concerned indicate that security considerations are dominant. Aid levels are, for the most part, viewed as being determined by base agreements, military objectives, and perceptions of communist threats. Following this budget process, the undersecretary manages the presentations to the Congress and subsequent adjustments in the allocations among countries and the specific conditions under which aid is provided.

The State Department's coordination process is well designed to relate aid resources to U.S. national security goals. However, national security goals have been narrowly conceived, with an overemphasis on politicomilitary security at the expense of the economic aspects of national security. This appears to be a result of the central policy concentration on the large military build-up and the relative neglect of the basic economic underpinnings of the U.S. position in the world.

What is needed is a fundamental rethinking of U.S. national security interests in the Third World countries of Asia, Africa, and Latin America, one that will achieve a better balance between military and security concerns, on the one hand, and the concerns of foreign economic and development policy, on the other.

Coordination by the Department of the Treasury. While the State Department has been preeminent in calling the shots for coordination of bilateral economic assistance, it is the Treasury Department that has had the lead recently for foreign economic policy, including Third World debt and multilateral aid.

Given budgetary pressures, the United States will need to emphasize burden-sharing among the advanced industrial countries in order to resolve the debt problems and meet the important capital requirements of the developing countries. The immediate economic and trade objectives of the United States require the mobilization of large capital flows to restore the financial stability and economic growth of the middle-income developing countries. The longer-term development of low-income countries also requires additional assistance. These needs can best be met by enhanced burden-sharing through the World Bank and the three regional MDBs for Asia, Latin America, and Africa.

Active participation in the multilateral banks has been a key element of U.S. economic policy for several decades and is likely to remain so in the

1990s. The Reagan administration initially called for a shift away from the MDBs in favor of bilateral programs but later abandoned that position in favor of greater support for the banks. The World Bank has been lending $15 billion annually, and, with completion of the current efforts to approve its capital increase, its position is likely to be more important in the future.

In channeling an increased proportion of assistance through the banks, the U.S. government has necessarily accepted reduced control over precisely how those resources are used and acknowledged that its influence will be used with discretion on broad policy issues of priority. For example, in addition to facilitating burden-sharing, the MDBs help to influence countries toward market-oriented policies and away from an inefficient emphasis on state planning. The banks have promoted structural adjustment and policy reforms that closely parallel the views of the U.S. administration.

U.S. influence over MDBs' policies and programs is primarily through formal policy and project reviews by the banks' executive directors, informal contacts with senior staff, and, most important, changes agreed upon during the periodic negotiations for funding replenishments. The Treasury Department's priorities in seeking to influence the banks' policies are often determined by the need to gain congressional support.

The secretary of the treasury has the authority to appoint and instruct the U.S. executive directors to the MDBs. In the past, the Treasury Department coordinated U.S. policies toward the banks, and financial matters generally, through the interagency Council on International Monetary and Financial Policies, which it chairs and staffs. In recent times, however, Treasury has come to rely more on meetings of the Senior Interagency Group for International Economic Policy (SIG-IEP), which it also chairs. SIG-IEP is little concerned with development issues, and USAID is not a member.

USAID as coordinator. U.S. bilateral economic assistance has been squeezed for funding between the high-priority security assistance programs governed by the Department of State and U.S. appropriations for the important programs of the MDBs. Increasingly, USAID has focused its direct activities on institution-building, training, and generating applicable technologies in agriculture, education, health, family planning, natural resources, and protection of the environment for low-income countries.

USAID coordinates a number of development cooperation efforts with the legal authority it inherited from the International Development Cooperation Agency (IDCA) and from the interagency Development Coordination Committee (DCC). This committee has interagency subcommittees on bilateral assistance, multilateral assistance, food aid, the development programs of the international organizations, human rights, food and agricultural programs, and international health programs—coordination structures that were authorized by Congress in 1973 (the Humphrey bill) and further elaborated by presidential directives in 1978.

IDCA was set up in 1978 as an independent government agency whose director—with a small staff of 30—had lead responsibility for U.S. policy and budget for USAID, the Overseas Private Investment Corporation, the UN development programs, and a trade coordination group. Opposition from the Treasury Department and other agencies prevented IDCA from assuming similar responsibilities for all U.S. bilateral and multilateral assistance, as had been initially proposed.

The director of IDCA replaced the USAID administrator as chair of the DCC, with essentially the same responsibilities for interagency coordination. He was to advise the Treasury Department on appointments of U.S. executive directors for the MDBs and on the "developmental" aspects of bank projects and policies. A potentially significant new responsibility for the IDCA director was to advise the secretary of state and the president on "all trade, science and technology, and other matters significantly affecting the developing nations."

The coordination authority of IDCA, though greatly reduced from initial congressional intention, was resented by State, USAID, and Treasury, which favored a more consensual style of interagency coordination. Consequently, in the transition to the Reagan administration the position of acting director of IDCA was assumed by the new USAID administrator, and the IDCA staff was not replaced. Some of IDCA's residual coordination activities are assumed by USAID's Office of Program Policy and Coordination.

Thus, IDCA continues to exist legally, and the interagency structure of the DCC, with its large array of specialized subcommittees, is still in place, but these groups seldom meet. Interagency working groups are set up from time to time to deal with special problems, and the groups on PL-480 and multilateral aid remain active.

USAID has made a sustained effort to improve the relationship between its own activities and those of the MDBs. Multilateral bank project reviews are conducted through the interagency Working Group on Multilateral Assistance. USAID has made efforts to obtain the views of its country desks and field missions on proposed multilateral bank projects and to relate them to USAID activities. This process is said to encourage more informal communications between USAID and bank staffs. USAID also has participated in the bank-replenishment meetings, contributing to and clearing briefing positions for the U.S. delegation and often attending the international meetings.

This coordination process has offered opportunities for USAID to seek changes in multilateral bank policies that seem at variance with USAID views on conditions for structural reforms. However, the agency is finding it increasingly difficult to influence World Bank country policies since the recent closer cooperation between the bank and IMF on their joint policy-framework papers on structural adjustment conditions and assistance for individual developing countries.

The special trade representative and trade coordination. The influence of the U.S. trade representative has become ever more dominant in coordination of international trade policy, though the State Department continues to be an important actor. Because U.S. policy on trade and investment is largely motivated by global considerations, it is difficult to coordinate such policy with USAID, whose activities tend to be country-specific. Consequently, USAID—despite its enhanced authority through IDCA—remains a minor actor in trade and investment issues.

AREAS OF DIFFUSED INTERAGENCY RESPONSIBILITY

Areas in which departmental responsibilities appear to be diffused among several agencies in terms of coordination between U.S. domestic and foreign concerns include public health, the environment, and natural resource issues. Legally, it could be said that the administrator of USAID, in his capacity as acting director of IDCA, has this responsibility. However, as previously noted, these coordination responsibilities have been selectively pursued in relation to USAID's program interests.

The Department of State functions intermittently as a coordinator in these areas, both in terms of budget responsibilities for U.S. contributions to the functional entities of the United Nations and under the aegis of the undersecretary of security, science, and technology for international negotiations on scientific issues.

Domestic line agencies are involved in advising on international issues and programs in such fields as health, drugs, and on environmental and natural resource issues. They work directly with the international organizations concerned with these fields, with USAID when funds for overseas programs are involved, and with the State Department in areas of negotiating internationally agreed standards.

Improving intragovernmental coordination can greatly enhance the impact of the U.S. government's foreign assistance programs in specific sectoral areas. The organizational problems, however, are considerable. Three leading environmental problems are explored below to demonstrate the relatively limited coordination efforts now in place and to highlight the opportunities for drawing more heavily on the experience and technical expertise in the domestic line agencies.

It is widely accepted that a variety of critical environmental problems are not bounded by local or national borders and require global solutions. The state of play of the U.S. government's activities relating to biological diversity, pesticide use, and global warming illustrate the fragmented lines of authority, oversight, and coordination on international environmental matters. In addition, except where U.S. domestic interests are directly involved, many domestic line agencies have neither the budget nor the mandate to address these concerns.

The protection and maintenance of *global biological diversity* has been of long-standing interest to Congress, the executive branch, and the international policymaking community. While the United States has passed landmark legislation and adhered to several international agreements concerned with biodiversity, policy and program approaches have traditionally been piecemeal. Past efforts have tended to be region-specific or to emphasize the protection of particular endangered species.

USAID plays the leading role in the U.S. government's biodiversity efforts abroad, but several other government agencies are also involved—among them, the Peace Corps, the Forest Service (part of the Department of Agriculture [USDA]), Fish and Wildlife and National Park services (Department of the Interior), the Department of Commerce, and the Smithsonian Institution. With a new authorization from Congress, USAID began a Biological Diversity Program in 1987 of roughly $5 million, additional to the $82 million in bilateral and food assistance provided for tropical forestry programs. However, the congressional mandate for the five-year-old interagency task force on biological diversity headed by USAID has ended, and the group has not met for over a year. Collaboration between USAID and domestic agencies is now on an ad hoc basis initiated principally by the environmental coordinators at USAID's regional bureaus. Much greater efforts could be made to maximize the talent pool available at domestic agencies such as the Forest or National Park services.

The State Department's Bureau of Oceans and International Environmental and Scientific Affairs (OES) recently resuscitated the interagency group on tropical forests, but this task force lacks a clear mandate and is mainly involved in exchanging information. Policy and program responses government-wide in scope and matched by the necessary resources will be needed to better coordinate the government's international efforts in this critical area. In addition, existing international agreements with respect to biodiversity need much more vigorous enforcement by domestic agencies.

The United States' *international pesticide policies* have recently come under strong attack by the environmental community. In the case of the Mediterranean fruit fly–eradication program in Guatemala, which is jointly implemented by USDA and USAID with PL-480 funds, conflicts arose between the two agencies over pesticide regulations and environmental review procedures. The program involved the use of controversial pesticides, including a known carcinogen banned in the United States. In addition, USDA's environmental-impact assessment did not meet the stricter review standards of USAID. When the two agencies failed to resolve their disputes, the matter was directed to the NSC, which ruled that funds could not be disbursed until a more thorough assessment was conducted and the program met the requirements of USAID's pesticide regulations.

Other U.S. government agencies implement projects that affect the use of pesticides and other chemicals in developing countries, including the Overseas Private Investment Corporation, the National Institute for Occupational Safety and Health, and the Environmental Protection Agency (EPA). Each government agency, according to executive order 12114, maintains its own environmental review procedures for overseas projects. The lack of coordination and conflicting regulatory standards, according to a recent report, "cost[s] time and money for the U.S. government [and] undermine[s] the United States' ability to encourage other donors to adopt environmental policies." The report also stressed that greater coordination is especially important to address urban pollution and industrial chemical problems faced by NICs.[2]

Fragmented policy approaches also characterize the government's response thus far to *global climate change*—perhaps the greatest environmental challenge humans may ever face. Scientists generally agree that it will take at least a decade to understand the effects of global warming. The administration has emphasized the need for research before making changes in its current energy policy, but mounting international and national pressure is forcing the United States to play a more active role in this area.

The Global Climate Protection Act of 1987 directs the EPA to work with the Department of State in developing a national policy by 1990. Its Interagency Committee on Global Change, however, has proved to be a nonstarter because the EPA lacks the needed authority for such coordination efforts and is not generally perceived to be a leader on scientific issues. Instead, much of the activity in this area is taking place in the Interagency Committee on Earth Sciences, which was convened by the White House Office of the Science Advisor and is chaired by the U.S. Geological Survey. Although its mandate is somewhat unclear, this interagency committee is coordinating the government's research efforts. The committee also formulated a position paper reviewed by the Domestic Policy Council for the U.S. delegation attending the World Meteorological Organization and the UN Environmental Program conference on global warming in October 1988.

One option for addressing the current fragmentation of policymaking and program implementation on international environmental matters is to give the White House's Council on Environmental Quality (CEQ) a stronger leadership role. The initial activities of the CEQ focused on domestic matters and the enforcement of the National Environmental Protection Act. The increasingly international scope of environmental problems, however, led the CEQ to expand its role. Its 1980 study, *The Global 2000 Report to the President: Entering the 21st Century*, was a timely reference on current international environmental concerns.

A new and expanded CEQ could play a valuable role in developing strategies to tackle global environmental problems. More specifically, the council should have the capacity to perform technical and policy studies, to develop government-wide environmental programs, to identify inconsistent implementation of environmental policies among U.S. government agencies operating overseas, and to call attention to long-range trends such as global warming.

A second option in the environmental arena is to strengthen the State Department's OES. Currently, OES is staffed largely by foreign service officers who lack the technical skills and authority for directing international environmental policy across government agencies or for spearheading research efforts among the scientific community.

OPTIONS FOR IMPROVING COORDINATION

Historically, coordination arrangements within the U.S. government tend to be most highly elaborated in areas of past central policy concern, such as politicomilitary security. It is difficult, perhaps impossible, to legislate policy attention and priorities for an unenthusiastic executive branch by elaborating complex structures of coordination. The IDCA experience illustrates this lesson. If Congress would improve coordination within the executive branch, it must first address, with the administration, the substance of policy priorities—for coordination is the handmaiden of policy, not its master.

The world and U.S. interests have been changing in ways almost certain to call for changes of emphasis in U.S. central policy concerns, and a consequent change in coordination arrangements. Among these changes is likely to be a far greater concern with economic and development policy issues and with developing regions as they affect the U.S. position in the world economy.

The new concerns have been well summarized by Arthur Schlesinger, Jr.:

> The decline in American competitiveness in world markets, our economy's growing dependence on injections of foreign capital, America's precarious position as the world No. 1 debtor nation—all these developments make us more vulnerable economically than ever before.
>
> Ecological and biological threats surge across national frontiers: acid rain, ozone depletion, pollution of the seas, the greenhouse effect, drugs, AIDS—all enlarge our national security agenda. Familiar problems remain (the Russians, the nuclear arms race, regional conflicts) but striking new possibilities emerge—above all for negotiation on a multitude of issues with the surprising new leadership in Moscow.[3]

There is need for an overall coordinating mechanism within the U.S. government to ensure policy and program coherence among the several instruments concerned with foreign economic policy and assistance. As previously mentioned, these include U.S. resources to the multilateral development banks backstopped by the U.S. Treasury, UN economic agencies backstopped by the International Organization, Bureau of Department of State, PL-480 aid administered by the USDA, the politically driven security assistance governed by the State Department, and U.S. economic development assistance administered by USAID. Additionally, there is need to orchestrate these programs in relation to U.S. trade, finance, and investment policies.

While organizational arrangements are best discussed within the context of objectives, it may be useful to postulate four broad organizational options in the areas of economic policy and development cooperation.

Treasury-Based Coordination

The power of the Treasury Department with respect to foreign economic policy has been growing for a long time, while the power of the State Department has been declining. As an institution, the Treasury Department inspires confidence in domestic and international financial circles and hence among many in Congress. In part, this is because Treasury tends to be unsympathetic to governmental interventions in the economy and to resist programs involving additional governmental expenditures.

The advantage of a Treasury-based coordination system is that it reflects present power realities and builds on the agency with the strongest economic policy expertise, as well as with the closest connections to private and international financial institutions.

However, the Treasury Department tends to see most issues in technical and financial terms. It lacks a core of development expertise and relies too heavily on analyses by the multilateral institutions. Hence, its disadvantage as a central coordinator of U.S. international economic policy is that it has too narrow a view to encompass foreign policy or broader development considerations. Nor is Treasury well positioned to deal with the trade, investment, and bilateral aid issues that affect U.S. interests in Third World development.

The State Department as Coordinator

The geostrategic orientation of the State Department and its concentration on security affairs has been matched by a decline of its influence in economic policy. The undersecretary for economic affairs, while playing a relatively limited role in budget formation and bilateral development programs, has generally followed trade, economic summit issues, commodity agreements, the multilateral institutions, and State's relations with Treasury.

The principal disadvantage of the State Department as a central economic policy coordinator is its long-standing traditional view of foreign policy, which downgrades the importance of economic policy issues. It would be difficult for the State Department to correct the imbalance of attention placed on political and security affairs in favor of more attention to such Third World economic issues as new responses to the debt crisis, problems of poorer countries, and domestic issues affecting U.S. trade performance.

In part, the State Department's stance of avoiding involvement in controversial international economic issues that engage domestic constituencies is defensive. The State Department lacks a constituency; its position in Congress and in public opinion is therefore inherently difficult, and its authority on issues of domestic concerns is frequently suspect and inescapably limited.

Reviving the IDCA Approach to Coordination

It would be possible to breathe new life into IDCA as a central policy staff and coordinating mechanism for linking international economic and development policies, as well as the range of interdependence issues. The legal authorities and interagency structure are all in place. This would require a new policy of greater emphasis on these issues and appointment of a prominent and well-qualified director of a newly constituted IDCA policy staff.

The disadvantage of this approach is that IDCA has been too closely associated with USAID and, earlier, was unable to establish its own identity because the key departments refused to cede or share authority with a subcabinet agency. An attempt to revive IDCA mainly to coordinate USAID as it did in the past would probably fail and would certainly fall far short of what is needed.

Coordination Directed by the White House

A strong case can be made that policies and programs affecting important U.S. economic interests with the developing countries can most effectively be coordinated from the White House: First, effective interagency coordination is less likely when the responsibility for coordination is lodged within any one of the participating or interested agencies; second, as international economic policy is increasingly politicized—at home and abroad—only the White House has the political authority to speak on these issues.

An international economic and development policy coordinating body within the president's executive staff is highly desirable. This could be achieved either by giving these issues weight equal to political issues in the NSC or by creating a separate structure modeled after the NSC. In either case, a person with experience in both domestic and international economic policies and with access to, and the confidence of, the president should be appointed as coordinator of economic policy and development. This person should be the chair of an interagency committee concerned with international economic and development policies and programs, be a member of all cabinet-level groups that address domestic economic policy, and have a close working relationship with the NSC staff to ensure coordination with foreign policy. International economic and development policy and its coordination with domestic policies would then attain the prominence its importance to national security interests fully warrants—an importance at least comparable to that of defense policy.

THE ROLE OF USAID

Whatever the structure chosen to improve the coordination of U.S. international economic and development policies, a successful outcome will depend in part on the ability of the U.S. bilateral aid agency to convey to the coordinating body sound and informed policy advice on the implications of international economic and development programs and policies for the Third World and the United States.

USAID could be in a better position to respond effectively to these requirements if it were restructured and given a new mandate. The essential reform would be an administrative separation of assistance for military and security objectives—which would be administered by the State Department—from assistance programs that address longer-term global and human development problems. Programs in this latter category would focus U.S. leadership and technology in concerted international efforts to eliminate poverty and sustain the environment.

Specifically, a restructured bilateral aid agency would need three capabilities:

1. A senior policy staff would be charged with advising the White House coordinating body on the development impact and implications of broader economic policies, particularly in the areas of trade and finance but also in environmental questions, and advising on the effectiveness of bilateral and multilateral aid programs in meeting U.S. interests.
2. A small staff would work on strengthening policy and program linkages between U.S. private institutions and middle-income countries that do not receive U.S. development assistance.
3. A capacity is needed to implement assistance projects in low-income countries, incorporating USAID's existing competence in field operations, particularly in Africa, Central America, and the Caribbean.

The new development entity would expand the engagement of U.S. private agencies in the development effort, especially for research and training by private companies, universities, and voluntary agencies. It is within these institutions that U.S. comparative advantage for development lies.

The director of the development entity would report to the White House coordinating structure for international economic and development policies and would be a full member of this White House coordinating group.

A reorganization of USAID along these lines and a stronger role by the State Department in foreign economic policy could provide a useful countervailing influence to the Treasury Department's dominant and overly narrow focus on the financial aspects of economic policy. In any case, more purposeful White House direction of foreign economic and development policy is required. New and improved coordination systems should be considered as a component of new policy directions. Without policy changes a redirection of coordination arrangements will not go very far.

NOTES

1. Robert Johnson, *Managing Interdependence: Restructuring the U.S. Government,* ODC Development Paper No. 23 (Washington, D.C.: February 1977).
2. *Report of the Committee on Health and Environmental Opportunities to Assist Developing Countries in the Proper Use of Agricultural and Industrial Chemicals,* prepared for AID by the Committee on Health and Environment and the Conservation Foundation (Washington, D.C.: 18 February 1988), p. 81. Unpublished.
3. *New York Times,* 25 August 1988.

TWELVE

USAID: Organizational and Institutional Issues and Effectiveness

ALLAN HOBEN

This chapter is about the fit between USAID as an institution and its task. It is concerned with the way that USAID's organization, procedures, personnel system, incentive structure, and informal work roles affect its capacity to support balanced agricultural and rural development in the LDCs. It is biased toward Africa because of my experience and because that is the region in which USAID faces the greatest challenge today. It is also biased toward development projects rather than nonproject assistance, long-term training, sectoral lending, food aid, policy dialog, relief, or other USAID modalities. Despite these limitations, I believe that many of the observations will be helpful in understanding USAID's strengths and weaknesses over a broad range of activities. Readers from other multilateral and bilateral agencies have indicated that they have found it helpful to consider the same type of issues in regard to their own organizations.

The discussion is also concerned with the way USAID as an institution has been shaped over the years by pressures from its external environment—from the administration, other branches of government (including Congress), the public, and a variety of special interest groups. This has been done both to draw attention to the fact that USAID faces significant constraints over which it has little or no control and to suggest that unless there are significant changes in the agency's external environment it cannot be expected to make significant improvements in its effectiveness in promoting development. This point is reinforced by examining recent management-introduced changes in USAID.

THE FIT BETWEEN USAID AND ITS TASK IN THE 1960s

Paradoxically, in some important respects USAID's organization, programming procedures, personnel system, and individual incentives were better suited to its task in its early years than in later periods or the present.

There is much evidence that effective donor assistance for agricultural and rural development must be based not only on an appropriate, balanced strategy, technical and analytical skills, a familiarity with what has been previously tried in the host country, and a comparative perspective, but also on a patient, persistent, flexible, and error-embracing approach.

The ability of donors to experiment, grope, take some risks, tolerate frustration, sustain a collaborative effort, and learn from experience has been especially necessary in the least developed nations. At independence, for example, Africa's new nations had very little trained manpower, their governmental institutions had little experience or capacity to carry out their tasks, and attitudes of professionalism and accountability were weak. Planning capacity was minimal. Since then, reliable planning data have remained scarce, and skilled manpower is still in short supply. As for agriculture, African cropping and farming systems are complex, diverse, and locally variable. They are unfamiliar to U.S. technicians, as are the social institutions through which rural Africans pool risks, conduct trade, save, and deploy their capital and labor. Under these conditions, it requires a good deal of patient experimentation to adapt Western technology and organizational forms to national and local conditions.

In its early years, USAID was able, to a remarkable extent, to adopt a flexible and error-embracing approach. It was decentralized, with considerable delegation of responsibility to its overseas field missions. Moreover, the missions had more employees in relation to the size of their programs than they have had in more recent periods.

In addition, USAID's Washington-based bureaucracy was less complex. Throughout the agency, lines of authority and areas of jurisdiction were blurred, access to superiors was easy, the agency's family-like missions fostered informal working relations (as they still do today), and considerable responsibility was assumed by subordinates. These are characteristics of an organization well suited to tasks similar to USAID's.[1] The agency was also less tightly bound by bureaucratic procedures and contracting regulations. Loans required fewer types of analysis and were subject to fewer restrictions than was later the case. Programming technical assistance required little analysis or documentation, and USAID/Washington's review and approval of requests was handled by a small, technically oriented staff. The process was therefore relatively rapid and flexible.[2] Contracting and procurement were less standardized, centralized, slow, and time-consuming than they have since become. Country strategy documents were less elaborate, and there was less pressure to conform to the Washington policy climate than has been the case since the early 1970s.

USAID's early personnel system and incentives for professionals also were well suited to its task. Because, in the optimism of the time, it was widely believed that self-sustaining development could be achieved in a decade or so, the new agency's personnel system was established on a temporary basis.[3] Most employees were hired as foreign service reserve (FSR) officers, a special category intended to give USAID the authority to hire professionals "on a temporary basis . . . with such specialized skills as may from time to time be required."[4] Under the FSR system, USAID was able to employ trained and experienced people quickly, without giving entrance exams, and it did not have to assume civil service obligations to those it employed. In addition to enabling the agency to stay flexible, this arrangement was intended to provide employees with the incentive to maintain a professional identity.[5] Some USAID employees were primarily concerned with administration and management, but many were involved in technical assistance. The line between direct-hire and contract personnel was less sharply drawn than it has come to be.

While there may be a nostalgic bias in memories of USAID's halcyon days, it seems clear that the agency was able to capitalize on the comparative advantage of its overseas missions in its early period. Employees had both the time and the incentives to devote a greater proportion of their energies to working with counterparts, implementing assistance, and thus learning about a country's needs and conditions. They also had more discretionary power to make changes and midcourse corrections, dropping extension work that proved inappropriate, for example, or initiating research.

The early system had weaknesses as well as strengths. Programs were unrealistically optimistic about what could be accomplished in a few years. This optimism, along with weak management planning and the desire to establish programs in newly independent nations, contributed to what Ambassador Korry in his 1966 report on USAID's African programs referred to as "scatteration, that is to say, our involvement in hundreds of projects dealing with almost every conceivable activity related to development and at many levels . . . in 33 countries."[6] As a result of the Korry report, USAID bilateral missions were closed in all but 10 nations. Other countries were assisted only through regional and multilateral programs.

INSTITUTIONAL TRANSFORMATION IN THE 1970s

By the early 1970s, USAID found itself operating in a changed and challenging organizational context.[7] The New Directions legislation altered USAID's objectives; at the same time, Congress restricted what the agency could do to achieve those objectives. Functional budgeting, earmarking, and additional reporting requirements subjected the agency and its missions to micromanagement by Congress. The elaboration of project design and approval procedures and the expansion of the Washington-based bureaucracy contributed to a marked centralization of decisionmaking authority. The role of direct-hire employees became primarily managerial. Most substantive work on project design, implementation, and evaluation was done by contractors. At the same time, contracting and procurement procedures became more standardized, more restrictive, and slower. Finally, the agency was spread thin since, in response to the Sahelian drought and the new congressional mandate, it once again established bilateral programs in most of the countries from which it had withdrawn in the late 1960s.

The effect of these changes on USAID's programming system was to reduce the comparative advantage of its overseas missions and to exacerbate a number of long-standing problems in project design and implementation. The missions' bureaucratic workload increased far more rapidly than did their work force. Employees were forced to devote a high proportion of their time to diagnosing the Washington "policy climate," packaging and promoting their programs, and overcoming arbitrary constraints in procurement and contracting. Their incentive to understand and address the distinctive, long-term developmental needs of the host country was reduced, as was their incentive to focus on project implementation. In sum, mission staff had to devote an increased amount of their attention to solving USAID's own problems. In this sense, the locus of decisionmaking for development shifted from host country institutions to USAID itself.

The reduction of mission autonomy and flexibility brought about by overcentralization was to some extent offset by an improved institutional memory and strengthened evaluation and learning processes in the agency. In time, these contributed to the formulation of more coherent and effective strategies in areas such as population and agricultural research. Here, however, I am primarily concerned with the effect of these changes in USAID's external environment on its institutional capacity to do its work.

Many circumstances contributed to the changes introduced in the early 1970s, including well-known political and historical factors beyond the scope of this chapter, and the recognition that USAID was no longer a temporary agency. The way the changes were introduced, however, was shaped by two features of the agency's external environment that had helped to shape U.S. foreign assistance programs from their inception: the absence of a strong constituency with shared goals, and the widespread assumption that most of the problems of developing nations could be solved quickly and easily by the direct transfer of U.S. technology and institutions. These features have forced the agency throughout its existence to be responsive to a wide variety of interest groups with differing and at times contradictory goals and to make unrealistic projections of what it could achieve. They have also contributed to ever increasing public disillusionment, tighter congressional oversight, and a more defensive posture by USAID and its employees.

Public support for foreign aid has generally been lower than for any other form of federal spending.[8] In the early postwar years, support was mobilized with the argument that the goals of foreign aid—containing communism, fostering democratic political institutions, promoting beneficial trade between rich and poor nations, and eradicating hunger, poverty, and ignorance—were mutually reinforcing and could be attained in a relatively short time. In addition, aid supporters argued, the United States was qualified by its unique historical tradition and its preeminent scientific and industrial capacity to exercise moral and technical leadership in fostering development.[9] Nevertheless, the passage of USAID's enabling legislation, the Foreign Assistance Act of 1961, under the charismatic leadership of President Kennedy, marks the last time an administration has successfully mobilized broad support for aid. By the early 1970s, in the wake of the Vietnam War, it was increasingly difficult to convince the public that USAID's humanitarian, commercial, strategic, and developmental goals were congruent.

To ensure the annual passage of USAID's legislation, administrations have had to forge a fragile coalition of special interest groups and to lobby key congressmen for their support. Some of the interest groups are committed to a particular goal; others are primarily concerned with having USAID use their products and services. Still others limit what USAID can do by sponsoring legislative amendments proscribing the agency's involvement with particular countries, commodities, or technologies.

USAID's dependence on special interest groups has had several effects: the proliferation of its legislated objectives, often unaccompanied by additional overall funding or higher personnel ceilings; the imposition of scores of special restrictions in amendments to USAID's enabling bill; dramatic shifts in the agency's regional focus and in its official policy, of which the New Directions mandate was an outstanding example. Reinforced by congressional mistrust of USAID's capacity and the administration's intentions, dependence on special interests has led to the introduction of functional accounts and increased earmarking in the agency's appropriations bill; has forced USAID to accept the nondevelopmental goals of other agencies, such as the USDA, Treasury, and OMB; and has subjected it to direct pressure from congressmen and high-level political appointees.

These increasing and often contradictory pressures influenced USAID's organization, personnel system, work force composition, programming and contracting procedures, and incentives. Its organization has become complex, flexible, and redundant. Over the years, many new organizational units have been created within the agency to cope with new goals or to show compliance with new thrusts. Thus, units have been created for new functional areas such as fish protein (when protein rather than caloric deficiency was considered most urgent), for new approaches such as private enterprise and voluntary organizations, and for new concerns such as Title IX, women, the environment, and energy. Other changes reflect a response to criticism or changing priorities. While units may be downgraded, moved, or merged, their functions are seldom altogether dropped.

The imposition of new objectives has also fostered functional redundancy and overlapping or poorly defined jurisdictional boundaries as units have added offices and positions for purposes of compliance, coordination, or protection of turf. At present, for example, African agriculture is the concern of the Office of Agriculture in the Bureau for Science and Technology, the Office of Policy Development and Program Review in the Bureau for Program and Policy Coordination, the Agriculture and Rural Development Division of the Africa Bureau, the Regional Development Support Offices in East and West Africa, and each of the African country missions. The same situation exists for other sectoral and special concerns.

In principle, of course, there are differences in the nature of the responsibility exercised over a functional area by different units. In reality, however, most policy and funding decisions are reviewed widely and discussed at committee meetings wherein employees with similar responsibilities (and perhaps similar professional qualifications) share ideas, dispute with one another, squabble over jurisdiction, trade support, and form temporary or lasting alliances. The impact of a reorganization, a new policy, or the reassignment of personnel is muted by this diffuse pattern of communication and decisionmaking.

Functional redundancy has been a source of institutional strength when the problems to be addressed are unclear, when multiple approaches are needed, or when effectiveness or protection against failure is more important than efficiency.[10] Redundancy has also contributed to USAID's resilience and organizational flexibility in the face of the reorganizations that tend to sweep across the agency after changes of administration. Since qualified personnel, as well as the responsibility for carrying out key tasks, are widely dispersed throughout the agency, USAID can lose a bureau or an office without seriously disrupting its overall functioning. Similarly, a unit in one bureau may be upgraded, merged, divided, moved to another bureau, or given new functions or a new name without causing serious problems.

Yet, redundancy can also be a source of difficulty if, as in USAID, personnel are not serving in positions for which they were trained, and if, as in the early 1970s, there is excessive centralization. Under these circumstances, decisionmaking is slow, and this inhibits USAID missions from quickly and flexibly responding to host country conditions and needs.

USAID's work force and personnel system have suffered from frequent changes in the agency's policy climate, substantive emphases, and regional focus. Changing objectives have made it difficult for the agency to maintain a work force appropriate to its tasks. Since the reduction in force following the end of the Vietnam War, USAID has been under almost constant pressure to reduce its complement of direct-hire employees and its operating budget. Efficiency-minded congressmen and administration officials tend to compare USAID's work with that of other federal agencies that, unlike USAID, are applying known techniques to well-understood domestic tasks.

One result of this pressure is that the agency has had to focus its recruiting efforts heavily on acquiring the professional skills needed to implement its most recent policy objectives. Over time, this has left USAID with acute shortages in some basic fields such as economics and agriculture. It has also fostered generational "stratification" in its work force; most of its anthropologists, for example, were hired in the mid-1970s. A second result is that the agency has had to reclassify many employees into skill categories for which they have had no formal training, so that they could be assigned to available positions. An agricultural officer in one of USAID's African missions in the 1970s was not necessarily an agriculturalist, much less one familiar with what was known at the time about African smallholder farming systems. A third result is that, regardless of their professional background, mission-based employees spend most of their time on bureaucratic and managerial tasks. Indeed, management is the only clear career ladder in the agency. Employees recruited because of other skills find it difficult to remain current in their field, to attend conferences, or to receive additional technical training.[11] This situation, plus the poor fit between the length of overseas assignments and the cycle of project development, contributes to frustration, poor morale, and deprofessionalization.

The complex and centralized programming procedures put in place in the early 1970s were shaped by USAID's vulnerability to criticism and the defensive posture it therefore adopted. At the time, USAID was under intense pressure to convince a skeptical Congress that it was conforming to the New Directions policies and that it was going to achieve positive results. As a consequence, the new system—which, with modifications noted below, is still largely in effect—requires missions to specify in considerable detail, before funds are obligated, what they propose to do, how they propose to do it, and how the activity will contribute to developmental goals. While changes can be made in the project during implementation, they require written congressional notification. The new system also requires each mission to prepare a more detailed and comprehensive justification of its country strategy in the annual budget submission and in the Country Development Strategy Statement (CDSS). Also in the mid-1970s, USAID management began to establish a strong, centralized database and a capacity for evaluating the impact of its activities.

The programming approach that had previously been used only for loan preparation was elaborated and extended to technical assistance. Virtually all development assistance was "projectized" so that it could be "targeted" on predominantly rural, low-income groups. In conjunction with the design of a project, the mission had to prepare a Project Identification Document, a Project Review Paper (which was subsequently dropped), and a Project Paper. Each of these was reviewed in Washington by the relevant regional bureau, the Bureau for Program and Policy Coordination, and the predecessor of the Bureau of Science and Technology. The completed Project Paper, which is still used with some modifications, includes a detailed project description, a logical framework relating inputs-to-outputs to a specified purpose and to a broad development goal, a detailed budget, an implementation plan, an economic analysis, a financial analysis, a social-soundness analysis, an environmental-impact determination, a procurement plan, and numerous briefer determinations intended to ensure that the project will not be contrary to U.S. policy interests nor conflict with the interests of one or another domestic lobby, as specified in USAID's enabling legislation.

This revised programming system has had a number of positive long-term effects on USAID's institutional capacity. Perhaps most important, it has enhanced the agency's capacity to learn from its experience and to introduce new ideas gradually into its mission programs through a process of creative dialog between its employees in Washington and overseas. The evolution of USAID's agricultural research, population, and health care–delivery strategies all exemplify this enhanced process of iterative learning.

Coming as they did, however, in the context of the New Directions policies, personnel cuts, and expanded country coverage in sub-Saharan Africa, the new procedures placed USAID's African missions in a very difficult position and exacerbated a number of endemic problems that have been found to be characteristic of all donors' technical assistance programs in that region. The new procedures took up much of the mission staff's time and energy, lessened its flexibility, and lengthened the time required to respond to host country requests, needs, and windows of opportunity.

Moreover, under increased pressure to "sell" their projects to an ever more skeptical audience, missions prepared documents that exaggerated what could be accomplished by applying known technologies and underestimated the difficulty of introducing significant institutional or technical change. Project advocacy in these documents not only fostered such distortions but also created strong incentives for field staff to "transform" the host countries' problems, capabilities, and commitments so that they would conform to the current Washington policy climate and review criteria, thus reducing employees' incentives to find out what was distinctive about a country and then to design interventions fine-tuned to its needs.

The overcentralized review process exacerbated the strain and suspicion between the missions and USAID/Washington. From the missions' perspective, distant and poorly informed bureaucrats "upstream" in the project approval and funding process second-guessed them on the basis of abstract ideas, personal predilections, or simply the wish to exercise their prerogatives. At times, the design and review process took on an adversarial rather than cooperative or constructive tone, and mission personnel found themselves assuming a defensive, risk-averse posture.

USAID's increased dependence on contractors for project design and implementation also created a number of problems, some of them characteristic of the federal contracting system and faced by all government agencies. As Thomas Rollis, assistant to the administrator for management, has noted in congressional testimony, concern about fairness and due process for the contracting community "requires, in large part, a face-value acceptance of the bidder certification of the types of services, the level, the quality, and just about everything except financial capacity." Unlike private sector firms, federal agencies are severely restricted in their ability to use generally available knowledge concerning the character, experience, knowledge, and past performance of potential contractors. They are not allowed to keep systematic records of contractor performance or to use poor performance as a criterion for nonselection. Indeed, it is very difficult and time-consuming to disbar a contractor for anything other than fiscal malfeasance.

Problems associated with the federal contracting system are exacerbated in USAID by the nature of its task and its relationship to its contractors. As I have noted, much of the agency's work requires in-depth knowledge of the host country and a flexible, trial-and-error learning approach rather than the direct transfer or application of known techniques. Yet, it is very difficult to establish nonsubjective quantifiable criteria for these qualities. For this reason, it is not surprising that much of the sensitivity to cultural, social, and institutional issues found in USAID's Project Papers is filtered out as they are transformed into contracts by Washington-based contract officers. USAID's comparative success with infrastructure projects and long-term training is probably due in part to the fact that they entail the use of known techniques and have outputs that are easy to quantify.

The rebidding procedures for contract renewals and the difficulty of enforcing more than minimal standards of performance also provide poor incentives for the contractor to be creative in meeting the unforeseen problems and opportunities that inevitably present themselves during project implementation. USAID missions, for their part, have little ability or incentive to enforce high standards of contractor performance. In addition to the costs and problems of terminating a contract for nonperformance or convenience, missions face a delay of from two hundred days to a year or more in obtaining the services of another contractor. Finally, USAID managers have proved understandably reluctant to offend contractors who are associated with any of the many special interest groups on which they feel dependent for the passage of their appropriations.

USAID's African missions have also had to cope with aid-tying regulations that direct them to purchase U.S. goods. In addition to the well-known economic costs of such regulations, in Africa these have regularly resulted in lengthy procurement delays and problems with service and spare parts. These problems have been particularly costly in the case of essential equipment such as vehicles.

CONFLICTING PRESSURES ON COUNTRY MISSIONS

By the early 1970s, a USAID mission had to cope with a very difficult organizational as well as host country environment as it played its pivotal role in the design and delivery of foreign assistance. It had to translate general policies into the host country context, develop a coherent rationale for its assistance program, and design a supply of plausible projects and programs, matched to funding available through two or more bills and numerous functional accounts—all within an arbitrary time frame. It had to manage the implementation of these activities despite the fact that it had little control over the personnel, logistic support, or other resources supplied by the host government or over interministerial coordination. Moreover, the USAID mission had to accomplish all these tasks in ways acceptable to a number of constituencies and agencies in both the United States and the host country.

Most of the constraints, pressures, and contradictions faced by missions in the 1970s are still present. Since they profoundly affect what the missions can do and what USAID employees are encouraged to do, it is useful to recapitulate them here:

1. Missions are under pressure from USAID/Washington to obligate appropriated funds in a timely manner or face program budget reductions in the following year.

2. Missions are under pressure from USAID/Washington to select and package their programs in accordance with the spirit of current policy guidelines or face time-consuming and delaying harassment in the review process. Failure to conform to the current "policy climate" makes projects more vulnerable to all types of technical and analytical criticism.

3. Missions have to design their projects in accordance with complex and standardized requirements and make dozens of determinations to ensure that they are in compliance with all the statutory regulations. In implementing projects, missions must comply with complex statutory regulations concerning contracting and disbursement, which were designed for use by federal agencies located in the United States. Compliance is monitored by the inspector general's office within USAID and by the congressional General Accounting Office, and consequently by USAID managers and lawyers up the line. Irregularities, no matter how technical, lead to serious sanctions and can have adverse effects on the career of mission directors and others. In contrast, ill-founded assumptions, faulty analysis, or even deliberate misrepresentation of facts about the host country in program or project documents, or suppression of negative evidence in evaluation reports, only occasionally elicits an official rebuke. And mission directors report that the developmental success or failure of programs has comparatively little effect on the careers of USAID personnel once they have left the host country for a new assignment.

4. If missions became involved in programming PL-480 food surpluses, they were, and are, subject to pressures from the USDA and other members of the interagency coordinating committee. Friction over the type

and quality of commodity to be supplied and over delivery dates is frequent.

5. Missions are occasionally directly pressed by a special interest group to fund a particular activity. More often such pressure is channeled through the personal, informal intervention of high-level USAID/Washington managers. The mission then requests funding for the activity through a central or regional program. Similarly, the mission may be under informal or formal pressure from USAID/Washington to use a particular type of contractor.

6. Particularly if the host country is considered important for strategic, political, or economic reasons, the mission is subject to pressures from the State Department and the U.S. embassy.[12] Pressures can have a variety of objectives: to shore up an unstable regime with general budgetary support; to obtain base rights or more limited strategic access; to "resettle" refugees to avoid another "Palestinian situation";[13] to help a government show concern for a dissident region; or to keep a personal commitment by a visiting U.S. official to the head of state. Regardless of whether the pressures are political, strategic, economic, or diplomatic, there tends to be a strain between the State Department view that USAID should have flexible, quickly disbursed resources and a very small in-country staff and the agency's view that long-term commitments and on-the-ground management are necessary to an effective technical assistance program.

7. The mission is subject to formal and informal pressures from host country leaders and, often, to competing requests for support from different host country ministries and agencies. In addition, it has to attempt to coordinate its assistance with other donors, with whom it is at times in competition for good project opportunities. (This problem was especially troublesome during the mid-1970s when all major donors were under pressure to reach rural people through targeted projects.) The mission also faces potential contradictions in its broader relationship with the host country: It has to assure host country officials that USAID is a reliable source of support for costly, long-term development initiatives and institutional changes yet must not "mortgage" its future program, and it has to work "collaboratively" with host country counterparts to make their planning more efficient, while requiring them to accept U.S.-made equipment, imposing on them USAID's latest developmental priorities and policies, and offering assistance that often favors foreign exchange over domestic savings and capital over labor.

More recently, missions have had to push for politically difficult policy reforms such as economic liberalization, reduced subsidies, and cuts in the government payroll. At the same time, the State Department may be seeking to stabilize the regime or reward it for loyalty in the arena of East-West relations.

PROBLEMS IN USAID's
PROGRAMMING AND PROJECT SYSTEM

The ways that USAID mission employees cope with these conflicting pressures as they allocate financial resources to programs and projects help to account for the persistence of a number of well-recognized problems associated with programming, project design, and implementation, including: lack of stability and continuity in country program size and content; neglect of social, cultural, political, and institutional issues; overoptimism about the suitability of shelf technologies; inflated estimates of economic rates of return; underestimation of the time needed to get project activities under way and to bring about change; underestimation of costs; delays in delivery, and servicing problems associated with tied-aid procurement; unrealistic assumptions about the availability of qualified and experienced technicians willing to live in remote areas or work under difficult conditions; unrealistic assumptions about the host country's absorptive capacity and ability to effect interagency coordination; neglect of project implementation or continuation, in favor of designing new projects; inadequate monitoring; failure to learn from previous USAID or non-USAID projects in the host country; and the repetition of projects and approaches that have previously proved unsuccessful.[14]

The fact that these problems have persisted and even deepened over the years strongly suggests that they cannot be resolved by exhortations "to do a better job" or by adopting additional guidelines or tighter regulations. Rather, they are symptomatic of the underlying and enduring structural contradictions in USAID's objectives, in its procedures, and in the incentives that shape the resource-allocation strategies used by employees as they carry out the tasks imposed by the program cycle.

The complex and time-consuming program cycle takes precedence over all other activities in the regional bureaus and overseas missions because it is both the context for most communication and coordination among different parts of USAID, and the decisionmaking arena wherein competing and intrinsically dissimilar objectives are reduced to the common calculus of fiscal resources. This process affects the career incentives of USAID employees by rewarding them for procedural and tactical knowledge and for becoming experts at moving money, regardless of their technical competence or the impact of their work on a country's development.

Within USAID's program cycle, it is useful to distinguish two types of allocation process at work: The first, enabling and top-down, establishes the broad parameters of country and sectoral funding levels and of development policy; the second, bottom-up and entrepreneurial, determines the content and recipients of specific aid activities.

The first process takes its direction from USAID's enabling legislation, State Department determinations, USDA projections, intermittent input from other agencies including OMB and Treasury, and policy guidelines developed by USAID management. Together these determine the funding level for a country program. The rationale for the funding level need not include developmental criteria. Early and enduring support for Ethiopia, the increase in funding for Kenya since the late 1970s, and huge appropriations for Egypt and Israel clearly did not.

Even when developmental criteria are significant in determining country funding levels, they are not necessarily consistent through time. Changes in the wake of the Korry report in the 1960s, the New Directions policies of the 1970s, and the free enterprise and policy reform thrust of the 1980s have resulted in significant fluctuations in program size and content for most USAID recipients. These changes make it difficult for missions to maintain existing programs while at the same time responding to new sources of funding and policy guidelines. The instability of USAID programs had particularly negative effects on institution-building activities such as agricultural research, and on livestock development—both of which require a comparatively long period of continuous support and entail a good deal of learning by doing.

From the perspective of most USAID employees, top-down allocation decisions are normally taken as a given.[15] Along with the procedures of the program cycle, these decisions determine the boundaries of permissible action and the rhetoric of discourse and justification. Together they may proscribe particular activities, but they do not prescribe them. Nor do USAID's country strategy and project design procedures in themselves determine the particular programs, projects, and approaches adopted by a mission since, as has been argued, they are so complex that they are often unworkable. In any case, their application is constrained by a great many exogenous pressures on the mission.

To understand the creative process through which resources made available through top-down allocation are fashioned into programs and projects—in other words, the way USAID's general policies and resources are operationalized and its working agenda defined—it is necessary to understand the strategies used by USAID's entrepreneurial, field-based employees in carrying out their work.

In principle, USAID's program cycle requires the mission to develop a country strategy informed by current development theory and policy, consistent with U.S. interests, based on USAID's comparative advantage, and responsive to the peculiar developmental needs of the host country. Projects and nonproject modes of assistance are then selected to implement the mission's strategy.

In practice, it has seldom been possible for USAID's country missions to follow this procedure. The mission's freedom of choice is limited by several considerations in addition to the external pressures discussed previously. Unless the country program is new or in a state of rapid expansion, the mission finds most of its forward funds encumbered by ongoing and approved projects that cannot easily be discontinued, even if they are no longer supported by Washington's "policy climate." The mission may also have committed itself to particular host country officials and priorities, or it may feel committed to extend an initiative in an attempt to make good on sunk investments.

Mission management is also constrained by the size and skills of its work force complement. Given the time-consuming complexity and time-driven nature of USAID's programming procedures, it is simply not practical to engage in extensive analysis or to explore alternative projects in more than cursory fashion. The mission is under more pressure to put together a plausible program and to obligate available funds than to consider the opportunity costs of potential options.

Paradoxically, missions with new or rapidly expanding programs, and therefore the widest options, generally have insufficient staff or time for thorough analysis. USAID addressed this problem creatively by mobilizing outside experts as advisors before starting major new programs in Nigeria, India, Southern Africa, and the Sahel. The results of this approach seem positive, but it has not generally been used once a country mission has been established.

The program strategies of missions have often been opportunistic, eclectic, and entrepreneurial—less the result of planning than the sum of their parts. Day-to-day problem-solving has left little time for long-term planning. In such cases, the strategy's coherence has been more in the way it has been described to Washington than in the way it has originated or functioned.

To be sure, many of the activities in the country strategy are the result of careful analysis and planning, but many others represent "targets of opportunity" that present themselves to mission management. Their origin may be a host country request, the politically determined selection of a region, the availability of funding and technical advice through a USAID/Washington centrally funded or regional project, pressure from a U.S. special interest group, or simply the enthusiasm of the mission director or an entrepreneurial individual on his staff. The final selection of projects cannot be based on a careful assessment of all the relevant variables in alternative courses of action. Because of the need to move ahead in the face of many uncertainties, choices must depend on a best-guess approach and the implicit use of a simplifying list of questions, most or all of which should be answered in the affirmative:

- Is the proposed project consistent with actual USAID policy—that is, the policy embodied in Washington project approval decisions rather than in policy papers?
- Is it consistent with the mission's analysis (in its CDSS) of the way that USAID policy should be adapted to host country conditions?

- Is it acceptable to host country political leaders?
- Is it acceptable to a host country ministry or agency that will be responsible for implementing it?
- Will the project complement or balance the mission's "portfolio" of projects?[16]
- Is the cost of the project consistent with the mission's budgetary levels or aspirations?
- Does the mission have a sufficient work force with appropriate skills to manage the labor intensive process of project design?
- Are there likely to be any special objections to the project raised by the U.S. ambassador or particular members of Congress?

Even though the planned-for development consequences of the project may be of great significance to the mission staff, USAID's organizational incentives do not necessarily give the potential impact a high priority in project identification and selection.

Regardless of its origins, a particular project usually takes the form of a fairly specific activity as a solution to a problem. As such, it soon gains a momentum of its own. Even in its early stages, the project idea may represent a commitment to a particular host government agency or to political officials to deliver more or less well-specified resources. Whether or not there is this sense of commitment, it becomes increasingly difficult to stop a project once scarce mission staff time has been invested in it, even if it becomes evident upon further analysis that the project presents many problems.

It occasionally happens that the mission becomes committed to a project that, rightly or wrongly, lacks a constituency in the host country or is even opposed by the ministry toward which it is directed. In extreme cases this has led to eleventh-hour high-level efforts by the mission director, or even the ambassador, to press the ministry to accept the unwanted project. Not surprisingly, such projects are often later the objects of benign neglect by the designated implementing agency.

In identifying and designing projects, USAID employees must, to some extent, use simplifying models. This strategy enables them to cope with the complexity of USAID's design and review requirements, the uncertainties of development work, and the diversity of local conditions. But it is not without costs. Models may be based in part on broad historical experience, such as the Marshall Plan in Europe or the U.S. experience with the land grant agricultural system, rural electrification, or range management. Often, however, they are grounded in past development projects or programs with which USAID employees and contractors are familiar. Such projects, or components of them, can be used to provide guidelines for everything from the rationale to the technology and institutional arrangements of a new project. Often, because of small mission size and the pressure to design projects, the same project design officers have been responsible for "families" of rather similar projects in several countries in the same region. This was the case, for example, with many of USAID's pastoral livestock projects and production-oriented area development projects in Africa in the 1970s.

The use of simplifying models rests on the explicit or implicit assumption that the context of the problem being addressed is similar to that of a problem addressed previously, and that the earlier project was successful in meeting its objectives. Such a strategy for allocating resources has proven reasonably efficient when these conditions are met—as they have been, for example, with projects involving many types of infrastructure as well as higher agricultural education.[17] In such cases, the use of familiar models not only simplifies USAID's work and ensures workable project design, but it increases the likelihood that USAID will be able to find contractors to implement the project who share the model's conception of the task. But when simplifying models are not well suited to the host country context, their use tends to short-circuit the project design process, to contribute to problems in project implementation, and to reduce the project's impact. This happened with many of the people-oriented, targeted projects of the 1970s.

The use of a project model generally means that fundamental decisions concerning design are made at a very early stage. The result is that alternatives tend to be ruled out without ever having been given serious attention, thereby vitiating the logic of USAID's design process, which assumes that project design entails a hierarchical, sequenced series of choices about the allocation of resources. Choices made early in the sequence involve a wider range of alternatives—for example, between sectors or regions—and require rather general types of data. Choices made later in the sequence involve a more restricted set of alternatives—for example, between crop varieties, techniques for extension, or user-cost rate structures—and require more specific types of data. Beginning with a model solution precludes many alternatives from the outset. Nevertheless, because of USAID's project documentation requirements, much design effort is devoted to rationalizing, post hoc, choices that in fact were never considered. Furthermore, depending on how great USAID's need is to approve the project, the project design team may find itself under pressure to disregard the views of technical and country experts, host country officials, and members of other groups whose interests will be affected by the project.

Incorrect assumptions introduced in the design process can be not only expensive for USAID in time and dollars during project implementation but frustrating and demoralizing for its employees, consultants, and contractors as well. For this reason, the tendency to use previous projects as models can be costly and can inhibit learning for many years. USAID efforts to draw lessons from project evaluations and to conduct evaluations some years after project funding has ended are directed to this difficulty and have led the agency to discontinue some types of projects. New project models may be based on experimental research findings (as was the case to some extent with farming systems research), on a new hypothesis about the nature of the problem to be solved, on a particularly successful local development initiative, or on the efforts of a contractor.

Designing projects within the USAID system gives considerable scope to the creativity of its more entrepreneurial employees. For this reason, USAID's projects are greatly influenced both by these individuals' substantive knowledge, experience, and familiarity with specific types of projects, and by organizational incentives generated within USAID to which they must respond. When a proposal is funded, USAID is committed to the particular conceptions, formulations, technologies, and approaches it promotes.

Entrepreneurs' bureaucratic skills are as important as, if not more important, than their expertise in development or knowledge of the host country. Successful entrepreneurs must capitalize on available funds, cast proposals in the current policy idiom and, to a greater or lesser extent, provide information and analysis that make them plausible if not compelling. But this is not enough. Entrepreneurs must also be adept at shepherding their proposals through the hazards of the review process through which funding choices are actually made, not so much by explicit bargaining as by attending meetings, writing memos, and mobilizing the support of a coalition based on previous association, common interests in development, commitment to a technology or contractor, or common professional background. Thus, they are members of task-oriented, crosscutting working groups, possess a well-developed information network, and can defend their bureaucratic turf. They have friends in key offices and bureaus in Washington and perhaps in Congress as well.

Entrepreneurial roles may be located anywhere in the organization—in the missions, the regional bureaus, or the support bureaus—though the beginner has more scope for action in the field. Roles are not restricted to the upper echelons of USAID's hierarchy. Indeed, able and enthusiastic individuals are often surprised at the initiatives they can take soon after "coming aboard." Many of USAID's more innovative activities originate with entrepreneurs located on the periphery of the organization—in the field, the Bureau for Science and Technology, or the Bureau for Policy Planning and Coordination, for example—who have been brought into USAID on a temporary or permanent basis because they have specific expertise thought to be needed after a policy change.

Entrepreneurs' professional background and experience have a direct bearing on the kinds of activities they promote. The secretary general of agriculture of one country has noted: "If they send a livestock man, you can be sure we'll get a livestock project." This observation applies not only to general sectoral interests but to specific definitions of problems and technical solutions. In a very real sense, USAID entrepreneurs "have solutions looking for problems." Particularly for entrepreneurs with a primarily technical background, this approach contributes to a persistent neglect of cultural and social factors, economic incentives, and opportunity costs.

IMPACT OF NEW DIRECTIONS ON COUNTRY PROGRAMS

The changes made in USAID's policies and procedures in the early 1970s made it difficult for missions to program additional funds for such activities as higher agricultural education and transportation, in which USAID had experienced considerable success. The New Directions thrust pushed them to undertake new types of projects that would directly benefit low-income rural people. It is clear that USAID management in most African countries would not have introduced this shift in their country strategies and project portfolios on the basis of their experience or knowledge of host country conditions or commitments.

The impact of the New Directions policies on the content of USAID's programs in agricultural and rural development differed from country to country, according to the status of the agency's earlier assistance program, pressure to increase the level of assistance on account of U.S. foreign policy concerns, and the mission management's perceptions of the host country context. In all countries, however, the new policy and programming environment led to an increase in what, in hindsight, appear to have been highly problematic projects.

New Directions, coupled with Congress's increasing concern about accountability, required USAID to "projectize" most assistance at a time when funding levels were rising. The task of designing and implementing targeted projects that would provide agricultural benefits directly to low-income rural groups presented USAID missions with a number of problems.[18] Some had to do with social and cultural factors, some with host country absorptive capacity, and some with USAID's capacity to carry out this type of work.

Attempts to change the behavior of low-income people in Africa must be based on a realistic understanding of how they make a living, how they view their needs and wants, and how they are organized to cope with risk, to control access to natural resources, and to deal with the government. Moreover, no matter how well project planners take account of such factors, project implementers must learn as they go, listen to people, and respond flexibly to the problems that arise. Since change is likely to be slow and uncertain, it is difficult to plan for it within a relatively fixed three- to five-year project framework. What is often needed is a long-term, incremental process rather than a project.

The proposed activities must be sequenced properly in relation to each other and to other developments in the host country. Appropriate technologies must be developed or adapted, not simply assumed to exist. Administrative and support services in the country must function and be coordinated. If the host government is expected to contribute to maintenance and recurrent costs during and especially after the life of a project, it must not only have the revenue to do so and share USAID's general objectives but must also view the project beneficiaries, intended or otherwise, as a significant political constituency.

Several other prerequisites must also be met. It is difficult for a mission to design and implement a project unless there are agreed-upon and appropriate models for its main component activities, and unless USAID can find contractors experienced in adapting them to a developing country.[19] Last, but by no means least, the project must anticipate and realistically address the logistic and procurement problems associated with activities in many African rural areas.

In light of these observations, it is clear that many of the tasks entailed in the targeted projects that USAID missions were urged to undertake in the early 1970s were inherently difficult, were out of sequence with agricultural research, infrastructure, and administrative capacity, and put unrealistic demands on USAID's design and implementation capacity under African conditions. At the same time, pressures to meet obligation deadlines and fit programs to available funding and political priorities created strong incentives for USAID's entrepreneurial managers, responsible for project design and approval, to downplay the problematic nature of these tasks.

Project success is linked to the ability of those who implement projects to carry out these problematic tasks. The effect is, to a large extent, cumulative. That is, the more unrealistic assumptions there are in a project's design, the greater the likelihood that severe problems will be encountered during implementation. Thus, for example, the approach taken by USAID to pastoral livestock development, crop production, and integrated rural development has tended to be based on many unrealistic assumptions and to be comparatively ineffective, while its approach to higher agricultural education and rural infrastructure has been more realistic and therefore more effective.[20] USAID's approach to some other activities, such as seed multiplication and agricultural research, has involved fewer incorrect assumptions, but, because of the linkages among components, those assumptions have been very damaging.

USAID's lack of success with these problematic tasks tends to override country-specific differences.[21] This suggests either that these tasks are inherently difficult, that USAID lacks the capacity to carry them out, or both. Whether other development agencies or private voluntary organizations (PVOs) have greater capacity to carry out targeted, people-oriented agricultural and rural development activities, and whether these are an appropriate part of a balanced strategy, is beyond the scope of this discussion. It is evident, however, that USAID's comparative advantage does not lie in this area.

Many of the problems I have been discussing have also proved troublesome in more orthodox types of USAID activity, including higher agricultural education and agricultural research, but they appear to be less acute in such cases. U.S. institutional models can be more easily transferred and adapted to African conditions in these modern sector activities. U.S. contractors familiar with these models and willing to live in Africa are easier to find. The activities themselves are generally of higher priority to African governments and their more vocal constituencies.[22] In addition, articulate constituencies for these types of activities in the United States put pressure on the Congress and USAID for continuing support, and they often maintain professional and institutional linkages with the institutions they helped to establish in Africa.

USAID PROCEDURAL AND ORGANIZATIONAL REFORMS IN THE 1980s

Since the late 1970s, USAID management has made a number of changes in organization and procedure.

To enhance the comparative advantage of its overseas missions, the agency undertook a program of decentralization. Middle management in Washington has been reduced, and mission staff size maintained as much as possible. Greater project approval authority has been granted to the missions. Project Papers have been shortened, and the average time for project design and approval has been reduced. The tour length of USAID employees overseas has been augmented by eight or nine months since 1981 to cut costs and increase mission staff continuity, and increasing use has been made of foreign nationals. USAID obtained the authority to "deobligate" funds from projects that are lagging and to "reobligate" them to other projects, though only for activities within the same functional account. Greater emphasis has been put on project implementation, as opposed to design, by hiring additional contract officers and administrative officers and by redesigning in-house training programs to emphasize the management of implementation.[23] In addition, USAID is providing more financial technical assistance to local administering units to foster their use of audit as a management tool.

To address USAID's weakness at designing and implementing small, flexible, people-oriented projects (and to facilitate compliance with budgetary earmarking) the agency has established "umbrella" cofinancing projects in five countries (as of June 1986), including Kenya and Senegal. Under this arrangement, a line of credit is set up between a PVO management unit and the host government; individual PVOs, both U.S.-based and indigenous, may then apply to have individual activities approved and funded without recourse to USAID's usual approval system.

To alleviate problems associated with project design, project proliferation, and recurrent costs, USAID has reduced the number of new projects in sub-Saharan Africa from about 63 in 1985 to about 33 in 1987, while increasing project size and duration. It has also relied more heavily on nonproject modes of assistance, which it tries to link to policy reforms and structural change. It has initiated the new African Economic Policy Reform Program to help African governments defray the costs and risks associated with such change.

To improve its "institutional memory," USAID has been seeking since the early 1970s to strengthen its evaluation and information capacity. Project evaluations, some of which have been cited above, are usually frank, self-critical, and as analytically sound as is possible, given severe data constraints and weak monitoring of the impact of projects. The agency's Center for Development Information and Evaluation provides information from agency evaluations and other sources in response to several thousand requests a year. Since the late 1970s, USAID has also conducted ambitious impact evaluations of projects, programs, and broader issues. The analysis in this chapter has made extensive use of all these sources of information.

While most of these changes are useful, their positive impact may be swamped by continued and even intensified pressure on USAID. As administrator Peter McPherson noted in his prepared testimony for the Congress in 1986, "The proliferation of 'priority' areas and the earmarks on assistance [still] create a web of constraints which reduce AID's ability to pursue coherent development strategies effectively responsive to individual countries."[24] Budgetary restrictions are of many types. For example, some 75 percent of economic support funds are earmarked for individual countries on nondevelopmental grounds; about 13 percent of development assistance funding is earmarked for PVOs and cooperatives; some 18 percent of commodity-import programs must be used for agricultural commodities; and 10 percent of development assistance is earmarked for minority-owned firms. The tendency to earmark has been on the rise during the 1980s.

Micromanagement by the Congress continues. In 1985 alone, USAID provided 849 congressional notifications totaling 1,700 pages. The agency estimates that it devotes more than 200 person-years per year to its interaction with the Congress.

Pressures on USAID from special interest groups are unabated. The head of the Africa Bureau reported,

> I just spend too much time fighting off the special interest brush fires, both, again, within AID and outside of AID. . . . Clearly, effectiveness and impact suffers from all of this. It is almost what I would call the "Johnny Appleseed" approach to development, where we merrily go across the continents, just dropping projects all over the place, without trying to figure out what is best or saying no.[25]

Despite USAID's increased emphasis on implementation, many problems remain. New regulations and set-aside requirements have made contracting more difficult than ever. Staff cuts have left mission personnel with less time to devote to project supervision. Indeed, the tendency to equate success in implementation with the ability to disburse funds does not necessarily encourage staff to focus on essential but difficult activities. Delegating authority to the missions is doubtless desirable, but it does not, in itself, provide mission personnel with development skills, in-depth country knowledge, or the incentive to undertake long-term programs that may be essential to balanced growth.

The increased funding of small-scale PVO projects may be appropriate for some activities but will not take the place of support for essential government services nor overcome those problems that trace back to overly optimistic assumptions about technology and institutional transfer.

Increased reliance on policy dialog and nonproject assistance may be desirable and necessary for a time, but it is not without risks as well as benefits: (1) past experience indicates that donor advice is not always correct; (2) USAID is not well staffed with economists and other social scientists who can anticipate the likely consequences of standard policy prescriptions in a particular country; (3) policy dialog coupled with conditionality often creates poor working relations between the mission and host country officials, as has been the case recently in Kenya; (4) many of the pressures and incentives that cause USAID entrepreneurs to make unduly optimistic assumptions or to be less than honest in their reporting can influence nonproject as well as project work.

CONCLUSION

Throughout this chapter I have tried to show that many of the well recognized and well documented difficulties constraining USAID project design and implementation are symptomatic of underlying and enduring structural contradictions in the agency's objectives that are reflected in its procedures and incentives. The analysis suggests that the best solution to these endemic problems lies in modifying the agency's institutional and individual incentive structure, rather than in issuing additional guidelines, imposing internal regulations, or adopting new management systems. Reforming USAID procedures will not be easy. Changes in procedures should be designed further to reduce the time and effort missions devote to designing and managing new and complex projects and preparing other advocacy documents, and should encourage them to give more attention to host country problems and to project implementation and impact. Official reporting requirements should be modified to create incentives for USAID staff to work with counterparts. There is a need, in short, to shift the locus of mission

mission attention from the agency's programming problems to supporting existing institutions and making them more effective. This shift would help to check the tendency of donor assistance to foster the proliferation of projects and the expansion of government. It would also encourage better coordination with other donors. Indeed, when several donors fund a technical assistance team, foreign advisors seem more likely to give priority to the needs of the host government than to the preoccupations of a particular donor.

Some simplifying modifications in USAID procedures have already been made. Others can be made without great difficulty. More fundamental changes will not be easy and cannot be made without the cooperation of Congress. In the longer run, Congress needs to find mechanisms for giving USAID multiyear appropriations and more flexibility in programming these funds, while at the same time holding the agency more accountable for the developmental impact of its programs. Such changes will require that USAID, together with other members of the development community, help Congress and the public to gain a more realistic picture of what needs to be done to promote development, and how long it will take.

The kinds of change I envision would encourage USAID to adopt a less defensive, more flexible, error-embracing approach and to welcome more participation in its deliberations by outside experts and critics, from both the United States and the Third World. Greater reliance on a more flexible approach, along with a greater emphasis on effective, informed, and patient policy dialog and nonproject assistance, would require greater analytical skills and country knowledge in the mission, but fewer personnel. Mission staff would have a greater incentive to update their skills and broaden their understanding of the host country and region.[26] And USAID/Washington would have the incentive to help them do so by providing short- and long-term training and by establishing coherent career ladders.

NOTES

This chapter draws heavily on material prepared for the World Bank study, Managing Agricultural Development in Africa, and presented in MADIA Research Report No. 12, *An Assessment of AID Activities to Promote Agricultural and Rural Development in Sub-Saharan Africa,* by Bruce Johnston, Allan Hoben, Dirk Dijkerman, and William Jaeger, which will be distributed by USAID. While I have benefited greatly from the comments and insights of Uma Lele, many USAID employees, and my colleagues on the report, the views expressed here are my own and do not necessarily represent theirs, or those of the World Bank or USAID.

1. The fit between USAID's organizational structure and its tasks is discussed in Judith Tendler, *Inside Foreign Aid* (Baltimore, MD: Johns Hopkins University Press, 1975), pp. 12–22, and in W. Siffin, "Public Technical Assistance—The Effects of the Inner Environment upon the Process" (manuscript, 1974).

2. Capital projects, clearly differentiated from technical assistance for historical

reasons, required economic and technical analyses and more complete documentation.

3. USAID did not request authority to include its personnel in a career system until 1966; see Tendler, *Inside Foreign Aid,* p. 16.

4. The FSR category, established by the Foreign Service Act of 1946 for the use of the State Department and USAID's predecessors, was incorporated into the Foreign Assistance Act of 1961, Section 522.

5. The Herter report, cited in Tendler, *Inside Foreign Aid,* p. 20, argues: They will be forced to identify with their profession. . . . The decisive reason not to include these specialists in an AID career system is that, in the main, the career contexts and career loyalties of the best professions and the whole range of activities with which those professions are associated.

6. The Korry report is summarized in *U.S. Aid to Africa: The Record, the Rationales, and the Challenge,* prepared by R. W. Copson, T. W. Galdi, and L. Q. Nowels (Washington, D.C.: Congressional Research Service, 1986).

7. Many of the pressures on USAID discussed in this section were not new. Their effect became more pronounced, however, and public disenchantment with foreign aid and policy increased, and the mounting costs of war limited resources devoted to development in nonstrategic areas.

8. A useful discussion of the determination of U.S. foreign aid policies is found in E. R. Morss and V. A. Morss, *U.S. Foreign Aid: An Assessment of New and Traditional Development Strategies* (Boulder, CO: Westview Press, 1982), ch. 5.

9. A good analysis of this concept of "manifest destiny" and its uses by U.S. presidents is found in E. Z. Berg, "The 1973 Legislative Reorientation of the United States Foreign Assistance Policy: The Content and Context of a Change" (Master's thesis, George Washington University, 1976).

10. David Leonard, "Choosing Among Forms of Decentralization and Linkage," *Institutions for Rural Development for the Poor,* D. K. Leonard and Dale Rogers Marshall, eds. (Berkeley: Institute of International Studies, University of California, 1982), pp. 209–210.

11. Each year, a few employees are granted long-term training leave.

12. Although it is surprising to outsiders, pressures from the ambassador are not necessarily the same as those from the State Department. The former not only feels he has a firsthand perspective on local conditions, but he also has a greater incentive to maintain cordial relations with host government officials. In either case, ambassadorial pressures can be much more specific and situational than is the general intervention of the administration in determining USAID levels, as discussed previously.

13. The State Department can make funds available for this purpose through the Migration and Refugee Assistance Bill.

14. All of these persistent problems are documented in the MADIA report. It is interesting that many of the same difficulties have constrained the efforts of other donors as well; see OECD/DAC, *Report of the Expert Group on Aid Evaluation on Lessons of Experience Emerging from Aid Evaluation* (Paris: OECD, 1984), p. 11.

15. Individual USAID employees with outstanding leadership qualities do occasionally manage to obtain higher funding levels for their mission or program. The genesis of the Sahel Development Fund, for example, owes much

to the efforts of one such individual.

16. For example, a mission that has a strong program in agriculture and health care delivery may desire projects in population or education. This desire for a balanced, or at least a mixed, portfolio is in part a reflection of USAID's congressionally mandated "functional accounts" and in part a risk-aversion strategy by the mission director, who does not want to put all his eggs in one sectoral basket.

17. Simplifying models have other functions in development agencies. Regardless of whether they are based on experimental evidence, disciplinary dogma, past experience, or merely professional folklore, the theories inherent in past projects have an important cognitive, evaluative, and expressive role in the world of the developer. Thus, these paradigms of and for development have provided the personnel of donor agencies with shared ways of thinking and talking about what they are doing and of explaining why they believe it will work to those on whom they depend for funding. Like other models, development models not only provide criteria for choosing between alternatives, but they define these alternatives and hence the kinds of information that are considered relevant to making the choice. In this way, they generate their own categories of data, which lend them a comforting aura of concreteness. For example, the "model farmer" paradigm, which held sway recently, rested on the self-fulfilling assumption that larger landholders have more land because they are progressive farmers, whereas smallholders are inherently more traditional. Aid should be given to those who have the attribute of being progressive; therefore, larger farmers received aid. Alternative hypotheses about the political-economic bases of wealth were not explored nor were data gathered that could have tested them. Like other long-used conceptual paradigms, development models are not challenged easily by factual evidence of failure, for they provide a rationale for explaining away their apparent lack of success and for shifting the blame to others. For example, since it is often assumed that pastoralists are not responsive to price, their failure to sell livestock in marketing projects is taken, prima facie, as evidence of their traditional values, and more rational explanations are not sought.

18. The problems noted here are those typically associated with projects that attempt to deliver a highly specific service or supervised technical package to farmers rather than funding generalized "enabling" activities such as the provision of rural infrastructure.

19. It appears that agreement or lack of agreement on the appropriateness of models is only partially an empirical question. U.S. interest groups differ sharply in their views of the desirable direction of change in African agriculture in regard to scale, crops, and mode of organization.

20. It is important to maintain the distinction between the goal of an activity and the approach taken to attain the goal. In development work this is often not done. USAID's lack of success with an inappropriate approach to pastoral livestock projects, for example, has led agency management to drop activities in this sector without seriously considering whether other approaches should be explored.

21. By extension, it appears that differences among USAID's performance in the six countries covered in the MADIA report are as much a function of the types of activities it happened to undertake as of host country factors or the quality of project design and management.

22. In the past this was less true of agricultural research than other activities, though Kenya was a partial exception.
23. This change was accompanied by a reduction in staff training in development.
24. McPherson's comment is found in *AID Oversight Hearings before the Committee on Foreign Relations, U.S. Senate, 99th Congress,* 21–24 April 1986 (Washington, D.C.: Government Printing Office, 1986).
25. *Ibid.,* pp. 137–138.
26. USAID might, for example, introduce a job classification called "country specialist," enabling the agency to reward individuals who acquire expertise in a country or a region such as the Sahel or East Africa. Country specialists would increase USAID's institutional memory and would be able to analyze a country strategy and projects in the light of USAID's past implementation experience in that country. They could also serve as the liaison officer with outside experts. Indeed, I believe that missions should be encouraged to make repeated use of outside experts with an intimate knowledge of a particular country. A funding mechanism could be devised so that missions and USAID/Washington could bring in such individuals for periodic consultations when strategic decisions are under consideration. Such an arrangement would contribute to building an institutional memory in a mission that would be longer than the time spent there by the USAID staff member who has been there the longest; it could also smooth discontinuities caused by staff and contractor rotations. These outside experts could perform a screening function, judging strategy components and project ideas against special circumstances in a particular country.

THIRTEEN

U.S. Delivery Systems for International Cooperation and Development to the Year 2000

DAVID SHEAR

This chapter presents recommendations for changes in the delivery systems for U.S. participation in international cooperation and development to the year 2000. In order to do this coherently it is necessary to set out some assumptions with respect to the way in which the United States is organized to support and in some instances operate programs for international cooperation and development. This organizational aspect is dealt with briefly because Chapters 8 and 11 in this volume examine these issues more extensively.

The analysis here is based on the premise that current U.S. foreign assistance objectives and the delivery systems for their realization need to be much more clearly defined to coincide with the following current realities:

1. Major changes that have occurred in the developing world since USAID was established in 1961, including the graduation of many countries, substantial progress of others, and the relative economic stagnation of the African continent;
2. Great concern relating to the exponential growth of population and the need to protect and renew the natural resource base upon which all long-term development depends;
3. Significant increases in the ranks of bilateral donors, ranging from the Netherlands and Italy to Japan and the OPEC states;
4. The growth in capacity and sophistication of international lending agencies such as the World Bank and the regional development banks;
5. The increase of debt as a major constraint to growth, occasioned by higher energy prices, world recession, attempts to sustain levels of domestic consumption, and faulty macroeconomic policies, affecting both the public and private sectors;
6. The growing importance of middle-income countries and NICs as partners in the development process; and
7. The relative role of the United States, substantially diminished with the

growth of other sources of assistance and the erosion of the concept that it is the world arbiter and the primary source of development capital, both financial and intellectual.

Because of the volume and diversity of assistance now available from other sources, the United States must select those areas where its assistance can have the greatest impact. While progress has been made by USAID and the Peace Corps in concentrating assistance, 35 years of experience working in economic development now compels U.S. policymakers to examine carefully how they can focus their efforts with even greater effect. Taking advantage of recent changes that have occurred outside of the United States, they must now select those arenas where the United States has a comparative advantage, and areas of special policy concern. I assume that overall levels of U.S. foreign assistance will not increase substantially, but that the percentage of the foreign affairs budget available for economic development cooperation will increase modestly. My recommendations also include ways in which development assistance can be managed at less cost and with greater impact.

I will draw a distinction between funding sources and mechanisms needed for long-term development, and the resources needed to achieve short-term political and military objectives. Also included is a brief assessment of the adequacy of the assistance mechanisms used by the United States in both supporting and cooperating with the international development community. I will examine how the United States may need to modify some of these delivery systems and mechanisms, especially with respect to increasing the efficiency of its interaction with these agencies and to altering the manner in which it cooperates with them.

I will outline the demand for different categories of development assistance and recommend a variety of delivery mechanisms relating to special U.S. interests, resources, and capacities in order to respond selectively to these needs.

ORGANIZATION

There is a growing and powerful consensus, derived from an overall agreement on the realities previously described, on the need for the total reorganization of U.S. assistance cooperation. This includes the need to rethink the entire process of how the United States supports and participates in development cooperation on a global basis. The consensus functions within an acceptance of the continued requirement to link international assistance and cooperation with U.S. political, economic, and institutional goals, with the understanding that these are best achieved by means very different from those prevalent when the USAID was founded 25 years ago.

Through the end of this century, the United States will need three delivery systems. They should operate as separate entities even though there will be a need to continue to coordinate them at the highest government levels. These delivery systems should function in support of long-term economic development and cooperation, shorter-term U.S. foreign policy objectives, and a set of military goals related to supporting U.S. foreign policy concerns.

Because the United States' global role is changing and increasing in complexity, there is an urgent need to improve internal government coordination. The experiment with a single foreign assistance agency—IDCA—demonstrated how difficult it is to include many of the responsibilities for international assistance and cooperation within one entity. It is, therefore, proposed that a coordinator for all foreign cooperation and assistance be located within the White House, having direct access to the president. The coordinator would chair a foreign cooperation and assistance committee, which would cover all aspects of the U.S. government's participation in overseas activities, including its coordination with the UN system and international financial institutions. The coordinator, in close concert with OMB, would guide the overall establishment of foreign affairs budgets, including those of a new Agency for International Development and Cooperation, the departments of State, Agriculture, and Treasury, the Export-Import Bank, Peace Corps, Overseas Private Investment Corporation, and the African Development Fund. The committee would include the Department of Defense in order to coordinate requirements for base-rights payments and other military-access costs.

The new Agency for International Development and Cooperation, while it would focus on long-term development and cooperation requirements differentiated by areas of geographic need, would concentrate mainly on policy planning and coordination, institutional development, human resources development, and science and technology.

In outline, the agency would be structured as follows:

Policy Planning and Coordination Office: This office, which would be relatively large, would include responsibility for policy and budget formulation, congressional relations, coordination with other U.S. agencies and with other donors both bilateral and multilateral, and review and approval of cofinancing allocations.

Office of Science and Technology: This would be the other principal organizational unit within the new agency and would concentrate on the transfer of science and technology at all levels and on a global basis. The office would include technical specialists organized within sector offices linked to the agency's objectives with respect to institutional and human resources development, science and technology transfer, support for international institutions, and cofinancing with the multilateral banks. The office would contract out most of its research and operations to nongovernmental institutions and organizations, both private and public. The selective use of cooperating-agency agreements with other elements of the U.S. government would continue. The Office of Science and Technology would also contain geographic units and specialists in order to assure continued access to the knowledge built up by USAID about country-specific requirements. Use of projects as currently formulated and implemented would diminish. The primary project design function of the new agency would be pilot-project formulation in areas of special innovation.

Private Enterprise Office: This office would be small and would contract out almost all of its functions to U.S. financial institutions and private organizations, both for and not for profit. There would be a continuing need for an office of personnel management and procurement as well as for an office of external affairs. The latter office would be expanded substantially beyond USAID's current effort to include a public education element in order to sensitize the U.S. public to broader U.S. interests with respect to international cooperation and development.

Field posts: These would be substantially reduced since the new agency would be undertaking many fewer projects. There would be the need, however, to continue overseas representation in order to take advantage of efforts of other agencies and international institutions as well as to coordinate efforts within developing country requirements and capacities. Regional offices would be established as *primary posts* in such key cities as Harare, Nairobi, Dakar, Cairo, and Manila. These primary posts would contain fairly large staffs of technical specialists whose primary responsibility would be to help identify areas of need and assist in planning efforts for the needs of individual countries. The primary posts would also have responsibility for designing pilot projects and for reviewing projects for cofinancing. Because of the much stronger policy thrust toward international liaison and cooperation, all U.S. embassies in both developing and industrialized countries would have a liaison officer for foreign assistance and coordination. Countries such as India, Brazil, and Indonesia would all have liaison officers assigned to the U.S. embassy. Because of the growing importance of the need to utilize existing international institutions more effectively, particularly within the UN system, staffs devoted to this purpose in such centers as Rome, New York, and Paris would be substantially increased.

Security assistance: All assistance relating to U.S. foreign policy objectives, including security aid, would be handled directly by the State Department, functioning within the Office of the Undersecretary for Security. Economic support funds would be considered as security assistance and would be managed directly by the State Department, with cash transfers being maximally used. Large, labor intensive, project-oriented but foreign policy–directed programs, such as those in Egypt and Pakistan, would be handled primarily through direct cash payments. Some project assistance would be continued bilaterally but with primary responsibility being transferred increasingly to international agencies such as the World Bank and the regional development banks.

Military assistance: Military assistance, which currently accounts for approximately one-third of the foreign assistance budget, would be transferred to the budget of the Department of Defense. This would include foreign military sales, military assistance and training, and payment for base rights. Most of these activities are currently financed from economic support funds. While the Department of Defense would continue to rely on assistance from the State Department for negotiating base rights and gaining access to new military assets overseas, the payments would be charged directly to the defense budget.

In summary, the current foreign affairs budget of $13 billion annually, which is divided approximately one-third each for economic, political, and military assistance, would remain about the same. Switching military assistance to the Department of Defense, however, would permit some substantial expansion of assistance to the international financial institutions, with primary emphasis on the World Bank and the regional development banks. Specialized UN agencies in areas of substantial U.S. concern—such as child survival, family planning, women in development, and the environment—would receive increased financing, accompanied by more direct participation by the United States in the formulation and oversight of their programs.

RECIPIENT AND COOPERATING COUNTRY REQUIREMENTS

For the purposes of this analysis, three categories of countries are identified. (It is understood that this categorization represents gross generalizations and that there are many variations within each grouping.)

1. Most African countries and the other *lower-income* nations of the world (such as Haiti, Nepal, and Bangladesh);
2. Countries characterized as *developing* (e.g., Jamaica, Jordan, Thailand, and Peru), which have per capita incomes around $1,000 per year;
3. *Middle-income* countries and NICs (such as Mexico, Korea, Brazil, and Taiwan).

The first category comprises those nations that are still primary recipients of major resources from external sources. These countries still require broad transfers of training, technical assistance, institutional development, concessional capital, and policy advice. The second category comprises those countries that have more selective needs—usually specialized sets of technological, institutional, and capital requirements. The third category comprises those nations that are in the process of economic maturation. They already have the capacity to become cooperators and sources of assistance themselves, while at the same time requiring specialized access to trade and capital markets. (Although both India and China should be treated separately here since they are very special cases, limitations of space preclude this; India is treated separately as part of the overall series of assessments within this exercise.)

MAJOR CATEGORIES OF ASSISTANCE AND COOPERATION

Technical Assistance

Training. Training programs respond to needs that can be met at three levels: training in the Third World, in the United States, or in other countries. The system proposed to meet these needs is a consortium of U.S. universities, community colleges, and private, for profit training institutions and companies.

Private contractors would be used to place students at the appropriate institutions. Many of these contractors would be in the LDCs since more training needs should be channeled through existing institutions outside the United States in order to ensure relevance and lower cost per trainee. Organization of training contractors would be by skill and sector needs.

For training in the United States, contractors will need to be linked to institutional consortia. Financing will need to be broadened so that specialized assistance will be available to students. Student advisors who are practitioners in the fields in which the students are studying must be provided. This means that students should be grouped in order to benefit from special faculty attention; currently, students are scattered, with little thought to providing them with concentrated faculty support.

Institutional development

Local level: PVOs, both foreign and indigenous, would continue to have a major role. Indigenous training institutions, U.S. and local cooperatives, labor organizations, and the Peace Corps would all be used. Also, the African Development Foundation should have a greatly expanded role, though substantial reorganization may be needed to accomplish this. Its programs should be focused on developing local institutional capacities.

The delivery mechanisms should be funded by direct multiyear grants to U.S. PVOs, cooperatives, and labor groups, which would be responsible for monitoring and evaluating subgrants to local institutions. Where possible, intermediary roles should be delegated to local organizations. Strong financial management would be needed so that the process is not discredited before the indigenous institutions can fully manage a larger quantity of resources.

A separate grant fund for project identification and design for the external cooperating organizations, such as U.S. PVOs, would be required and would permit a higher quality of project development and design than is current.

Since many of the private organizations providing the technical assistance to local institutions cannot be expected to have all the technical skills necessary, there would be need for a series of back-up contracts. These should include both for profit and nonprofit organizations, which would provide consulting services for all the levels of expertise required. Local organizations would also be an approved source for consulting services, as would those from other donor states.

The U.S. sister cities programs should be expanded substantially to link U.S. cities with appropriate Third World communities. The capacity and skills of the sister cities organization would need to be increased considerably to accomplish this. Improvement of local government administration would be the major aim of this program. Sources of community financing would be broadened through such an effort, and private voluntary agencies such as Lasting Links greatly encouraged to expand their operations.

Central government and provincial level: The U.S. role in institutional development should be limited to agricultural universities, community colleges that emphasize continuing education, school administration, and testing systems. The aim would be to strengthen regional associations of universities, such as Midwest Universities Consortium for International Activities and the Consortium for International Development of the arid land western U.S. universities, and to encourage fuller development of the Southwest Universities Consortium for International Development concept, i.e., the linking of 1890 and 1864 land grant institutions.

The Collaborative Assistance Mode (CAM) of institutional project design combined with implementation as a single process should be more widely used. Universities or consortia of universities undertaking major institutional development must be involved at both the design and the execution stage.

A 10-year time frame for the development of land grant college institutions is required for successful transfer of this concept to other countries. A conscious effort should be made to build U.S. geographic expertise through the mechanism of these contracts—essential in order for postcontract linkages to be continued between and among cooperating universities. Special funds will need to be made available in order to promote such continuing linkages.

A separate program of research grants to U.S. institutions for program development and evaluation in key sectors will be required. Examples include adaptation of agricultural research, environmentally sustainable agriculture, renewable energy, and improved science education. Grants should also be made for technical assistance and training provided by non-U.S. institutions that have successfully embodied the land grant concept.

Consortia of U.S. community colleges would be established in order that practical, locally based education, at lower cost and geared toward employment, can be developed.

For school administration, special consulting contracts would have to be established. Most local school districts do not have the capacity to transfer their own experience and success to LDCs. Outstanding school districts that excel in administration will need to be linked with these consultants in order to help bring about the transfer of this knowledge. It may also be advisable to create nonprofit organizations to help analyze and transfer cost-effective school administration.

Testing, its relation to quality education, its cost, and the control of results is another area in which the United States can make a major contribution. Both for-profit and nonprofit organizations, which have been exceptionally successful in the United States in designing and managing large-scale testing at low cost, need to be applied to improving the quality of education and ensuring the objectivity of the results.

SECTOR NEEDS IN AGRICULTURE, HEALTH, PRIVATE ENTERPRISE, AND TECHNOLOGY

Agriculture

The United States should continue a heavy concentration in agriculture. The emphasis must continue to be on food production within the context of sustainable agriculture but should also include exports, increasing rural income, and environmental rehabilitation including reforestation.

The delivery mechanism should be an increased emphasis upon using U.S. land grant colleges. This will not succeed unless the land grant colleges undertake a major restructuring of the ways in which they relate to the institutions they assist. Longer-term posting of key personnel will be needed in order to help develop faculties and research facilities. At the same time, a much fuller range of short-term assignments relating to specific technical and managerial needs, including curriculum development and applied research, is needed. As noted elsewhere, technical assistance should be provided over a much longer time frame than has typically been the case. A postproject assistance phase also needs to be established, linking U.S. colleges with recipient institutions on a more collaborative peer relationship that encompasses the continuing exchange of faculty, students, and research. U.S. land grant colleges should also link up with Third World land grant colleges that have been successfully established in order to form programs of joint technical assistance to help establish new institutions in those countries in which the land grant concept is alien.

The consortium approach to specific crops, embodied in the

Collaborative Research Support Program, should be intensified. Successes in such areas as cow peas, peanuts, and small ruminants indicate the utility of a product-focused approach, applying the technical resources of a number of U.S. institutions in a specific developing country setting.

As food production increases, opportunities for local enterprises in the processing of food and other agricultural products will become increasingly important. Therefore, special programs in support of rural entrepreneurs will need to be established. The most effective delivery mechanisms would be local enterprises in concert with foreign technical experts. Here, special technical assistance and credit would be principal factors. Intermediate credit institutions also would become increasingly important and could be directly assisted by the U.S. cooperative movement, particularly by those cooperatives that have had experience in encouraging local production with a high degree of commercialization and marketing. The U.S. cooperative movement has in recent years been underutilized toward these development ends. In food and agricultural product processing, U.S. commercial firms have no peer in the world and should be extensively used.

A major area of continuing frustration is the development of local research capacity. While there has been little success to date, there is no substitute for locally adapted research. Therefore, national research programs will have to be pushed to the regional and local levels.

For extension of information, LDCs should be encouraged to pursue a parallel approach rather than follow the historical U.S. pattern based upon county and state extension systems. LDCs should seek connections with the commercial sector for both extension services and seed production, as well as other inputs such as fertilizer, in addition to using conventional public institutions.

Health

Health is one area in which the United States still retains some substantial comparative advantages. U.S. leadership in family planning and demography is widely recognized. Both the global and individual impact of unchecked population growth is now being increasingly accepted. While the United States needs to recommit itself to support and expand major funding allocations in this area, it should continue to do so through intermediary systems, many of which it helped to develop. Private agencies, international organizations, and, increasingly, local institutions should be the primary vehicles through which family planning and other population programs are implemented.

The United States' efforts in the future should focus on fostering research in critical new areas such as the application of genetic engineering for new vaccines to treat malaria and other major parasitical diseases. These are problems that are appropriate for U.S. government support and in which the private sector does not have a substantial interest.

Within the reorganization of U.S. foreign assistance and the creation of the new foreign assistance act, there should be a fusion of the disparate and overlapping accounts for child survival, health, population, and AIDS. Intermediaries should be used increasingly to carry out the objectives of these four categories and U.S. government agencies with special expertise, such as the Center for Disease Control and the Bureau of the Census, should continue to play an important role.

There is increasing need to integrate feeding programs, particularly for mothers and children, with child survival activities. The development of a new methodology is urgently needed. The delivery of this system should be the primary responsibility of PVOs, especially local ones, but the WHO, particularly its regional arms, such as Pan American Health Organization, should be used more extensively—especially for programs of immunization.

The major focus of the foreign assistance health office should be one of supporting critical research, identifying and helping to develop local and international delivery systems, and focusing on health policy, especially with respect to locally financed and managed health care.

Private enterprise

Private sector development is treated separately from technical assistance and institutional development because so little progress has been made in this area by USAID and other involved U.S. agencies. The existing organizational units in the U.S. government should be combined into a single, relatively small office whose major functions should be contracted to private companies and banks.

Leveraging U.S. private capital for investment in Africa and other low-income areas would be one major objective. This is a difficult assignment, given the risks and the relative ignorance of the U.S. investing community of many of the geographic areas involved. An important inducement, however, would be access to large existing and prospective local-currency accounts in Africa and elsewhere. Wherever possible, U.S. private capital investment should be tied to local investors in order to provide a degree of local knowledge, as well as to share risk and exposure.

Significant support for local entrepreneurship is only just beginning after many years of frustration and false starts, and needs in this area, for both technical assistance and credit, are great. Existing U.S. mechanisms likely to be successful include small investor incubators (such as those currently being promoted by Control Data Corporation and other U.S. private companies). Computer-assisted learning systems already well developed should be used extensively in order to increase the overall skill levels of entrepreneurs. Special programs in support of the informal sector, using local organizations, should also receive special emphasis. In this regard, local PVOs and existing local small business associations in Africa should receive special attention. The African Development Foundation, U.S. PVOs, and the Peace Corps would have a special role in this area. Support for the local private sector in rural and urban areas must be viewed as a major effort seen in the context of ongoing and prospective policy reform programs.

While job creation would be a normal function of both investment and support of entrepreneurship, it will require additional attention. Increased use of technology should not be allowed to bring about a reduction in job opportunities but rather an increase. Job creation can also be related to the U.S. special educational effort emphasizing practical education through community colleges.

Technology

Most African nations and many other low-income countries have not been able to take advantage of the great mass of usable technology already available. Therefore, a new Foundation for Technology Cooperation should be established, dedicated to transferring existing technologies in order to accelerate economic and social development. The foundation must find ways of applying modern scientific and managerial solutions to the major development bottlenecks. It could do so by providing bridges between the scientific/industrial progress of the United States and an appreciation of local social and political circumstances, thus allowing greater emphasis on a full understanding of and by the people being affected by the new technology.

U.S. private sector success in popularizing new technologies, processes, and products would be an important aspect in effecting the transfer of this technology. While the foundation would be a nonprofit institution, it would seek to establish financially self-sustaining programs. This could be accomplished by using the private sector whenever possible and by having the beneficiaries pay for the services and goods received.

The foundation would build upon a unique aspect of modern corporations, i.e., their ability to turn the results of research and development into broadly utilizable products and services and to get these rapidly accepted by the general public. The history of technology transfer to much of the Third World is exactly the reverse of this. The enormous body of scientific and technical knowledge available for development has been virtually untapped because the customers of this technology have seldom been consulted, and an institutional interface between their needs and available knowledge has never been developed. As a result, no methodology for the application of modern scientific and management knowledge to basic development needs has ever been established. This would be a primary goal of the foundation.

Initially, the foundation would attempt to improve health, increase food production, and arrest or reverse environmental decline. Over the longer term, it would foster the modernization of science education, and the gathering, management, and dissemination of data and information. By focusing on health, food production, environment, and education, the foundation would seek to strengthen and build upon the synergisms among these four areas.

Management affects all aspects of development and change. However, one of the major constraints at the present is the limitation of local organizations and institutions both to gain access to and effectively to use available resources. Therefore, an important goal of the Foundation for Technology Cooperation would be the application to management of modern technological change. This can increase local institutional capacities, providing a marriage between modern data accumulation and information transfer and the needs of local communities. Communities, such as villages and cooperatives, are frequently much more effective in identifying and responding to local requirements than are government agencies. They also form historically important linkages with the local culture and history and, therefore, can process change in a way compatible with local usage. In order to achieve this, however, a new process needs to be established that links basic management requirements at the local level with the new, available tools. This is an extremely difficult task but one that needs to be undertaken since the very concept of management is being fundamentally altered by the application of computer-related sciences and techniques. The understanding of this process is still at an infant stage. However, an intensive analysis needs to be undertaken in order to assist in bringing both modern management and technology to beneficiaries at the grassroots level.

Management will, of course, remain an extremely important requirement at national levels. Here, however, more conventional approaches such as decentralization, privatization, and the introduction of national and regional schools of management remain the most cost-effective means of transferring management skills to large public and private organizations. The efforts of U.S. institutions that have had success in management training at the project, organizational, and macro levels should be continued and enhanced.

A special pilot program to help achieve replicable breakthroughs for activities in sectors of concentration will be needed. Pilot projects would receive great care, both in design and in evaluation; this is essential for adaptation and application elsewhere. Examples of such projects include low-cost, self-sustaining health delivery systems, successful family planning efforts, agricultural production, food processing and preservation, and small-scale entrepreneurial projects.

FOOD AID

Food aid presents a special series of issues. There is a need to revamp existing PL-480 legislation completely. As currently written, it fosters conflicting objectives. U.S. agricultural exports are seen in the short term by farm groups as being reduced by the very economic development that is being encouraged. A longer-term view needs to be taken—i.e., that U.S. food aid can help overall economic growth in developing countries, which will, over time, bring about increases in U.S. agricultural exports, providing U.S. products remain competitive.

The Department of Agriculture also frequently dictates program content and direction based on immediate domestic production, thereby making food aid a very unreliable development tool. Existing food aid–delivery systems need to be changed.

Title I, dollar-repayable loans should be eliminated for Africa and lower-income countries. It borders on the absurd to make dollar loans, even on concessional terms, to countries overburdened by debt. Existing Title I loans should be renegotiated into Title III grants, which should concentrate on supporting either ongoing or proposed policy reform in agriculture. In those few countries where agricultural reform is no longer needed, Title III programs should be used in policy areas of special U.S. interest—for example, institutional development, technology transfer, and health.

Local-currency accounts should be used to leverage U.S. private investment and to support local entrepreneurs. Local currency should *always* be utilized in support of U.S.-related policy objectives and should not be treated as a budgetary free good. It should also be available for use in cofinancing projects with MDBs. The United States should agree to use local-currency accounts for part or all of the host country contribution to World Bank or African Development Bank foreign exchange loans.

A special local-currency account should be established to support local PVOs, which can be linked with U.S. PVOs in order to provide assistance in technical areas, project development, and financial management.

Increases in monetization of donation programs should be encouraged. Currently, funds generated in this manner are limited to project uses. Use of these funds also should be permitted to support organizational growth and, in some instances, to meet recurrent financing needs of private local development agencies. The institutional development potential for the use of these funds should be emphasized.

There needs to be developed a new and more complete methodology with respect to food-for-work programs. Food-for-work projects should be directed toward alleviating rural unemployment, and the use of local currencies as partial cash payment should also be permitted. Food-for-work should also be used as a training instrument. USAID should borrow from the experience of the International Labor Office in labor intensive rural development activities. U.S. PVOs, as well as Peace Corps volunteers, can play an important role in food-for-work activities, though both groups would need special training for effective utilization. These activities should be concentrated in rural infrastructure, agriculture, job creation, skills training, and health.

USAID should take a more active role in working with the World Food Program to revamp its food-for-work policies and methodology in order to make it more effective in alleviating rural unemployment and in developing economically sound rural infrastructure activities.

Special welfare programs in support of maternal and child health and family planning should be continued but should be more directly related to health and nutrition training.

CAPITAL ASSISTANCE, POLICY REFORM, AND DEBT RELIEF

Financing of infrastructure should be left to the World Bank and the regional development banks as well as those donors with special interests in this area, such as the European Common Market Fund, the OPEC Funds, and Italy. Capital transfers from the United States for economic development assistance should be limited to helping to mobilize other donor resources to coincide with U.S. foreign assistance priorities. These include special environmental programs, building technical and agricultural research capacity, specialized institutional development, and health programs such as low-cost delivery systems and family planning. There is substantial capital aid available from many donors that do not have a special analytical capacity to direct their assistance; they should be encouraged to target their aid to the critical development areas selected by the United States.

Some exceptions to this principle will be necessary—e.g., cofinancing or direct participation in major regional programs in which several other donors are participating, such as transport in Southern Africa. In this instance, U.S. participation also has important direct policy implications.

The United States should concentrate on cofinancing policy reform at both the macroeconomic and sectoral levels. It should leave to the World Bank much of the analytical and design work in determining the details of these programs. The role of the United States in cofinancing should be to help influence World Bank policy directions as well as financing to those policy areas and geographic zones where the United States has special interests and knowledge and where the provision of additional capital can have a significant effect.

A strong policy office within a new Agency for International Development and Cooperation would have an important review function in examining projects being proposed by the bank with respect to both policy direction and content. Such a policy group would also have a major role in interacting with other donors to leverage funding into areas of greatest need. A significant percentage of the Africa Development Fund resources should be programmed in this manner rather than as separate, policy-directed projects.

The problem of debt provides a major constraint to achieving progress in many of the areas described above. The function of this chapter is not to deal extensively with solutions to this complex and difficult problem. Therefore, I will only note that the failure of the United States to respond to this problem in any effective manner is a product of policy inertia resulting in part from organizational issues within the U.S. government. Basic differences between the State Department and the Treasury on how to deal with the problem are at the root of this paralysis. In sum, the following actions need to be taken:

Commercial interest rates need to be rescheduled on near concessional terms and over much longer periods of time—up to 20 years.

Multilateral debt poses an especially difficult issue. The creditworthiness of the World Bank is at issue in the bank's rescheduling of its own loans. Arrears to the IMF are reaching alarming proportions. While reluctant to do so, the fund must stretch repayment periods, even with the expanded structural adjustment facility. Just as important, the fund must also expand its staff capacity in order to undertake much more detailed and realistic analyses of the structural problems of the developing countries. More realistic policy packages and more imaginative approaches geared to the specific needs of the countries must be developed. This cannot be accomplished without a substantial expansion of fund staff capacities.

Regional development banks should be asked to play a larger role in helping with structural adjustment lending and reform packages in order to stimulate growth and thereby give countries a greater capacity to pay back their debts.

Debt-for-equity swaps should be encouraged. Programs such as the investment of Club Med in Mexico and the environmental programs in Colombia are examples of imaginative debt-for-equity transactions.

U.S. PVOs working in concert with U.S. private banks and the central banks of the debtor countries need to be encouraged to find opportunities for *debt write-offs* under recent Internal Revenue Service rulings. A U.S. private bank can now take a tax reduction by writing off its debt to a central bank, which, in turn, will make the funds available to a U.S. PVO for development activities.

The Policy Planning and Coordination Office in the proposed Agency for International Development and Cooperation would be charged with providing the White House coordinator with the primary staff work relating to U.S. economic assistance and would provide direct support for the chair on the committee composed of all U.S. government agencies involved in foreign assistance. The staff function of this office is considered essential in order to ensure proper coordination of U.S. economic assistance efforts, both with the U.S. government, with international fora, and in relation to the areas of U.S. geographic concern.

Because of the number of African countries and their relatively small size, there is a need for special support for multicountry cooperation. This is also important because of the fragile political and economic structure of many African nation-states. Therefore, regional and subregional cooperation should be much more vigorously promoted through organizations such as the Southern African Development Coordination Conference. Donors should act in concert much more seriously. African regional organizations fostering economic cooperation, such as the Economic Community of West African States, also will need support. A special function of the U.S. foreign assistance agency would be to foster coordination and cooperation among donors.

POLITICAL ASSISTANCE

Development professionals, policymakers, and the public should accept the fact that politically motivated assistance is a legitimate and necessary tool for the achievement of U.S. foreign policy objectives and not attempt to blend it with economic assistance objectives even though they sometimes interact. The major difference between the utilization of political and economic assistance is that the former is of a short-term nature, while sound economic assistance is long-term in character. As a result, I propose the following:

A fund for security and political objectives related to U.S. foreign policy needs. Such a fund should be kept separate from the African Development Fund and the development account for other regions. Economic support funds as currently conceived should be replaced by a political/security fund controlled by the State Department, which will need to take account of U.S. economic assistance policies and programs in order to assure nonconflicting uses and impact. This fund would have clear political objectives (examples are payments to Israel, Egypt, and Jordan).

Base rights and military access. The payment for U.S. base rights and access to military facilities should be made directly from the Department of Defense budget and should not be cloaked in other rationales. The Department of Defense will need assistance from the State Department in negotiating these agreements. However, it should be very clear that the United States is buying military and security-related assets, and that such Department of Defense funds function to this end.

DEVELOPING COUNTRIES

Countries with per capita incomes of around $1,000 per year have a different set of needs from those of the lower-income states and, for the most part, have a degree of institutional development that permits more rapid utilization of external technical and financial resources. One of the keys for effective U.S. assistance is more efficient delivery of these resources and access to private resources in the United States by the countries. At the same time, these states still need a reasonable degree of concessional assistance. They can, however, accept a mix of long-term loans and grants, as opposed to all grants. Even though many of them have significant debt problems, soft loans are still an appropriate assistance mechanism, especially when the loans are used for productive purposes. Illustrative of the countries under discussion are Jamaica, Jordan, Thailand, and Peru, each in the process of more accelerated development.

While it is always difficult to generalize about any grouping, developing countries tend to have stronger regional commercial and trade relationships, providing greater prospects for cooperation with peer nations. Members of organizations such as the Caribbean Community and the Andean Pact tend to take greater advantage of possibilities for regional economic cooperation and trade than do the lower-income countries. The Inter-American Development Bank and the Asian Development Bank are also stronger regional development institutions, providing a higher volume of lending as well as designing projects with a greater degree of sophistication.

Assistance from the United States, therefore, should be different both in degree and in kind from that received by lower-income countries. The developing countries are better able to utilize capital transfers to support both infrastructure needs and policy reform (as noted elsewhere, this should be accomplished through MDBs). Development of exports and job creation are important requirements. Because local institutions are more highly developed, they could receive larger volumes of external assistance more directly and with less emphasis upon projects. While they still would need capital, technology, and improved management, these needs could be met by direct linkages with banks, private investors, foundations, and universities.

The enormous reservoir of scientific, technical, and management expertise in the United States needs to be made more accessible to the developing countries, and their indigenous institutional capacity to use these resources must be strengthened through special programs established to facilitate access to U.S. resources. Here, a Foundation for Technology and Cooperation would have an extremely important role.

U.S. assistance to the regional development banks should be of primary importance for macroeconomic reform and sector programs. In addition to normal direct financial support, the United States should emphasize cofinancing; while the risk is somewhat higher in cofinancing with the regional development banks than with the World Bank, this should still be an important element of U.S. assistance strategy. Such cofinancing would strengthen the institutional capacity of the regional banks, as well as provide them with important capital. USAID regional field posts and liaison offices should have an important role in reviewing proposed projects, and cofinancing should be undertaken on a selective basis and in direct relation to areas of U.S. development policy. Cofinancing should also be used to encourage direct participation by other donors.

Debt problems in these countries are a function more of private than of public debt. Hence, the United States must find ways to promote commercial rescheduling along more realistic lines, including softer terms. USAID should encourage U.S. banks with substantial debt exposure to use the debt–write-off possibilities now available to them under recent Internal Revenue Service rulings to finance PVO programs.

Because debt is such a big problem for developing countries, direct, private investment has slowed greatly. Hence, a major role for the United States is to help develop investment opportunities in these countries. U.S. merchant banks, PVOs, and corporations with technology-based training and job creation programs need to be joined in partnership. Access to concessional financing is required to make many private investments attractive.

Interregional trade, while often difficult to achieve, needs to be emphasized. Merchant and trading banks could be especially useful, providing analysis, technical advice, and access to lines of credit established by the regional development banks, the United States, and other donors.

The creation of jobs in these countries is an especially crucial issue. Access needs to be encouraged, with those organizations mentioned elsewhere specializing in job-related training. These include consortia of U.S. community colleges, private sector firms, agribusiness, and private sector food-processing companies.

Job training is needed to attract foreign investment. In rural areas, the Peace Corps and local PVOs could take a special responsibility. In urban areas, both PVOs and U.S. for profit training organizations should be enlisted.

MIDDLE-INCOME AND NEWLY INDUSTRIALIZED COUNTRIES

Despite severe debt problems in some of the middle-income nations such as Mexico and Brazil, these countries form a large and relatively untapped source of training and technical assistance for both the lower-income countries and the developing nations.

Within the context of a growing, interdependent world economy, based upon access to and utilization of new technologies, the role of the middle-income countries and NICs with respect to both trade and economic transformation is becoming increasingly important. Technology transfer is part of a broader world economic linkage. There is a great danger that the lower-income and even the advancing countries will be left behind as change becomes ever-accelerating as a result of the world technological revolution. The middle-income states and NICs provide a source for lower-cost and more relevant transfer of basic institution-building, information, education, and training.

Because the resource middle-income and newly industrialized countries represent is so great, and the cost of providing access and sustaining the transfer from that resource is so enormous, the United States cannot expect to finance this process alone. It is appropriate, however, for the United States to take a leadership role in establishing a Fund for Technical Cooperation in order to provide access to the substantial resources from these nations. This fund could be established either within the context of a UN agency or the World Bank. A central location would facilitate contributions to the fund by other bilateral donors. Recent entrants into the world of bilateral assistance, such as Japan and Italy, are looking for mechanisms through which to channel substantial resources. Such a fund could very rapidly become an important vehicle for their assistance.

Assistance from the middle-income countries and the NICs should take a wide variety of forms. At one level, these countries can provide operating personnel in larger numbers and at relatively low cost. This has recently been seen to be successful in Zimbabwe, where managers from the Indian National Rail Corporation assisted in the maintenance and operation of Zimbabwe's rail system.

The middle-income states and the NICs have many training institutions with available capacity and appropriate skills for utilization by the lower-income countries and the advancing states. Special areas, such as small business development, local management and training, small-scale agriculture, and locally based health delivery systems lend themselves to the utilization of these institutional resources.

The multinational Fund for Technical Cooperation could be used to catalog the availability of these institutions, their costs, and the way in which they can be made accessible. These institutions, rather than training facilities based in the United States or other industrialized countries, should increasingly be utilized.

The fostering of trade between the middle-income and newly industrialized countries and the lower-income states of the world is becoming increasingly important, and the former should therefore be made approved sources for the supply of commodities, services for structural adjustment loans, and commodity-import programs financed by the U.S. government. For example, small-scale Chinese farming implements are probably more appropriate and cost less than does similar equipment made in the United States, or even in Japan.

In certain others areas, also, particularly with respect to improvements in agricultural processing, NICs and middle-income countries are becoming increasingly important. The transfer of forest products into higher-value commodities, agricultural processing, food production, and storage have all shown marked advances in these countries. Of special importance are on-farm and commodity storage and regional food security.

Countries, such as Brazil, with substantial success in developing small-scale industry and private investment should be encouraged to provide direct assistance to the private sectors in developing states.

This approach to encouraging the relationship of NICs and middle-income countries with the Third and Fourth worlds will probably find substantial resistance in the United States. In the short term, increasing trade among these countries and lower-income nations that form the fastest-growing market for U.S. export products will be seen as having a negative impact on U.S. exports. At the same time, there is indisputable historical evidence that the overall growth of the lower-income countries will most certainly increase their demand for U.S. products and services.

IMPROVING OPERATING PROCEDURES WITH THE UN SYSTEM

Despite many inefficiencies, the myriad of UN agencies involved in international development represent an enormous resource for improving and increasing the effectiveness of U.S. foreign policy. With the exception of the Child Survival Campaign, fostered by UNICEF, the UN system has had little direct influence on U.S. assistance mechanisms. In turn, except for child survival, family planning, environmental concerns, and the role of women, the United States has not had enough impact upon the direction of UN development policies, despite the fact that the United States has historically been the single largest funder of these efforts.

There are many opportunities to use the UN system and, in so doing, influence both its direction and its efficiencies. As noted elsewhere in this chapter, the International Labor Organization has had a high degree of success in labor intensive rural works programs in many of the least developed countries of the world. These programs lend themselves to joint efforts through the utilization of local currency for food-for-work activities and the use of Peace Corps volunteers on these projects. Despite the fact that this program is now almost 10 years old, it is almost unknown among U.S. development agencies, including USAID.

The FAO, rather than being seen as a political problem, should be used for its substantial expertise in such crucial areas as reforestation and on-farm storage. FAO represents the single largest organized pool of agricultural talent in the world. It is self-defeating not to pursue policies that draw on this talent and move it in ways consonant with U.S. foreign assistance objectives.

The IFAD, with its emphasis on small farmers and cooperatives, also should be a vehicle for greater U.S. cooperation. This organization, the creation of the United States and the OPEC states, is currently underutilized in terms of its potential for joint programming. IFAD also could provide an excellent opportunity for the more effective utilization of Peace Corps volunteers in fostering local agricultural production.

The UNDP resident representatives, and the more recently established resident coordinators, need to be strengthened. Their potential role in coordinating not only UN programs but also in assisting host governments to track and manage the large number of bilateral and other multilateral agency efforts should not be underestimated. The impact could greatly improve overall donor effectiveness, especially with respect to clustering projects in support of both macroeconomic and sector objectives.

An effective, on-site resident coordinator could help to alleviate the enormous management burden placed upon host governments in keeping track of hundreds of externally financed activities. A knowledge of these activities would be of great importance for understanding the implications for future recurrent costs. It is very unfortunate that so little is known about the overall budget impact of ongoing development projects on virtually all recipient countries.

Even more difficult, but worthy of greater attention, is an attempt to develop some uniformity with respect to project documentation. Each donor has its own special set of requirements, both for documentation and procurement. This management burden on recipient governments cannot be overemphasized: Conforming to project documentation and procurement regulations is a problem of enormous complexity. However, it would not be inappropriate to ask UNDP, or some other UN agency, to take on this task. The OECD has, from time to time, attempted to come to grips with this problem, without much success. This does not mean, however, that the objective should not be attempted.

A more active role by the United States in the community of UN development agencies could also have substantial effect on the plans of Japan and Italy to channel massive funds through UN agencies over the next five years. For example, Japan plans to provide $400 million over five years for 10 African countries through the UN systems, apart from its own regular UN contributions. Much of this money could be moved into areas consonant with U.S. development interests and expertise without affecting the independence of the UN agencies involved, or Japan's desire not to lose control of the programming of these monies.

The area of information exchange among bilateral and multilateral development agencies needs attention. There is no excuse, in an age of highly sophisticated data management and information transfer, for there to be such a paucity of information about the assistance programs of other countries and international agencies. The UN secretary-general cannot be provided with a single document that shows the programs of all the UN development agencies in any one country. There is not only a need for the United Nations to be able to provide such information, but there should also be a system whereby *all other donors*, both bilateral and multilateral, could funnel their assistance data into a single information source so that the total amount of financing being made available in any given year can be known. In addition, information by sector and by type of financing is invaluable for ministries of both planning and finance in order to keep track of the level and future costs of development aid. Such information is also useful for all donor agencies, the better to channel their assistance, synergistically, into areas of need.

In sum, the resources of the UN system have not been adequately utilized by the United States in supporting its own assistance objectives. A major effort in this area would be exceptionally cost effective and would improve the impact of U.S. bilateral efforts.

REMOVING LEGISLATIVE CONSTRAINTS

A major constraint on moving forward with the new mechanisms and systems described above are the many limitations imposed by foreign assistance legislation. There are over 106 limitations in the annual appropriations legislation, and another 100-plus in the authorizing legislation, resulting in 136 annual reports, plus separate congressional notifications on increases in annual budget appropriations for every activity. The Foreign Assistance Act is now over 300 pages long, and the annual appropriations bill usually exceeds 100 pages. Such constraints constitute a major hindrance to pursuing the effective modernization of U.S. foreign assistance and its delivery systems.

Major areas that need to be modified or eliminated include annual appropriations. Multiyear authorizations are required in order to provide an appropriate planning horizon and to prevent funds from being obligated at the last minute for poorly conceived activities. By making funds available until they are expended, it will also be possible to design pilot projects with greater care and with much more participation by the beneficiaries.

The elimination of functional accounts will help in minimizing earmarking, which is a favorite congressional policy-management tool. There are many special interest groups with many good causes supporting functional accounts. Nonetheless, a unitary budget makes it infinitely easier both to plan and to manage effective foreign assistance. Micromanagement by the Congress, especially with respect to earmarking of funds, has been a major problem in the past. An overall agreement must be negotiated between the executive branch and the Congress in order that the general directions of foreign assistance are agreed upon, overall policy concepts created, and the executive branch permitted to undertake its work.

The untying of goods and services would not only lower the cost of U.S. foreign aid but also would greatly increase its effectiveness and efficiency. An important side effect is the economic effect of procurement for local development with concomitant beneficial economic effect.

Other less constraining but still irritating and important limitations include:

- The 30-day notification of Congress prior to initiating debt relief by the executive branch;
- Restrictions on assisting countries with the production of agricultural commodities in surplus in the United States;
- Limitations on publicizing U.S. foreign assistance in the United States to any extent;
- Three million–dollar limitation on revolving-fund projects;
- The limitation on PVOs that 20 percent of their resources be derived from non–U.S.-government sources (especially onerous for small and newly established PVOs);
- Restraints against using developing countries for architectural and engineering services;
- Termination of assistance because of loan-payment arrears; and
- The continuing insistence on using U.S. cargo ships for both regular commodities and PL-480, the latter requiring 75 percent U.S. bottoms.

This list could be extended almost ad nauseam but represents the major constraints that need to be removed in order to make U.S. assistance more effective.

FOURTEEN

Beyond Aid:
Alternative Modes of Cooperation

PRINCETON N. LYMAN

For nearly 30 years, the United States has defined its relationship with the Third World largely in terms of foreign aid. Part of the rationale for aid has been developmental, part has been security related. In either case, an image of the Third World has been firmly planted in U.S. minds: poor, unstable, and—more recently—ungrateful.

U.S. government organization has mirrored this pattern; the budget for Third World policy and programs has been almost exclusively the aid budget. The principal institution for addressing Third World problems is called USAID. Efforts to overcome this approach have foundered on institutional rigidity and the defense of bureaucratic and professional stakes in the status quo. Not only in the bureaucracy, but in the Congress and academe, as well as the community of PVOs, the preservation of the aid mentality has been an indispensable part of the struggle by important groups in U.S. society to control U.S. policy toward the Third World. Sometimes the motivation is developmental, sometimes humanitarian, sometimes it is just a question of power.

In the 1990s, however, the relevance of the aid approach that has characterized U.S. policy for the past 30 years will be minimal in all but a few parts of the Third World. Few Third World countries of significance to the United States will be aid recipients, especially of bilateral aid. Those who do command large aid allocations will do so more for security than developmental reasons, and the gap between economic "need" and allocation of resources will grow. Trade issues will become of steadily greater importance. Financial issues, such as debt, already overshadow other developmental concerns and thus increasingly make aid less central to the most fundamental economic decisions that have to be made affecting the Third World for the next decade. New problems also compete increasingly for determination of U.S. policy in the Third World: drug production and trafficking, AIDS, terrorism.

Finally, and perhaps most significant, are the changes in technology coming so rapidly and having so fundamental an effect on the future of Third World countries that traditional aid agencies and experts are unable to keep up with them. These changes, moreover, are dissolving the traditional relationships between developed and developing countries and creating new ones that will basically affect developmental strategies and prospects.

To address the challenges of the 1990s, the United States needs to redefine its interests in the Third World. In this redefinition, traditional aid concerns, including development, must be only a subset, and perhaps a small—if significant—one. The interests that should inform U.S. policies and institutional responses include:

- The Third World's potential for weakening the international financial system;
- The need to capture more of the rapidly growing Third World market for U.S. exports;
- The instability and potential for conflict in the Third World, directly affecting U.S. interests;
- Problems of drugs, disease, crime, and migration that operate in and from the Third World and that impinge directly on U.S. lives and interests; and
- The problem of persistent poverty, especially in the least developed countries, and how to deal with it on a long-term basis.

In addressing this set of interests, the United States will need new bureaucratic structures. No "super Third World agency" is possible. U.S. interests are too diverse and involve too many legitimate actors throughout the government, but new, stronger, and more effective coordinating mechanisms can address these interests effectively. The new structure should, moreover, provide for a diverse set of responses to Third World issues, including new uses of aid and other resources. These responses should include special programs for the least developed, programs in science and technology targeted on the middle-income NICs, and resources devoted specifically to export promotion. There will need to be less direct bureaucratic control of some of these programs, and less centralization of control over the diversity of U.S. relationships with the Third World as a whole. Security programs have to be an indispensable part of the total and recognized as such.

With this approach, the United States would still face problems of poverty, instability, trade deficits, debt, drugs, and migration—problems that will all be part of the environment of the 1990s. But, the United States would have a more differentiated policy and programmatic capacity to address them; it would have more specialized and differentiated instruments. It would, too, have involved a larger part of both the government and public in addressing U.S. interests in the Third World. That in itself may lead to a better response to the truly enormous challenges of the 1990s.

THE AID MENTALITY

In 1961, in a period of exceptional intellectual creativity, the U.S. government created its first consolidated agency dedicated to the objective of development in the Third World. Embedded in this decision was not only a bureaucratic reorganization, but a decidedly new approach to development based on an outpouring of academic and other studies of development economics.

It was a heady time. People believed they understood the dynamics of development. And they believed that if they could put together the various technical inputs and financial resources, within an overall conceptual and policy framework, there could be a steady progression of success stories. The model was Taiwan, which was just then emerging as an extraordinary (and unexpected) success story. The targets were countries such as India, Pakistan, Indonesia, Brazil, and Colombia.

The United States, however, made a fundamental error in an otherwise noble and wise move. It chose to name the new entity the Agency for International Development. Thus, it stamped on the U.S. psyche (and on the minds of those in the Third World) the association of the Third World, and U.S. interests there, with aid.

Equally important, it associated development with aid. Indeed, it has become difficult for development practitioners and professionals to accept any form of economic activity not associated with (if not downright funded by) aid as truly "developmental." One sees this in Percy Mistry's admirable contribution to this volume, "Financing Development in the 1990s." Mistry struggles with the practice of export credits, accepting them as legitimate but refusing to accept them as development assistance. Somehow, they can be useful, even desirable, but not "development." The latter is reserved for aid, meaning concessional aid, or ODA in the language of the fraternity.

The problem in this is that for the U.S. public, development—rather than being an objective of distinction and value to the United States—is something that can only be achieved in these Third World countries by aid, or (to put it bluntly) charity. Third World countries cannot develop by competing in the international economic sphere nor by participating directly with the United States in mutually beneficial commercial enterprises (as France and England do), but only through special concessions.

It is no surprise, therefore, that when these countries do achieve a level of development that enables them to compete, there is resentment in the U.S. mind: These countries made it on U.S. charity and are now ungratefully taking away U.S. markets and jobs. The problem is highlighted in Charles William Maynes's chapter, "U.S. Foreign Policy Interests in the Third World in the Years Ahead." Maynes points out that "most people in the United States believe that over the longer run people and nations fundamentally get what they deserve. The rich are rich because they have earned their wealth; the poor are poor because they have not tried hard enough."

From time to time, of course, as the limitations and disadvantages of this association of development and aid have become manifest, there have been efforts to overcome it. But these attempts have foundered on confusion of objectives and on the ambivalence of those making them. For example, throughout the history of aid legislation, there has been a constant struggle between the more clearly "security" aspects of assistance and the more purely developmental or humanitarian. When the administration leaned too far in the direction of security, as in the early 1970s, the Senate reacted so sharply as to defeat the basic authorization bill and later rewrote the legislation with a strong separation of security and development objectives. On the other hand, when the aid rationale became too closely associated with issues of equity and humanitarianism (basic human needs, for instance) the Congress reacted by earmarking much of the funds for special security-related countries and—while applauding the humanitarian emphasis—virtually made it second priority in funding. The same conflicts and ambivalence exist when commercial interests are introduced into the equation.

Efforts to broaden the basis of U.S. interests have also encountered opposition from one of the strongest constituencies for foreign aid, the PVOs. They have argued not only against greater political and security rationales for assistance but even against macroeconomic approaches and the allocation of significant funding for nonproject support of structural adjustment, lest such allocations take away from PVO activity on a people-to-people basis. For PVOs, the image of Third World countries as poor, deprived, and needing aid is central to their raison d'être and, to be frank, to their fund-raising activities. This is not meant as a criticism of their motives. PVOs contain some of the most dedicated and selfless people in the United States, and their humanitarianism is a credit to the best in the nation. But the image of poverty and helplessness that flows from this approach has its cost in the attitude of U.S. voters toward the Third World. As I wrote in an essay on the images of Africa in the U.S. mind:

> It is an image of disaster, of drought, starvation and death. It is the picture of millions of helpless people, clutching stick-figured babies to dried breasts, without hope unless outside help arrives. It is an image that calls forth our sympathy, indeed brings forth incredible acts of generosity and giving. But it is not an image that creates admiration. Nor one that conjures up much hope.[1]

In summary, we have tried to squeeze within a single response mechanism—aid—a complexity of interests in a great part of the world. There were good reasons for trying to do so. And indeed, efforts to broaden that focus foundered as much on congressional and public ambivalence as on conflicting motives within the various administrations or among Third World "experts." But in the 1990s, this approach will not suffice. The problems have changed, U.S. interests have multiplied, and, perhaps most important of all, the Third World has changed.

THE CHALLENGES OF THE 1990s

Development and aid: Development will of course remain one of the most important objectives of the United States in the Third World. The stake in development is multiple: economic, humanitarian, commercial, political, and security-related. However, even in terms of development, aid will be less significant to U.S. policy than previously, confined largely to a few countries that are very poor or are of special interest.

What is true of development is even more true of political and security concerns. Already, bilateral aid programs have been phased out or greatly reduced in many of the most important Third World countries. The United States has no significant bilateral aid program in Argentina, Brazil, Colombia, Chile, Mexico, Venezuela, South Korea, Taiwan, Zimbabwe, Algeria, Saudi Arabia, Iraq, Iran, Singapore, or Malaysia.

Debt: In both aid recipients and other Third World countries, the debt problem is beginning to overwhelm all other development-financing considerations. Of the 17 largest Third World debtors, only eight are recipients of U.S. bilateral financial aid. Even in those debtor countries where aid is important, it is becoming more and more marginal to solving the debt problem.

For a while, in the 1980s, there was an effort to use aid to overcome the debt problem. Multidonor aid packages were being put together to fund IMF- and IBRD-inspired programs of recovery in which irreducible (not able to be rescheduled or already rescheduled) debt was one of the most difficult gaps to cover (e.g., in Sudan, Zambia, Liberia, Zaire, Jamaica, Ecuador, and the Philippines). Pressure was brought to bear on donors to increase the proportion of nonproject financing for this purpose. In some cases, aid was used directly to repay debts to other aid entities.

By the end of the 1980s, however, this approach proved untenable. The debt problem multiplied, beyond the capacity of aid resources to cover it. Aid constituencies, including the U.S. Congress, rebelled at the use of development aid for this purpose.

The debt problem, moreover, is not managed within the U.S. government by USAID. It touches on critical issues of U.S. international (and domestic) financial and monetary policy and is largely in the province of Treasury. For much of the Third World—i.e., outside Africa—the problem is commercial debt and thus even more distant from USAID's operation. In summary, as debt looms larger in the development equation, the aid response has to be seen as less directly relevant and less centrally controlling.

Trade: Another major change that has taken place in the U.S. relationship with the Third World is that trade issues now loom very large. They cut two ways. On the one hand, Third World countries represent the fastest-growing market for U.S. goods and services and thus are an important export market. Representing 40 percent of U.S. exports already, they are one of the most important ways out of the U.S. trade deficit. Development becomes relevant here, for if these countries cannot grow, neither can U.S. exports to them. Resolving the debt problem will also be crucial to this, as Percy Mistry aptly points out.

However, the other side of the coin is that some of these countries are either strong competitors or are blocking U.S. exports. In either case, aid programs, where they exist for such countries, will be subject to restrictions and conditions related to trade. Already, Congress has reverted to a restriction, dropped in the 1960s in the face of fears of world famine, that prohibits U.S. aid to production of crops or products that would compete with U.S. exports. We can expect more such restrictions. The dilemma will become especially acute in cases where agricultural exports from the United States, an important economic and political interest, are restricted by developing countries seeking to boost their own food production. Nigeria now bans the importation of wheat, denying the United States its previously largest export to that country. Malt has just been added to the list. For how long will the United States turn a blind eye to such restrictions?

But aid is not the main consideration in this matter. The principal competitors or restricters are no longer aid recipients: South Korea's trade practices became an election issue in the United States; Taiwan (which I nostalgically remember as an aid recipient when I joined USAID in 1961) now has the fourth largest holding of foreign exchange reserves in the world—some $90 billion; Brazil is a major exporter to the United States of shoes and textiles. The principal trade issues with the Third World cannot be handled, even badly, through the aid mechanism. They are part of another dialog and must be handled through other parts of the U.S. government.

Drugs: Yet another problem with a focus in the Third World is becoming more important to the United States: drugs. Production of heroin and cocaine is almost exclusively in Third World countries; trafficking is being taken over by Third World criminals; whole political systems are being corrupted by the trade. U.S. relations with some Third World countries are coming to be dominated by this issue. Panama, Bolivia, Colombia, Mexico, and Pakistan are deeply affected, and the problem is growing in Malaysia, the Bahamas, and the smaller countries of Africa. It is approaching alarming proportions in such countries as Nigeria and Kenya.

USAID aid plays an important role in antinarcotics programs, but it is a secondary role. And USAID is on potentially dangerous grounds when it argues, though with justification, that narcotics production is partly a development problem in that these crops are often grown by poor farmers with few comparable alternatives.[2] Poverty cannot be an excuse for moral turpitude; there are many poor people in the world who neither grow poppies nor stuff their body cavities with narcotics and act as "mules" in order to meet their economic needs. Nor can the U.S. public accept that the narcotics problem cannot be overcome until all the developing countries are developed. Drugs (the supply side of the problem, at least) will in the end be a moral, legal, and enforcement issue. Development consideration will be secondary and, where conflict between these objectives occurs, may be sacrificed.

CHANGES IN THE WORLD ECONOMY

Perhaps nothing in U.S. relationships with the Third World is so challenging as the changes taking place in the nature of the world economy.[3] Many of these changes are the result of technological change; others have come through major policy shifts by the industrialized countries. The result, as Peter Drucker has pointed out, is a "decoupling" of the primary products economy from the industrialized economy, and a "decoupling" of manufacturing production from manufacturing employment. The implications for Third World countries are enormous.

In terms of primary products, we are seeing in the world today a staggering surplus of food production and production capacity. Induced largely by subsidies in the industrialized countries, along with technological breakthroughs (with more on the way through biotechnology), this surplus poses major challenges to the economic health of the EC and major budget problems for the United States. It makes export competition in the agricultural area extremely keen and often contentious. There arises even greater competition than before (and the conflict has long existed) between the goals of self-sufficiency in food production, promoted by aid agencies and developing countries alike, and the political and commercial interests of donors. Even the economics of food self-sufficiency is questionable if supplies are available from industrialized countries at a fraction of their production costs in the developing countries (rice in West Africa being a prime example).

But the implications are greater when one looks at this phenomenon beyond food. Demand for nonfarm primary products is weakening, and the prospects are for a continuing trend in this direction. According to the IMF, the amount of raw material needed for a given unit of economic output has been dropping steadily since 1900. The trend is being accelerated by technological changes. For example, 50 to 100 pounds of fiberglass rod can transmit as many phone messages as a ton of copper cable. And manufacture of that fiberglass requires only 5 percent of the energy needed to produce a ton of copper. The new research on ceramics and superconductivity could profoundly affect one of the most critical raw material demands of the modern world: energy.

Supply is also changing in this area. New iron ore discoveries in Brazil may have eliminated the rationale for further iron ore investment in Guinea and Liberia and has perhaps rendered obsolete the iron mines of Liberia on which that country has relied for 50 years for a large part of its earnings. Copper producers face, in addition to the technological changes noted above, another problem. The United States, which is the largest consumer of copper, now obtains virtually half its needs from scrap.

What these changes mean is that raw materials, on which many Third World countries still depend for their export earnings, will become less significant, not only economically but in the political calculations of industrialized countries.

If these sources of earnings (and influence) are diminishing, what are the most promising alternative prospects for developing countries? Here, too, changes in the world economy are instructive, and for some countries ominous. Just as there are changes in raw material input, there is a similar trend going on in labor input. Industry is becoming more knowledge intensive than labor intensive. For example, research, development, and testing accounts for 70 percent of the cost of producing semiconductor microchips; labor, for only 12 percent. As Ambassador Edward Streator has concluded, "the declining contribution of labor to the final cost of a product obviously will affect especially the prospects of developing countries which have gained market access because of comparative advantage in labor costs."[4]

These changes are likely to differentiate more sharply the comparative advantage of some developing countries over others. In examining Japanese investment trends, David Wheeler found that Japanese investment abroad, to the extent that it was attracted by low wages, was attracted increasingly to highly skilled workers, not unskilled ones. Most Southeast Asian nations can compete in this market, some least developed countries cannot.[5] Equally important, if modern technology is knowledge intensive rather than labor intensive, what are the implications for employment? Even as structural adjustment programs argue forcefully for efficiency, one noted economist suggests that employment of "supernumerary hands" may be a rational "incomes policy" for developing countries that cannot afford massive social transfer schemes.[6] But what does that say for longer-term competitiveness for these developing countries?

One final change needs to be noted, emphasizing another conclusion of Peter Drucker's of which development planners need to take note—i.e., that individual economic policies of nation-states are becoming less important than are developments in the world economy. We have seen this already in the technological, supply, and production trends noted above. It also arises from the interlinked nature of modern production. In a recent address, Secretary of State Shultz quoted the shipping label for some integrated circuits produced by a U.S. firm: "Made in one or more of the following countries: Korea, Hong Kong, Malaysia, Singapore, Taiwan, Mauritius, Thailand, Indonesia, Mexico, Philippines. The exact nature of origin is unknown." If one needed further evidence of the interlinked rather than strictly national nature of the modern economy, one only has to take another passage from Secretary Shultz's speech: "The amount of money that changes hands in the global financial market in one day exceeds one trillion dollars—more than the entire budget of the U.S. government for a year. Such flows transcend national boundaries and can overwhelm rigid economic policies."[7]

Such changes in the world economy are continually taking place and are often outside the ken of development or national policymakers. For purposes of this chapter, these changes suggest that even the tasks of development cannot be encompassed within the purview of development or aid agencies. The changes that are perhaps most far-reaching are occurring in laboratories, companies, and trading practices; and often their impact is evident only years after they have begun to be employed.

Development thus is becoming more challenging, not less. And it is becoming more dependent on openness to new trends and flexible policy responses (including those of aid agencies) than ever before. Relationships on which developing countries once relied are disappearing (raw material interdependency), and theories of comparative advantage have to be reexamined. Trade, investment, monetary, and exchange policies will have more pronounced effect on development than in the past. And education, scientific, and technological exchange will become more critical to any country's competitiveness than ever before.

A NEW APPROACH FOR THE 1990s

The changes taking place in the world demand that we take a fresh look at U.S. interests in the Third World. These interests have become so diverse, as indeed has the Third World, that we need to redefine rather fundamentally what U.S. interests and objectives are. In this redefinition, the traditional aid concerns should be an important part, but only a subset, of the United States' principal objectives, and in many cases a means not an end.

These interests, with appropriate goals and objectives that should be attached to them, include the following.

1.   The Third World is a critical but dangerously weak element in the international financial system. That weakness threatens U.S. prosperity and economic security. Alleviating the debt crisis and creating conditions for long-term growth are critical objectives in overcoming this weakness.

2.   The Third World must be a major target for U.S. exports. It is the fastest-growing market, but one fraught with weaknesses as well as prone to

protectionism, and is an arena of almost unregulated competition. The United States is singularly unrepresented in many of these economies and needs new tools, resources, and organizational structures to meet this challenge.

3.   The Third World is a major source of political and military instability. Regional problems, as they are now called, should continue to be on the agenda with the USSR and with U.S. allies. We need to establish a clear framework for security assistance to appropriate parts of the Third World in order to protect our interests. This assistance can in some instances be developmentally oriented, but the security rationale will be overarching in other cases.

4.   The Third World is increasingly the locus of other problems directly affecting U.S. society: drugs, crime, and migration (both legal and illegal). These conditions are likely to persist, even increase, during the 1990s. The United States needs to develop instruments and structures to address these problems on a long-term basis.

5.   Parts of the Third World will remain desperately poor and dependent on outside assistance as far into the future as we can see. Policy changes and other developmental activities will reduce that dependence over time; but for many countries, basic needs will continue to be an overwhelming preoccupation and not be domestically sustainable. These countries also offer little to the United States in terms of markets or other advantages. In recognition of continued humanitarian concern with these countries, and their political role in the world community, the United States should develop structures of assistance appropriate to their needs.

This list is not exhaustive nor are the more specific goals and objectives spelled out. But it is illustrative and reflects the discussion earlier in this chapter on the nature of the challenges we face in the 1990s.

Note, moreover, that in this approach, development becomes one means of advancing U.S. objectives—it has a place in nearly all these objectives—but it is not an objective in itself, nor is it the only tool for advancing them. That means, of course, that aid, in its traditional sense, is of much less significance, except in the last objective.

This approach may seem harsh, overly concerned with self-interest, and not very humanitarian. Indeed, the developmental and humanitarian aspects of U.S. policy seem to get lost. That is not the intention; humanitarian interest in the Third World is an important part of U.S. concerns, and one very significant in the public's and Congress's reaction to the aid budget. But it carries U.S. policy only so far. Moreover, it does gross injustice to the complexities of the Third World today, which contains countries of sharp competitiveness, industriousness, financial ability, and, in some cases, significant military capability.

Moreover, as long as development and aid are inextricably linked, in minds and in programs, there will be a limit to U.S. support for the developmental objective. We need to break that link. We need to see development as in the United States' self-interest and as an objective the country can promote at the same time as it promotes its other interests. That means that tools other than aid—e.g., export credits, scientific and technological exchanges, financial market reforms—must be recognized and promoted as useful development tools along with—indeed, in many cases more important than—aid.

Finally, this approach argues against too much emphasis on regional specialization to be allocated among the United States and its allies (as proposed, for example, by Maynes and Mistry in this book). That idea is simple and beguiling, especially in an age when the country is feeling its own limitations. But the concept is in itself anachronistic, harking back to an era when the world economy was less interdependent and when U.S. allies were less internationally capable than they are today. Nor does it take account of issues that are of special political importance to the United States outside of geography.

Should the United States be less concerned with Southern Africa because Europe is far more dependent on the minerals from that region? Should the United States oppose the new, rather significant amounts of Japanese aid and capital going to the largest Latin American debtor countries? (Can the United States match it?) Who is most concerned with security issues in the Far East—U.S. policymakers or the Japanese, who give no military assistance and have no overseas defense capability? Finally, can the United States afford to relinquish markets in large parts of the Third World because it has had no historical participation there?

Rather than making some arbitrary geographical division, U.S. policymakers need to assess what their interests are. In one region, they will have one interest (in Central America, security); in another, they will have another (in southern and Southeast Asia, and now in Africa, drugs).

On the other hand, the importance of *shared responsibility* in the 1990s cannot be overestimated. In virtually none of the areas we have discussed is the United States capable of carrying the responsibility alone. Japan surpassed the United States as the largest nominal aid donor (and the United States has long been surpassed in percentage of GNP), and its recycling proposal was welcome news. Problems such as drug trafficking are international and demand a multilateral approach. In summary, U.S. policymakers have learned in the last few years (or should have) that we cannot tackle the development, security, or financial needs relevant to U.S. interests in nearly any part of the Third World without the strong role of the multilateral agencies and the support of allies.

Thus, as the United States defines its interests carefully, it must also shape its tools and its bureaucratic response to the realities of greater dependency on cooperation with its allies and friends and on the importance of multilateral institutions. Here too, traditional aid mechanisms are inadequate to the task.

Bureaucratic Responses

New policies need to be reflected in new bureaucratic structures and mechanisms. Without such changes, new directions will not go very far. Each agency presently involved in Third World programs or cooperation will cling to its special concerns and modes of operation.

Yet, the idea of a "Super Third World Agency" is unrealistic and in fact undesirable. The different bureaucratic structures that now play a role in Third World policies and programs represent real interests (and interest groups) in the U.S. body politic. The experience with IDCA is instructive. Intended as the agency with full responsibility for U.S. developmental policy and programs in the Third World, IDCA failed even to gain control over U.S. policies in the multilateral aid agencies, an indispensable part of such responsibility. Indeed, beyond the bilateral aid program, IDCA was unable to move.

Even within the bilateral aid program, a single agency would have difficulty encompassing the full range of U.S. interests in the 1990s, at least if it paralleled how USAID is now configured. USAID's history is instructive. Since it was founded in 1961, USAID has struggled with this objective and has either lost ground or been put in the position of blocking valuable programs. It has resisted independent activity in developing countries by domestic agencies such as the Agriculture and Labor departments, or the Federal Aviation Administration. At a minimum, it sought to channel such activity through its country programming and prioritization process, the more so as USAID became the source of funding of such activities.

While the motives were understandable, this approach inevitably narrowed U.S. interaction with Third World countries. If it did not fit USAID's priorities (which themselves shifted), it was not supportable: Airport safety went in and out of vogue, as did advanced scientific research, labor programs, legal assistance, university development, industrial research, and so on. Even more significant, as USAID came to focus more on the least developed and the poorest, its ability to interact with the increasingly important middle-income countries diminished. USAID often was in the position of insisting on reviewing proposals for cooperation with these countries and then blocking them because of its own funding and policy constraints.

The problem is mirrored in the Congress, where channeling our Third World interests through the aid oversight committees similarly narrows the focus. From 1978 to 1980, the administration and Congress debated a proposal for a new Institute for Scientific and Technological Cooperation (ISTC). One of the objectives of ISTC would be to open up lines of cooperation with middle-income countries with which the United States no longer had an aid relationship, an objective supported by the congressional committees concerned with science and technology. But congressional members and staff on the aid oversight committees attacked it on that ground, arguing that a middle-income focus detracted from aid's focus on the poorest. As a result, the ISTC proposal was gradually modified to correspond more with the existing priorities of the USAID program, and the rationale for ISTC's separate existence diminished. In the end, the programmatic proposals for ISTC were folded back into USAID (and the middle-income–country initiatives were lost).

Finally, USAID has always had trouble with the security and political rationale for aid. Development purists felt this emphasis tainted the motives and uses of aid. In actuality, it does distort programming decisions away from purely developmental criteria, especially in overall allocations among countries. But as a result of this ambivalence, USAID became largely irrelevant to some of the major programming decisions with regard to its own funds. Today, the programs for Israel and Egypt are determined without any real USAID leverage, and the one in Israel, though nearly a quarter of the agency's budget, is not even administered by USAID but simply handed over as a check. USAID is largely outside the programming loop (in determining levels) for such countries as Pakistan and Turkey, and for some in Central America. The point is that, while developmental criteria and focus on the poorest is emphasized by both USAID and its congressional oversight committees, both the administration and Congress engage in a decisionmaking process that bears little relationship to those criteria overall. That reflects a reality of U.S. interests, and we cannot ignore it.

When we move to areas such as drugs and trade, these limitations on USAID, or any proposed aid agency, as the overall coordinating body become even more apparent. Other existing agencies, moreover, have similar limitations.

Treasury, which has always played a dominant role in U.S. policy with the MDBs and the IMF, has assumed even greater responsibility for Third World policy with the debt crisis. Moreover, the IMF, which was once more isolated from Third World development strategy and more narrowly a Treasury focus, has, since its deeper involvement in Latin America and Africa (with U.S. encouragement), become deeply enmeshed in cooperative programs with the IBRD on structural adjustment and other development objectives. Thus, the line between monetary/financial policy and development policy has become increasingly blurred. Treasury's and USAID's foci have correspondingly further overlapped.

Treasury, however, lacks a core of development expertise. It relies more on analyses from the multilateral institutions than on those from USAID's staff overseas. Its focus is on the stability and viability of the international trade and monetary system, less on development of Third World countries. Its congressional audience is quite distinct from the aid oversight committees, except when contributions to the MDBs are involved. And, of course, the

Treasury does not have responsibility over the administration of U.S. bilateral aid.

The Export-Import Bank has also assumed greater importance in U.S. Third World policy. Its outreach has been decidedly more limited because of the debt crisis, which has put a number of Third World countries off limits. But as the U.S. trade deficit has become more acute, the importance of export promotion to Third World countries has grown. The role of the Export-Import Bank shows clearly the division between U.S. policy toward less developed and middle-income countries: The bank will not risk credit to many of the poorer or debt-distressed countries. As a result, there has been more pressure on USAID to introduce export subsidies within its program, something the agency has stoutly resisted. As a result, export promotion in a large number of Third World countries is a virtual no man's land of responsibility or budgeting.

The U.S. Trade Representative (USTR) will also figure more prominently in U.S. Third World policy in the 1990s, as the discussion of trade has shown. Already, developing countries such as Mauritius have, to their amazement, found themselves on the Office of the U.S. Trade Representative's list for "consultations" as their share of exports in a certain category of textiles crossed the 1 percent mark. As the export strategy, being actively promoted by the international development agencies, with U.S. support, takes hold in more Third World countries, this situation will become more commonplace. Conflicts between domestic protectionist pressures and development policy will become more acute, affecting all aid recipients, not just the middle-income countries.

USTR works directly for the president and is responsive largely to domestic concerns. On the other hand, it is not a protectionist-oriented entity. It is as concerned with opening up markets for U.S. exports, and thus keeping the trading system open, as it is with regularizing import growth. Thus, there is room for cooperation and coordination with development agencies. But, at present, the two types of agency operate in different worlds, with little comparable expertise or experience.

Other agencies play a role that crosses the lines separating development, export promotion, and domestic concerns. The Department of Agriculture is a prominent example, with its role in budgeting and allocating PL-480 commodities. The history of coordination and sharing of responsibility between Agriculture and USAID is, however, a commendable one, with a generally respectable balance between U.S. interests in exports and in development. Congress has helped in this regard with its guidance on conditionality for PL-480 food aid.

The State Department, by function and outlook, has both a coordinating and mediating role among these several, sometimes competing interests. But it is not uniform in its own approach. In general, State's role has varied with the personalities and preferences of particular officeholders, and its role in development policy has waxed and waned accordingly. At the undersecretarial level, there are three offices with strong interest in Third World issues: Political, Security Assistance, and Economic Affairs. In the Reagan administration, it was the undersecretary for security assistance who played the dominant role in coordinating the foreign affairs budget, with support from the Political-Military Bureau. The undersecretary for economic affairs was, by contrast, generally more focused on trade, international economic issues (economic summits), and commodity agreements than on development policy or budgets. At the next level, the Economics Bureau, while playing a relatively limited role in budget formulation of bilateral development programs, has had the formal responsibility for managing the contacts of USAID and other State Department branches with Treasury and, through Treasury, with the MDBs and the IMF. This has the laudable purpose of coordination, but in practice it produces a cumbersome game of message passing (the Africa Bureau calls the Economics Bureau, which calls Treasury, which calls the IBRD to set up a meeting to hear about the IBRD's program in Sierra Leone—and of course everyone has to come to the meeting).

The State Department, of course, does not administer the resources for either bilateral or multilateral aid programs. Significantly, however, it established much greater control over the foreign affairs budget, including all forms of aid, during the Reagan administration. It remains to be seen how, or whether, this is translated into greater leadership in development policy and the integration of that within the United States' overall concerns with the Third World.

There have been some extremely effective cases of State Department coordination of U.S. policy on Third World economic issues. Deputy Secretary Whitehead, in a series of breakfast meetings in 1985 and 1986, played an important role with his counterpart in Treasury, fashioning new responses to the debt crisis including special attention to the problems of poorer countries in Africa. Much of the thinking that went into the second Baker Plan, i.e., the proposals that focused on the poorer countries, grew out of this process. USAID played a prominent role in these meetings, and the integration of bilateral, multilateral, financial, and political policy was commendable.

The point of this rather extended discussion of the bureaucratics of Third World policy is that we have to accept a multiplicity of actors. The bureaucratic solution has, therefore, to be one that blends a desirable pluralism of responses reflecting the United States' various interests in the Third World with clearly defined policy guidance and effective coordinating mechanisms.

Charting the New Course

The first step in charting this course might be for the Bush administration to have the NSC commission and direct a study of U.S. interests in the Third

World. Presumably such a study would be along the lines expressed earlier in this chapter. No single study could, of course, encompass all U.S. interests, but, if it clarified U.S. interests in the Third World in terms that took them out of the range of poverty, instability, and ingratitude—in other words, beyond the traditional aid concerns—it would open the way both to new policy directions and to instructions on new bureaucratic responsibilities and mechanisms.

A new development structure. One result of a bureaucratic restructuring should be a new development agency (or agencies) with appropriate legislative changes and (God willing) a new name. The mandate of the agency (or agencies) would differentiate among several categories of countries: (a) least developed countries with their special problems and special types of assistance; (b) development-potential countries of economic and political importance to the United States; (c) countries in which the United States has base rights and similar security interests; and (d) countries outside the aid framework altogether, but wherein the United States has important trade and other interests demanding programming of resources.

To respond to these several categories, several types of programs would be needed; for example:

1. Bilateral assistance programs, especially in the least developed countries, that focus on health, education, agriculture, population, and research are justified. Structural adjustment, and similar macroeconomic reforms, would be encouraged for the purpose of improving efficiency and creating incentives. But, in the least developed countries, one would not be so rigid or ideological, since many of these countries will not make it to self-sufficiency in the foreseeable future despite the most sweeping adjustment programs.

2. Development-oriented programs, including both project and nonproject funding, aimed at countries of greater potential, are needed. In large part, these countries correspond to (b) above. Here, policy reforms and adjustment efforts would be very relevant and would deserve appropriate dedication of staff and resources.

3. Financing of base rights and similar security arrangements would be a separate category of assistance. In recent years, there has been a disintegration of the consensus needed between the administration and Congress over the requirements for these arrangements. As a result, the United States has been placed in the position of not meeting obligations entered into by the executive branch, with corresponding risks to some of our most important overseas relationships. It is critical that a new consensus be established between the executive and legislative branches, and that the next round of negotiations with the affected countries proceed on the basis of consequent understandings. Further, this category of assistance need not be administered by a development agency. In any case, payments should be

made for the most part in cash, treated as service costs. If these countries are also of development importance and part of the U.S. multilateral concern over financial stability, structural adjustment, etc., there are other mechanisms by which the government can pursue those ends. Payments for base rights and so on only add to the United States' right to use overseas security facilities. Trying to link base payments with development conditionality is a losing proposition and of increasingly doubtful value.

4. A special allocation to PVOs, not restricted to use in the least developed countries, should be made. The United States has a concern with poverty in many parts of the world, and people-to-people relationships such as those fostered by PVOs serve many valuable ends. PVOs also provide flexibility in programming and, if kept distant (and they should be made more distant than they are now) from government control and cross-conditionality, they offer an alternative to the all-or-nothing posture that arises when the government has to confront another country on drugs, nonpayment of debt (as provided for by the Brooke amendment), or any other matter that would require cutting off aid.

5. A separate program, not necessarily administered by a development agency, aimed largely (but not exclusively) at middle-income countries and emphasizing science and technology cooperation is needed. The objective should be to enhance U.S. interaction, and therefore trade potential, with such countries through their greater knowledge and use of U.S. technology, services, and goods. As such, the program would go well beyond present USAID emphases and would encompass industrial and related technology. While enhancing U.S. contacts with these countries, it would serve to help them cope with the rapidly changing nature of the world economy and its technology. For that reason, it cannot be narrowly construed to fit current or future aid priorities: The world is changing too fast and from too many directions. U.S. interaction has to be as diverse. This program could be administered as grants to universities, private institutions, and even businesses, which would do the actual programming. No U.S. government bureaucracy would review and approve individual programs; rather, they would be evaluated regularly to see whether they met objectives and targets. (The United States Information Agency's university linkage program offers a valuable example, compared to USAID's programming practices. The National Science Foundation and National Academy of Sciences models are also instructive.) Liberal use of scholarships, fellowships, internships, etc., should be featured.

6. An additional development financing program, either direct or through guarantees (at terms less concessional than those offered to least developed countries) and linked to export promotion, should be instituted. Such a program might be administered by the Export-Import Bank (in addition to its regular funds), so as to meet the special circumstances of, say, debt-distressed countries. A mechanism would be in place to review projects

in terms of their development value. Already, European export-financing agencies are moving in this direction. In recognition of the place of export credits in financing for Third World countries, especially as aid budgets are likely to remain constrained, there should be a major effort to establish common criteria with European and Japanese agencies to direct this large and necessary source of capital to the most developmentally effective projects.

7.   There should continue to be significant programming of funds for the multilateral agencies, including IDA, the IMF's Structural Adjustment Facility and Expanded Structural Adjustment Facility, and other mechanisms that come into being to alleviate the development and debt crisis in the Third World. Multilateral fora offer perhaps the best means to address the debt overhang more effectively than has been possible so far. This clearly will be one of the greatest challenges of the 1990s.

8.   Finally, there will be continued need for special funds to address such problems as drug trafficking, terrorism, and global environment issues. These funds can be administered by the agency with the most pertinent expertise.

Coordination. At the risk of sounding parochial, it is hard to see which department other than State could act, in most instances, as coordinator of U.S. Third World policy. Nevertheless, coordination does not mean direction or control. The State Department does not, and never should, administer such things as narcotics programs. Nor does it have to "coordinate" when there is no conflict of purpose or objective among agencies.

Coordination, in fact, is often done best when done with the lightest hand. With some appropriate executive guidance, and building on existing coordinating mechanisms (policy-coordinating committees, the integrated foreign affairs budget process, etc.), State could play a more effective role in bringing to bear the United States' several Third World interests. Informal coordinating mechanisms should be used more frequently: The Africa Bureau's experience with the "Wheeler Group" (purposely not formally named even long after its founder, Joe Wheeler, had left Washington), in which each agency enters and leaves with its bureaucratic prerogatives intact, is instructive. Although not a substitute for formal mechanisms to resolve serious interagency differences, the Wheeler Group served throughout the 1980s to bring together the disparate parts of the U.S. government working on development, debt, and financial reform in Africa, and led to more systematic and coordinated policy positions. The deputy secretary's breakfast meetings among State, Treasury, and USAID, which, as noted earlier, helped shape the Baker Plan proposals, is a more prominent example.

In any case, it seems logical to restore, in the Bush administration, the role of the undersecretary for economic affairs as the principal coordinator on Third World economic issues within State. Particularly if some of the security-related transfers could be separated from other financing, as suggested above, the integration of economic issues (development, trade, debt) seems to be the most challenging issue in the next decade.

The State Department's role is enhanced because the authority of ambassadors flows from the president through this department. Overseas, coordination is easier than in Washington: The ambassador is the president's representative and oversees all U.S. government representatives. Policy-coordinating mechanisms, though of uneven effectiveness, already exist in overseas missions (the secretary's letter to each ambassador, the goals and objectives paper, the reporting plans, etc.) to which each agency contributes. But ambassadors and country team members will need clearer guidance on Third World policy, and ambassadors more training in the various issues affecting the United States in the Third World, if such coordination is to be effective.

We can nevertheless already see in the field, if Nigeria is any example, that integrated or coordinated multiagency efforts are possible in tackling such new problems as drugs, AIDS, and even export promotion. In Nigeria, a narcotics coordinating committee consisting of State, the Drug Enforcement Agency, United States Information Agency, and USAID, has addressed enforcement, legal cooperation, health, public awareness, and political issues related to the drug problem. There is no friction and little overlap. The same is happening regarding AIDS. And having different instruments, indeed different agencies, under these arrangements is not a disadvantage, but a source of flexibility and a wide variety of skills.

CONCLUSION

We need to broaden our horizons in the 1990s. The problems and challenges the United States will face in the Third World will increase in complexity and importance. Issues such as drugs and migration will directly affect U.S. domestic affairs. Trade prospects will have a major bearing on the United States' continued prosperity. The traditional development concerns and constituencies will no longer be adequate to the task.

To meet these challenges, new actors and constituencies are needed; instruments and response mechanisms within the government must be diversified. The arbitrary distinctions between domestic and overseas concerns with the Third World have to be dissolved.

This will, of course, create new challenges: Development will no longer necessarily take pride of place; development experts will not be the guardians of wisdom on the Third World; and there may be sharper conflicts among the United States' several objectives. There will be a greater burden on the U.S. government of coordination and management.

But, if the United States invites a larger constituency into its interests in the Third World, the basis for support of its efforts, including development, should be strengthened, and the effectiveness of U.S. interaction with the Third World should improve immeasurably.

NOTES

The views expressed here are those of the author and not necessarily those of the U.S. government or any of its departments.

1. See The *Crisis and Challenge of African Development,* ed. Harvey Glickman (Westport, CT: Greenwood Press, 1988), p. 112.
2. Agency for International Development, FY 1988 *Congressional Presentation* (Washington, D.C.: USAID, 1987), p. 273.
3. I am indebted to an article by Peter F. Drucker, "The Changed World Economy," *Foreign Affairs* (Spring 1986): 768-791, for some of the ideas in this section.
4. *Ibid.*
5. David Wheeler, "African Development in the Information Age: Understanding the New Economics of Comparative Advantage" (unpublished manuscript, Boston University, 1984).
6. Wassily Leontieff, quoted in *ibid.,* p. 4.
7. George Shultz, *National Success and International Stability in a Time of Change,* Current Policy Series No. 1029 (Washington, D.C.: Department of State, 4 December 1987).

PART FOUR

Appendixes

Summary of the Recommendations of the Report of the Project on Cooperation for International Development

RALPH H. SMUCKLER
ROBERT J. BERG
with DAVID F. GORDON

The United States, more than any other nation in the world, stands to gain from a global system that promotes broadly based growth, an effective attack on poverty, and an end to degradation of the world's environment. We have the most to gain for the same reason that we would have the most to lose if, in the years ahead, we do not realize such goals. In the decade ahead, we must cooperate effectively with the nations and the peoples of the Third World to attain these ends.

The world of the 1990s, and that of the twenty-first century, will be substantially different from the one in which a worldwide enterprise known as "foreign aid" was launched 40 years ago. New circumstances make the concept of foreign aid less appropriate. To much of Asia and Latin America, the concept of "cooperation for development" fits better. If we are to address difficult issues successfully, we must encourage cooperation for mutual gain as an essential step toward maintaining a progressive global system.

By development cooperation, we mean that the United States shares responsibilities widely and appropriately. The primary responsibility must lie with the developing countries themselves. But the people and governments of other countries, including the United States, should expect to join in this endeavor by contributing resources and helping to shape policies. If we stand by, if we take a shortsighted view, pursuing only narrow and immediate interests, we will allow the uneven progress of development in Third World countries to let hundreds of millions of people sink further from decent standards of life. Is that what we want to leave as our heritage?

Developing countries have a rich legacy of experience, both in projects and policies, from which to draw in future planning. We can point out many

This report was published in 1988 as "New Challenges, New Opportunities: U.S. Cooperation for International Growth and Development in the 1990s," by The Center for Advanced Study of International Development, Michigan State University, 306 Berkey Hall, East Lansing, Michigan 48824-1111.

internationally supported success stories: large-scale public health campaigns such as smallpox eradication and oral rehydration to treat diarrheal disease; broad-based improvements in agricultural productivity in much of Asia as a result of the green revolution's introduction of high-yielding grain varieties and related technology; and the vast experience of smaller-scale projects. In Asia and Latin America, we can point to countries that have graduated from being recipients to become potential aid donors. This range of successful policies and efforts in all parts of the developing world offers lessons for the future. Demonstrably, development has a positive learning curve. One of the lessons is the need for patience; change is not an overnight process.

U.S. INTERESTS

Most broadly, our interests lie in the growth of a healthy global system that will help to sustain the values we cherish. By any measure, the Third World is now an important part of that system. If the United States is to play its role well, we must forge a new national consensus on the importance of Third World issues and international development goals; and we must chart our course sensitively, marshaling our capabilities in recognition of new circumstances. There are humanitarian, economic, and political interests at the base of such a consensus.

We have both an economic and a humanitarian interest in seeing that the world grows economically with minimum damage to the natural environment. With others, including developing countries, we share an interest in maintaining a global economic system that enables our type of market-oriented economy to continue and to prosper. We also have a national economic interest in resolving the Third World debt crisis.

The United States also has important political interests in developing countries. In the world we wish to pass on to the next generation, we seek to promote and protect values of widespread citizen participation, respect for civil and human rights, and the rule of law. The United States has an interest in cooperating with the Third World in the resolution of a series of pressing contemporary problems. Some of these are domestic problems with an international dimension: drugs; crime; and diseases such as AIDS. Some problems are international but affect the quality of life at home: maintaining a livable global environment; controlling infectious diseases; eliminating locusts and other infestations; meeting the challenge of terrorism; and managing common property. All require a multinational approach as part of the solution.

For all of these reasons, the United States has an important interest in a wide array of Third World countries and in their development. The Third World is too important a component of the global economy and environment to be analyzed in isolation. We must rethink fundamentally the meaning of our national security. In an earlier era, strategic and military considerations dominated the concept of security. Today, it rests also on protecting the global environment, maintaining a viable global economic order, and dealing effectively with widespread social problems that could be as overwhelming to our societal well-being as military actions or confrontations.

GUIDELINES FOR COOPERATION

U.S. programs should be cast in long-term perspective. Most tasks cannot be accomplished in three or even five years. In some cases, we must consider the proper planning cycle to be 10 years or more. Development cooperation between the United States and Third World nations should involve the public, private, and voluntary sectors both in the United States and abroad. We must respond to real needs and to informed voices in developing countries. These voices will come from various sources. With rare exception, we should not design bilateral programs on our own diagnosis or initiative, with only passive approval coming from the developing country.

The U.S. program should be capable of diverse responses. The situation should guide our response. We should design program instruments and management arrangements with this flexibility. We should work in ways that will strengthen the growth of pluralism in Third World societies. We should consciously include, therefore, a number of nongovernmental organizations, private sector entities, and other decentralized units as is often as is feasible in planning and implementing cooperation.

U.S. responses to developing countries should be both bilateral and multilateral. Both have advantages. Multilateral agencies are best in some circumstances (such as the World Bank for macroeconomic adjustment and the WHO for smallpox eradication); bilateral U.S. programs are best in other situations.

Finally and above all, our programs in the decade ahead must reflect a commitment to cooperation for development. This pervasive theme must guide our actions with the poorest countries, where certain assistance instruments will still be appropriate, including straightforward relief at times, as well as with those countries at a more advanced stage, where cooperative linkages and joint research on global problems may be the predominant pattern. We must be willing to plan jointly, establish goals together, and share financing and other responsibilities. This cooperative style must prevail and become the basis of our interaction with the Third World in the 1990s.

URGENT ISSUES

Before we suggest four important substantive themes for U.S. development cooperation for the 1990s and a number of approaches to them, we feel that urgent attention must be directed to three tasks. They concern development but go far beyond. They require more than U.S. action and, within the country's official stance, far more than just development agency action.

Third World Debt

In the 1990s, for a substantial number of Latin American and African countries, real development progress will depend upon reducing the burden of debt service. Politically, the debt is the source of increasing demagoguery aimed at the United States. The Third World debt burden also hurts the global economy at large and the U.S. economy because it restrains further expansion of U.S. exports to the developing countries. Thus, there is a strong case for new initiatives to break the bottleneck of the Third World debt crisis.

We leave to others the writing of the prescription to ease this difficult, complicated problem. We do note, however, that in the past several years market forces have lowered the value of Third World debt. The task is to create mechanisms and opportunities for the indebted countries themselves to reap a share in the de facto market devaluations. Such a solution calls for U.S. leadership.

Africa

Africa presents a second set of urgent issues. For two decades, population growth has outstripped agricultural productivity. Economic growth rates have plummeted. We do not exaggerate when we say that the basic building blocks of societies—education, food, and health—are at risk in large parts of sub-Saharan Africa. Unless deteriorating conditions are turned around, an increasing number of African countries will suffer economic stagnation, increasing poverty, environmental degradation, and decay of their already fragile social and political institutions.

Africa's complex problems must be attacked on a number of fronts. Basic policy, institutional, and infrastructure questions must be addressed. We must encourage attention on five fronts:

- Sharply reduce debt burdens for many countries
- Lay the base for locally relevant agricultural research
- Address health and population problems that are interrelated but demand both independent and joint action
- Confront Africa's environmental degradation directly
- Counter the devastation of continued warfare in Southern Africa

Global Environment

Global environmental issues go well beyond what a U.S. development cooperation program can handle. They call for concerted international efforts and a major role for the United States both in reforming its domestic performance and in helping construct effective international action. Without such an approach, the long-term viability of a good many international development strategies is open to serious doubt.

SUBSTANTIVE CONTENT OF FUTURE U.S. PROGRAMS

In view of the wide array of conditions that prevail in Third World countries, the United States should be prepared to apply a range of approaches. In some of the poorest countries, U.S. cooperation will focus primarily on alleviating poverty, expanding productivity, and building capacity for growth. In the more advanced countries, our attention should focus on mutually beneficial gain, including trade development, joint research, and energy efficiency.

The four themes that we suggest were drawn from the colloquia and analyses that have been part of this project. They are our best estimate of developing country needs in the 1990s, and key in on the areas that provide the best opportunity for the United States to contribute—and to gain. The first two are continuing themes of the past; the latter two are new, and reflect the needs of the future:

- Physical well-being: health and population
- Sustainable food supplies: agriculture and forestry
- Enhancing the environment
- Urban development

Each of these themes can proceed on a basis of cooperation for mutual gain. But each is important, also, for attacking poverty conditions. Historically, the alleviation of poverty and the expansion of opportunities for mutual gain go hand in hand as poor countries grow economically.

Physical Well-Being: Health and Population

Since World War II, we have seen dramatic improvements in human well-being and a remarkable increase in life spans. In recent years, however, profound economic changes combined with the global emergence of new health problems such as AIDS, substance abuse, and illnesses related to environmental degradation are causing a major reconsideration of health policies and strategies. During the past decade, two developments have led to important redirections and strategies for provision of health services: first, there is the primary health care movement; second, there are the revolutionary developments in biomedical research.

Effective and inexpensive technologies are the keys to primary health care improvement. The new research tools in immunology and molecular biology offer the promise of a larger array of vaccines, chemotherapeutic agents, and diagnostic tests that have the potential of markedly transforming health conditions in tropical countries. Effective primary health care programs require strengthened leadership and management capacity in ministries of health to establish policies and define strategies to improve health.

Efficient use of tight U.S. funding will require strengthening capabilities to mobilize technical, managerial, and financial resources available nationally and internationally. Academic centers in the United States have substantial resources and potential for conducting biomedical research, and extensive capacity for training and assisting researchers from developing countries. Nongovernmental organizations and commercial enterprises represent other stable resource bases we should call upon. Multilateral agencies such as the WHO, UNICEF, and the United Nations Fund for Population Activities (UNFPA) bring strength in their ability to discern a worldwide strategy on issues that transcend national boundaries, such as primary health care, child survival, population, and, most recently, the global AIDS program. We must strengthen capacities to set priorities, plan strategically, and provide financial analysis in the developing countries as well as in the donor community.

The world's population will grow by another billion people in the 1990s. No one greets this as good news. Nations cannot achieve the social and economic goals they seek with extremely high population growth. That is why some 64 developing countries have policies favoring lower rates of population growth.

Successful population programs depend on the commitment and resources of countries themselves. But, though this commitment is absolutely necessary, it is often insufficient. In the 1990s, we believe it imperative to reaffirm the historic U.S. commitment to family planning. Particularly, we should resume support of the two most respected and widely connected population agencies: the UNFPA and the International Planned Parenthood Federation.

Sustainable Food Supplies: Agriculture and Forestry

Given the growth of grain production in the world in recent years, we know that hunger results from poverty and environmental degradation, not just from a lack of food production. Deaths from starvation and malnutrition still outnumber deaths from all wars. Yet the war on hunger goes on at an intolerably slow pace in a world of substantial wealth.

We need major policy changes, indeed new development strategies, to restore and protect the water, land, and forests on which the survival of the rural poor depends. Our attention should be given to research, to policy analysis that underpins programs to attain food security, and to training and institution-building in selected countries and regions.

Agricultural research has consistently had one of the very highest rates of return to development, but it still suffers from serious underinvestment. Developing countries and donors need to renew their dedication to rapid improvement of national research capacities in the developing countries. We should encourage and support universities and other agricultural research institutions in the industrialized nations, especially those in the United States, to give priority to research that addresses needs in developing countries.

Environmental Improvement

People do not understand the scope of the environmental challenge facing the world. Although single trends are often seen, rarely do we grasp the cumulative nature of the adverse trends in temperature, radiation, desertification, deforestation, species reduction, and pollution of the air, soil, and water.

In the developing world, 10 trees are cut down for every one that is replaced (29 for one in sub-Saharan Africa), and forest animal and plant species are disappearing at an unprecedented rate. Fuelwood shortages now affect an estimated 1.5 billion people in 63 countries. Often, old strategies to attack these problems—settlement of fragile tropical forests, large dams, and continuous irrigation schemes—failed because they could not be sustained economically or ecologically over the long run.

There is a need to build capabilities to provide Third World governments with reliable analyses, to assure that programs supported by the U.S. government operate with environmental insight, and to help launch special programs in Third World countries of national or global environmental importance.

Some of these actions will defy conventional economics, conventional obligations of the state, conventional roles of multilateral institutions, indeed conventional notions of security. Fresh thinking and innovative action will be necessary. Business as usual would mean a virtual neglect of these issues, and that can be entertained as an option only at our long-term peril.

Energy issues will become more urgent in the 1990s. The United States should continue its leadership in promoting sustainable energy strategies and programs within the multilateral agencies. We must avoid treating energy issues as a fad linked only to the prices OPEC is able or not able to set for oil. For Third World countries, as for the United States, the issue is far more significant and requires long-term, consistent approaches.

Urban Development

In the past, U.S. programs in developing countries have largely ignored urban issues. We cannot stop the growth of Third Would cities. Eighty-five percent of the Third World's population growth in the 1990s will be in urban areas. Rather than working to retard urban growth, we should help shape policies to maximize the economic contributions cities make, to maximize their residents' well-being, and to minimize the impact of the concomitants of urbanization such as air and water pollution.

International financial resources will be needed, particularly to respond to massive urban infrastructure needs. Working with others, the United States should play its part. Initially, we should be cautious as we build linkages with sources of U.S. expertise, promote policy research, organize dialogs with Third World authorities, and help with policy development.

APPROACHES TO THESE SUBSTANTIVE AREAS

What approaches should be followed in addressing these four substantive themes? We believe that the United States can help most by drawing on its national strengths and its comparative advantages in the following crosscutting activities:

- Human resource development
- Science and technology
- Policy and institutional development
- Mobilizing diverse energies for development

In each, there are strong Third World interests where our talents can complement local resources. For the most part, these cut across all the substantive areas.

Human Resource Development

People are the bottom line, both as contributors and recipients of any successful development strategy. To strengthen a nation's human resources requires three complementary elements: The first is the commitment to raise general education levels; the second is vocational and advanced training capacity for adolescents and young adults; the third is the institutional and policy environment capable of mobilizing and using the nation's talent productively and equitably.

For the United States, the pioneer both of high-quality public higher education and of an uncompromising commitment to universal access to schooling, education is a natural area for emphasis in programs of cooperation. We believe it is now time to confirm unambiguously U.S. support for basic education for all children and for the school as the basis for any system of such education.

Advanced training is a key to practically every aspect of development. It is essential to build capacity for advanced training in many fields in a number of countries. We see the building of management capacities as an important component of a human resource development strategy in the 1990s. The United States has strong training and technical assistance resources to improve management in the Third World. Increasingly, these U.S. strengths should operate as peer supports to Third World managers through networking and long-term linkages.

Science and Technology

The Third World, with over two-thirds of the world's population, has a mere 13 percent of its scientists. This limits Third World ability to create wealth. The United States has major public and private sector strengths in science and technology that Third World nations recognize and frequently desire. These cover a wide range of fields. Biotechnology in its various forms now offers much promise. The rapidly growing areas of informatics and communications are central to many development tasks and will certainly contribute in the 1990s. U.S. bilateral programs should tie U.S. strengths to Third World opportunities and needs.

For the poorest countries, we should help increase capacity through training and institution-building. In the more advanced developing countries, science and technology have progressed to the point where we can pursue mutual gains, working together on problems such as global ecology, alternate energy technologies, diseases, and agricultural research, as well as industrial technology issues.

Policy and Institutional Development

The adjustment crisis of the 1980s will continue into the 1990s for most developing countries. With support from donors, many countries undertook economic policy reforms aimed at improving the setting for development at the macro and sectoral levels. In the 1990s, we must build upon the lessons, both positive and negative, of these experiences.

The United States should continue to engage in active policy discussions with a broad range of governmental and private sector leaders in the Third World. A general lesson is that only if countries wish to undertake policy changes will they do so. A second lesson is that only where institutional growth has been commensurate with policy changes have these changes been sustainable.

The United States should emphasize its support of policy-relevant research in developing countries. It should support the strengthening of autonomous policy research centers and encourage governments to use the technical expertise resident in such centers.

Mobilizing Diverse Energies for Development

Over the longer term, nations that encourage freedom and open opportunities for economic participation (coupled with rules that assure that private actions are socially responsible) progress further than those that restrict participation. These nations also create growth that is politically more sustainable.

Mobilizing diverse energies means fostering decentralized development and selecting local initiatives (embodied in local government, private groups, and individuals) over central initiatives. More pointedly, we mean the expansion of the role and participation of a number of organizations and segments of society in addition to government agencies. We place special emphasis on four categories: the private sector; nongovernmental organizations; women in development; and human rights.

Private sector. U.S. bilateral economic cooperation should focus particularly on helping to establish fair rules of the game for domestic and international investment. Barriers to new formal and informal enterprises must be reduced, and access to easier credit, especially for small enterprises, must be provided. This should be a major focus of U.S. policy dialog. The United States can also assist in organizing capital markets and in promoting the role of financial intermediaries within Third World countries.

Nongovernmental organizations. Collectively, and in several cases individually, nongovernmental organizations are significant development actors. It should be a more prominent part of U.S. policy to foster these local centers of program initiative. In the years ahead, we should help U.S. nongovernmental organizations both to strengthen their links with local organizations and to foster the development of these local organizations. So, too, official U.S. programs should more fully assess the lessons of the nongovernmental organization community to help shape future U.S. programs and policies.

Women in development. Women are central in each of the substantive themes discussed above. For example, in terms of health and population, women are the key actors in health education and practices within the family and the key to effective family planning programs. In terms of hunger and food, women produce, process, and prepare much of the world's food. In terms of economic growth, women's roles in production and marketing are underappreciated and could expand greatly if credit and other services were assured. In terms of environment, women are primarily responsible for the collection of fuel, fodder, and water and are, therefore, much involved in prevention of environmental degradation.

Enhancing the participation of women in technical assistance programs must become one of the starting points in development, not a minor afterthought. Mobilizing the energies of women becomes an important means of attacking a number of basic constraints to development. What is required is not only strong commitment, but an effective strategy that acknowledges gender differences and is based on principles of equity.

Human rights. For over a decade, the United States has fostered human rights as a matter of national policy. This is not a new concern, but one that calls for continued attention and support, especially in view of positive trends observable in much of the world. The United States should organize a positive approach to help peoples and groups currently discriminated against because of race, religion, or gender become more directly involved in development activity.

In summary, we believe that the four substantive programs and suggested crosscutting approaches will serve well the three goals of broad-based economic growth, the attack on poverty, and sustaining the environment. But are they sufficient to attain the goals? They are not. The efforts of Third World countries themselves will be crucial. We should seek to help their efforts become increasingly effective, not to impose U.S. ways. Genuine cooperation for development will be important; and coordination with others, especially with multilateral banks and organizations, will be essential if we are to meet these goals.

REGIONAL BALANCE

Bilateral programs designed to meet national circumstances and interests should continue to be the building blocks for the U.S. development program in the decade ahead. However, both U.S. interests and Third World needs call for distinctly regional approaches and differentiated commitments.

The United States has a great deal at stake in its ties with Latin America: large economic interests; security concerns; and the disruptions to its own society that result from poverty at its doorstep. The United States must adopt three broad priorities in this region: to help relieve debt burdens so that growth can be accelerated; to help reconstruct postwar Central America; and to assure an effective Caribbean Basin Initiative.

We have discussed Africa's special needs and see a large role here for development assistance, a much different balance of activities than in the case of Latin America or Asia.

Generally, southern Asia is institutionally capable of putting large amounts of foreign resources to good use. We should respond with programs that address both southern Asia's poverty and its trade and investment opportunities. We have practically no programs in India. This is inappropriate. India is a large democratic country with massive poverty where there is clearly room for innovative programming including cooperation for mutual gain.

Eastern Asia also offers complexities and opportunities for the United States. Investment, trade, and other activities for mutual benefit should be the order of the day with the "four tigers" and, increasingly, Thailand. Long-term development cooperation efforts will be appropriate for the Philippines and Indonesia.

For the Middle East, it would be preferable to find ways of expressing our deep commitment to the area so that the proportion of bilateral development aid going to the region, currently virtually half of the total U.S. aid appropriation, is reduced or treated in a manner that will more accurately present our overall development fund level.

MODE AND STYLE OF OPERATION

The way the United States carries out programs in Third World countries can be as important as the substance. Our policies and programs in the 1990s should build on the lessons we have learned in sensitive situations—careful attention to collaborative style, consultation, and emphasis on shared gains.

Development cooperation programs in the 1990s must emphasize high quality. We must draw our very best scientists, agriculturalists, environmentalists, and social and economic analysts into the challenge. Comparatively small in size compared to past years, U.S. development efforts must make up in quality what they have already lost in quantity.

Development cooperation should work increasingly through cooperating organizations and institutions. The balance of effort should rest with intermediate organizations. Such intermediate organizations would demonstrate in practice the pluralistic approach we propose. U.S. policy should encourage growth of intermediaries within countries abroad, especially units that can generate ideas and operate as nongovernmental organizations independent of direct government control.

We should strengthen and expand the scope of the Peace Corps as a vehicle for encouraging cooperation on development matters, and as a way for U.S. citizens to experience life in a broad range of countries, even in some where we may not have development assistance programs.

ORGANIZATIONAL CONSIDERATIONS

A temporary agency, USAID, has managed the U.S. development assistance program since 1961. USAID has served the nation and the development process well. However, as we move from an era of aid to a period stressing cooperation for development and mutual benefit, we need to change.

It is timely and appropriate now to rename the agency and to redesign some aspects of its structure in order to say to all, at home and abroad, that different goals and operational style now prevail; the Development Cooperation Agency would be a good new name.

The Development Cooperation Agency should operate through a policy center plus regional counterparts to the State Department's regional bureaus. The new agency must have a stronger ability to do economic and macropolicy analysis, and should spend more time on the larger issues and program strategies, less on budget and management.

The administrator of the agency should have a single high-level advisory council that should draw top people from the private sector, academia, nongovernmental organizations, and the environmental community. The aim would be to build bridges between key sectors that must work together more successfully.

It is time to consider creating a new entity, resembling a foundation, one that would promote research on issues and technologies of broad consequence to the United States and to developing countries. This foundation would fund the U.S. share of multicountry, jointly planned lines of research. Its use of the best in science and technology would apply across the range of developing countries. The foundation would provide easier access to U.S. talent and a healthy balance to the country and regional programming approach.

The Security Assistance Dilemma

U.S. relations with the Third World present a difficult dilemma: the contrasting needs of development progress on the one hand; and traditional security considerations on the other. Both are legitimate, but together the two can confuse goals. Historically, we have called on bilateral aid appropriations to serve our military/security tasks such as those in South Korea, Vietnam, and, more recently, Central America. Aid funds also finance payments on base rights and underpin our approach to Middle East issues. As a result, the majority of funding for foreign assistance is based heavily on political or security needs and definitions, and is mainly directed to advanced developing countries.

It is now desirable to separate development cooperation funding and management. Separating military from development program funds would clarify the goals of the United States abroad and for the U.S. public. It would help to clarify just what we are spending, in comparison with others, to bring about growth, to attack poverty, and to attain other development cooperation purposes.

Our share of defense expenditure markedly exceeds that of our Western European partners and Japan, whereas their proportion of development aid is increasing and ours is diminishing. The balance is disadvantageous to the United States. What we are paying for (defense) is immensely more expensive than what they are paying for (aid). For our relations with the Third World, this arrangement costs much and gains little.

The largest funding area in which confusion persists is the Middle East, where economic support fund allocations totaling over $2 billion are provided to Egypt and to Israel. The U.S. contribution to these two countries should be placed in a separate account to cover Middle East peace programs.

Coordination Within the U.S. Government

U.S. interests and effectiveness are not well served when trade policies operate at cross purposes with development programs and when goals to increase agricultural productivity are countered by subsidized food sales. We need expanded coordination because of the involvement of new domestic actors, such as the EPA, the Food and Drug Administration, and various other agencies.

In view of the importance and complexity of development issues, some form of council for international development policies would be appropriate and timely. In such an effort, the White House would appoint the chairperson; members would be the heads of the critical agencies involved in trade, finance, development cooperation, agricultural sales, and so on. We would expect the agency principally devoted to development, the redefined Development Cooperation Agency, to be very active in the council in order to assure a strong development voice. The White House must lead such a council because only at that level can overarching national interests be well articulated, providing both a single voice and the strength to follow through.

More effective coordination between the executive branch and the Congress is also needed. Instead of micromanagement, Congress should move toward broader policy review and a focus on strategies and results. The changes in style and substance we have recommended will require greater trust by Congress. Congress could begin by reducing its notification procedures.

An Agenda for Domestic Coordination

The United States greatly influences Third World development prospects. The greater impact does not come from government programs of development assistance. Rather it comes from nonaid policies—trade, finance, interest rates, investment rules, and patent rulings.

The U.S. agency charged with the main responsibilities for development should be in a position to command respect in high-level discussions of such issues. Policymakers should at least know when a proposed domestic action will undermine a Third World development policy being pursued by the United States so that issues can be weighed within a broadened perspective. It is important in the 1990s that U.S. trade negotiators listen to those who hold development policy responsibilities. Many Third World nations depend on U.S. leadership to maintain an open international trading system.

MULTILATERAL AND BILATERAL BALANCE

The United States must continue to play an active and supportive role in the multilateral agencies devoted to international development cooperation. Given the financial challenges facing developing countries, U.S. interests and those of the Third World are well served by a strong IMF and World Bank. Key UN agencies, such as the WHO, the FAO, IFAD, the UNDP, and UNICEF also deserve expanded U.S. support. A strong multilateral system will not be subject to the U.S. dominance that may have existed in the past, but it is an essential component of a global assault on serious issues, including development, that affect all of us.

While supporting a strong multilateral system, the United States cannot limit its development cooperation activities to the multilateral approach, as some have urged. We need a strong bilateral program to assure our interests and to gain access to top expertise and capacities within the United States that cannot be fully harnessed in the multilateral system. Both types of programs serve our interests as we move toward our three broad goals.

FINANCIAL IMPLICATIONS

Polling data confirm that U.S. citizens think of themselves as almost uniquely generous international citizens. This is no longer the case. In the comparison chosen by Western donors to gauge their performance, i.e., percent of GNP allocated for ODA, the United States, which had been first among the donors, now ranks almost last and is also outpaced by a number of OPEC donors.

In the 1990s, the need for funds to sustain development cooperation efforts will not diminish. Private flows are likely to remain weak and are unlikely to be directed to the poorest countries. Budgetary pressures should not blind us to the need for development cooperation or to the benefits, both to the United States and the Third World, that are to be derived from it.

Although the immediate future will require level financing and sorting out of priorities and opportunities, our goals are sufficiently important to our future to justify increases during the 1990s. It would be foolish to argue that more resources go into ill-defined and poorly executed programs. But with sharper definition of goals and effective programs to meet them, we would expect to see a higher priority for development cooperation in the 1990s. The larger Western European nations provide an average of .42 percent in ODA. It would be reasonable to consider the fair share of the United States to be closer to that average to be achieved by the mid-1990s.

The reasons to increase our financing are based not on what others do, but on the critical importance of meeting the goals we have suggested. If proposed new programs and modes are effective and the nation can see progress toward economic growth, an impact on poverty, and environmental improvement, it will be natural and desirable to provide increased U.S. funding.

Accomplishing the gradual funding increase we recommend will require a new agreement between the executive branch and the Congress on the shape of our future programs of economic cooperation with the Third World. The primary way of obtaining increases in these programs is for the president to work for them. If they become important for the president, they will generally become important for Congress.

BUILDING A NEW CONSENSUS

We believe the policies and programs suggested in this report can help regain broader public support. To start the process of building a new consensus, there is absolutely no substitute for an active White House. Silence is the wrong signal. These issues require an active president and support from the White House communications infrastructure.

Beyond this, the U.S. public must be educated to the changed world of the 1990s and beyond. Here, our needs for a more competitive society and one that acts as a good global citizen merge around educational issues of geography, language, area studies, and study of international issues. A number of citizen groups have been expanding nonformal education on these important issues. We urge major sectors of U.S. society (business, labor, civic groups) to consider strategies in their councils to educate their constituencies on these issues. Federal support can also be helpful.

In this report, we have explored serious problems and opportunities facing the United States in its economic relationships with the Third World. We have stressed broad-based growth, lessening of poverty, and improvement of the environment. We have urged a new, mutually beneficial cooperative stance.

Some will object to this formulation, saying, "Work either for poverty alleviation or for your own gain, but do not mix the two. What does their condition of life mean to us?" To that we reply by paraphrasing a statement made by the religious sage Hillel some 2,000 years ago:

> If we are not for ourselves and our peoples, who are we?
> But if we are not for other peoples, what are we?
> And if not now, when?

Meetings, Papers, and Presentations of the Project on Cooperation for International Development, 1987–1988

I. **Association for Women in Development: "Gender Issues in Development Cooperation"**
   Colloquium Summary Report: Jaquette, Jane S. "Gender Issues in Development Cooperation." Available from the Association for Women in Development, c/o Office of Women's Programs, 10 Sandy Hall, Virginia Tech, Blacksburg, VA 24601.
   Colloquium Papers:
   Chen, Marty and Mary Anderson. "Integrating WID or Restructuring Development?"
   Joekes, Susan. "Macro-Economic Policies: Gender Impact and Policy Implications."
   Schultz, T. Paul. "Investment in Women: Priorities and Prospects."

II. **Board on Science and Technology for International Development (BOSTID) of the National Research Council: "U.S. Policy for the 1990s: Science and Technology for Sustainable Development"**
   Colloquium Summary Report: "Symposium on U.S. Policy for the 1990s: Science and Technology for Sustainable Development." Available from Board on Science and Technology for International Development, National Research Council, 2101 Constitution Avenue, Washington, DC 20418.
   Colloquium Papers:
   Baruch, Jordan. "Issues in Technology Development."
   Brady, Nyle C. "The Role of Science and Technology in Development."
   Prewitt, Ken. "Strategic View of Science and Technology for Development."
   Sagasti, Francisco. "Science Policy and Technology Assessment."
   Working Group Reports:
   "Advanced Development Countries."

"Assessment, Management & Policy."
"Development of Technology."
"Mechanisms and Institutional Issues."
"Pure and Applied Research."
"Least Developed Countries."

III. **The Futures Group: "International Cooperation in Population Programs in the 1990s"**

Colloquium Summary Report: Stover, John. "International Cooperation in Population Programs in the 1990s: The U.S. Role." Available from The Futures Group, 76 Eastern Boulevard, Glastonbury, CT 06033.

Colloquium Papers:

Baldi, Patricia. "Foreign Assistance in the 1990s and the Role of Population."

Dunn, John. "Twenty Years of A.I.D.'s Experience in Population."

Hoogenboom, Hugo. "U.S. Population Assistance into the 1990s."

Spiedel, Joseph. "Budgetary Requirements in the 1990s."

IV. **Institute of International Education: "The Role of Education and Training in Development in the 1990s"**

Colloquium Summary Report: "The Role of Education and Training in Development in the 1990s: Policy Report and Conclusions." Available from Institute of International Education, 809 United Nations Plaza, New York, NY 10017.

Colloquium Papers:

Heyneman, Stephen and Bernadette Etienne. "Higher Education in Developing Countries: What, How and When."

Krasno, Richard. "International Students in the U.S. as an Instrument of Foreign Assistance and National Policy."

Zagorin, Ruth K. and David M. Sprague. "Education: The Cornerstone for Development. Let's Capitalize on Our Comparative Advantage."

V. **Johns Hopkins University School of Hygiene and Public Health: "International Health in Development in the 1990s"**

Colloquium Summary Report: Mosley, W. Henry. "International Health in Development in the 1990s." Available from The Johns Hopkins University School of Hygiene and Public Health, Institute for International Programs, 615 North Wolfe Street, Baltimore, MD 21205.

Colloquium Papers:

Akin, John S. "Recession, Structural Adjustment and Innovative Health Financing."

Howard, Lee M. "Trends in United States and International Financial Support for Health in Developing Countries."

Jamison, Dean T. "International Aid in the Health Sector: Program,

Project and Research Investments."

Mosley, W. Henry and Christine Mauck. "Technical Assistance: Professional Development and Career Structures in International Health."

Nabarro, David. "Bilateral Versus Multilateral Aid."

Roemer, Milton. "Strategies in International Health: The Health Model."

Smith, P. G. "Technology Development and Adaptations: Challenges for Field Research in the 1990's."

Taylor, Carl. "The Role of the Private Sector."

VI.   **Michigan State University, Center for Advanced Study of International Development: "The Changing Nature of Third World Poverty in the 1990s"**

Colloquium Summary Report: Derman, William. "The Changing Nature of Third World Poverty in the 1990s: A Policy Focus." Available from Center for Advanced Study of International Development, Michigan State University, 306 Berkey Hall, East Lansing, MI 48824.

Colloquium Papers:

Annis, Sheldon. "What is Not the Same About the Urban Poor: The Case of Mexico City."

Bandarage, Asoka. "The Feminization of Poverty."

Bratton, Michael. "Poverty, Organization and Policy: Towards a Voice for Africa's Rural Poor."

Cernea, Michael. "Poverty Creation Through Projects and Their Alternatives."

Crone, Donald. "Asian Government Policies Toward Their Poor."

Martin, Atherton. "The Changing Nature of Poverty in the Caribbean."

Pollak, Molly. "The Changing Nature of Poverty in Latin America."

Starr, Martha. "Macroeconomic Adjustment and Third World Poverty."

Uphoff, Norman. "Organizational Capabilities of the Poor in Asia" and "Para-Projects as Alternative Modes of International Assistance for Self-Sustainable Development in the 1990s."

VII.   **Midwest Universities Consortium for International Activities: "The Role of U.S. Universities in the Development Task in the 1990s"**

Colloquium Summary Report: "U.S. Universities in Internaitonal Development." Available from the Midwest Universities Consortium for International Activities, 134 Derby Hall, The Ohio State University, Columbus, OH 43210.

Colloquium Papers:

Ahmad, Muzaffer. "An LDC Perspective on Development Assistance."

Fahs, Margaret. "How Can Universities Influence Development Assistance?"

Lipman-Blumen, Jean. "The U.S. University—What Should be the International Involvement in the 1990s?"

Morss, Eliott. "The Development Task."

Schuh, Edward. "What are the Modes of Assistance Appropriate for U.S. Universities?"

VIII.   **U.S. Council for International Business: "U.S. Policy for the 1990s: Promoting Private Director Investment"**

Colloquium Summary Report: Dunn, Paxton. "Promoting Private Investment." Available from U.S. Council for International Business, 1212 Avenue of the Americas, New York, NY 10036.

IX.   **Virginia Tech College of Architecture and Urban Studies in cooperation with the Washington Chapter of the Society for International Development: "Urbanization in Developing Countries: Potentials for U.S. Development Cooperation"**

Colloquium Summary Report: Van Huyck, Alfred. "Urbanization and Settlement Policy in Developing Countries: Strategies for U.S. Development Cooperation in the 1990s." Available from Center for International Development Planning and Building, 101 North Columbus Street, Alexandria, VA 22314.

X.   **Winrock International Institute for Agricultural Development: "Future of U.S. Development Assistance: Food, Hunger, and Agricultural Issues"**

Colloquium Summary Report: "That Damn Foreign Aid." Available from Winrock International, Petit Jean Mountain, Morrilton, AR 72110.

Colloquium Papers:

Avery, Dennis T. "Tomorrow's Environment for Agricultural Development."

Brady, N. C. "Reevaluating Substance and Process Priorities in Development Assistance."

Cesal, Lon and Ed Rossmiller. "Development Assistance and Trade: Lessons Learned from Forty Years of Experience — The Way It Was, the Way It Is and What the Difference Means."

Cloud, Kathleen. "Women, Development, Equity and Efficiency: In Pursuit of Constrained Bliss."

Denlinger, Nelson. "Market Development and Economic Development: Contrasts and Comparisons."

Harwood, Richard R. "Developing Sustainable Agriculture in the Third World: Lessons from Indo-U.S. Experience."

Johnson, Glenn. "The Urgency of Institutional Change in

Agriculture."

Johnson, Stanley. "The Emerging Production/Demand/Policy Scenario."

Johnston, Philip. "Re-defining National Security."

Kleckner, Dean. "U.S. Agriculture and Foreign Agricultural/Economic Development."

Kleis, R. W. "The Case for Refocusing on Development of Human Resources and Institutional Capacity."

Lele, Uma. "A Comparative Analysis of Eight Major Donors in Agricultural Development in Six African Countries."

Mellor, John W. "Global Food Balances and Food Security."

Paarlberg, Don. "Forty Years of Food Aid and Development Assistance: What Have We Learned."

Pellett, Peter L. "Nutrition, Health and Agricultural Development."

Richardson, Len. "International Agricultural Development: Benefits or Myths?"

Rossmiller, George. "Lessons From Trade Development Experience: New Opportunities and Challenges."

Trostle, Ronald G. "Prospects For Food Aid Needs and Global Food Supplies."

Williams, Maurice. "Famine Prevention—Lessons from African Experience."

XI. World Resources Institute: "U.S. Policy in the 1990s: International Cooperation for Environmentally Sustainable Development"

Colloquium Summary Report: Brown, Janet Welsh. "Poverty and Environmental Degradation: Basic Concerns for U.S. Cooperation with Developing Countries." Available from World Resources Institute, 1709 New York Avenue, N.W., Washington, D.C. 20006.

The Contributors

ROBERT J. BERG, an independant international consultant, also is president of the International Development Conference, a national coalition based in Washington, D.C. A former official of USAID, Berg chaired the OECD Committee on Donor Evaluation. He was the codirector of the Committee on African Development Strategies, and is a member of the steering committee of the North South Roundtable.

COLIN I. BRADFORD, JR. is currently on the staff of the World Bank. He is on leave from Yale University, where he is associate professor in the School of Management. He has written extensively on international trade and development issues.

WILLIAM U. CHANDLER is senior researcher at Batelle International. He was formerly a senior member of the Worldwatch Institute, for which he wrote a series of policy-oriented reports on energy, health, and other environmental issues.

DAVID F. GORDON is associate professor of international relations in James Madison College at Michigan State University. A political economist, Gordon has served as a consultant to the World Bank, USAID, and other public sector and private sector organizations. He is the author of *Decolonization and the State in Kenya*.

JOHN MAXWELL HAMILTON, a historian and journalist, is a public affairs specialist at the World Bank. Hamilton is the author of *Main Street America and the Third World* and *Edgar Snow: A Biography*. He has served with USAID in Asia and on the House Foreign Affairs Committee.

ALLAN HOBEN is director of the African Studies Center at Boston University. An applied anthropologist and specialist on Africa, Hoben has worked as a participant–observer at USAID, at the World Bank, and with other donor agencies.

LINDA Y. C. LIM is research director of the Southeast Asia Business Education Program at the University of Michigan. A specialist on the economies of the Asian NICs, Lim has served as a consultant to the ILO, the World Bank, and other international organizations. She has written widely on industrialization and on the role of women in the NICs.

PRINCETON N. LYMAN has had a distinguished career in the Department of State and in USAID. Most recently, he served as U.S. ambassador to Nigeria. A former deputy assistant secretary of state for African affairs, he is an expert in Asian as well as African affairs.

CHARLES WILLIAM MAYNES is the editor of the influential journal *Foreign Policy*. A former assistant secretary of state and development official, Maynes has written extensively on a wide range of foreign affairs topics.

PERCY S. MISTRY is senior fellow of international finance at Queen Elizabeth House, Oxford University. He was formerly senior financial advisor to the vice-president of finance at the World Bank. He has worked for the World Bank on operational assignments in Asia and Africa and as an advisor to the governments of Tanzania, Zambia, and Sweden.

DAVID SHEAR is senior vice-president at the International Management and Development Group. A former official of USAID, Shear served as mission director in Senegal, and has also been a leader in the private voluntary international sector. He is an adjunct faculty member at Princeton University.

RALPH H. SMUCKLER is dean of International Studies and Programs and assistant to the president at Michigan State University. He is also chairperson of the Board on Science and Technology for International Development of the National Research Council. A political scientist by training, Smuckler has worked extensively for USAID, including chairing its Research Advisory Committee.

JOHN STOVER, a forecaster of long-term trends and a policy analyst, is vice-president of The Futures Group. He has developed a number of methodologies used in population forecasting, economic and social trends, and environmental analysis, and he has consulted and published extensively in these fields.

PAUL STREETEN is director of the World Development Institute at Boston University and editor of the respected journal *World Development*. An eminent international economist, he has served as special advisor to the president of the World Bank.

JOSEPH C. WHEELER is the chairperson of the Development Assistance Committee of the OECD in Paris. He was formerly deputy administrator of USAID and served for many years in Asia.

MAURICE J. WILLIAMS is senior associate at the Overseas Development Council and also secretary general of the Society for International Development. A former deputy administrator of USAID, Williams was chairman of the Development Assistance Committee of the OECD and executive director of the World Food Council.

Index